Violent Belongings

Kavita Daiya

Violent Belongings

Partition, Gender, and National Culture in Postcolonial India

TEMPLE UNIVERSITY PRESS
Philadelphia

TEMPLE UNIVERSITY PRESS
Philadelphia, PA 19122
www.temple.edu/tempress

⊖ The paper used in this publication meets the requirements of the American National
Standard for Information Sciences—Permanence of Paper for Printed Library Materials,
ANSI Z39.48-1992

Library of Congress Cataloging-in-Publication Data

Daiya, Kavita, 1970–
   Violent belongings : partition, gender, and national culture in postcolonial India / Kavita Daiya.
   p. cm.
   Includes bibliographical references and index.
   ISBN-13: 978-1-59213-743-5 (cloth : alk. paper)
   ISBN-10: 1-59213-743-1 (cloth : alk. paper)
   1. English literature—South Asian authors—History and criticism.   2. American literature—
South Asian authors—History and criticism.   3. Motion pictures—India.   4. India—History—
Partition, 1947—Influence.   5. Group identity—South Asia.   6. Gender identity—South Asia.
7. Ethnic relations—South Asia.   I. Title.
   PR129.S64D35 2008
   820.9'3585404—dc22
   2007049481

2 4 6 8 9 7 5 3 1

ISBN-13: 978-1-59213-744-2 (paper : alk. paper)

Printed and bound in Great Britain by
Marston Book Services Limited, Didcot

For Devyani and Dilip Daiya

Contents

Acknowledgments

There are many to whom I owe gratitude for the support and inspiration that have made this project possible. My gratitude is unbounded for Homi Bhabha whose rigorous readings, extraordinary support, and warm generosity have animated and nurtured this project from its inception. Lauren Berlant generously shared her time and work, and energized my thinking about gender, capital, sexuality, and nationality. Dipesh Chakrabarty's tireless engagement and conceptual contributions always brought new insight and good cheer. I have benefitted from many others who have been rare interlocutors, readers and friends: Arjun Appadurai guided me when I first began exploring the relationship between urban communalism and globalization in Bombay in 1996. Arjun, Jacqueline Bhabha, and Rashid Khalidi gave me the opportunity to be a Fellow at The Globalization Project at the University of Chicago, enabling me to explore the transnational dimensions of the histories and refugees of Partition. I have benefitted from the engaged responses to early presentations of this research at UC Berkeley, University of Michigan, University of Chicago, the Provisions Library in Washington DC, and Georgetown University. Support from the Andrew W. Mellon Foundation, the Committee on South Asian Studies at the University of Chicago, The Ford Foundation, the Globalization Project at the University of Chicago, the Junior Faculty Support Grant and the University Facilitating Fund at George Washington University has enabled the completion of research on three continents. I thank the dedicated staff at the India Office Library, British Library, Maharashtra State Government Archives, National Film Archive of

India, Library of Congress, and Center for Research Libraries in Chicago. I am grateful to my interviewees who generously agreed to share their time and their memories of witnessing the Partition of 1947. My graduate and undergraduate students at GW have offered many excellent questions and conversations that indelibly mark this project.

I thank my fabulous editor Janet Francendese at Temple University Press for so wonderfully shaping this project with her superb insight, patience and many kindnesses, and the meticulous and generous reviewers at Temple University Press. My thanks also to Marianna Vertullo, David Wilson, and Gary Kramer at Temple University Press for their kind and efficient assistance. Excerpts and early versions of this manuscript have appeared in different sites. A shorter version of Chapter 2 appeared as "Postcolonial Masculinity: 1947, Partition Violence and Nationalism in the Indian Public Sphere," in *Genders* March 2006. Portions of Chapter 6 appeared in "Provincializing America: Engaging Postcolonial Critique and Asian American Studies in a Transnational Mode," *South Asian Review* vol. 26, no. 2 Dec 2005: 265–275. A section of Chapter 6 is based on "'No Home But in Memory'" Brinda Bose, ed., *Amitav Ghosh: Critical Essays* (New Delhi: Pencraft International, 2003). An early version of the argument in Chapter 3 first appeared in "'Honourable Resolutions': Gendered Violence, Ethnicity, and the Nation," *Alternatives: Global Local Political* vol. 27, no. 2 April–June 2002. The editors at *Genders, Alternatives: Local, Global, Political,* and *South Asian Review* have been prompt and helpful, and I owe a special thanks to Brinda Bose, Ann Kibbey, Sankaran Krishna, Kamal Verma, and the anonymous readers of this work.

Colleagues and friends from Washington DC to Bombay have shaped this project with their engagement and encouragement. Judith Plotz has been a wonderful mentor and extraordinary friend and Marshall Alcorn, Linda Bland-Stewart, Patty Chu, Jeffrey Cohen, Maria Frawley, Jennifer Green-Lewis, Gil Harris, Jennifer James, Dane Kennedy, Ivy Kennelly, Diana Lipscomb, Melani McAlister, Robert McRuer, James Miller, Dan Moshenberg, Faye Moskowitz, Linda Salamon, Chris Sten, Gayle Wald, and Tara Wallace have given me an intellectual and collegial community that has supported and invigorated this work. Constance Kibler has unfailingly supplied good cheer and perfect assistance over the years. Many institutional spaces besides the English department at GW have been enabling: the Department of English Association of Students of Color and the Center for the Study of Gender and Sexuality at the University of Chicago, the South Asia Workshop and the Women's Studies Program at GW. I have learned much from conversations with Surendra Gambhir, Ron Inden, C. M. Naim, Geeta Patel, Amit Rai, Lawrence Rothfield, Henry Schwartz, Mrinalini

Sinha, Zohreh Sullivan, and Ken Warren. All have been generous friends and impeccable interlocutors.

I have been fortunate to have the love and support of friends and relatives too numerous to mention, including the Daiya and Karia clans. Some of them are: Teresa Becker, Vikram and Melanie Chandra, Rinki and Anudeep Chauhan, Darshana and Sanjay Doshi, Zahid Hasnain and Supriya Madhavan, Gul and Harsheela Mansukhani, Madhavi Menon, Alero Ogedegbe, Jay Pandhi, Kalpana Peddibhotla, Dimple Rao, Priya Taori and Carmen Vergara. I am thankful to my various uncles and aunts here in North America, especially Malti and Yash Pandhi, Bhupen and Nirmala Karia, Bharati and Vijay Thakkar, Kamlesh and Kalpana Karia, and Pravin and Kapila Karia who have all helped me through my migration to the United States. My loving brother Dhiren has warmly helped me to laugh and enjoy life in many trying moments. This book is dedicated to my parents Devyani and Dilip Daiya without whom it would not have been possible. My gratitude for their unending patience, their serene faith, and their exemplary love is boundless. I thank them for their sacrifices and wisdom which have sustained me through the most difficult times in this endeavor. And finally, I am grateful to my paternal grandfather Shri Mulji V. Narsi and my maternal grandmother Laxmiben Karia, whose extraordinary energy, memory, and spirit animate this work.

Beyond this book, I thank Sunny, my home in the world, whose unwavering faith, witty inspiration, and enduring love have sustained me on this long journey, and my daughter Riya, for shining unimaginable joy into my life, every single day.

I

Train to Pakistan 2007

Decolonization, Partition, and Identity
in the Transnational Public Sphere

What difference does it make to the dead, the orphans,
and the homeless, whether the mad destruction is
wrought under the name of totalitarianism or the holy
name of liberty and democracy?

—M. K. GANDHI[1]

The task of a critique of violence may be summarized as
that of expounding its relation to law and justice.

—WALTER BENJAMIN[2]

If the humanities have a future as cultural criticism,
and cultural criticism has a task at the present moment,
it is no doubt to return us to the human where we do
not expect to find it, in its frailty and at the limits of its
capacity to make sense.

—JUDITH BUTLER[3]

On March 21, 2000, in the war-torn state of Kashmir in India, Islamic militants massacred thirty-five Sikh men from the village of Chitti Singhpora. It was Holi, the festival of colors. Militants with bright Holi colors on their faces wore Indian military uniforms, arrived in the village, told the villagers they were from the army, and dragged the Sikh men out of their houses on the pretext of an "identification parade." All the Sikh men, young and old, were lined up against two walls in the village, and then shot to death. Since the targeting and subsequent exodus of Hindu Kashmiri Pandits from Kashmir, this was the first time the Sikh community was targeted and brutally massacred.

This incident immediately evoked the British Partition of India in 1947: As one newspaper headline remarked, "Ghosts of Partition Return to Haunt

Sikhs." Many of the Sikhs in the villages in Jammu and Kashmir were migrants from Pakistan, who had been displaced during the Partition, due to large-scale ethnic violence between Muslims, on one hand, and Hindus and Sikhs on the other. The killing of the male members of the family also evoked Partition: Once again, it left so many women without any traditional male support. Several women, young and old, were now faced with utter poverty, bereft of the breadwinners in the family. The Sikhs constitute only 2 percent of the population in the valley (around 80,000), and this massacre—in what has largely been a Hindu–Muslim conflict in Kashmir—filled the Sikh survivors with terror. Kashmiri Sikhs were forced to contemplate an exodus similar to that of the Kashmiri Hindu Pandits over the past decade. For many, this was a double displacement due to ethnic violence—once in 1947 and again, fifty-three years later, in 2000.

This event is exemplary in many ways. Caught up in the midst of writing a cultural account of post-1947 South Asian nationality, I understood with indelible force and clarity how the 1947 Partition continues to haunt contemporary life in India. This is true not only for discourses that debate the place of religion in India but also for the historical interpretation of justice and minority belonging, and for the tension-ridden struggle over the production of secular national culture in the subcontinent. After all, in this instance the militants chose not Hindus, Christians, Parsis, Buddhists, Tibetans, or other minorities in Kashmir as targets: They targeted Sikhs—Sikh *men*, as if re-iterating the violence of 1947. Furthermore, the narrativization of this massacre in public culture made visible how it is to Partition that we often turn, even today, as an evocative repository of the meanings, metaphors, and conceptions of contemporary ethnic belonging in South Asia. Even though the massacre repeated the similar and more recent ethnic violence in North India against Sikhs in November 1984, which followed the assassination of Prime Minister Indira Gandhi by her Sikh bodyguards, it was through the 1947 Partition that the massacre in Kashmir was historicized and politicized in middle-class public culture. Like the demolition of the Babri mosque in Ayodhya (Northern India), which was attacked and vandalized in 1992 by Hindu nationalists who believe it is the birthplace of the Hindu god Ram; like the ensuing Hindu–Muslim ethnic violence, which spread across India in December 1992; and like the series of riots and state-supported mob violence against Muslims, which occurred in the Indian state of Gujarat in 2002 in the city of Godhra, this attack on Sikhs in Kashmir represents a crisis that refracts the ethnicization of territory and national belonging that marks the checkered history of secularism in the subcontinent.

Cut to 2007. On February 19 2007, the Samjhauta Express, a bi-weekly train running between India and Pakistan, became the target of a devastating bomb explosion that left sixty-seven dead and scores wounded. The Lahore-bound train was routed by the explosion in Panipat, about 100 km from the capital Delhi. In an ironic twist, the two antagonistic nations became united in their grief, as out of the sixty-eight dead, only eleven bodies were identified: four Indian, seven Pakistani. Running between Amritsar in India and Lahore in Pakistan, the Samjhauta Express is the oldest train link between India and Pakistan. As such, it represents a fragile move towards peace as its passengers travel back and forth between the two nation-states to be briefly united with family members across the border, families that were forever fragmented when the British partitioned the Indian subcontinent in 1947. Among the passengers were Pakistanis who had come to India to visit relatives, Indians who were going to Attari in Pakistan to attend a wedding, and Sikh pilgrims for whom key religious places ended up on the other side of the national border drawn by Sir Cyril Radcliffe. Generally, the train's passengers tend to be mainly poor and lower-middle-class Muslims from families divided by the India-Pakistan border, but also Pakistani and Indian Hindus, and over a million passengers are estimated to have used this train since it began. The attack happened on the eve of the start of peace talks to be held between India and Pakistan, and days before the fifth anniversary of a fire on a train carrying Hindu pilgrims that killed fifty-nine people in Godhra in Gujarat and led to ethnic riots across India in which around 2,500 people died, most of them Muslims. Immediately following the terrorist attack, the symbolic import of it was clear: The national Hindi news channel Sahara Samay ran headlines like "Aman par Chot" (A Wound to Peace), "Insaniyat Ki Maut" (The Death of Humanism), and "Samjhauta Ke Dushman" (The Enemies of Friendship). On February 19 and 20, 2007, newspapers around the globe narrated the event differently: *The Hindustan Times* story was entitled "66 Killed as Samjhauta Express Becomes Terror Target"; *The Hindu*'s report was "Evoking Horrors of Partition—and hopes of a peaceful future"; *Dawn* in Pakistan ran a story "President Musharraf Says Train Blast Won't Stop Peace Process" on February 21, 2007. The elite consensus was that this was an effort to derail the Indo-Pakistan peace process, even as popular media representations of these blasts in both India and Pakistan yoked together the memory of 1947, the discourses of peace and humanism, and the rhetorics about terror and "terrorism" that increasingly permeate current discourses about political violence across the world.

It is obvious that contradictions mark the violent complexities of these varied national scenes. Described as "the first crack in Kashmir's equivalent of the Berlin Wall, the first fissure in south Asia's iron curtain since the 1947 partition divided British India into two nation-states," Indo-Pak cooperation recently made possible on April 7, 2005 the first bus journey since

1947 across the national borders, or Line of Control (LOC) that divides the Indian state of Kashmir, and united many families and friends.[4] Yet, as David Ludden has noted, while Hindu nationalist political parties garnered relatively few votes prior to 1980, since 1980 in India, "killing classified as 'communal' increased rapidly and so did the Muslim body count."[5] Cut to the United States. The U.S. State Department reported a 25 percent increase in "terrorist incidents" worldwide in 2006, while the National Counterterrorism Center (NCTC) suggested that terrorist attacks around the world resulted in 20,498 deaths. While violence in Iraq accounted for 45 percent of the overall attacks, the next highest concentration of terrorist incidents was in South Asia, including Islamic militants' attacks in Kashmir.[6] At the same time, the BBC noted that the Hindu nationalist organization Rashtriya Seva Sangh (RSS), founded in 1925, today is the largest voluntary organization in the world. The chief proponent of anti-minority activities in India, the RSS today has 25,000 branches in India and over sixty branches abroad in thirty-four different countries. In part, it is in this contradictory legacy of ethnicized geopolitical conflict that the Partition of India in 1947 by the decolonizing British endures.

This book is about the relation between culture and violence in the modern world. In particular, through a focus on South Asia, it examines the relation between contemporary ethnic and gendered violence, and the questions about belonging that haunt nations and nationalisms today. In an increasingly globalized world, the widespread problem of ethnic violence and its attendant displacement of peoples have gained prominence, if not center stage, in academic scholarship and public policy, generating new and urgent consideration primarily in the social sciences. In 1947—the moment with which this inquiry begins—and today, the issues of ethnicity and belonging violently haunt the life of nations across the world, be they postcolonial nation spaces like India, or world powers like the United States. Ethnicity, often used interchangeably with race, religion, and culture, has become an increasingly intensified site of identification—in what seems to be an apparently contradictory development, as globalization and transnational flows transform the remotest cultural forms on the planet. In spite of the globalizing spread of modernity, and of its avowed values of secularism, humanism, and individualism, how is it that people continue to invest and re-invest intensely in ethnic and raced identities? Why does ethnic violence, always experienced by men and women differently, continue to become a prominent part of political life across the world?

In order to understand the workings of ethnicity, gender, and violence through the specific case of India, I take as my point of departure the event of "1947"—the simultaneous decolonization and partition of India into two countries: India and Pakistan. This book examines South Asian ethnic violence and related mass migration in and after 1947, through its representation in postcolonial Indian, and more broadly, global South Asian literature and cultures. This inquiry, then, is necessarily transnational: It articulates accounts of violence and refugee experience from South Asia as well as its diasporas in the U.K. and North America. My interdisciplinary exploration proffers that the 1947 Partition experience of gendered violence and displacement critically shapes the contemporary ethnic nationalisms that prevail in transnational South Asian political life today. The Partition constitutes a field of transformation and a discourse that became the condition of possibility for the gendered ethnicization of citizenship and belonging in postcolonial South Asia. It also created the framework for the recent resurgence of gendered, ethnic nationalism in India and the Indian diaspora.

In other words, if there is a singular moment in the history of South Asia and Britain that had a profound and lasting effect on the politics and societies of many of the nations that make up contemporary South Asia, it is the 1947 Partition. The decolonization of India in 1947 was accompanied by its partition into two nations, India and Pakistan. Partition granted independence to a supposedly Hindu India as a secular democracy, and created a new nation, Pakistan, to be predominantly populated by Muslims. After August 6, 1946, ethnic riots involving Hindus and Sikhs against Muslims escalated all over the subcontinent. This escalation of violence, combined with pressure from Hindu and Sikh communalist groups in Bengal and Punjab, led the Congress Party (the secularist party which had emerged dominant in the anti-colonial struggle) to finally accept the partition of the subcontinent demanded by the Muslim League (which had managed to gain majoritarian Muslim support). In June 1947, Congress President Kripalani informed Viceroy Mountbatten: "Rather than have a battle we shall let them have their Pakistan, provided you will allow the Punjab and Bengal to be partitioned in a fair manner."[7] The British Prime Minister Attlee had famously announced in the Commons on February 20, 1947 that June 1948 was to be the deadline for decolonization; he also appointed India's last Viceroy Lord Mountbatten. In an ill-fated move in March 1947, Mountbatten determined that the date of Indian independence was to be moved ahead, from June 1948 to August 1947. Shortly thereafter, it was also decided to partition India.

Thus, even as 1947 marked the freedom of the South Asian population from British rule and the emergence of India as an independent and secular nation, it also marked India's simultaneous partition into two different nations, India and Pakistan. Over a span of three months, Sir Cyril Radcliffe drew borderlines on the map of India that split up the regions of Punjab and

Bengal into two nations: India flanked on both sides by the nation of East and West Pakistan. Pakistan was born at midnight on August 14, 1947, a day before India. As the location of the territorial division was announced, whole villages were forced to migrate and relocate themselves (depending on whether they were Hindu, Sikh, or Muslim) in territories that were in the process of being marked as India or Pakistan, in what was, as Sumit Sarkar has aptly noted, the world's biggest mass migration in less than nine months.[8] It is a remarkable fact that the exact location of the borderline was announced by radio on August 16, 1947, *after* the two nation-states had been declared independent. Lord Mountbatten did not want the announcement of the borderlines to interfere with the independence celebrations, and so decided to postpone the radio announcement until afterword. As a result, the nation-states formally came into being as political entities before their citizens knew what their territorial frontiers were. Incredible confusion, mayhem, and violence followed, because many people did not know whether their villages were now in Pakistan or India, and did not know in which direction they were to migrate.

What made this simultaneous partition and independence a singular event thus was the large-scale ethnic violence and mass migration that accompanied it. In the nine months between August 1947 and the spring of the following year, by unofficial counts, at least sixteen million people—Hindus, Sikhs, and Muslims—were forced to flee their homes and became refugees; at least two million were killed in ethnic violence.[9] Many of these refugees eventually migrated to the U.K. and the United States. As the borders were drawn and sporadic news traveled of the lines which marked one village Pakistani and another Indian, huge populations were "exchanged" according to their religious affiliations. The bulk of this migration and consequent violence occurred in Punjab in the west, while the division of Bengal in the east remained relatively less violent. Whole villages proceeded on foot or by bullock-cart, with their meager belongings, to areas where their 'co-religionists' were; groups of men from the antagonistic communities (Muslims, Hindus, and Sikhs) massacred and looted villages, and also abducted, raped, and mutilated women, men, and children; families were separated and lost; thousands of people were forcibly converted; and a dominant trope of Partition's exemplary violence is the image of trains arriving from each country laden with the slaughtered bodies of refugees who had tried to get across to the other side. A singular aspect of this violence was the large-scale abduction of over 150,000 women by men often, but not always, from a different community. In the end, millions were left, to borrow a phrase from Amitav Ghosh's *The Shadow Lines*, "with no home but in memory."[10] Freedom was accompanied by traumatic loss, nations gained through homes lost forever for millions.

already a crowded field of study.

The scale and nature of violence that India's partition involved thus makes it one of the most violent events in the history of modern nation-formation.

Seen largely as an aberration in modern Indian history, this Partition is little memorialized by the state or by those affected by it. Urvashi Butalia has noted the silence on Partition in *The Other Side of Silence*: "In India, there is no institutional memory of Partition: the State has not seen fit to construct any memorials, to mark any particular places—as has been done, say, in the case of holocaust memorials or memorials for the Vietnam war."[11] After 1965, the Indian Partition—especially its violence—largely disappeared from discussion in the Indian public sphere; apart from a few films and novels, it was relegated to the past that was, from the perspective of the Indian state. It is best forgotten to maintain harmonious ethnic relations within the nation.[12] Popularly perceived as irreconcilable with India's history of peaceful, non-violent anti-colonial struggle that Gandhi led, it suggested its very failure. Moreover, because responsibility for the violence lay with all the constituencies involved—British, Hindus, Muslims, Sikhs—Partition has ultimately been disavowed historically as an aberration, a moment of "insanity" in an otherwise remarkable story of non-violently achieved freedom from British oppression.

In addition, state ideology about the Partition in the early national period represented it as both inevitable and in the past, and the need to preserve law and order and peaceful inter-community relations was cited by India's first Prime Minister Jawaharlal Nehru as early as 1948 (and has continued to be cited by the state in the postcolonial period) as the grounds for censoring published and filmic accounts of Partition violence. These were seen to incite communal conflict. Even in his momentous speech on the eve of independence, the Indian Prime Minister Jawaharlal Nehru elides the magnitude of the traumatic violence and mass displacements that pervaded that time for tens of millions of South Asians:

> Before the birth of freedom we have endured all the pains of labour and our hearts are heavy with the memory of this sorrow. Some of those pains continue even now. Nevertheless, the past is over and it is the future that beckons to us now. . . . We think also of our brothers and sisters who have been cut off from us by political boundaries and who unhappily cannot share at present in the freedom that has come. They are of us and will remain of us whatever may happen, and we shall be sharers in their good [or] ill fortune alike.[13]

Nehru's reference to the "pains of labour" can be read as an indirect reference to the trauma of Partition; it problematically naturalizes the ethnic violence and forced migration experienced by so many South Asians as inevitable labor pains of a feminized nation giving birth to "'freedom.'" Moreover, by describing the violence and displacement in August 1947 as a "memory" and a "past" that is "over," Nehru minimizes their magnitude and elides state responsibility for the imminence and continuity of violence and migrations that endured well into at least 1949. Similarly erasing the epic scale of this dispossession, the then Home Minister Vallabhbhai Patel once described the Partition as "the disturbances after Independence Day."[14] In a speech in January 1948, he further argued, "I can tell you that if we had not accepted Partition, India would have broken into bits."[15] This naturalizing state discourse about the trauma of Partition as unavoidable for the attainment of postcolonial nationhood, combined with state concern about internal order and unity, and the emergence of new secessionist movements (linguistic and regional) in different parts of the country, both erases the responsibility of the British in engendering Partition, and grounds the Indian state's failure to remember the Partition experience. The words of Rajendra Prasad, the first president of India, evince this official state discourse. In his introduction to a collection of Mahatma Gandhi's essays, he asserts:

> It is remarkable how by his honest and fearless advocacy of communal unity he has enraged many of the Muslims and a negligible few among the Hindus. . . . This is the long and tragic history of Mahatma Gandhi's attempts to establish Hindu-Muslim unity which ended with the establishment of Pakistan on the one side and his supreme sacrifice on the other. The problem has, however, not been solved inspite of the creation of Pakistan. We have still some 40 millions of Muslims in this country, spread all over the vast area of what is called India today.[16]

Like Nehru, Prasad reproduces the naturalizing ideological assumptions about Partition and the making of India. In spite of India's constitutional commitment to secular democracy, his words signal the incipient ethnicization of Indian citizenship as "Hindu," whereby the Indian Muslim becomes an anomaly by her very presence in the nation-state. Eliding the imminence and enormous complexity of the ongoing mass migrations and refugees' problems, Prasad's writings indicate the state's ambivalence towards the minoritized Muslim citizen-subject in India as a "problem." This conception of Muslim (un)belonging in India reappears in the nineties in Hindu nationalist political discourse, and it foreshadows the contemporary violent contestations around ethnicized citizenship that garner popular support in Hindu middle-class India and its diasporas. For example, Partition as a discourse is frequently mobilized in the Bharatiya Janata Party's political rhetoric. In 1997, *The Economic Times* carried a report, "Partition Still Remains a Curse," in which it quoted the then Bharatiya Janata Party (BJP) President L. K. Advani suggesting that Partition effects contemporary ethnic violence in India: "'If the idea was to avert the recurrence of communal riots in the country, then the propagators of the two-nation theory had miserably failed in their effort,' he said."[17] Further, conflicts around regional and language struggles emerged in and dominated through the late sixties and seventies; the new postcolonial Indian state's focus on addressing these divisive and often violent politics may have contributed to the official and public elision of Partition and its memorialization. This question of memorializing Partition can be raised with respect to the British machinery as well; an account of the administrative failure to ensure a peaceful transfer of power, and of British complicity in fomenting the ethnic politics of Partition and the uncontrolled unfolding of ethnic violence, are part of the story of Partition's erasure. Partition violence was typically narrated in British circles, and especially in the British press, by invoking Orientalist ideologies: as evidence of the inherent lack of civilization of Indians, and of the necessity of a benevolent British colonialism.

Accompanying the official Indian erasure of the violence of Partition has been the historiographical lacuna on the moment until recently. Despite the magnitude of violence that characterized the duality of independence from British colonial rule and partition into two nation-states for the Indian subcontinent in 1947, few scholars have studied the role of this essentially constitutive ethnic and gendered violence in colonial and postcolonial history. As Gyan Pandey has acknowledged, "[i]n much of the historiography of Partition, the history of violence has scarcely begun to be addressed."[18] Indeed, Urvashi Butalia has asked, "Why had the history of Partition been so incomplete, so silent on the experiences of the thousands of people it affected? Was this just historiographical neglect or something deeper: a fear, on the part of some historians, of reopening a trauma so profound, so riven with pain and guilt, that they were reluctant to approach it?"[19] Seeking to explain this silence, Purnima Mankekar has suggested that "[p]erhaps the modernist language of social science and its myth of detached objectivity render the horrors of Partition difficult to analyze."[20] For an event that has been the single most defining moment for the social and political relations that mark modern national life in most of South Asia, it has received scant scrutiny until recently, when subaltern studies historians, feminists and translators began to initiate numerous transnational conversations about what happened, how and why. Early work on colonial and postcolonial history and the Partition primarily documented the consolidation of empire and the concluding Indo-British political negotiations that led up to Partition and formal decolonization; these accounts largely end at the transfer of power that occurred in 1947.[21] The protagonists of these historiographical narratives are largely the male, nationalist elite—namely, Nehru, Gandhi, and Jinnah; of these, the studies of Partition often focus on the regional—rather than urban or national—impact of this violence and displacement in the partitioned states of Punjab and Bengal.[22] Historical and political science scholarship on postcolonial India often begins in 1947 with a brief mention of the Partition and its unfortunate violence, moving on to the socialist direction of Nehruvian policies, the Five Year Plans, and the regional politics of post-1947 India.[23] In this approach, where the story of Indian history either ends at or begins in 1947, the dramatic transition that was "1947" itself is largely elided. It is this field of transition and transformation, and the forms of its persistent appearance and material effects in the global present, that this book hopes to illuminate.

In contrast to the earlier elision of Partition's ethnic violence and displacement, recent revisionist work that has returned to the scene of the Partition has primarily taken two directions. In one, the translation into English of Hindi, Urdu, Punjabi, and Bengali literature about the Partition experience has resulted in a range of new novels and edited collections of short stories and poetry becoming available for those interested in the Partition, most notably through the valuable work of Mushirul Hasan and Alok Bhalla.[24] In the second direction, feminist and subaltern studies research has focused on recording the oral testimonies of Partition survivors and witnesses (much like those of Holocaust survivors) and making audible the silences in the histories and memories of Partition, especially for women and ethnic minorities in India. In particular, pioneering work in anthropology, history, and feminist historiography by Veena Das, Urvashi Butalia, Ritu Menon, Kamala Bhasin, and Gyan Pandey, among others, has investigated women's and refugees' experiences of the violence in 1947; they have mapped out the complex forms of agency at work in women's negotiation of memory, nationality, and state ideology and functioning in the aftermath of Partition.[25] Through a detailed exploration of accounts of events in and around 1947, Gyan Pandey has identified the limitations of official history and "the enduring concern with unity in Indian historiography" that has led to the dominant erasure of the events of Partition.[26] In the current pre-occupation with memory, translation, and testimony, however, the large body of literary and cultural texts about Partition is often seen, at best, as supplementary evidence of experience. Moreover, what remains unanswered is: What happens to the formation of ethnic/religious identity and its gendering—Hindu, Muslim, and Sikh—in 1947 for South Asians? How are ideas of national citizenship and narratives about belonging collectively created and contested in such moments of violence and mass migration? How does the public, cultural negotiation of violence and displacement, in various media, shape and impact current ethnic nationalisms, which are transnational in their support and reach thanks to globalization? Going beyond a humanist condemnation of violence and violent migrations, how do we understand its working, its meanings, and its effects in the modern nation? After all, "1947," which ushered independence, freedom, and nationhood in South Asia, still reverberates today across the subcontinent. Its effects are starkly visible in the Indo-Pak conflict over Kashmir, terrorism in Kashmir and elsewhere in India, and in the resurgence of bloody Hindu–Muslim ethnic politics in the subcontinent which have now become a routine part of daily news.

In her ethnography of Indian television, Purnima Mankekar has argued that "[f]or those of us committed to feminist and secularist praxis, however, perhaps the time has come to use our revisionist histories to interrogate (nationalist) History. . . . [W]e need to confront contending narratives of the past in order to analyze the configurations of power that led to the violence surrounding Partition and continue to result in the violence ravaging the postcolonial polity."[27] Pandey has similarly observed, "There are numerous ways in which the life and conditions of India and Pakistan, and perhaps Bangladesh too, have been obviously remade by that violence and the curious memory-history we have of it."[28] To understand the diverse and complex legacies of the Partition for contemporary life, we must re-examine the cultural and political transformation that the 1947 Partition was. In order to explore the preceding questions, to bridge the gap between the political history and oral testimony, *Violent Belongings* takes up varied media representations of gendered violence and displacement in the postcolonial public sphere. In the process, it hopes to show how Indians and, more recently, South Asians in the diaspora, fashion belongings, perform citizenship, and survive nationalisms.

The Postcolonial Public Sphere

> The public sphere is the site where struggles are decided by other means than war.
>
> —Negt and Kluge [29]

Social theory after Habermas has begun to re-examine the relation between various local, political and social affiliations and the nationally framed bourgeois public sphere. If Habermas posited the disintegration of the public sphere which brought citizen-subjects face-to-face in the articulation of community following the shift to cultural consumption made possible by the new technologies of mass media,[30] Negt and Kluge revisit Habermas' formulation towards a new theory of public life in an age of mass media and Internet technologies. Moving away from the critique of mass culture articulated by the Frankfurt School, Negt and Kluge identify the existence of a proletarian public sphere which has emancipatory and utopian possibilities, and which is distinct from the exclusionary classical liberal and hegemonic bourgeois public sphere. This proletarian public sphere consists of counterpublics—alternative publics formed by working-class subjects creatively reappropriating, resisting, and refashioning their horizons of experience in an oppositional relation to the limits and exclusions of the classical hegemonic and the industrial-technological public spheres. They argue: "[W]e believe that what is at issue here is not a variant of the bourgeois public sphere, but rather an entirely separate conceptualization of the overall social context, which has been established in history but not included within the parameters of the term public sphere."[31] Although, as Miriam Hansen has pointed out, they end up reinscribing the idealization of female subjectivity as maternal and familial in their formulation of a feminine, "maternal mode of production," Negt and Kluge nonetheless offer a useful way of conceptualizing the processes of the formation of contingent, alternative publics or collectivities that harness the potential of mass-mediated technologies.[32] Their analysis recognizes the multiple, competing counter-publics that exist in a sometimes collusive and sometimes critical relation to the hegemonic bourgeois public; these counter-publics are saturated with everyday experiences and fantasy of citizen-subjects who participate in the social collective process, create relationality between everyday life and politics, and counter the alienation and fragmentation of social life. It enables us to reconceptualize the public sphere as a process and a *context* of social experience imbricated in relations of power, rather than an arena of rational consensus—as an unstable mixture of different types of publicity, as a modern hybrid site of discursive contestation, as a mode of organization grounded in material structures which enables translation among diverse publics.

Rita Felski reworks Negt and Kluge's theorization of the plurality of the proletarian public sphere towards a feminist politics of critique. She suggests that, "[u]nlike the bourgeois public sphere, then, the feminist public sphere does not claim a representative universality but rather offers a critique of cultural values from the standpoint of women as a marginalized group within society. In this sense it constitutes a *partial* or counterpublic sphere."[33] While Negt and Kluge's Marxist formulation takes as the horizon of transformation the social relations of production, then, following Felski, I want to suggest that it can be usefully engaged for postcolonial feminist struggles. While there is much scholarship focused on public spheres in American and

European contexts, there has been no book-length investigation of what I call "postcolonial public spheres." As such, this book appropriates Negt and Kluge's theorization of publicity to describe the complex network of "postcolonial publics"—hegemonic and alternative—that mark South Asian cultural life; these postcolonial publics are now inherently diasporic and transnational given the reach of mass media, and they illuminate how minor (as used by Deleuze and Guattari) subjects critically negotiate the violent legacies of empire and the oppressions of postcolonial nationalisms.

Recently, Dietrich Reetz has analyzed the role of Islamic organizations in negotiating and contesting the dominant public sphere in pre-1947 India, to explore the historical shape of their contemporary role in ethnic politics.[34] Francesca Orsini has also uncovered the emergence of a nationalist Hindi literary public sphere in North India in the early twentieth century, in which literary associations and schools consolidated a new national, anti-colonial, political consciousness.[35] In contrast to such religious or linguistic foci, this book intentionally draws upon cultural representations in multiple languages, including English, that appear across urban India. I use the concept of the postcolonial public sphere to refer to those processes in a formerly colonized, democratic society by which postcolonial subjects articulate a new framework and discourse for their everyday experience, motivations, actions, and fantasies in decolonization. Excluded from the hegemonic narratives of neo-colonial power of raced global capitalism in the West and native nationalisms in ethnic South Asia, the minor postcolonial subject fashions an oppositional relation to dominant political and cultural ideas through this postcolonial public sphere. This postcolonial public sphere is not always subaltern, or always oppositional; rather, through various media like newspapers, magazines, literature, film and the Internet, it enables minor subjects to contest, re-imagine and resist the conditions of their oppression. These can be of the "proletarian" or working class that Negt and Kluge focus on, but also, I suggest, of caste, colonialism, gender, sexuality, race, ethnicity, and disability. The discourses uncovered here—in the bourgeois nationalist public sphere, the industrial sphere of production marked by institutions of journalism and cinema, and what I call the counter-public of the "postcolonial public sphere"—reveal the official rhetorics as well as what Foucault has called "subjugated knowledges"[36] about ethnicity and minor citizenship, gender and belonging in postcolonial India and its diasporas. As such, they also illuminate how ethnicized and gendered subjects navigate the processes of governmentality, which, Foucault shows, participate in the subjectification of people—as refugees and minor citizens—in the postcolonial state. The minor subject, Homi Bhabha has brilliantly reminded us, is "always a partially denationalized political subject"; the narratives I consider evince this liminality to nationality, which emerges from an intimacy with imperial and nation-state violence, that marks the postcolonial Partition migrant's experience in both India and Pakistan.[37]

In the Indian context, several historians and cultural critics have analyzed how the Indian nation is represented in popular literature, drama, and other public media; the formations of literary nationalisms particularly in Bengali and Hindi have received considerable attention, revealing in the process the gender, caste, and class exclusions of nationalist discourse in colonial and newly independent India.[38] As Benedict Anderson emphasizes, print media (novels, journals, and newspapers) become key technical means for representing the modern nation, and so for both contesting colonialism and constituting national consciousness. These media texts create a public sphere that mediates between the state and civil society, and they generate mass reading publics that form a collective *cultural* imagined community—the nation.[39] In addition to literature and the institutions of the press, film technology emerged as a powerful and popular means of representing the nation in the fifties in the early national period in India (due to mass illiteracy, among other factors). If, in the colonial period, colonial governmentality politically controlled modern institutions like the press, and marked the racialized limitations of the indigenous public spheres, then in postcolonial urban India, despite their institutional censorship by the postcolonial Nehruvian state, print media and film emerged as powerful forces that bridged public and private, elite and minor, local and national, in the mediation of civil society and citizenship.[40] As such, these cultural texts (like literature and film) both registered the impact of Partition on everyday life in urban India not recorded by official histories and mediated and shaped collective memory and survivors' oral testimonies being gathered today, through their stories about national history. Moreover, in the Indian context, it is hard to separate early national literary and film culture, simply because many films about Partition are based on novels; many Indian writers also wrote or directed Hindi film scripts; they worked in multiple languages, including English and Hindi. For example, writers like Saadat Hasan Manto, Ismat Chughtai, and Rajinder Singh Bedi often used their film work to support their literary endeavors; and at yet other times, they thought that the mass appeal and reach of film made it an ideal medium to disseminate positive social values and progressive political messages to the illiterate masses. Rather than focusing exclusively on either literature or film, then, it became imperative to examine South Asian literature and film in conversation, as commodities and cultural texts with different narrative conventions that inhabit and transform inter-articulated urban public spheres, constitute postcolonial counter-publics, and illuminate the cultural imagination of subjectivity and community in postcolonial national modernity. Hence, this account would be incomplete if it considered only one or the other; to tell the story about violence and belongings that I want to tell, literature and film have to be examined together, as a part of the transnational publics in which the middle class meditated issues of gender, ethnicity, migration, and nationality.

This book thus tracks the formation of transnational South Asian public spheres by taking up the Partition as both historical event and what Foucault has called "discursive formation." In the process, it connects the ascendancy of ethnic identities and ethnic violence in 1947 South Asia with contemporary diasporic discourses in South Asian American and British Asian communities about ethnicity, gender, and racial discrimination. Foucault has reminded us that genealogy, which is necessarily "disordered and fragmentary," is "the reactivation of local knowledges—of minor knowledges, as Deleuze might call them—in opposition to the scientific hierarchisation of uncovering and gathering together of knowledges and the effects intrinsic to their power."[41] In part, then, this project is genealogical: One of the arguments of the book is that the cultural scenes and texts examined here, some discontinuous and others marginal, reveal how Partition enabled the cultural ethnicization and gendering of belonging in the nation in India and Pakistan; this cultural ethnicization and gendering of belonging in turn became articulated with the ambivalent ethnicization of citizenship by the Indian state, and became the condition of possibility for the contemporary, popular Hindu nationalist minoritization of non-Hindus—especially Muslims—in India.

Modern Migrations: Representing Refugees, Citizenship, and Rights

While revisionist studies of Partition have focused on the experience and narration of violence, the experience of Partition refugees' migration has received relatively less attention. Today, it is estimated that large-scale movements of voluntary and forced migrants have uprooted more than 190 million people worldwide. Correspondingly, there has been increased scholarly and policy attention to the complexities of these migrations, caused by varied reasons ranging from economic opportunity or ethnic violence to social and political persecution. Economic globalization and the end of the Cold War have led to the steady rise in cross-border flows since 1990, when there were an estimated 120 million migrants. Experts warn that the twenty-first century is likely to continue to see large-scale movements of people, both voluntary and forced. The top ten receiving countries include the United States, India, France, Germany, Canada, Saudi Arabia, Australia, the United

Kingdom, Kazakhstan, and Poland; these ten accounted for 55 percent of all international migrants in 1990, and they continue to host large immigrant populations. The impact of this movement on the transformation of processes of creating cultural and ethnic community, the invention of diasporas and imagined nations, necessitates going beyond the focus on the borders and boundaries of nation-states which contain migrants, to examine the links among different "areas" or "regions" which send and receive flows of people. Rather than focusing on particular nation-states, Arjun Appadurai and Saskia Sassen have recently theorized the effects of the transnational movement of people and commodities given globalization.[42] In the light of the resurgence of a transnationally linked ethnic violence since the 1960s in India, and the international rise of violence and "terrorism" in both Western and decolonized nations in the twentieth century, the re-examination of ethnic violence and its generation of temporary and permanent migrations of both individuals as well as communities is imperative. Furthermore, the construction of categories and communities like "citizenship," "refugees," and "nation" needs to be reconceived in a less regional and more transnational context—in the case of India, in relation to both the history of Partition and the largely post-1950 history of global migration. In this, the different experience of women and children has attracted substantial attention, as women now make up 47.5 percent of all international migrants. Recent research on refugees and human rights by Jacqueline Bhabha and Liisa Malkki, among others, illuminates the social and juridical processes by which migrants become refugees, and makes visible refugees' gendered experiences in forging new relations of diaspora, assimilation, and belonging.[43]

In addition, internal displacement within nation-states comprises a significant part of the world's migrations, yet receives less attention given its confinement within a particular nation-state's borders. Since the end of the Cold War, increasing numbers of people have been forced to leave their homes as a result of armed conflict, internal strife, and systematic violations of human rights: witness the Biharis in Bangladesh who migrated there 1947 but are still not granted citizenship, or the Kashmiri Hindus languishing in camps in India for over a decade now. Whereas refugees crossing national borders benefit from an established system of international protection and assistance, those who are displaced internally suffer from an absence of legal or institutional bases for their protection and assistance from the international community.[44] Examining the historical transformations that led to the production of large numbers of people as refugees in the twentieth century, Hannah Arendt argues that "[m]uch more stubborn in fact and much more far-reaching in consequence has been statelessness, the newest mass phenomenon in contemporary history, and the existence of an ever-growing new people comprised of stateless persons, the most symptomatic group in contemporary politics."[45] Arendt illuminates how the lack of powerful institutions and nation-states willing and able to guarantee what were once believed to be inalienable human rights—the Rights of Man—has led to the contemporary condition where the loss of citizenship itself constitutes a loss of all rights, and of one's humanity and personhood: "The calamity of the rightless is not that they are deprived of life, liberty, and the pursuit of happiness, or of equality before the law and freedom of opinion—formulas which were designed to solve problems within given communities—but that they no longer belong to any community whatsoever."[46] I take this insight about the modern overlapping of the loss of belonging with the loss of human rights to the particularity of Partition migrations, to track how the Partition refugee—officially constructed as ethnic citizen by India if she was Hindu or Sikh, and by Pakistan if she was Muslim—was negotiated in the cultural representation of community, state practices of rehabilitation and rights, and political discourse about national belonging. The discourse around the liminal Partition refugee in postcolonial South Asia illuminates the increasing political and cultural ethnicization of national belonging that today generates Hindu–Muslim ethnic violence in India. Here, Victor Turner's theorization of liminality and transitional beings is relevant: "Liminal entities are neither here nor there; they are betwixt and between the positions assigned and arrayed by law, custom, convention, and ceremonial."[47] He suggests that such "transitional beings are particularly polluting, since they are neither one thing nor another; or may be both; or neither here nor there; or may even be nowhere in terms of any recognized cultural topography."[48] Insofar as Partition refugees were migrants who were simultaneously hailed as citizens in transit by the postcolonial states of India and Pakistan in 1947, their juridical and existential liminality illuminates the shape of incipient belongings in the new postcolonial states.

In her study of Hutu refugees in Tanzania, Liisa Malkki has pointed out the structural absence of the refugee in the study of nationalism, and problematized the humanistic universalization of the figure of the refugee that generates "the discursive externalization of the refugee from the national."[49] In the process, she has argued, "the homogenizing, humanitarian images of refugees work to obscure their actual sociopolitical circumstances—erasing the specific, historical, local politics of particular refugees, and retreating instead to the depoliticizing, dehistoricizing register of a more abstract and universal suffering."[50] Keeping this in mind, I re-examine here the discourse about Partition migrants in 1947, who were both refugees and citizens, depending on ethnicity and gender. To counter the homogenizing abstraction and erasure of Partition refugees' suffering, the chapters that follow uncover the heterogeneous, multi-layered, and discontinuous local experiences, as well as the popular media representation of Partition migrants. The case of these gendered and ethnicized Partition refugees—in their simultaneous marginality to postcolonial Indian history even in the sheer epic scale of their migrations—becomes a useful site from which we can explore what Rajeswari Sunder Rajan has called "the overlaps and pulls between the concepts and practices of citizenship-as-rights and citizenship-as-national identity (and, even, as compulsory residency) in the case of the subaltern gendered subject."[51] It is my argument that the crisis of Partition violence and its refugees critically informs contemporary, dominant conceptions of ethnic agency, and subaltern citizenship in India and its diasporas. In other words, I propose that the public and cultural negotiation of ethnic, gender, and state violence and displacement illuminates how political identities like "Indian," "Muslim," "Sikh," "Hindu," "refugee," "citizen" etc., are both created and contested, locally and abroad, in and after 1947. The national emergence and cultural interrogation of these categories thus reveals to us the forms of subaltern agency and politics imaginatively mobilized in the postcolonial public sphere.

In South Asia, two nations were created in 1947 on the basis of Hindu–Muslim ethnic difference and fears of Muslim minoritization after independence. Although India is constitutionally secular, the Indian Ministry of Rehabilitation Reports until 1954 expressly state that only non-Muslim refugees are to be aided by the government. This puts into a troubling frame the ambivalent place of Jewish and Muslim refugees within the new nation-state given the ethnicization of refugee rights, even as Indian cities like Bombay had earlier been welcoming refuges for Jewish refugees fleeing the Holocaust who were denied entry in other European countries and the United States. Moreover, the status of Hindu refugees coming to India from Pakistan (and of Muslim refugees in Pakistan) was unique because they were not placeless like most refugees: The state's official rhetoric offered them both national identity and a place—a new nation—to come to. Thus, they were simultaneously citizens and refugees; yet, fifty years later, as the Sharanarthi [Refuge] Action Committee reported, post-Partition refugees from Pakistan in Kashmir continue to be denied citizenship rights in the name of Kashmir's "permanent residents," even as its Hindu residents fleeing ethnic violence are denied refugee status by the state. These complex forms of dispossession make it imperative to rethink the narration of the past in terms of refugee experience, the writing of subaltern histories of violence and displacement, as well as the very production of the immigrant as "refugee" and/or "citizen" in the scene of the nation-state.

Furthermore, this complex and contradictory history of the present raises important questions for rethinking the role of refugees and violence in the cultural landscape of the nation in the twenty-first century: What kinds of new knowledge about modern citizenship and displacements can be gleaned from the refugee, the survivor, and the migrant? How do they enable us to rearticulate the political vocabularies of citizenship, human rights, and personhood in national geographies, especially given the contemporary "War on Terror" and the racialization of religion in the "West"? Exploring the relation between historiographic narratives and cultural ones, this book proffers a genealogy of the emergence of gendered ethnicity as a category and technology that critically shapes citizenship and belonging in postcolonial democratic life. In doing so, I foreground the problems and politics of representing violence—be it war, domestic, or collective—and its role in the production of public memory, the consolidation of state power, and the writing of national culture.

Recasting Gender: Masculinity, Intimacy, and National Coupledom

This book takes as its point of departure the popular translation of "gender" as "woman" in the study of gender and nationalism, in which the norms of masculinity often come to bear an implicit givenness. In the conversation about how women as raced and ethnicized subjects often come to represent both the colonized landscape and the nation ("the motherland") in colonial and nationalist discourse, as many critics from Sangeeta Ray to Anne McClintock and Partha Chatterjee have valuably illuminated, this book intervenes with attention to the role of men as gendered subjects, and to the production of sexuality and intimacy in the postcolonial public sphere discourses about belonging and nationality.[52] In her critique of law and the postcolonial state, Rajeswari Sunder Rajan has recently elaborated the complex dispossessions engendered by the contemporary inter-articulation of differences of ethnicity, class, and age in women's experience of citizenship in the postcolonial Indian state.[53] By tracking the imbrication of gender and ethnicity in the literary figuring of the nation, Sangeeta Ray has usefully demonstrated that "the discursive construction of the Indian nation by both nationalists and imperialists was often inseparable from their idealization of a Hindu India epitomized in a particular Hindu female figure."[54] This book explores the postcolonial shape of this feminization of the nation; it turns to the representation of male and female experiences of violence and displacement, and the cultural fashioning of intimacy and coupledom to uncover the transnational imagining of belonging and citizenship in its hegemonic as well as counter-public forms. This marginalized issue of the colonial and postcolonial production of masculinities has recently attracted attention from scholars like Mrinalini Sinha, Rosalind O'Hanlon, Sikata Banerjee and Sanjay Srivastava.[55] Contributing to this emergent postcolonial engagement with masculinity studies, one of the claims of this book is that like the female body, male bodies also become symbols of decolonized and postcolonial nationality—albeit in different, often heteronormative ways. Moreover, it shows that both men and women, depending on whether they are ethnically Hindu, Muslim or Sikh, become differently ideal citizens or troubling bodies in the new Indian nation. This ethnicized subjectification is of course recast in the Euro-American diaspora through its encounter with the minoritizing practices of racialization that dominate Euro-American subject formation.

Lauren Berlant and Michael Warner have problematized how "community is imagined through scenes of intimacy, coupling and kinship"[56] in the rhetorics of citizenship in heteronormative, official U.S. national culture; they point out that "[i]ntimate life is the endlessly cited *elsewhere* of political public discourse, a promised haven that distracts citizens from the unequal conditions of their political and economic lives."[57] Taking up this issue of intimacy, Laura Kipnis critiques the imperatives of modern American coupledom. She proposes that "[r]omance is . . . a socially sanctioned zone for wishing and desiring, and a repository for excess. Mobilized as it is by unconscious fantasy, it is potentially a profoundly antisocial form as well—when unharnessed from the project of social reproduction."[58] What happens when we re-examine postcolonial normative intimacies in the Partition discourse produced in the postcolonial public sphere? How is the imagining of national belonging tied to particular, heteronormative constructions of ethnic and secular intimacy and coupledom? Berlant describes heteronormative culture as "a public culture, juridical, economic, and aesthetic, organized for the promotion of a world-saturating heterosexuality."[59] In addition to the troping of ethnic masculinity in particular ways, this book's analysis of gender examines how discourses of intimate relations and inter-ethnic romantic coupledom are deployed to constitute political relations that involve the historical production of secular Indian nationality under siege. As such, the dominant and the counter-public public sphere and their media forms become critical sites for the gendering consolidation and critique of the postcolonial nation in the context of partitioned South Asia.

Narrating the National Through the Transnational

In part, then, this book is about how diverse identities—for men and women; locals, migrants, and refugees; Hindus, Muslims, Sikhs; and Jews, Indians, and Pakistanis—are collectively created and contested, through various media, in postcolonial India and ethnic America. *Violent Belongings* brings to light the rich, contradictory, collusive, and productive relation between the literature and culture of South Asian public spheres that dealt with Partition, on one hand, and the emergent public discourses of national identity and belonging that shape the memories of survivors being interviewed today. Linking together newspaper reports and literature, the political writings of Gandhi and Nehru with films/this book hopes to offer a new account of how gender and ethnicity have come to determine who belonged, and how, in the Indian nation/ It is my contention that the silence that many historians claim marked the event of Partition in public memory was not as prolific as they proffer; indeed, I argue that the early national narration of Partition around and after 1947, as well as today, is a rich and valuable archive of the discontinuous processes by which certain discourses about ethnicity, gender, and citizenship came to become dominant—and indeed defining (if also much-debated)—rhetorics for postcolonial South Asian nationality.

Towards this aim, the chapters that follow take up transnational South Asian literature and culture primarily from 1947 onwards—spanning the Indian subcontinent as well as the diaspora in the U.K. and United States. They explore how post-1947 literature, film and journalism represent violence, migration and the nation; the book as a whole argues that these representations challenge our contemporary historical and political explanations about the relationship between ethnicity, gender and nation in the postcolonial world. In the preface to their edited volume *Postcolonial Theory and the United States,* Amritjit Singh and Peter Schmidt have acknowledged that we are now "in a 'transnational' moment, increasingly aware of the ways in which local and national narratives, in literature and elsewhere, cannot be conceived apart from a radically new sense of our shared human histories and our growing global interdependence. To think transnationally about literature, history, and culture requires a study of the evolution of hybrid identities within nation-states and diasporic identities across national boundaries. How best to understand these global matrices is a source of intense debate and urgency."[60] *Violent Belongings* takes up this urgent challenge and historicizes the contemporary and transnational politics of Hindu nationalism through the cultural history of the 1947 Partition. In the process, it links the scene of decolonized Indian national belonging with South Asian American and British Asian histories of gendering and racialization in the diaspora.

This book thus sets out to demonstrate that the cultural and political narration of Partition violence is critical to understanding the contemporary salience of ethnicity in South Asian national and transnational life, especially in the resurgence of gendered Hindu–Muslim ethnic violence post-1980. Indeed, as Sugata Bose and Ayesha Jalal have suggested about the RSS- and

BJP-driven destruction of the Babri Masjid in 1992, "Partition seems to be the demon the Bharatiya Janata Party-led Hindus are trying to exorcise by felling a mosque and erecting Ram's temple in its place."[61] Contrary to the view that the violence of 1947 was a unique aberration, this book shows that it was a formative moment that consolidated particular narratives about citizenship, belonging, and gendered ethnicity in postcolonial India. Furthermore, gender difference articulated this patriarchal conception of ethnic citizenship in important ways: Citizenship for the female refugee/migrant was presumed, politically, to be determined by the voices and religion of their families of origin. This rhetoric of women as property of family and ethnic community, then, articulated the realization of political subjectivity and citizenship for women in complex and often disempowering modes. Simultaneously, the chapters pay particular attention to the role of normative intimacies, inter-ethnic coupledom, and ethnic masculinities in the cultural construction of the nation and the discursive critique of nationalism, as well as the historical and anthropological silence around the gendered violence done to male bodies.

Postcolonial Critique and U.S. Ethnic Studies

This book engages postcolonial studies with ethnic American studies and South Asian area studies, and connects the humanistic study of the postcolonial public sphere with recent historical and anthropological work on violence, displacement and oral testimony. It connects the apparently disjunct scenes of the increased salience of ethnicity in India, the racialization of South Asian immigrants in the West and the renewal of ethnic investments in transnational public spheres of the Indian diaspora. For the story I want to tell about the relationship between the rise of ethnic nationalisms in South Asia, the history and legacy of the Partition, and the discriminatory experiences of minoritized South Asian immigrants in the U.K. and United States, an engagement of postcolonial studies of India and U.S. ethnic studies is critical. Henry Schwarz has already argued in a different context for the need to interrogate "the imaginary divide between postcolonial and other ethnic studies in the U.S.," towards challenging dominant rhetorics of American exceptionalism in the academy and outside.[62] Similarly, Rajini Srikanth cautions against simplistic generalizations that might pit U.S. ethnic studies and postcolonial critique against each other; she also reminds us that "the forces of global capital, the forces of global labor distribution, and the multiracial and multi-ethnic communities that have been created in different parts of the world are the undeniable effects of colonialism."[63] Thus, Srikanth argues for the necessity to situate the struggles of racialized subjects in relationship to the histories of European colonialism and to present-day American imperial-ist involvement in global affairs—increasing as its "War on Terror" continues to territorialize the globe in new ways. Speaking to the racialization of religion and attendant discriminatory discourses about Muslims in the United States, Robert Stam and Ella Shohat have remarked, "The shrinking of civil liberties in the post 9/11 period was first tried out on Americans with Muslim names or of Muslim religious background."[64] In the Indian context, caste-ist and religion-based cultural minoritization is not only pervasive, but also is a site of discursive disenfrachisement and material violence. As Partha Chatterjee has argued in his indictment of contemporary India, "[t]he continuance of a distinct cultural 'problem' of the minorities is an index of the failure of the Indian nation to effectively include within its body the whole of the demo-graphic mass that it claims to represent."[65]

The new history of global migration also makes imperative an engage-ment of ethnic American studies and postcolonial studies that recognizes the transnational circulation of people and products that both inhabits and constitutes national communities and their everyday life. Research on inter-national migration reveals that around 190 million people currently reside in a country other than where they were born, thus doubling the number of international migrants in twenty-five years, while there are 24.5 million internally displaced persons in the world.[66] According to a 2003 report of *National Geographic*, at least 35 million people in the world—more than the entire population of Canada—have been forced to become refugees and are either temporarily or permanently exiled from their homes. Approximately half of them are women and children.[67] That the question of citizenship and its signification of belonging is an urgent issue today ever more than before—today, one in every thirty-five human beings in the world is a migrant—is evident in the varied attempts to theorize a comfortable mode of living with complex affiliations that has marked recent postcolonial cultural studies, from Kwame Anthony Appiah's "cosmopolitan patriotism" to Aihwa Ong's "flexible citizenship," Bruce Robbins and Pheng Cheah's "cosmopoliti-cal," Benedict Anderson's "long-distance nationalism," and James Clifford's non-nostalgic "discrepant cosmopolitanisms."[68] Of course, the national and the transnational are often mutually constitutive, rather than exclusionary forms; for example, the popular anti-Muslim Hindu nationalist organiza-tion the RSS in India has, for a couple of decades now, garnered substantial economic and ideological support for its political activities in India from the Hindu diasporas in the United States and the U.K. First established in 1925 as an anti-colonial organization, the RSS rose to power in the sixties and seventies and helped constitute one of India's most powerful political parties, the BJP, as well as the VHP—the World Hindu Council—specifically set up to mobilize support to build a temple on a sixteenth-century mosque site in Ayodhya, North India. Today, the RSS has over 25,000 branches in the world, becoming the largest voluntary organization in the world. It aims to transform India from a secular country into a Hindu nation; towards this, it has regularly been inciting anti-Muslim violence and anti-Christian violence across India, leaving thousands dead and displaced.

In his article on this new, transnational Hinduism, Benedict Anderson has called this long-distance nationalism "a rapidly spreading phenomenon whereby well-off immigrants to the rich, advanced countries (and their children) are becoming key sources of money, guns, and extremist propaganda in their distant, putative countries of origin—in perfect safety and without any form of accountability."[69] Others, like Sucheta Mazumdar, have also pointed out that many Indian immigrants in the United States are also aggressive supporters of political Hinduism. Mazumdar uncovers how the VHP (World Hindu Congress) and its affiliate organizations in the United States provide community services to immigrants such as youth and summer camps, formulate plans for building a university in America, and fund Hindu student councils on over sixty college campuses. Further, she observes, "most recent immigrants are devout Hindus, turning patios and bedrooms into Hindu shrines and prayer rooms, starting Hindu versions of Bible studies and Sunday schools, sponsoring priests for functions at home, rushing to temples to witness miracles, and helping build temples. About 200 temples have already been built, and another 1,000 are in various stages of planning and construction."[70] Several South Asian American immigrants have donated extensive funds to Hindu ideological causes both in the United States and in India, pointing to the renewal of ethnic investments in transnational Hinduism in the context of racialization and minoritization as Asians in the West: "The class insecurities of an immigrant bourgeoisie in fact foment a more aggressive definition of Hinduism as culture, religion, heritage, and tradition; even loyalty to the 'motherland' becomes linked in this definition of identity and family."[71] So the question this book also grapples with is: What can we glean from uncovering how the hegemony as well as subversion of the (ethno)nationalist is produced transnationally? How can this transnational perspective enhance our understanding and dealing with the problematics of gendered ethno-racial identities and nationalist violence that dominate the globalization of culture?

Genealogy, Culture, Nation

I have two general aims, then, to summarize, in writing this book. My first aim is to excavate the transition and transformation in cultural meanings and effects wrought by Partition and decolonization, violence, and displacement. This cultural story of the role of violence and refugees in shaping national histories has largely been marginalized in the focus on oral testimony or elite history in Indian historiography in general, and early Partition historiography as well. Given the official account of refugees' seamless assimilation into Indian national life, it is imperative to tell this story about violence, refugees and postcolonial citizenship if we are to create a space for Partition migrants' own particular history. My second aim is to track the genealogy of contemporary languages of ethnic nationalism and belonging in South Asian communities—in India, as well as in diasporas in the U.K. and North America. In other words, I will show how the origins of the complex and always contested transnational discourses of a resurgent Hindu nationalism, the politics of terrorism and "security" in India and its diasporas, can be traced in part to the modes by which the cultural and political negotiation of Partition violence institutes and consolidates hegemonic, if contradictory, ways of determining citizenship based on gendered ethnicity.

Among the several broad areas of emphasis in the book are the feminist critiques of nationalism, the representation of masculine citizenship and ethnic/secular coupledom, refugee and immigrant experience, the South Asian diaspora in North America, urban public culture, and the increasing transnationality of what I call the postcolonial public sphere. The early chapters of the book focus on the rich and hitherto little know cultural history of Partition: I examine the representation of the partition experience in literature, cinema, and journalism in order to track how Partition functions as a discursive formation. Through this exploration, I show how partition becomes both an iconic event as well as battleground for the competing construction of national belonging, community, and gender in South Asian public spheres post-1947. How gender difference and sexuality shape this varied story about belongings is enunciated by tracking the differential production of rhetorics about the feminized nation "Mother India," which are accompanied by surprising constructions of the heterosexual Sikh male refugee as ideal citizen and national victim. The later chapters explore questions about historicity, modernity, and the Partition: How do the cultural and political narratives of belonging produced during Partition inform the contemporary resurgence of ethnic nationalist politics—what Gayatri Spivak has named "the failure of decolonization in India"—in South Asia?[72] How does the re-historicization of Partition as a cultural field enable us to interrogate contemporary equations of gendered ethnicity and citizenship? Given the importance ascribed to ethnic identity globally, including in the U.S. national context after the terrorist attacks of September 11 2001, how do we understand the growing apparent salience and power of ethnicity as a location of identity, in a world that is increasingly globalized? After all, the questions about ethnicity, gender, and nation that generated the Indian Partition are troubling questions that have not yet been resolved, in India or elsewhere. They remain, to haunt us, across the globe—in the Israel–Palestine issue, in the Middle East, in Ireland, Indonesia and South East Asia, in Pakistan, Iraq and Afghanistan—making it increasingly clear that it is a problem that will not go away easily. The dominance of ethnicity in various postcolonial parts of the world as a central mode of identity is as much a colonial legacy as it is a modern mode of identification.

Violent Belongings is an effort to understand the cultural, imaginative working of gendered ethnicity in the modern and late modern world. It is my hypothesis that in this age of migration—local, national and transnational— gendered ethnicity has become increasingly important for the articulation of identity and community. In other words, the modernization of the world, even if it has led to the proliferation of plural, alternative modernities, has also led to the simultaneously growing power of ethnicity in the formation of gendered identities and communities—local, regional, national and now, transnational. Since ethnicity, as a category, and the processes of constructing religious or ethnic difference are not about to go away, and in fact have become progressively more powerful in global discourses of identity—both individual and collective—it is imperative that we re-examine the cultural and political production of ethnicized belongings, and how it is articulated with norms of gender and sexuality within and across cultural and national contexts. Through such a re-examination, we can perhaps invigorate and revitalize the utopian potentialities invested in our conceptions of human rights and secular democracy, even as we challenge, following Gandhi, the violence done in their name.

In his meditation on the effects of the terrorist attacks on September 11, 2001 on global politics, Homi Bhabha has valuably suggested that we defamiliarize "democracy" as a hegemonic value term circulating in both policy and public-sphere discourses about Islamic communities, terror, war, and Euro-American politics. He argues that "[i]f we attempt to de-realize democracy, by defamiliarizing its history and its political project, we recognize not its failure but its frailty, its fraying edges or limits that impose their will of inclusion and exclusion on those who are considered—on the grounds of their race, culture, gender or class—unworthy of the democratic process." Bhabha urges that "[i]n these dire times of global intransigence and war, we recognize what a fragile thing democracy is, how fraught with limitations and contradictions; and yet it is in that fragility, rather than in failure, that its creative potential for coping with the trials of the new century lies."[73] It is such a revisionary, sideways re-examination of gendered ethnicities—the categories that we take for granted in the institutions of Indian democracy, and indeed, American democracy as well—that this book also hopes to enact. In engaging the subaltern, the minor, the refugee toward the critique of the failures of the colonial state and the postcolonial state, this book works towards provincializing the postcolonial nation and, appropriating Dipesh Chakrabarty's words, ends with provincializing Euro-America.[74]

This book does not claim to be the definitive study of the violent transition to postcoloniality that is named Partition. It does not offer a comprehensive account of the literature and film about Partition in various Indian languages—English, Hindi, Punjabi, Urdu, Sindhi, and Bengali. It does not cover the vastly different experience of independence in the southern part of India that, for the most part, escaped the violent upheavals witnessed in the North—both west and east. In that sense, it is necessarily a partial story about the political, historical, and cultural transitions marked by "1947" in India; a story about how its cultural representation in various media both illuminates and memorializes in specific ways the experience of violence and displacement in new national cultures. I also remain aware of the difficulties in speaking of the different Indian and Pakistani stories, and certainly do not intend to claim an identity between "India" and "South Asia." While my study does pay more attention to the Indian nation-state post-1947, I intentionally resist the confining frame of national borders and articulate the experience of the two nations—India and Pakistan—together. Since the entire subcontinent was called India prior to its division in 1947, and since I do not claim to adequately attend to the literature of what is now Bangladesh (formerly East Pakistan), I hope to remain aware of the inadequacies of deploying such terms when speaking about a moment of transition and flux. This book also intentionally moves away from the tendency in scholarship to focus on regionalism—and on the regions of India most directly impacted, namely, Bengal or Punjab. Instead, I have traced a transnational story of the 1947 Partition—as event, metaphor and memory, to borrow Shahid Amin's words—and mapped how that story can illuminate for us the complex and contemporary, ambivalent and antagonistic articulation of national belonging in our globalized and diasporic worlds.[75]

The chapters that follow track key issues—gender, ethnicity, citizenship—as they play on the Partition scene. In particular, Chapter 2 explores the representation of partition by focusing on the cultural articulation of masculinity and ideal masculine citizenship in South Asian literature about partition and nation-formation, from the subcontinent and the diaspora. Examining a range of literary texts, I show how the representation of violence done to male bodies played a critical, symbolic role in the production of nationalist sentiment in the public imagination. This chapter thus points to the fissures between history and literature, in bringing to light how violence to the sexual male body remains elided in the contemporary historical investigation of gender and nationalism, even as literary and popular cultural texts deploy it to articulate a secular political critique of nationalist politics. In particular, I show how the postcolonial nation-state's sustained economic exploitation and political disenfranchisement of the Indian Sikh male and the Indian Muslim male is engendered through popular stereotypes of hypermasculinity and feminization, respectively, that exemplify what David Eng has called "the technology of gendering . . . centrally linked to processes" of ethnic-racial formation and sexualization.[76]

Chapter 3 tracks the representation of women's experience of Partition violence and displacement in literature, political documents, and oral histories. During and immediately following 1947, Hindu, Muslim, and Sikh women in India suffered both sexualized ethnic violence, as well as state violence. Large numbers of women were kidnapped by rival communities, often across the India/Pakistan borders, forcibly converted, raped, bought and sold, mutilated, and in many cases, married by their abductors. In the early fifties, as per an agreement between the governments of India and Pakistan, these women were tracked down and forcibly repatriated by the two states, largely to families that no longer accepted them due to their rape, which is seen as "dishonor." I explore how this violence against women is narrated, addressed and critiqued in the postcolonial public sphere in literature and political discourse, both then and now. In the process, I argue that postcolonial feminist criticism today needs to go beyond the ideological critiques of gendered violence articulated in recent feminist writings, to challenge and undo the very language of "honor" and "dishonor" that marks our critiques.

Chapter 4 takes up the cultural representation of migration, displacement, and refugees in the postcolonial public sphere in major Indian cities like Bombay. Examining literature and popular cinema, as well as British administrative records, newspapers and film magazines, I show how the Partition migrations not only transformed urban culture and industry in the Indian city-space like Bombay, but also produced hitherto unprecedented narratives of cultural belonging and citizenship in the public sphere. Here, I uncover the fragmentary and ambivalent narration of refugee experience in public and political discourse, to argue that it was around the figure of the refugee that debates about citizenship and about the place of ethnicity and gender in determining nationality coalesced in the early national period in India. Thus, the minor subject, the itinerant, stateless migrant became critical to the shape and form of early national discourse in South Asia, as well as its critique.

Chapter 5 deals with the representation of the Partition, Pakistan and ethnic citizenship in contemporary Hindi cinema. It focuses on how contemporary Bollywood films represent Partition—in period films, as well as films about war and inter-ethnic coupledom. In so doing, they attempt to melodramatically reconfigure contemporary questions about Indo-Pakistan geopolitical war and peace, the relation between ethnicity and citizenship in national culture, and to memorialize women's experience during Partition in transnational public spheres. Through an analysis of recent films like Chandraprakash Dwivedi's *Pinjar,* Farah Khan's *Main Hoon Na,* Farhan Akhtar's *Lakshya* and Yash Chopra's *Veer Zaara,* this chapter explores the futures of ethnicity and patriotism and uncovers the contemporary mappings of heteronormative coupledom and geo-political peace in these globally circulating texts of the hegemonic public sphere.

Chapter 6 argues that it is postcolonial literary and cultural production by diasporic South Asians in the U.K. and United States that returns to raise questions that link the 1947 Partition with stories about secularism, contemporary ethnic and racial violence, and post-September 11 belonging in South Asian American lives—from India to Bangladesh to the United States. The narratives taken up here, like Salman Rushdie's *Shalimar, the Clown* and Jhumpa Lahiri's *The Interpreter of Maladies,* connect the 1947 partition to other global scenes of violence; in doing so, they inscribe politicized transnational affiliation, provincialize America, and critique state terror. In the process, these transnational stories provincialize the nation form. They carve out a non-national humanistic account that measures the distance between history and memory, between the politics of contemporary ethnic nationalisms and racialized patriotism in places as diverse as India, Sri Lanka, and the United States.

Foucault reminds us that genealogy "does not pretend to go back in time to restore an unbroken continuity that operates beyond the dispersion of forgotten things." Instead, he argues that to do a genealogy is "to maintain passing events in their proper dispersion; it is to identify the accidents, the minute deviations—or conversely, the complete reversal—the errors, the false appraisals, and the faulty calculations that gave birth to those things that continue to exist and have value for us." This, he suggests, leads us to the recognition that truth "does not lie at the root of what we know and what we are, but in the exteriority of accidents."[77] In this book, I have attempted to take up this task to locate some of the textures and accidents, fragmentary accounts and "forgotten things" that made up what we call Partition, in order to interrogate the increasing violence and dispossessions—ethnic, national, racial, gendered—of contemporary South Asian life for its minor subjects. By engaging transnational scenes and diverse aesthetic texts of violence and migration, I propose that the emergence and ascendancy of gendered ethnicity as a dominant technology of identity, citizenship, and belonging is not only a feature of Indian history, or indeed of South Asian and postcolonial histories, but of national modernities across the world. The humanistic exploration of violence internationally—its representation, naming, remembrance, and reproduction—is essential if we are to uncover the sites and strategies to challenge the discourses that engender it, and that it engenders.

Finally, it is my hope that this book will make visible the urgency of understanding the inter-articulation of art and history, and the centrality of the literature and film of the postcolonial public sphere in writing the relation between postcolonial history and memory. Aesthetic texts like literature and film enable us to interrogate the narratives of dominant cultural memory; they are representations of everyday life that often mark the limits of historicist and social scientific accounts of historical experience. Dipesh Chakrabarty has noted about "the new histories of the Partition" that their "exploration of history and memory shows that only a capacity for a humanist critique can create the ethical moment in our narratives and offer, not a guarantee against the prejudice that kills, but an antidote with which to fight it."[78] Questions of history and memory are now strongly in play in contemporary India and the diaspora (particularly in North America), such that literary and cultural histories are themselves part of a political struggle over the meaning of nationality, cultural identity, and freedom. I have been interested in locating how literature and film constitute a counter-memory and an archive for measuring the discontinuity between hegemonic ideologies of nationalism and their often violent, gendered embodiment in everyday life. By mapping the articulation of national violence in different registers and in a transnational form in the public sphere, this book reexamines the terms and transformation of national life and citizenship through internal and international migration. In this critical project, our aesthetic and cultural texts open up a new space for rethinking the ethical and political articulation of the democratic, the human and the humane in the public sphere, civil society, and international history.

Violent Belongings began as an effort to trace "the political economy of memory"[79] and to understand the senseless losses of those who have endured, inhabited and survived ethnic violence and displacement both in contemporary South Asia and in the Indian subcontinent of 1947. I hope that the struggle to write these histories and memories into the present will contribute, in some measure, to a new understanding of their enduring legacies. Inspired by the stories of my grandfather, who was from Karachi, now in Pakistan, who was never able to return there after Partition, this book is also a desire to understand how Karachi came to be an ideal, fabled city in my imagination and his.

What are you contributing?

2

Re-Gendering the Nation

*Masculinity, Romance, and
Secular Citizenship*

Khushwant Singh's 1956 novel *Train to Pakistan* features a crucial moment in which Hukum Chand, the magistrate sent to maintain law and order in the village Mano Majra during the Partition of India in 1947, reflects critically on the dominant image that emblematized Indian independence internationally:

> What were the people in Delhi doing? Making fine speeches in the assembly! Loud-speakers magnifying their egos; lovely-looking foreign women in the visitors' galleries in breathless admiration: "He is a great man, this Mr. Nehru of yours. I do think he is the greatest man in the world today. And how handsome! Wasn't that a wonderful thing to say? "Long ago we made a tryst with destiny and now the time comes when we shall redeem our pledge, not wholly or in full measure but very substantially."

He then goes on to remember the contemporaneous experiences of three Sikh acquaintances: a colleague, Prem Singh, who is murdered in Lahore by "a dozen heads with fez caps and Pathan turbans"; recently married Sundari, the daughter of his orderly, who was raped by a Muslim mob and handed the penis of her castrated husband; and Sunder Singh, who Hukum Chand had recruited for the army, and who shot his family to relieve them of hunger and thirst during their migration. In ruminating upon how Prem Singh "made his tryst at Falletti's hotel," how Sundari "had made her tryst with destiny on the road to Gujranwala," and how Sunder Singh "came to his tryst by train, along with his wife and three children" such that "[h]e did not redeem the pledge. Only his family did," Hukum Chand indexes his cynical distance from the prevailing nationalist rhetoric about independence.[1]

This narrative moment offers a number of useful starting points for thinking about ethnic violence and Indian national modernity. First, it links the Indian state and its official formation with the experiences of its citizens. Hukum Chand recounts Nehru's momentous political speech only to test its romanticization of nationalism against the minor experiences—of death, bodily violence, displacement, hunger—of its subaltern citizens. Second, this scene addresses the invisibility of the suffering, mass violence and death that accompanied the Indian partition, in the celebratory official and international discourse on Indian independence. Thus, it connects the story of national independence to the twin axes of an international global community and Partition's violence. The cynicism towards the barely incipient nation-state manifests itself through the denigration of Nehru and his momentous speech that invokes race as well as sexuality, by describing his words and appearance as objects of white women's admiration and desire. Moreover, Hukum Chand's description of ethnic and sexual violence not only suggests the absence of ordinary peoples' experiences of violence in dominant accounts of 1947, but also indicts the failure of the nationalist elite to usher in a peaceful transfer of power. Finally, this scene raises questions about the representation of the Indian nation and history. As he describes the newly married Sundari's gang rape by a mob of Muslim men who first castrate her husband, it is clear that for Chand, this gendered and sexual violence marks the failure of a patriarchal nation-state to protect both its male and its female citizens from gendered, bodily violence. Thus, in this bureaucrat's cynical ruminations, national politics betrays the nation's normative patriarchal family.

Before exploring the questions about nationalism and gendered violence raised by cultural accounts like Khushwant Singh's novel, the pre-history of the Partition conflict is worth considering briefly. The relationship between the anti-colonial nationalist movement in British India and the rise of communalism (or ethnic nationalism) is a long and complex one, and there were many factors that culminated in the concrete demand for a separate nation-state on the part of the Muslim League in the 1930s in India. Though 1885 saw the organization of the first Indian National Congress, the anti-imperialist movement in India at the time was a heterogeneous formation of extremist activity, diverse labor and tribal organizations and protest, Hindu revivalism, and some cautious bourgeois reformist moves amongst the middle classes as manifested in the Congress. In the 1880s and 1890s, anti-British activity increased and began to organize around the call for swaraj (self-rule) and limited reform-oriented demands; simultaneously, these years also saw "communalism" acquiring a national dimension, principally through the twin issues of language (Urdu-Devanagri) and cow protection.[2] As Bernard Cohn, Susanne and Lloyd Rudolph, and Dipesh Chakrabarty have argued, the British policy of designating the Indian population into separate "Hindu" and "Muslim" communities was motivated by both the need for administrative organization and management of colonial populations, as well as the more invidious political policy of divide and rule. The latter especially attributed a mythic homogeneity to these communities and set up a structural antagonism between them through both (a) colonial political policies, and (b) the discursive construction of "Hindus" and "Muslims" as separate communities for enumeration.[3]

Both Hindu revivalism—the indigenous response to British orientalizing discourses about Hindu civilization and reform—and a pan-Islamic assertion of a distinctive Muslim culture and civilization emerged towards the end of the century as powerful and popular discourses for mobilizing Indians along ethnic lines. Moreover, the Indian nationalist movement's struggle to create a sense of a unified, Indian cultural identity in opposition to the British resulted in a Hinduized mainstream nationalism which, though Hindu in its imagery, was committed to a secularist, modernizing vision of India.[4] Yet political debate was saturated with issues emerging from religious practices which had become the object of colonial control, and consequently, sites for asserting indigenous resistance: For example, the cow-protection issue, many have argued, articulated elite and popular Hindu communalism.[5] During this period, and indeed for the first twenty years of its life, the Indian National Congress was a moderate, annual platform from which the professional classes (criticized by both extremist groups and revivalists for the swadeshi cause, including writers like Rabindranath Tagore) appealed to British public opinion for administrative reform, native participation, and gradual constitutional change. This movement's secular moderate character attracted support across religious lines, and included Hindus and Muslims, as well as Sikhs. Their cross-ethnic solidarity during mass anti-imperialist action, even in the Muslim majority districts like Punjab and Bengal, surprised even the British.

In the early 1900s, in a bid to break the strength and communal solidarity of the swadeshi movement, the British did two things. Following their policy of divide and rule, they suggested to, and enabled, elite, land-holding Muslims in the UP to establish the Muslim League in 1906 to represent Muslim interests, which they claimed were different from and opposed to Hindu interests. Second, the British consolidated their position through the Indian Council Act of 1909, which provided separate electorates for the Indian population along communal lines for Hindus and Muslims: eight out of twenty-seven elected seats were reserved for the Muslim separate electorate. As Sumit Sarkar has recorded, the period from 1905 to 1917 saw both Hindu revivalism and Pan Islamism oscillate between anti-imperialism on one hand, and on the other, the expression of class discontent and communal conflict over issues like cow protection, the playing of music near mosques, and the Urdu language.[6]

It is important to note here that both Hindu and Muslim communalism—their discourses and practices—are by no means uniform, homogeneous, and singular in their constitution. Ayesha Jalal and others have reminded us that they contained within them a range of political positions and religious views which cannot be easily assimilated into a monochromatic picture of either; what is more interesting to note is that throughout the 'teens and twenties, they co-operated unevenly with each other in an effort to assert cultural interests as well as wrest political power from the British. Gandhi's return from South Africa in 1915, and his rise to power in the Congress by 1920 with the non-cooperation movement (and its alliance with the Khilafat movement from 1919–1922), was the most powerful articulation of Hindu–Muslim alliance in the anti-imperialist struggle.[7] After 1922, communal riots on a large scale disrupted the Hindu–Muslim alliance between the Congress and Khilafat; political reforms in this period broadened the franchise but preserved and even extended separate electorates.

Historians of South Asia largely agree that separate electorates encouraged the growth of communal organizations and discourses which mobilized members around religious, regional and caste difference. In addition, economic and social tensions like mass unemployment following the spread of education, and landlord–tenant antagonism, were sometimes manifested, suggest Sarkar and others on the Left, in "a distorted communal form." As Sarkar proffers in an oblique mapping of class and communalism, "[l]ower down the social scale, economic and social tensions, as before, could often take a distorted communal form."[8] As Jawaharlal Nehru, who became India's first Prime Minister, wrote about the role of the British in the rise of communalism, "[i]t is a political question of the upper middle classes which has arisen partly because of the attempt of the British Government to weaken the national movement or to create rifts in it and partly because of the prospect of political power coming into India and the upper classes desiring to share in the spoils of offices."[9] Thus, Nehru also describes communalism as generated by economic and political conflict. This middle-class contest for power, compounded by Muslim fears of minoritization in a Hindu-dominated democratic India, eventually contributed to Jinnah's demand for a separate nation-state for Muslims in 1946. It is worth noting that the Hindu Mahasabha (a strong pro-Hindu organization) had also passed a resolution in 1937 to the effect that Hindus and Muslims are two nations and cannot co-exist harmoniously. This two-nation theory, communalist in nature, was posited as the ideological counterpart to secular nationalism. However, the relationship between secular nationalist discourses and communalist politics was complex: Many members of the Hindu Mahasabha, like Madan Mohan Malaviya, were also influential members of the swaraj movement and were close to Gandhi and Nehru. Dominant nationalist discourse was also often inflected in Hindu terms and imagery. For example, independence from colonial subjection was often named Ram Rajya,[10] an idea that probably alienated Muslims. Yet, the decision to partition India on the basis of the two-nation theory, and the ensuing violence (especially the large-scale violence against women) came as a surprise to even the Indian nationalists, and only as late as early 1947.

Recent historical analyses have revealed the multi-layered, overwhelmingly successful manipulation of Muslim perception in favor of a separate homeland, based on purportedly radical differences between Hindus and Muslims.[11] This production of Hindus and Muslims as inimical, politically opposed, and homegeneous communities that belonged in two different nations was engendered through both the British constitutional provision of separate electorates and the generation of fear in colonial discourse—fears of Muslims being minoritized and marginalized in independent India. This two-nation theory, even though it did not emerge from a mass consensus, became the basis for the partition of India in 1947—a partition that was only suddenly seen as inevitable in 1947 after the riots of March 1947, and a partition that was remarkable in its failure "to satisfy the interests of the very Muslims who are supposed to have demanded it."[12]

Rethinking Communalism: The Modernity of Ethnicity

Early nationalist historiography and state discourse has generally represented Partition as an unfortunate outcome of ethnic/communal politics that tragically, and sometimes inevitably, attended the courageous Indian anti-colonial struggle for freedom. In particular, the writing of the Partition has dwelled more on the ethnic violence that marked this moment than on the experience of the accompanying migration and its effects. Marxist historians like Bipan Chandra describe the communalism that led to the Partition as evidence of the failure of nationalism (configured as secular, rational modernity) and of nationalism's incomplete reach and penetration of Indian society. Thus, Chandra asserts that both nationalism and communalism are modern, post-eighteenth-century phenomena; however, nationalism in India "was a correct reflection of an objective reality: the developing identity of common interests of the Indian people, in particular against the common enemy, foreign imperialism." In contrast, he argues that communalism is not "a remnant of the past or the revival of traditional ideology"; it emerged in South Asia because of the failure of certain "sections of society" to "develop the new national consciousness." As such, Chandra proffers that "communalism was generated by the lack of deeper penetration of nationalist outlook and ideology . . . Communalism was and is, the false consciousness of the last 100 years."[13] This was, and continues to be, a common as well as an influential response on the part of the left Indian intelligentsia to the 1947 Partition as well as the rise of contemporary Hindu nationalism: Communal violence is false consciousness and an atavistic remnant of "backward" pre-modern ideas, and evidence of the failure of "true" modern nationalism. Marxist historians, on the other hand, like Asghar Ali Engineer, have described communalism as the effect of elite manipulation of the masses, as "generated by the conflicting interests of the educated elite,"[14] and as socio-economic conflict taking a "distorted communal form."[15] The account of the development of communal ideology as the organization of political and economic interests along religious lines fails, however, as Veena Das has also pointed out, to explain how and why this ideology might suddenly give rise to communal violence.[16]

In the contemporary moment marked by terrorism and international war, many scholars from Edward Said to Bill Brown have called for a reexamination of the critical and new role that religion plays in the formation of cultural communities and national politics; the workings of religion and the ethnic/communal identities derived and consolidated from it deserve urgent attention, if we are to take seriously and understand the resurgent role of "religion" in public life. Towards this end, I am less interested in tracing out here the origins and causes of communalism in South Asia. Instead, one might ask: What do "communalism:" and "secular nationalism" mean in this context? Dumont has defined communalism thus: "Communalism supposes a group of adherents of the same religion but it gets the edge of its meaning through parallelism in which the nation, so to speak, is replaced by the community. In other words, communalism is an assertion and affirmation of the religious group as a political group."[17] In this view, communalism mimics the logic of nationalism, with the desire to replace the nation with the religious community. Furthermore, in some instances, communalism can develop into a communalist nationalism, as is evident in the ascendancy of the Hindu right in India since the 1980s. Nationalist historians like Chandra and others have criticized and castigated communalism as "a distorted ideology" and "a farce," and even Nehru saw it as a temporary aberration, "a side issue" that would wither away with the progress of science, technology, and industrialization.[18] In contrast, secularism in the Indian context has been understood not as state neutrality towards all religious matters, but as equal respect for and recognition of all religions by the state.

In the conventional contours of the debates about ethnic nationalism in the South Asian context, then, the story of ethnic violence—during Partition and after—is often narrated as one of the conflict between communalism and national secularism. Recently, historians have tried to shift the terms of this debate to challenge the simplistic binary division between secularism or secular nationalism and communalism in two ways: on one hand, recent feminist- and subaltern studies research has demonstrated the Hindu influence on the Congress' rhetorics of secular nationalism.[19] On the other hand, a move to re-describe communalism as a "culturalism" has sought to open up a way to think of religious difference as a modern problem of cultural or ethnic difference through which identities are mobilized. For example, Ayesha Jalal argues that the gravitation of Muslims in India towards the idea of a Muslim community in the early twentieth century is less "communal" or religious, and more a "cultural" move—a gravitation towards an assertion of cultural difference and a "religiously informed cultural identity."[20] Further, she contends that the binarism between secularism and communalism has tended to manifest itself in the tendency to name the Muslim as the communalist in South Asian history. In order to correct this tendency, she suggests that what is named Muslim communalism should be seen as an inevitable Muslim "cultural nationalism" "in an inclusionary religious mode," engendered by the Hindu-dominated Congress' refusal to share political power in independent India.[21]

This last argument is disturbing and problematic in its desire to legitimate communalism or communalist politics "in a religious mode" by renaming it cultural nationalism. It not only elides the violence that such exclusionary movements centered upon religion or cultural exclusivism engender, but it also leaves unanswered the feminist questions about the control as well as deployment of women as social and political symbols and objects in the construction of these "cultural nationalist" narratives. This lack of analytical distinction between "religion" and "culture" unwittingly reinforces the very distinctions between Hindus and Muslims that Jalal argues we need to dissect in their complexity and articulation of regional and class interests. As Aamir Mufti usefully cautions, "[e]ven as we are forced to use the antinomies normalized by the state—Hindu and Muslim, majority and minority, Indian and Pakistani, citizen and alien—our task is to make visible the work of this normalization, to reveal its unfinished nature."[22]

Jalal's suggestion that communalism's religiosity be seen as an issue of "cultural" difference is productively countered by Dipesh Chakrabarty's more compelling argument to think of communalism in terms of ethnic difference. Chakrabarty asserts that communalism is a form of racism, and we need to rethink communalism as a modern problem of ethnicity that inevitably becomes a part of Indian political life, once religion is reified as a category marking difference by colonial practices like censuses and separate electorates. Such techniques of power homogenized and consolidated religious and caste identities through their institution in colonial administrative life and their insertion into the public sphere. Thus, he argues, "The very structure of modern governmentality carries with it the seeds of ethnic bloodbath."[23] This is a useful reminder of the modernity of ethnicity, and accordingly, I deploy the terms "communal," "religious," and "ethnic" interchangeably, in order to hold onto the historical valence of the term "communal" in the public-sphere languages of identity in the South Asian context, even as we rewrite the "communal" as a modern problem of *ethnic* rather than religious difference. Furthermore, the problem that preoccupies much of South Asian literature and culture—namely, the representation of ethnic difference or religion in the nation—is one that I will explore through the public-sphere responses to Partition.

Much Partition historiography has been engaged, as Gyan Pandey points out, in "making a case for how this [Partition's genocidal violence] goes against the fundamentals of Indian (or Pakistani) tradition and history: how it is, to that extent, not *our* history at all."[24] Towards interrogating the disavowal and disappearance of Partition violence from dominant national historiography, Pandey has argued that history writing needs to address and incorporate Memory, as both History and Memory are practices of recollecting partition.[25] Discussing the difference between historical, statist accounts of Partition and popular, "non-disciplinary" remembered accounts like oral narratives and memoirs, he points out that the former render violence as both obvious and invisible, banishing it as outside history and community. The latter, on the other hand, "use the event [Partition] to describe a set of other relations and constituencies—which may be called 'community.'" Thus, for Pandey, Memory, or non-disciplinary constructions of the past, uses Partition to account for communities that do not necessarily coincide with the nation, and moreover, are fluid, contingent and in process. For example, in my interviews of Partition refugees from 1947 in Bombay conducted in 2006, the interviewees recounted their individual circumstances of forced dislocation, hardship, and loss but by continually weaving them into a broader narrative of how the Sindhi community had suffered and survived the Partition. Recently, feminist historians and anthropologists, through a concern for the figure of

the woman in community construction, have shared this interest in the production of alternative, non-national forms of community, and in the workings
of community and communality. Scholars like Veena Das, Urvashi Butalia,
Ritu Menon, and Kamala Bhasin have variously addressed the problem of
communal violence; while Das has examined Sikh women's experience in
the 1984 anti-Sikh riots; Butalia, Menon, and Bhasin have taken up the relationship between communalism and nationality and the elision of Partition
violence by focusing largely on the experience of women and children during
Partition, and through a turn to oral testimony.[26]

In response to the elisions and occlusions of disciplinary practices whose
subject is the community and the nation, and in order to tell the story of the
ambivalence of secular nationalism, of the complexities of desire and identification that engendered sexual violence against women, of the violence done
to male bodies during this undeclared civil war that was Partition, I turn to
the postcolonial public sphere. Into Pandey's useful map of the difference
between history and memory, I want to posit the importance of public sphere
cultural texts like literature and film—an archive which is a part of the public memory of Partition, and that constitutes a discourse of what Foucault
has called "counter-memory" to the hegemonic public sphere. A discussion
of Memory, which Pandey locates in the individual and her "community," is
incomplete without a discussion of the special role of literature and film as
an archive of memory in the public sphere—a public, collective, non-statist
memory. As I have argued earlier, these imaginative literary and filmic narratives not only give testimony about the public, aesthetic and collective *translational* understanding of the Partition experience, but also shape contemporary
individual narratives of memory (oral testimony, memoirs) from which Pandey
argues history writing needs to learn. For example, Khushwant Singh's realist
novel *Train to Pakistan* not only remembers a peaceful, syncretic rural community of Mano Majra before Partition, but it also illuminates the ambivalent,
contest-ridden production of everyday life in the postcolonial nation-state. The
novel negotiates the tension between History, whose subject is the nation, and
Memory, whose subject is the individual, to articulate an imaginative resolution of the contradictions of postcolonial freedom and dispossession, national
independence and a deathly failure of homeliness. Such cultural texts reveal
as well as critique the varied forms of violence that inhabit and measure the
distance between the nation and the individual, History and Memory, making visible, in the process, the production as well as destruction of gendered
subjectivities, belongings, and identities—ethnic and national.

The literary and film representations of the everyday experience of
Partition violence and its impact on national identity and citizenship
challenge the simplistic binarisms of liberalism/fundamentalism and secular

nationalism/communalism that have so far dominated political discourse in the modern world. As Allen Feldman has suggested in the Irish context, rather than taking communalism and nationalism to be static, pre-constituted ideological formations, we need to understand them as relational effects of productive networks of power, and as cultural constructions enacted and contested through specific, material and somatic practices of violence in this moment.[27] It is only by taking communalism and nationalism as not necessary but contingent, ambivalently articulated, *materially constructed* and productive relations of power that we can open up a space for the critique of their violence. The cleavages and alliances that Partition literature and film make visible enable us to complicate the traditional cast of a binary oppositional relationship between secularist nationalism and communalism and track the potential of building non-oppressive social relations through the recognition of difference.

In this, my approach differs from Urvashi Butalia's in her ground-breaking book *The Other Side of Silence*.[28] In her book, Butalia presents remarkable oral accounts of the Partition experience of women, children, and *dalits,* painstakingly recorded between 1987 and 1997. Butalia asserts that she "would like to place them [the oral narratives] *alongside* existing histories" rather than placing "these voices *against* the conventional, factual histories of the time"[29] (my italics). However, I suggest that the contestatory power and memorializing testimonies of such oral narratives, and of narratives of literature and cinema, in fact make it imperative to intercept and interrogate hegemonic nationalist histories of colonialism and postcolonialism, if we are to harness the translational power of these other, non-official archives of Partition. These cultural narratives, as practices of political intervention, enable us to historicize and challenge the violent minoritization that marks ethnicized and gendered political identities in contemporary subcontinental nationalist discourse. Thus, it is urgent and necessary to intercept and interrogate hegemonic nationalist histories through them: It is only when we contest conventional textbook histories (as Shahid Amin has also suggested[30]), that we can make visible the production of subjects and communities, as well as the disavowals and contradictions that inhabit nationalist histories.

Postcolonial National Masculinities and Coupledom

Much of the current scholarship on the vexed relationship between nationalism and gender, especially feminist cultural criticism and the postcolonial critique of nationalism, has illuminated how women are constructed as signs and symbols of the nation or ethnic/cultural community in nationalist discourses. As such, women's bodies often begin to bear the symbolic burden, as valuably illuminated by literary critics like Sangeeta Ray and Henry Schwartz and colonial historians like Partha Chatterjee and Lata Mani, among others, of signifying culture and tradition, community and nation.[31] For example, in her study of colonial narratives by British as well as Indian writers, which concludes with a consideration of the postcolonial fiction of Anita Desai and Bapsi Sidhwa, Ray has demonstrated how ethnicity and gender are deployed in the narration of the Indian nation across these diverse cultural texts. "[The] articulation of a Hindu India is intrinsically bound up with the production of the Indian woman as Hindu, and who then becomes the epistemological and ontological cultural principle against which the history of British India is enacted."[32] Ray uncovers not only the gendering of the nation as a feminized space, but also its dominant ethnicization as Hindu; the Hindu woman in this discursive formation embodies the Indian nation. In his study of the formation of anti-colonial nationalism in India, Partha Chatterjee has also shown how the nationalist construction of the new Indian (and Hindu) woman was central to the invention of "tradition" and cultural difference between East and West posited by Indian nationalist discourse. His analysis, in his words, "shows how, in the confrontation between colonialist and nationalist discourses, the dichotomies of spiritual/material, home/world, feminine/masculine, while enabling the production of nationalist discourse, nonetheless remains trapped within its false essentialisms."[33] In the process of examining the gendering of nationalism, feminist scholarship has often translated the relation between "gender" and nation as one between "woman" and nation. This leads us to questions we are now prepared to and need to address, about men and masculinity in the production of gendered identities: What happens to men's roles, male bodies, and conceptions of masculinity in the discursive articulation of nationalism in the postcolonial public sphere? How are male bodies represented, deployed and refashioned in the creation and contestation of postcolonial nationalism?

To complicate the equation of "gender" and "woman," to offer a fuller account of the gendering of nationalism, I want to argue that it is imperative to examine the construction of both masculinity and femininity together in the articulation of cultural and national belonging in public and political discourse. Thus, while recent feminist work has argued that women become symbols of the nation in moments of ethnic conflict—not only in South Asia but around the world—I suggest that a new look at the narration of violence against men in the postcolonial Indian public sphere reveals that masculinity and men as gendered subjects can also become critical sites for the symbolization of nationality and belonging. While the violence perpetrated by men against women's bodies in ethnic conflict has received much attention, this chapter deliberately focuses on the cultural representation of violence suffered by male bodies in the public sphere. This is not to elide or minimize the role of men as agents of gendered, sexual, and ethnic violence against women, but to complicate that discourse by attending to the ideological production of, and material violence to, male bodies in the postcolonial nation.

In colonial discourse studies, Frantz Fanon's work has illuminated the fantasmatic dynamics of inter-racial colonial desire, and shown how European racist discourse about black masculinity marks a fear of the black male subject's perceived hyper-sexuality. This racial discourse about desire turns on binarisms (black/white, potent/impotent, female/male) that indicate a fear of miscegenation and racial degeneration through the imagined potential sexual union of the white woman and the black man.[34] Building upon his analysis of racial masculinity and desire but contrary to the misogynist views that mark much of Fanon's work, new directions in feminist studies have begun to take up the construction of masculinity, towards reconceptualizing the project and politics of feminist and queer struggles.[35] Masculinity-studies scholars like Rachel Adam and David Savran have sought to initiate the re-examination of masculinity and eroticism, and elucidate the formation of "socially-sanctioned, patriarchal—but not necessarily heterosexualized—masculinity" in primarily Euro-American scenes.[36] While these studies largely explore the historical and cultural construction of masculinity in Euro-American contexts, Mrinalini Sinha has illuminated the complex and contingent racial articulation of colonial masculinity in nineteenth-century India.[37] Taking up the colonial rhetorics about British masculinity and the stereotype of the "effeminate" Bengali babu, Sinha uncovers the historical production of specific dominant masculinities—the "manly Englishman" and the "effeminate babu"—as categories that mark colonial contestation and signal colonial power. As mentioned earlier, Sinha, with others like Rosalind O'Hanlon, has thus foregrounded masculinity as a discursive construct in colonial and postcolonial studies.[38] In his psychoanalytic work on queer masculinity in Asian America, David Eng explores the production of Asian American male subjectivity in "the dominant heterosexist and racist structures" of U.S. national culture.[39] Tracking "Asian American male subjectivity as an especially contradictory identity within discourses of national citizenry," Eng posits queerness and diaspora as sites through which racist and heteronormative exclusions from national belonging can be challenged. Drawing upon the insights of Fanon, Sinha, and Eng, this chapter explores the hegemonic and counter-construction of masculinity and nationality in decolonization and postcolonial diasporas. Special attention is given to the rhetorics about postcolonial coupledom and citizenship in South

Asian cultural texts from the subcontinent and diaspora. In interrogating the slide from "gender" to "woman" by re-examining masculinity in the narratives about ethnicity, coupledom, and belonging offered up in the hegemonic Indian public sphere as well as postcolonial counter-publics, I hope to contribute to and complicate our understanding of the relation between gender and the postcolonial nation.

Many scholars, like Anne McClintock and Elleke Boehmer, have suggested that in the nationalist scenario, women "are typically constructed as the symbolic bearers of the nation" while in contrast, men are "contiguous" with each other and with the national whole.[40] However, in the literature of the 1947 Partition of India, it is notable that often, men become symbolic national icons; through their suffering masculinities, they index the violence of both colonialism and elite nationalism. These texts critique British colonialism as well as postcolonial Indian nationalism through the loss of belonging endured by masculine subjects and inter-ethnic coupledom. In excavating the gendering of nationalism in the Indian public spheres post-1947, then, one encounters an ambivalent, complex construction of both male as well as female subjects as symbolic representatives of (ethnic) community and nationality. In particular, the literature that engages the history of decolonization, Partition and independence in India deploys the gendered body, marked by ethnic difference, as the literal and symbolic site of national violence. This literature, as a part of postcolonial public spheres that become increasingly transnational, critiques nationalism through the representation of violence and displacement experienced by its heterosexual male and female subjects, by the heteronormative couple and the patriarchal family. In the process, these narratives make visible how both male and female bodies are subject to intimate violence and disabling displacement. By showing how the state thus generates suffering citizens and resisting subjects, these cultural accounts illuminate new contours of gendering that mark discourses of ethnic identity, nationalism, and postcolonial citizenship. Thus, while Chapter Two takes up the cultural and mass-media representation of women's experience of Partition violence and displacement, I have begun this book deliberately with a topic that has not been taken up in feminist postcolonial studies and especially in Partition studies: the cultural account of men's experience of Partition violence.

Secular and State Masculinities

Salman Rushdie's novel *Midnight's Children* (1981) and Yash Chopra's popular Bollywood film *Veer Zaara* (2004; discussed in Chapter Five) are especially interesting works in their representation of postcolonial national experience in South Asia, and of the suffering masculinities they code as heroic citizenship. *Midnight's Children* came out in 1981, and was, apart from Anita Desai's *Clear Light of Day* (1980), one of the first South Asian novels in English that returned to the question of nation formation and partition in the South Asian public sphere; this turn to reconsidering 1947 emerged in the South Asian diaspora, and after Partition had largely disappeared from discussion in public life in India for over a decade. Thus, Rushdie's return to the meaning and effects of Partition marks the diasporic turn to questions about national history and memory, a turn paralleled by subsequent work by feminists, subaltern studies historians and anthropologists on Partition. In Salman Rushdie's novel *Midnight's Children*, the story of the male narrator Saleem Sinai's body, "buffeted by too much history," becomes an allegory of a divided subcontinent in which the past as Partition is continually reiterated in the present.

Midnight's Children is about the 1,001 children born in India in the novel at precisely the moment India gained independence from British colonialism and became a nation-state. The protagonist and narrator, Saleem Sinai, is one of the 531 children who survive adolescence and so represent the post-independence generation. When Saleem is born at midnight on August 14, 1947, newspapers designate Saleem as "MIDNIGHT'S CHILD" and "the Happy Child of that Glorious Hour," and a personal letter from Prime Minister Jawaharlal Nehru also claims him as the representative citizen of the new nation: "Dear Baby Saleem, My belated congratulations on the happy accident of your moment of birth! You are the newest bearer of the ancient fate of India, which is also eternally young." Furthermore, the letter ominously offers, foreshadowing the state violence inflicted upon resisting citizens, "We shall be watching over your life with the closest attention; it will be, in a sense, the mirror of our own" (138). Nehru's congratulatory note and its denouement emblematize the collusive and conflicted relation between the nation form and the everyday life of its citizens. The nation's address to Saleem in this note not only writes him as the nation's present and its representative citizen subject, but also subjects him to the disciplining scrutiny of the nation-state apparatus as its pedagogical object. Thus, the allegorization of Saleem's masculine body as nation is suggested throughout the narrative. As Saleem puts it, "the cracks in the earth . . . will-be-have-been reborn in my skin" (125). Accordingly, "as the body politic began to crack," Saleem begins to be physically mutilated: for example, his finger is lopped off in an accident (coinciding with the bloody language riots in Bombay); as he lives through Pakistan's civil war of 1965 and India's Emergency in 1975, Saleem ends up forcibly lobotomized and sterilized. Nehru's note makes Saleem nation embodied, and foreshadows how the dismembering, bodily violence suffered by Saleem will be an allegory of national history. As regional and linguistic conflicts rip the fabric of national unity, Saleem's mutilated body symbolizes the spatial and social partitions of South Asia. Saleem's impotent and dismembered body, in scenes scattered throughout the subcontinent, becomes the effect of state violence on the dream of secular Indian nationalism. In the process, it is his wounded, emasculated and disabled male body that stands as witness and victim of the violence of nations and nationalisms.

Thus, on one hand, the 1947 Partition appears throughout the novel as the event that splinters and spreads Saleem's extended family over two countries, as many of his parents' siblings choose to migrate to Pakistan. Simultaneously, it remains present in the novel in its reiteration in the minor citizen's disabled body. Partition is both a historical event and a metaphor of national experience; the parallel dismembering of the nation's body politic and the narrator's own body mark Saleem as a postcolonial mirror-citizen who somatically performs the critique of postcolonial nationalisms. Early on in the novel, Saleem says, "Please believe that I am falling apart." This fragmentation, he insists, is literal, as like the cracking of postcolonial India into regional and language conflicts, he has "begun to crack all over like an old jug—that my poor body, singular, unlovely, buffeted by too much history . . . has started coming apart at the seams." Then, he exhorts the reader, "I ask you only to accept (as I have accepted) that I shall eventually crumble into (approximately) six hundred and thirty million particles of anonymous and necessarily oblivious dust" (37). Clearly, the phrase "six hundred and thirty million particles" refers to the population of India; as Saleem disintegrates, he predicts the disintegration of the myth and body politic of the nation. Narration—through which Saleem enacts his "vengeful irruption into the history of [his] age"—becomes an act that counters the violent effects of "too much history" (317). Gayatri Gopinath has also noted "[t]he centrality of a failed or impotent masculinity as a metaphor for the postcolonial condition" in the work of diasporic fiction—both modernist and postmodern—by V. S. Naipaul and Salman Rushdie. Indeed, she argues that "[t]he impotence of Rushdie's narrator Saleem Sinai reflects his inability to effect historical change and institute an alternative vision of the nation."[41] While my consideration of Rushdie's *Midnight's Children* is brief and necessarily partial—for example, it does not address the extensive discussion in earlier scholarship of the representation of women in *Midnight's Children*—what it nonetheless tracks is the postcolonial literary symbolization of suffering, minor masculinities as embodied and disabled secular nationalism.

Partition produces Saleem's body as an iconic victim and exemplary critic of the postcolonial nation-state and its political elite. For example, Saleem's body is at once the body of the upper-class and minoritized Indian Muslim in Bombay in terms of his social identity as Saleem Sinai, and also a racially hybrid body. The narrative suggests that he is the product of an adulterous fling between the working-class Hindu Vanita and the British colonialist Methwold, even though he is born as the son of the working poor couple: Wee Willie Winkie and Vanita. Michael Gorra has argued that Saleem's "British ancestry functions, rather, as a trope, for his hybrid cultural heritage, for the different forces that the novel suggests have shaped modern India."[42] I would add that, in addition to his genetic hybridity, his class and cultural hybridity also make Saleem an embodiment of a utopian vision of secular Indian nationalism, much like Jugga in Khushwant Singh's account from the early national period. But if Jugga in *Train to Pakistan* (which I will discuss shortly) is very much a secular peasant *Sikh* hero, Saleem is a minor, Muslim, not-quite-heroic, urban, middle-class, and mongrel mirror-citizen of the nation.

Saleem's suffering Muslim masculinity and his increasing disenfranchisement in postcolonial India at the hands of the state is contrasted, late in the novel, to another midnight's child, Shiva. The narrative reveals and problematizes the heroicization of the violent masculinity of late, statist, Hindu nationalism, represented in the figure of Major Shiva—"India's most decorated war-hero"—from the seventies onwards (486). We are told that "once he led a gang of apaches in the back-streets of Bombay; once before he discovered the legitimized violence of war, prostitutes were found throttled in gutters" (486). Here, the narrative links sexual violence against women and the state production of violence in the form of war, implicitly critiquing the masculinist aggression engendering both. Shiva, who is raised as Wee Willie Winkie and Vanita's son, not coincidentally, reappears in the narrative in 1974 when India conducted its first nuclear tests. This portends the emergence of a militant, masculine Hindu nationalism that overshadows once-hegemonic ideas of secularism in the Indian public sphere from the late seventies onwards with the Janata government (1977–1979) and the discursive formation of a political "Hindu majority" cresting in the eighties. Shiva's origins in Bombay crime hint at a critique of Bombay's dominant political party Shiv Sena, notorious for its links with underground crime. Saleem remarks, "There are ironies here, which must not pass unnoticed; for had not Shiva risen as Saleem fell? Who was the slum-dweller now, and who looked down from commanding heights?" (486). This reversal of fortunes for both characters thus allegorizes the transformation of hegemonic political discourse in India and foreshadows the meteoric rise to state power of a once-marginalized, now-militant Hindu nationalism. As Michael Gorra has remarked, "a newly prosperous and self-consciously Hindu middle-class, has turned away from Congress and toward the BJP in what has become, in the

years since the publication of *Midnight's Children*, a far greater challenge to
Nehru's legacy than that posed by the separatists of Kashmir or Assam."[43]
Described as a charismatic ambassador, the figure of the muscular Major
Shiva acquires a mythic quality and becomes a legend among the Hindu
bourgeoisie: He is "elevated in social status as well as military rank," only
"to be applauded and monopolized by the noblest and the fairest in the land"
(487). Thus Rushdie explicitly problematizes the popularity of chauvinistic
Hindu nationalist rhetorics, as they capture state power and bourgeois support; the ascendancy of the hyper-masculine, sexually potent, sexist, and
muscular Hindu masculinity of Shiva—who is, ironically, the biological son
of Muslim parents Ahmed and Amina Sinai—in this narrative also indexes
the increasing disempowerment of the minoritized and partitioned Saleem
as citizen. His suffering masculinity now marks the marginalization of early
national secularism, cultural hybridity, and nationalist optimism in postcolonial India.

Amy Kaplan has offered a compelling account of the spectacular construction of embodied masculinity in the 1890s American representations
of the U.S. empire as disembodied national power. Describing the early-
twentieth-century reinvention of the male body in American romances, she
points out that "in the figure of a revitalized male body, geographic disten-
tion, and overseas conquest figure as a temporal return to origins, literally,
as nostalgia, nostos, the return home."[44] In contrast, in much South Asian
postcolonial literature, the male body is not revitalized, but is instead disabled and destroyed in and through geopolitical violence. In Saleem Sinai's
mutilated, minoritized body as the mirror of the nation, Rushdie describes
the historical legacy of that first, violent, national partition of 1947. National
fragmentation is reproduced upon the masculine bodies of its male citizens,
and Rushdie's urban, hybrid bourgeois male subject's impotence represents
the failure of the promises of postcolonial India—reconfiguring in the process, the nationalist discourse of the nation as "Mother India." Hence, in
Midnight's Children, Rushdie imaginatively pictures for us not only a magical
realist revision and remembrance of the violent territorial splitting of 1947,
but also its historical continuity and repetition in national life upon embodied
national subjects.

The Early National Moment: Suffering
Masculinities and Inter-ethnic Romance

Khushwant Singh's novel *Train to Pakistan* (1956), from the early national
period, is a prize-winning novel about how Partition violence in different

parts of India eventually creeps into the once syncretic village community, an oasis of peace: Mano Majra. A small village near the Indo-Pakistan border, Mano Majra's seventy families include one Hindu (a moneylender, Lala Ram Lal) and about an equal number of Sikh and Muslim families. The Sikhs are largely landowners, and the Muslims are tenants who shared the tilling of the land. The novel's melodramatic plot centers upon the transgressive inter-ethnic romance of Juggut Singh, a Sikh ruffian, and Nooran, a Muslim girl. Set in the summer of 1947, the novel describes Mano Majra as initially untouched by the Partition, its harmonious everyday life regulated by the rhythms of the trains that rattle across the nearby river bridge. When, in this peaceful haven, the moneylender is murdered by some thieves, suspicion falls on Juggut Singh, who is a known village thief. In the meantime, even as a Western-educated Communist political worker, Iqbal, arrives in the village to preach class struggle and communal harmony, a train comes over the bridge at an unusual time, and the villagers discover it is full of dead Sikhs. When the same thing happens a few days later and another train carrying dead Sikhs arrives, the village's peace becomes another casualty of Partition.

When the large-scale migration or "exchange" of populations began in 1947, large numbers of people went across the new national borders in every imaginable way: by train, by air for the elite, by ship for those going from Karachi to Bombay, and most common of all, by foot. Once the ethnic violence escalated, organized gangs of Hindus and Sikhs, as well as Muslims, ambushed and attacked trains carrying people of the "other" community across the border. For instance, news reports like this one in the *Times* from September 26, 1947 were very common: "On the train, the refugees were riding outside and on the roof, and a stone thrown at such a bulging, writhing target generally killed. No army could supply complete protection."[45] Often, attackers stopped trains, and systematically killed every man, woman, and child on board, leaving the engine driver alive to carry "the gift" (as they would call it) to India or Pakistan.

Set in this moment, *Train to Pakistan* makes visible how, locally and individually, the villagers of Mano Majra begin to rearticulate their identities and alliances following the advent of trains laden with dead Hindu and Sikh refugees' bodies from Pakistan. From being unified as a stable, rural community of Mano Majrans, they now become polarized into new ethnic groups—Hindus and Sikhs versus Muslims—in an abstract nation. When the former's desire for revenge violence is questioned, "[W]hat have the Muslims of *this* village done?" (my italics), many, from native Sikh Mano Majrans to the local sub-inspector say, "They are Muslims." Thus, neighbors become marked ethnically, and in that process, othered—a familiar story in many other global scenes of ethnic violence.

Following this chain of events around the train from Pakistan—a symbol, until now, of West-ushered scientific modernity—events proceed very dramatically. As Hukum Chand, the magistrate newly arrived in Mano Majra "to maintain the peace," plans, the Muslims of Mano Majra are forced to leave the village. They are evacuated first to a refugee camp in a nearby town, Chundunnugger, and then to Pakistan by train, with only as many belongings as they can carry in hand. Their property is ransacked and taken over by local dacoits and Sikh refugees from Pakistan that had taken shelter in the village. Finally, these same people hatch a plot to kill as many Muslims as they can when the train carrying the Muslim refugees from the Chundunnugger refugee camp passes through Mano Majra's railway station.

Refugee trains at this time overflowed with passengers, some traveling even on the rooftops of the trains because the compartments were overcrowded. Their plan is to stretch a strong rope across the span of the bridge, a foot above the height of the funnel of the engine, such that when the train passes under it, the rope will sweep off all the people (at least five hundred) sitting on the roof of the train. The plan is foiled when Jugga uncovers it, and discovers that his beloved Nooran (who, unbeknownst to him, is pregnant with his child) is on that same train. He heroically cuts off the rope just as the train arrives; wounded, he falls and is crushed under the train even as it passes safely on to Pakistan. Jugga's love for his departing Muslim beloved saves the lives of hundreds of refugees. The novel thus valorizes heroic interethnic love, and envisions it as the only redemptive, secularizing force in the midst of this senseless violence.

On one hand, *Train to Pakistan* registers the rhetoric of avenging women's dishonor that many men from both communities voiced at this time. The conversation between the sub-inspector at Mano Majra and the magistrate Hukum Chand early on, when Chand arrives there, is pertinent. As government employees, both are responsible for maintaining law and order; Chand is expressly sent to the district for this purpose. However, the conversation between them sheds light on a much regretted but underplayed aspect of Partition violence: that despite the purported official condemnation of violence on the part of both the Indian and the Pakistani states, the workers and officials that constituted the state apparatus were not always neutral or secular. In fact, they often deployed their positions as state officials and representatives to engineer ethnic violence and displace people from the other community. The sub-inspector says, "Sometimes Sir, one cannot restrain oneself. What do the Gandhi caps in Delhi know about the Punjab? What is happening on the other side in Pakistan does not matter to them. They have not lost their homes and belongings; they haven't had their mothers, wives, sisters, and daughters raped and murdered in the street" (31). However, like the "Gandhi caps" or nationalist politicians he is criticizing, the sub-inspector has not lost his home or belongings, or seen his wife, sister, or daughter raped and murdered in the street either. On the other hand, then, this scene also makes visible the distance and dissonance between elite, secular nationalist politics, and the alienated, resentful actors in the state apparatus entrusted to translate that secular national vision into reality—actors voicing popular communalist rhetoric and for whom local, ethnic, class, and caste affiliations were often more compelling than the imagined nation.

To the sub-inspector's outburst Hukum Chand responds, "I know it all. Our Hindu women . . . so pure that they would rather commit suicide than let a stranger touch them" (31). Chand's response not only erases from the ethnic community the presence of the raped Hindu woman, but also endorses the contemporaneous popular ideology (voiced even by Gandhi initially) of suicide as the only option for women raped, or about to be raped.[46] Chand thus not only reinforces the common Hindu nationalist rhetoric about women's purity and defilement, but also locks the "Hindu woman" into a discourse where sexual violence is a form of "dishonor": a dishonoring which amounts to social death, and therefore supposedly makes the very victim—the woman—of that violence desire physical death. The novel's heteronormative structure reinforces this symbolic violence to the figure of the "Hindu woman": the Hindu and Sikh women who are raped die in the novel's account. In contrast, both the Muslim women—Nooran and Haseena Begum, who have sexual relations with non-Muslim men (Juggut Singh and Chand)—do not die, but migrate to Pakistan—their troubling bodies banished beyond the Indian national border. In addition, Nooran, the new Muslim citizen of the incipient nation Pakistan, is pregnant with a Sikh's child.

Hukum Chand's machinations to displace Muslim Mano Majrans and his relationship with a 16-year-old Muslim sex worker, Haseena Begum, both reveal Chand to be a depraved, corrupt bureaucrat. He rationalizes away his misgivings about Haseena's age, because she has been procured for him at his own behest. He reminisces that she reminds him of his daughter, and then deliberately dismisses those thoughts to proceed to be intimate with her. Later, he realizes that he has developed feelings for Haseena, whom he had sent away to Chundunnugger after a couple of days with her in Mano Majra: "'No fool like an old fool.' It was bad enough for a married man in his fifties to go picking up women. To get emotionally involved with a girl young enough to be his daughter and a Muslim prostitute at that! That was *too* ludicrous." Chand feels embarrassed and stupid at this: "He must be losing his grip on things. He was getting senile and stupid" (200). Chand's sexual encounter has turned into emotional attachment; when he realizes that as per his own plans, she was being evacuated along with all the Muslims in the district to Pakistan, he becomes remorseful: "Why had he let the girl go back to Chundunnugger? Why? He asked himself, hitting his forehead with his fist. If only she were here in the rest house with him, he would not bother if the rest of the world went to hell. But she was not here; she was in the train." (204) Then, the narrator reveals the depth of Chand's grief and regret, as he turns to God to pray for his "beloved": "Hukum Chand slid off his chair, covered his face with his arms and started to cry. Then he raised his face to the sky and began to pray" (204). Thus, the end of the novel redeems Hukum Chand's communalist acts through his realization of his "feelings" for the Muslim girl sex worker. His act of praying, presumably for forgiveness and for Haseena's safety, signals his moral transformation through inter-ethnic intimacy. In other words, his sentimentality about the Muslim sex-worker and refugee mitigates his communalist sentiments. This representation criticizes communalist ideology, but it fails to challenge the production of women as sexual objects and cultural symbols that grounds ethnic sexual violence. Ultimately, the novel's ambivalence towards Chand perhaps exemplifies the middle-class sentiment about ethnic violence in this moment: The narrator both embraces Chand's criticism of nationalist politicians and the price that ordinary Indians paid for their so-called freedom and tryst with destiny, as well as reveals Chand to be a communalist, mean, and corrupt state representative who destroys Mano Majra's peace. In this ambivalence, where Chand is almost but not quite a hero or a villain, the novel articulates the middle-classes' ambivalence towards communalism—and consequent complicity with its ethnic violence—at this time. Herein lies the novel's failure in transcending and envisioning a beyond to the patriarchal and communalist discourses of its time.

Although the state official Chand ends up being partially redeemed by his love in the narrative, it is Jugga—a common criminal—who is good-hearted, sincere, and ultimately the novel's secular hero. Jugga is seen to be ethical, in that he does not commit crimes against his fellow Mano Majrans, and ultimately a hero because he sacrifices his life for true love. Chand mistakenly claims that the raffish Jugga would never risk his life for a woman, but would merely replace her with another. Jugga proves this class and ethnic prejudice wrong. It is significant and ironic that it is Jugga, the young, hyper-masculine, sexual "bad" man, and not the government bureaucrat Chand, seen as "the Government" by the uneducated villagers, that ensures the safety of Muslim refugees going to Pakistan. Jugga's heroic act of saving the life of hundreds of Muslims thus undercuts Chand's best efforts to engineer the saboteurs' violence. However, if Jugga's lower class criminality is redeemed by his heroic true love, it is done only through the dematerialization of his body. It is on his crushed, rural, masculine body that the triumph of secularism—figured as inter-ethnic love—is inscribed.

It is notable that all the inter-ethnic sexual relationships that appear in the novel's heteronormative frame are between Sikh/Hindu men and Muslim women. Like much Indian literature and film of the time (and I must add, with few exceptions, of today) nowhere is the Muslim man a figure of embodied masculinity and heroism, involved with a non-Muslim woman. The Muslim woman here is represented through the paradigmatic opposition of either girl-whore (Haseena Begum) or mother (Nooran). Nooran's pregnant body carrying the product of Sikh–Muslim love becomes not only symbolic of the birth of the Pakistani nation, but also suggestive of the impurity of ethnic and national identities. At the same time, this birth of the Pakistani nation is inscribed as symbolically enabled through the violent sacrifice of Jugga's potent and heroic body—the Sikh male peasant's body. Jugga's wounded, hyper-masculine yet minor body represents both the region of Punjab and secular Indian nationalism; however, this embodiment of the "real" India becomes a victim of nationalist politics and its failures. In the epic romance of this novel, it is the sincere, secular, and suffering male peasant who is both a victim and an authentic representative of true India. In other words, through the performativity of sexed masculine identities, reinforcing codes of chivalrous masculinity, the novel produces Jugga as both a secular hero and a suffering victim of the nation. The violence to the heterosexual, male, peasant citizen's body thus becomes the evidence of the failure of the Indian nation-state as a utopian site for granting freedom from colonial and communal violence, and the failure of nationalist politics in much contemporary literature. Moreover, it is important to attend to the ethnicity of Jugga as Sikh, and not Hindu, in this melodrama. The production of a gendered Sikh subjectivity in Indian public spheres has a long history. As Brian Axel has noted, in the colonial period, "Sikh men had come to be known as extremely courageous soldiers and the strongest challenge to the British."[47] Popularly represented as the fighting arm of the Hindu nation, it was only in the eighties, Axel points out, that the separatist militancy in Punjab and the assassination of the Prime Minister Indira Gandhi led to Sikhs being seen as national enemies in India, even as there emerged a discourse of persecuted Sikh subjectivity in the Sikh diaspora. *Train to Pakistan* participates in the popular discourse of its time by heroicizing Sikh masculinity as national strength and iconic citizenship; however, by mourning its destruction by the state-enabled Partition violence, this postcolonial novel critiques both elite nationalism and ethnic discrimination.

Train to Pakistan draws upon a familiar motif of epic romance: the lover takes care of the beloved, at the cost of his life. Jugga's secular love, transcending communalism, is banished from the structural-symbolic world of nations secured through ethnic difference in this novel; yet, Jugga's somatic sacrifice is not simply an imaginary contestation that engineers the failure of communalism in this moment of crisis. It is also, in the shape and form of Nooran's pregnant body and his own crushed one, a troubling return of a humanist, non-national, non-communal force illuminating the violent and contingent boundaries of communalist nationalism. As Judith Butler puts it in a different context, it is "an enabling disruption, the occasion for a radical re-articulation of the symbolic horizon in which bodies come to matter at all."[48] Jugga's male body takes the wound of the nation-state, in an embodied performance of a sensate, secular democracy; however, Nooran and Haseena's bodies, sexually and culturally "othered" through prostitution and pre-marital pregnancy, are deployed differently, They are not coded as heroic. Both male as well as female bodies are being worked in this novel's narrative; yet, if the male body is heroicized, the female body is a transitional object, a symbolizing site of intelligibility in the rhetoric of nationalism. In other words, the imminent temporality of the Indian nation can exist only through the traumatizing banishment of inter-ethnic love, and of impure, unintelligible, inter-ethnic identities whose future possibility is embodied by a pregnant Nooran. The novel brings out the uncertainty and impurity of ethnic national identities which communalism disavows through the figure of Nooran;[49] yet it displaces this uncertainty and hybridity of ethnic location embodied by Nooran's fetus elsewhere, on the other side of the national border, in Pakistan. If Jugga's suffering masculinity is ideal and honorable, then Nooran's fecund femininity, because of its Islamic origins, must both inspire it (to symbolize the secular) and disappear (to stave off the threat of ethnic impurity in the "secular" nation).

The theme of inter-ethnic romantic love as the only transcending force in the face of ethnic violence was also popular in other novels, short stories and films. It also resurfaces in contemporary representations like Deepa Mehta's 1999 art film *Earth* (discussed later), which was based on Pakistani writer Bapsi Sidhwa's novel *Cracking India*. Inter-ethnic love, between a Hindu/Sikh man and a Muslim woman, is also a dominant theme in popular Bollywood films like *Bombay* (1995), *Dahek: A Burning Passion* (1999), *Gadar: Ek Prem Katha* (Mayhem: A Love Story, 2001), and *Veer Zaara* (2004). That such literary narratives of inter-ethnic love usually end in tragic ways suggests the limits of imagining a way of living with ethnic difference in domestic intimacy. Perhaps because inter-ethnic romance potentially threatens the ideological family purity upon which ethnic communities are built, the realist fictional narrative—unlike popular Bollywood cinema—often forecloses the imaginative realization of inter-ethnic love.[50] However, in *Train to Pakistan* the origins of this motif of inter-ethnic love lie, at least in part, in the tropes of urban middle-class secularist discourse about ethnic difference in India:

the syncretism of religious social life in rural India; the fabled peaceful and harmonious communal relations pre-Partition; the rural as both destroyed by urban politics and as the site of "real" India.[51]

In accounting for the collective, historical production of nationalist discourse in South Asia, it is also important to examine how certain kinds of oppositions, like Hindu–Muslim, men–women, and secular–communal become conventional and iconic, and become the norm in our historicist accounts. The literary recollection of Partition violence, as in *Train to Pakistan*, shows how these terms are not opposite but aligned to constitute the nation on the body of the couple. The literature of this crisis in general, and this novel in particular, shows how communality and nationality do not always coincide or work in tandem. *Train to Pakistan* illustrates that often, people cared little for the nationality being thrust upon them, and responded ambivalently to communalism, in a political situation where one nation (Pakistan) was being explicitly founded on the basis of religious commonality—*for Muslims*. It is this very anxious and ambivalent space between the communal and the national that the state seeks to fill through the figure of the ethnicized man and woman. The ethnicized woman, Hindu, Muslim, or Sikh, enjoins nation-state and community as both property owners (of women's bodies) and masculine authority. *Train to Pakistan*, in placing Nooran squarely within the territorial limits of Pakistan, re-inscribes dominant Indian patriarchal social and ideological discourse. Such texts' ambivalence towards inter-ethnic love emerges in their movement from the valorization of inter-ethnic romance, to their inability to allow its realization in their representations—all such romances end in heroic-tragic ways.

Manto and the Urban Modern: Everydayness and Embodiment in Violence

If Partition renders impossible the realization of romantic inter-ethnic intimacy in the national imagination, it also disfigures intra-ethnic domestic intimacy in partitioned South Asia, suggest Saadat Hasan Manto's short stories from the early national period. Khushwant Singh's contemporary, Saadat Hasan Manto (1912–1955) is a writer who has now also become somewhat of a cultural icon in South Asian literary and cultural spheres, having left behind a remarkable and searing corpus of Partition stories. He wrote in Urdu, and his works have been translated into several languages. Recently, Manto's work has seen a revival: For example, in the early 1990s his collected works were compiled and published in Hindi in India as well as in Urdu in Pakistan. Several translations of his short stories into English have also been published throughout the 1980s and 1990s; among these are three volumes of selected stories published by well-known publishers in South Asia.[52] Furthermore, many of his stories have been included in an increasing number of anthologies on the Partition and ethnic violence in South Asia.[53] Indicative of the renewed international attention to Manto's work is Salman Rushdie's description of Manto as "the undisputed master of the Indian short story" and the only subcontinental writer writing in a language other than English who would compare with the more internationally renowned post-independence Indo-Anglian writers.[54] Manto is widely praised as a humanist who, despite the savagery of Partition that he witnessed, "never lost faith in the essential rightness of human nature."[55] Indeed, Manto's short stories have also been taken up by subaltern studies historians and other scholars of South Asia as narratives that offer documentary evidence of the 1947 experience.[56] However, rather than taking up these stories as documentary, I take them up here as literary texts that are experimenting with realist and modernist forms, in order to illuminate the everydayness—the banality of evil—that inhabited Partition, that lies beyond the pale of documentary, historical writing. In the process, Manto's stories return us to the human and its gendered violence as it transforms urban everyday life in 1947.

Manto lived in Bombay from 1941 on, where he wrote not just short stories but also film scripts, autobiographical sketches, articles, radio dramas, and essays; his relationship to the Progressive Writers' Group in Bombay was conflict-ridden, as he often came under attack for his explicit representations of sexuality. His work traversed various media in the urban public sphere of Bombay, where the Indian film industry provided a means of livelihood for struggling writers. Although Manto was very successfully involved with the Bombay film world through his writing, he moved to Lahore in Pakistan after Partition, because he was "deeply disturbed by the intolerance and distrust that he found sprouting like a poisonweed everywhere, even in the areligious world of cinema."[57] He could not tolerate that after Independence, he was no longer seen as Manto, but as a Muslim. Since the film industry in Lahore was nearly destroyed by the Partition and mass migration (most of the film producers from Lahore were Hindu and so had been forced to migrate to India after Partition), Manto and his family became indigent. Depressed at his circumstances and the loss of his city Bombay, he became an alcoholic and tragically died penniless at a relatively young age.

Many of Manto's stories are located in urban spaces, and Indian as well as Pakistani cities like Bombay, Amritsar, and Lahore figure prominently in his work. Most of his characters are ordinary people—working class, poor, students, pimps, and prostitutes living on the fringes of society. His depictions of gender and inter-ethnic relations unequivocally endorse the idea of a vernacular cosmopolitan subject that, from the location of a minority, disavows gender discrimination as well as ethnic and national affiliation. Unlike Singh's work, Manto's short stories scathingly critique the multiple forms of discursive and embodied violence that saturate women's lives during the Partition. Through irony, many of his stories make visible the female subject's dehumanizing reduction to a sexual object of communal consumption and ethnic exchange. Concurrently, Manto's representations of ethnic masculinities in the scene of violence uncover how gendered ethnic violence disfigures its agents and domestic, marital intimacy at home: For example, the desire to enact sexual violence in the story "Colder Than Ice" ends up turning its Sikh perpetrator impotent and engenders his murder by his own wife.[58] In this story, Ishwar Singh, a Sikh man, has been going about an unnamed city looting gold from and killing Muslims. After one such visit to the city, he returns anxious and confused, and says, "I feel strange." His wife, Kalwant Kaur, presses him and demands an explanation for why he has been unable to be intimate with her: "Ishr Sian, you're not the man you were eight days ago. Something has happened" (25). Trying to avoid this discussion, Ishwar Singh decides to make love to her. Even as she becomes receptive and responsive to this, the narrator says, "Like a wrestler who is being had the better of, he employed every trick he knew to ignite the fire in his loins, but it eluded him. He felt cold" (26). Kalwant's efforts to arouse him also fail; furious, she angrily asks him if there is a woman involved. When she repeatedly presses him on this point, he nods his assent. At this, in rage, she kills him: "[L]ike a wild and demented creature, Kalwant Kaur picked up Ishwar Singh's kirpan, unsheathed it and plunged it in his neck" (27). Then, she demands to know the woman's name. Ishwar Singh reveals that when he had gone to the city and joined a gang attacking Muslims, he had broken into a home and with the same kirpan, killed six Muslim men he found there. The seventh Muslim, a beautiful young woman, who was also there, he abducted: "I said to myself, Ishr Sian, you gorge yourself on Kalwant Kaur everyday. . . . How about a mouthful of this luscious fruit!" (28–29). Thinking that she had simply fainted, he carried her to a secluded area to rape her. But when he "[threw] his trump," he realized "She was dead. . . . I had carried a dead body . . . a heap of cold flesh . . . jani, give me your hand." When in response, Kalwant Kaur places her hand on his, "It was colder than ice" (29). When Kalwant kills him with the knife, Ishwar Singh acknowledges ironically that he deserves being killed by his wife for his "infidelity" with the same weapon that he used to kill six Muslim men. Yet, what is more interesting in this narrative is that Singh's inability to rape the beautiful Muslim woman through sexual violence, because she is dead, not only shocks and horrifies him, but also makes him impotent. The cold, abjected, dead body of the beautiful Muslim woman and Ishwar's inability to violate her sexually because she is already dead, constitutes the failure of her apparent "abduction" by him. His literal sexual contact with death through her "cold flesh" not only makes him impotent, but also leads to his own literal death (as he becomes "colder than ice") at the hands of his beloved wife, because he became "cold"—unable to be aroused again.

This story signals how Ishwar Singh's violent intimacy with his ethnicized victim permanently alters his own domestic, marital intimacy and sexuality. Here, his masculine peasant body is meted out death by his wife for his apparent infidelity; if the dead Muslim woman as a "luscious fruit" cannot be consumed, Ishwar Singh as the masculine consumer ends up dead. Postcolonial masculinities, then, do not remain unchanged in the encounter of gendered violence; their enactment and failure—in the failure of the ethnicized rape—becomes the traumatic transformation of a disfigured domestic coupledom and intimacy. The irony of his name "Ishwar" which means "God" in Hindi, and its association with an agent of ethnic and sexual violence, becomes a powerful indictment of this social violence marked by religion.

Sanctioned Sexualities and Sentimental Secularism in Diasporic Cinema

If secularism and inter-ethnic politics in Indian cultural production are often popularly negotiated through the figuring of inter-ethnic heterosexual romance—witness both "high" literature and popular Bollywood films mentioned earlier—this sentimental secularism about national history also persists in new forms in diasporic South Asian culture. Among these diasporic cultural texts is Indo-Canadian filmmaker Deepa Mehta's *Earth*—the second film in Mehta's trilogy of the elements, *Fire*, *Earth* and *Water*. Based on Pakistani writer Bapsi Sidhwa's novel *Cracking India* (1991), *Earth* was shot by a transnational crew in New Delhi, India, in January of 1998, though its story is set in Lahore.[59] It had its world premiere as a Special Presentation at the 1998 Toronto Film Festival where it was received with a standing ovation and critical acclaim. It went on to win several prizes at film festivals in France and Italy in 1999, and was sold to twenty-two countries: Its awards include the Prix Premiere de Public at the Festival du film asiatique de Deauville and the Critic's Awards at the Schermi d'Amore International Film Festival. *Earth* was released in Europe and India in August 1999 and in North America in September 1999. The *New York Times* reviewer Stephen Holden wrote that *Earth* "is bathed in a deep golden light that at moments recalls the orange sky silhouetting the sweaty faces of Vivien Leigh and Clark Gable in *Gone With the Wind* during the burning of Atlanta." Commenting on this cinematographic aesthetic, Holden argues that "This amber glow gives the film, which remembers the tragic events surrounding the partition of India in 1947, a ruddy twilit sensuality along with a sense of nocturnal foreboding."[60] Calling Deepa Mehta "courageous" for her choice of subjects, the *Chicago Sun-Times* review observes that "*Earth* is effective because it doesn't require much history from its viewers, explains what needs to be known, and has a universal message, which is that when a mob forms in the name of a religion, its first casualty is usually the teaching of the religion."[61] While *Earth* earned such laudatory reviews in North America, which claimed for the film both cinematic sensuality and historical insight, it was banned in Pakistan, and some Hindu extremists in India unsuccessfully called for its ban in India. With promotional materials describing it simultaneously as "an epic romance set against the blood-stained canvas of partition" and exhorting the viewer to "witness history" through the film, *Earth* has carved a remarkable, successful space for itself in transnational public spheres while also being nominated by an Indian state controlled largely by BJP Hindu nationalists as India's official entry for the Oscar Academy Awards. As a representation of the Partition, the film's critical reception has also often turned on its comparison with cinematic representations of the Holocaust in the "West": As Dorothy Barenscott points out, Mehta "draws intentionally on the potent visual vocabulary of Holocaust films" and "has been quoted often as saying that, 'The partition of India was a Holocaust for us . . . it was our Holocaust.'"[62] *Earth* thus has become an important text, in its simultaneous global popularity and its official, Indian state-sponsored status. Its hybrid cinematic invocation of a dominant discourse about trauma, memory, and Holocaust history crucially informs its engagement with the contemporary contemplation of the meanings, experiences, and impact of Partition's ethnic violence.

The novel *Cracking India* by Bapsi Sidhwa is about the experience of Partition and its transformation of everyday life from the perspective of a Parsi family in Lahore, the cultural capital of Pakistan. An eight-year-old Parsi girl, Lenny Sethi, from an upper-middle-class Parsi household, narrates her family's experiences as the Partition becomes a political reality that accompanies freedom from British rule in 1947. The novel thus has two threads in its narrative: One is the story of the domestic, everyday conflicts and concerns that mark Lenny's coming of age; the second is the story of how partition, ethnic violence and migration dramatically change the lives and relationships centered upon Lenny's Hindu nanny, Ayah. Ayah is popular among the working-class men that frequent their neighborhood and their daily haunt, Queen's Garden. While both Ice-Candy Man and Masseur (both Muslim) compete for Ayah's affection, it becomes subtly apparent that she has chosen Masseur. One day, Ice-Candy Man's relatives, coming to Lahore on a refugee train from India, are brutally massacred; only a train laden with dead bodies and gunny sacks filled with Muslim women's breasts arrives. In revenge, Ice-Candy Man begins to participate in acts of ethnic violence against Hindus and Sikhs. Soon, ethnic violence and the subsequent migrations shatter the community formed around Ayah. One day, Masseur is murdered. Ultimately, having manipulated the innocent Lenny into telling him where Ayah is hiding in the Sethis' house, Ice-Candy Man engineers the forcible abduction (and subsequent gang-rape) of Ayah with whom he is in love, by a mob of Muslim men of which he is a part. In the novel, Lenny's grandmother eventually traces Ayah's whereabouts in the red light district of Lahore, now in Pakistan; at Ayah's request, she helps Ayah to get away from Ice-Candy Man and go to India.

According to Hamid Naficy, diasporic filmmakers in voluntary (or forced) exile, like Deepa Mehta, "as partial, fragmented and multiple subjects, . . . are capable of producing ambiguity and doubt about the taken-for-granted values of their own home and host societies. They can also transcend and transform themselves to produce hybridized, syncretic, performed, or virtual identities."[63] However, in her translation of the novel into film, Mehta fails to harness this potential power to destabilize conventional South Asian rhetorics around ethnicity, gender, and identity. *Earth* largely relegates the first thread of Lenny's (portrayed by Maia Sethna) coming of age in a bourgeois household to an idealized, romanticized family life depicted in sepia tones, soft focus, and lighting in warm colors. The filmic plot itself elides the complex relationships and betrayals that Lenny slowly apprehends in her family, like her father's extra-marital affair, her mother's protests, and the bruises on her mother's body from domestic abuse. *Earth* thus sanitizes the multiple stories of betrayal, violence and love in the novel, creating an idyllic, romantic pre-Partition picture of middle-class domestic bliss and communal harmony "bathed in a deep golden light." In the heteronormative ideological rhetoric of *Earth*, Lenny's father and mother are deeply in love, and Masseur/Hasan (Rahul Khanna) loves the Ayah/Shanta (Nandita Das) so much that he is a good Muslim man, unlike Ice-Candy Man/Dil Nawaz (Aamir Khan), and he chivalrously offers to convert to Hinduism in order to marry and accompany Ayah to India. Very much the opposite of the more aggressive, dangerous, resourceful, and outgoing Muslim Ice-Candy Man, Masseur is depicted as a soft-spoken, shy, sensitive, simple and quiet man.

It is important to note that two contrasting types of Muslim masculinities are offered in this film: Ice-Candy man's sinister, violent, hyper-sexual one, dia-

metrically opposed to Masseur's good, docile, and self-effacing one. Masseur's
Muslim masculinity is effectively feminized, and he is rendered the ideal Muslim
lover for the Hindu Ayah but also, ultimately, a dead one. *Earth's* simplistic message of communal harmony and secularism through inter-ethnic romance thus
simply reproduces and reifies contemporary stereotypes of Muslim masculinities
and identities in India: Muslim male sexuality is threatening, and so rendered
evil (Dil) or evacuated (Hasan). Further, *Earth* represents Partition's historical
violence by aestheticizing it—its "oversaturated cinematography" propagates an
aesthetics of romance which dehistoricizes the everdayness of lived ethnicity.
In particular, the scene of Ayah and Masseur's lovemaking is central to the
narrative. The rustic, amber sensuality of the lovemaking shot in the soft-focus,
romantic glow of dim lamps indexes the contrasting horror of Ayah's later abduction. In this scene's representation of sexual intimacy, which follows a wedding
song and celebration, romantic love is implicitly realized after the traditional
wedding. It suggests their future, inter-ethnic, married coupledom in free South
Asia, only to be shortly countered by Masseur's death and Ayah's abduction. As
one critic charges (thus going against the grain of the popular reception of the
film in the West), "From the lurid reds and purples coloring a tableau of blood-
ied bodies on a train car, to the warm yellow glow suffusing every household
scene, Mehta has made a film at once exploitative and nostalgic."[64]

Figure 2.1. Romanticizing inter-ethnic intimacy between Masseur and Ayah in Deepa
Mehta's *Earth. (Earth. Dir. Deepa Mehta. Cracking the Earth Films Inc., 1998. Nandita Das as Ayah, Rahul
Khanna as Masseur.)*

Moreover, the film's representation of the migration and Partition refugees is static and problematic: The refugees in *Earth* remain anonymous, faceless masses. They merely form the backdrop to the epic failure of Hindu–Muslim romance at the hands of violent Muslim masculinities. *Earth's* sanitizing, simplifying, and ultimately stereotyping discrepancies from the novel also include a troubling representation of Ayah's abduction. Unlike the novel, *Earth's* melodramatic epic story of Partition *ends* with Ayah's abduction; *Earth's* account of national history ends with the end of secular romance and the failure of the inter-ethnic marriage to be realized. This failure is followed up by a documentary-style turn to the figure of the narrator and author, Bapsi Sidhwa, reminiscing in the present, which is 1998, discussing the anniversary of fifty years of Indian and Pakistani independence and their betrayal of Ayah. This is a significant narrative choice: In the novel, Ayah is found after much searching by the Sethi family in the red light district of Lahore. When she meets Lenny's grandmother, she insists on being sent away to her family in India. Eventually, Ayah is rescued and sent to India as she had desired. Ultimately, then, *Earth* both circulates the potentiality of an inter-ethnic non-national romance, and undermines it by returning to the horizon of nationalist ideologies, for which ethnic identities and stereotypes are reified constructs and a woman as national citizen and subject is socially dead after her rape.

Earth does very important work in bringing to the screen and international cinematic audiences this violent scene of abduction and Partition. By making visible the everyday contexts in which both innocent betrayals and "the pitiless face of love" generated gendered and sexual violence against women, Mehta illuminates the multiple betrayals before the translation of sexual violence into ethnic violence in this cinematic representation of Partition. Indeed, in her discussion of Deepa Mehta's earlier controversial film *Fire,* Jigna Desai enumerates the complexity of Mehta's position as a postcolonial migrant, which she describes as "the ambivalent position of the diasporic cultural producer who is framed as native informant in the West and in the postcolonial nation-state and who must vacillate between national celebrity and contaminated Westerner."[65] Mehta's diasporic positionality, on one hand, has enabled her to effectively deploy the technology of film in a transnational collaborative project; this transnational and translational aesthetic allows Mehta to make visible a comparatively little known history of violence and mass migration in public spheres around the world. On the other hand, however, by ending the story about the history of Partition it purports to make visible with the scene of Ayah's abduction, *Earth* reproduces the dominant, nationalist construction of women's abduction by violent Muslim masculinities as the final and ultimate moment of horror and unintelligibility.

Ayah's abduction becomes a visual spectacle not only for Lenny and the Sethi family, but also for the film's spectator subject. Ayah as the raped woman disappears from the horizon of national history in this film after sexual violence; her abduction and implied rape in this nationalist discourse mark her death as a social subject, a citizen, and an agent. *Earth*, in effect, refuses to represent *Cracking India*'s account of Ayah's life after abduction—her life in a brothel in Lahore, her rejection of the love and married respectability after rape offered by Ice-Candy Man, and her willing embrace of the likely rejection by her family in India after her "dishonoring."

Terry Eagleton has suggested, in a different context, that rape is "unrepresentable," because "the 'real' of the woman's body" is "the outer limit of all language."[66] *Earth* reiterates just such a rhetoric of rape as the end of history, narrative, representation—fetishizing and mythicizing rape in the process. While the film does make visible the sexual violence done to women during Partition, this implied sexual violence becomes the final spectacle of horror and unintelligibility in the visual narrative of history framed by the film; unlike the novel, the film remains unwilling or unable to imagine its beyond. *Earth* thus reproduces the very silences that feminist historians and anthropologists like Urvashi Butalia, Ritu Menon, and Kamala Bhasin have encountered in their attempt to recover and record oral testimonies about the experience of abduction and sexual violence by female survivors. These silences have long been overlaid by patriarchal nationalist rhetoric of death as the only honorable option for women raped during Partition.

Bapsi Sidhwa's *Cracking India* marks a unique and critical attempt in Anglophone literature's attempt to write into the story of Partition the aftermath of women's experiences of abduction and rape, to write into South Asian history the abducted and raped woman as citizen and agentive minoritized subject. In contrast, *Earth* not only achieves a neat, melodramatic closure to this "tragic epic romance," but also reproduces patriarchal, Hindu nationalist discourse about the abducted woman as "dishonored," "impure,'" and ultimately, socially dead—for which Muslim masculinity is held responsible. Unlike its melodramatic and pedagogical 1949 filmic predecessor, *Lahore* (discussed in Chapter Three), which insists on creating an "honorable" space for the raped woman as equal subject and citizen, an international production in 1998 like *Earth*, despite its tremendous potential, fails to offer a critical, non-misogynistic, non-nationalist vision of national history. In reiterating the trope of failed heterosexual inter-ethnic romance figured as secular nationality, *Earth* simply reproduces the middle-class ideologies of Khushwant Singh's early national text, *Train to Pakistan*, from 1956. It is also important to note that the rhetorics of masculinity, suffering, and citizenship we encountered in the work of writers like Khushwant Singh also persist into the present moment. They reappear in contemporary South Asian cultural production to articulate a critique of postcolonial ethnic nationalisms. However, if, in the early national period, Partition literature constructed the male peasant as secular hero and suffering citizen in the new nation, in the contemporary counter-publics of transnational South Asian cultural production, the suffering secular masculinities that index national violence are by and large marked Muslim—urban and middle class in Rushdie's *Midnight's Children*, urban and working class in Mehta's *Earth*.

Re-Gendering Histories of Violence

Elsewhere I have written about how Pakistani writers like Bapsi Sidhwa also grapple with scenes of violence suffered by gendered bodies.[67] The next chapter also focuses on the scholarly, literary, filmic, and political negotiation of violence experienced by women during the Partition. In focusing on the representation of masculinity and the allegorization of the male body as nation in this chapter, I am not endorsing it. Nor am I suggesting that we erase men's role as agents of violence against women, or overlook the specificity of women's experiences of sexual and gendered violence. I am also not suggesting that women and men are subject to intimate violence in identical or equivalent ways. What I am arguing is that it is urgently necessary to explore the intertwined and pluralized discursive emergence of both masculinities and femininities, and their performance and deployment in conjunction with other discourses about class, ethnicity, and heterosexuality, in order to expose the pressures of nationalism on the lived experience of gendered embodiments.

In June 2000, while researching this topic, I was listening to the stories of the 1947 Partition recounted by some Indian-American friends, who now lived in Chicago. They were Sikh, and had grown up in Delhi with these stories of their families' experiences of that traumatic time. One of them described how he remembered overhearing the mention, in hushed tones, of an uncle who had been castrated by some Muslim attackers as he had tried to escape across the border to India from his village in what is now Pakistan-occupied Kashmir. He did not know if anyone in the family had dared to ask about or discuss this experience with his uncle, who survived and made it to Delhi; all my friend remembered was that he had heard this uncle's experience alluded to or mentioned several times, in the circulation of the family stories.

While somatic violence to men's bodies as sexual subjects is represented in considerable postcolonial Indian writing, and this often includes scenes of forced circumcision and castration, there has been little historical work done on this experience of violence to male bodies. Recently, abducted women's experiences and memories of 1947 have been the object of interviews and investigations by anthropologists and historians. However, the intimate violence done to men's bodies has yet to be investigated. Perhaps because its effects remain invisible in public life, unlike the woman whose social presence simply vanished when she was abducted, men's experiences of ethnic violence, and the cultural reinvention of the ethnic male body as citizen, have yet to be written into the story of gender and nationalism. Through these complex and varied representations of masculinity, inter-ethnic heterosexual coupledom and violence in postcolonial literature and film, then, I want to suggest that we must begin to problematize the discourses of nationalist and feminist histories that assimilate gendered violence and violence against women.

3

"A Crisis Made Flesh"

Women, Honor, and National Coupledom

Reports current in Delhi [say] that Kashmiri Hindu women
carried away by Muslim raiders were being sold in Pakistan
in NWF towns and Kabul for four rupees each.
—GANDA SINGH[1]

We are not only constituted by our relations but also
dispossessed by them as well.
—JUDITH BUTLER[2]

Disenfranchised as sexual objects, communal commodities, and
patriarchal property, by both the nation-state and their relations,
hundreds of thousands of South Asian women experienced multiple forms of gendered and sexual violence during the Partition. This
chapter tracks the cultural negotiation of this violence in literature, film
and political discourse, and uncovers its impact on the narratives of national
belonging invented by and for women as citizens and refugees in postcolonial South Asia. Roughly overlapping with the resurgence of regional and
often religious politics in the eighties in India, the publication of Anita
Desai's *Clear Light of Day*[3] and Salman Rushdie's *Midnight's Children* from
1980 onwards signals the cultural return to the moment of independence,
decolonization and nation formation; this literature by diasporic writers,
however, enjoins the transition to nationality with the history and memory
of Partition.

Critical to the diasporic return to 1947 is the silenced memory of the
sexual and gendered violence experienced by women during the Partition
which has been the focus of recent research on the Partition experience in
India and its diasporas in the U.K. and North America. The previous chapter
argued that while Hindu, Sikh, and Muslim men were agents of horrifying
forms of violence against women during Partition, the critique of Partition

and indictment of Indian nationalism in transnational South Asian litera-ture has often been articulated through the trope of minoritized, suffering masculinity—often either Sikh or Muslim. In this literature, I showed how the ethnically minoritized Indian male body becomes a site for figuring both the desire for national belonging and the failures of postcolonial citizenship; in particular, I tracked how inter-ethnic intimacy and coupledom emerge as popular tropes for figuring national secularism in South Asian literature and cinema. Here, taking the transnational counter-public narrativization of 1947 as a discursive formation that illuminates South Asian modernities, this chapter asks: How did Partition violence impact the new gendered national identities and the narratives of citizenship being forged in independent India and Pakistan for women? In particular, how does the literary, cultural and political representation of violence against women during the Partition illu-minate and complicate current conceptions of belonging, nation, subaltern agency, and historical representation?

The work of Urvashi Butalia, Ritu Menon, and Kamala Bhasin has been influential in drawing attention to the differential history of women's experi-ences during the Partition. Recording the oral testimonies of women who witnessed and experienced the migration and violence, they have revealed the complex dispossessions—psychic and material, state-supported and famil-ial—that mark women's experience in 1947. Butalia focuses on the partition of Punjab, and uncovers the traumatic, oral "hidden histories" of mass rape, abduction, and state "recovery" of women and children, to make visible the trauma, anguish, pain, and ambivalence that mark the lived experience of Partition. Exploring abducted women's experiences in the late forties and early fifties, Butalia shows how abducted women were "denied the right—theo-retically, every citizen's right—to choose where they wished to live" once they were "recovered" by the state operations of both countries.[4] Given the gender-ing of nationalist discourse and its ideology of a feminized "Mother India," she argues that "partition represented an actual violation of this mother, a violation of her (female) body."[5] Critiquing the role of the patriarchal Indian state and dominant ideology in abducted women's disenfranchisement and exploitation, she suggests, "If colonialism provided Indian men the rationale for construct-ing and reconstructing the identity of the Hindu woman as a 'bhadramahila,' the good, middle class Hindu wife and mother, supporter of her men, [then] Independence, and its dark 'other,' partition, provided the rationale for making women into symbols of national honour."[6]

In their feminist historiography of the Partition of India, Ritu Menon and Kamala Bhasin have also similarly pointed to the question of "honor" in the sexual and gendered violence that prevailed during Partition: "The most predictable form of violence experienced by women, as women, is when the women of one community are sexually assaulted by the men of the other, in an overt assertion of their identity and a simultaneous humiliation of the Other" by "dishonoring" their women. They note that, as in other moments of ethnic conflict in the world, "the rape and molestation of Hindu, Sikh, and Muslim women before and after Partition probably followed the familiar pattern of sexual violence, and of attack, retaliation and reprisal."[7] Furthermore, they show how the project of "recovering" abducted women that India and Pakistan began reproduced the ethnic objectification of women and disallowed abducted women complete agency in their own rehabilitation. Juxtaposing oral testimony, memoirs, and government papers, Menon and Bhasin's analysis valuably uncovers the ideological and material violence of the state response towards women who experienced ethnic violence and displacement during Partition. Drawing upon and taking as my point of departure this illuminating feminist research on state history and oral testimony on women's experiences in 1947, this chapter takes up the articulation of gendered violence in literary and cinematic representations in transnational postcolonial public spheres. Exploring the heteronormative narration of female subjectivity, ethnic embodiment and modern coupledom in the postcolonial public sphere, I will argue that the aesthetic representation of this history not only illuminates the discursive production of Hindu, Muslim and Sikh women as ethnic citizens and embodied "honor" identified by Butalia, Menon and Bhasin, but also challenges it. It demands that we complicate the historiographical narrativization of gendered and sexual violence as "ethnic," at the same time that it illustrates the emergence of ethnic citizenship that marks contemporary political discourses in South Asia. In the process, this South Asian cultural production makes visible the fissures and the contradictions in nationalist discourse about women's citizenship, secularism and inter-ethnic coupledom.

Narrating Abduction and Nation: The Production of Gendered Ethnic Identities

I deliberately begin this re-examination of Partition's gendered violence, ethnicity and historicization with a consideration of the contemporary Pakistani-American writer Bapsi Sidhwa's novel *Cracking India* (1991).[8] As a novel that returns to the origins of Pakistan as a nation-state, in order to interrogate and uncover the genealogies of minoritization and gendered citizenships in South Asia, *Cracking India* occupies an important place in the aesthetic and political contemplation of current hegemonic discourses about postcolonial citizenships in South Asia. As mentioned in the previous chapter, *Cracking*

India represents the transformations of Partition from the perspective of a Parsi family, the Sethis, in Lahore. The narrator is an eight-year-old, disabled Parsi girl, Lenny Sethi, from an upper middle-class household, whose account offers a double elite and minoritized perspective on how Partition transforms everyday life in decolonizing India. In the novel's account, Parsis or Zoroastrians were politically neutral in a conflict whose central agents were Hindus, Muslims and Sikhs. Through the literary device of a child narrator, the Parsi perspective purports to present a dispassionate account of the transformations wrought by Partition, and in the process, signals the forgotten minoritization of the Parsi community itself in this history.[9] As Jill Didur has suggested, the female narrator's satirical perspective on Parsi culture illuminates both how the minority Parsi community's privileged relationship to the British ruling class gets transformed by Partition as well as the "patriarchal and majoritarian underpinnings" of dominant accounts of national history.[10]

Cracking India is set in 1947 in Lahore, and the story is told in the present tense as the events unfold before the young polio-stricken girl's eyes, although at times the narrator appears to be an older Lenny looking back. While Sangeeta Ray has usefully analyzed the representation of nationalism and bourgeois betrayal in this novel, my reading will focus on the novel's representation of ethnic violence as witnessed by Lenny. Lenny's nanny, Ayah, with whom she spends considerable time every day, is not only beloved by her but is also sought after by her multi-ethnic working-class group of male friends, Masseur, Ice-Candy Man, Butcher, and others that frequent their neighborhood and their haunt, Queen's Garden, every evening. They all compete for Ayah's attention, but soon it becomes evident that she is in love with Masseur. When the Partition becomes certain, ethnic violence in the form of arson, lootings and murders begins to generate the migrations of non-Muslims from Lahore. Soon, the cosmopolitan community of friendship that articulated different religious backgrounds around the Sethi family and around Ayah begins to fall apart. One day, Masseur is murdered, and his body is found with his head severed in a gunnysack on the street.

As Partition draws nearer and the violence escalates in Lahore, there comes a day when a mob of Muslim men roaming the city to attack Hindus arrives at the doorstep of the Sethi bungalow, thinking they are Hindu— Sethi tends to be a Hindu last name. In the exchange that follows, we witness how particular practices of encoding the identity of "co-religionists"[11] and others rearticulate a cosmopolitan community of friendships into abstract, polarized relations of ethnic difference. All the members of the household (except Ayah, who is Hindu) gather before the mob to confront it, and Lenny notes that the men in the mob look like "calculating men, whose ideals and passions have cooled to ice" (Sidhwa, 190). The mob demands that the Hindus in the household come forth; the Muslim cook, Imam Din, tells them that there are none in the house. Then, someone from the back of the mob asks for Hari the Hindu gardener, and Imam Din genially informs the mob: "Hari-the-gardener has become Himat Ali." Hari has obviously converted to escape the violence, as was common; his conversion to Islam is signified by his taking on an Islamic name. But this name change does not convince the mob of his true conversion: "'Let's make sure,' a man says, hitching up his lungi, his swaggering gait bent on mischief. 'Undo your shalwar Himat Ali. Let's see if you're a proper Muslim'" (192).

Because Hari has recently been circumcised, and is also able to also recite the Muslim prayer *kalma* on demand, the mob spares his life. The circumcised or uncircumcised penis in this moment of anxiety of identification and ethnic conflict becomes an exaggerated, material sign of "religious" identity upon the other's male body; further, the propriety of religious identity is marked "male." The public visibility of the penis becomes a mode of ascertaining true Hindu/Muslim identity, which is at the same time always already a masculine identity in this discourse. The visual marking of Hari's sexual body in ritualized ways, and the performance of the kalma are thus signifiers of a masculine Muslim identity that is less religious and more ethnic for Hari/Himat Ali. This transaction dramatizes not only the somatic intimacy of ethnic identity, but also its immanent production. This production of new intimate identities occurs not through the conversion of faith and belief that have to do with the transformation of the modern subject's interiority. Instead, it materializes through "proper" bodily mutilation and the accurate performance of religious practice in everyday life. Hari's conversion probably constitutes the humiliating, symbolic emasculation of Hindu men for the mob, as well as legitimizes his presence in the new nation-state, Pakistan.

This is the scene of violence that becomes ordinary during Partition and refashions everyday life. In addition to literature, memoirs and verbal accounts of Partition are replete with incidents of castration and both voluntary and forced conversion of men, women and children.[12] As is also vividly depicted in Khushwant Singh's *Train to Pakistan*, castrating the man became a way of emasculating and humiliating the ethnic community and foreclosing its reproduction. To address the anxiety of the masculine other's "proper" ethnic identity, forcing men (before killing, castrating or converting them through circumcision) to strip in order to examine whether they were circumcised or uncircumcised was seen to be the ultimate, foolproof test of whether they were Muslim or Hindu/Sikh. Forced circumcision, shaving facial and head hair (for Sikh men), and shaving off the Hindu Brahmin's traditional, short, plaited hair (on an otherwise bald head) were routine Muslim conversion tactics for men and boys.[13]

In the discourse that produces the test of a "proper Muslim," this incident reveals that women never inhabit that identity of a proper religious subject. Women's bodies are not marked in canonized ritual ways, for women are never "properly" ethnically identified except through their relations with Hindu, Muslim, or Sikh men. Hence, the signs of women's ethnic difference appear at the sartorial level (through their dress, makeup, jewelry), already one level removed from the somatic marking of male bodies. Of course, during Partition, many women who were abducted and raped by men from the "enemy" community were branded with religious symbols on their bodies. However, I contend that these symbols, like "Om" or the crescent moon on the women's bodies, did not signify the women's conversion; instead, these symbols represented their "otherness" (or their prior, other identity as Hindu, Sikh, or Muslim) before the violence, and their "other" identity as shamed, conquered, and violated by the ethnic community with whose symbol they were branded. Paradoxically, then, unlike in the case of Hari's circumcision, this violent encoding of religious signs on the woman's body also reinstated her previous ethnic identity and location in the present.

The narrative moment of Hari's encounter with the mob unveils the instability of masculine ethnic identity, when the male sexual body becomes the site, limit, and evidence of ethnic identity and national belonging. This instability is heightened when Hari/Himat Ali recites the Islamic *kalma* with "the cadence and intonation of Hindu chants" (193). This hybridized proof of faith—the performance of an Islamic prayer inflected with the cadences of the Hinduism which the prayer's meaning purports to have replaced—ironically asserts the impurity of identity. Hari's past re-emerges as the banal cadence of everyday recitation and haunts the dehistoricization of his body; it persists as a memory, and a residual, material trace of the Hindu other in Himat Ali's now Muslim masculine body.

In *Imagined Communities*, Benedict Anderson argues that the cultural roots of nationalism and death are linked in two ways: first, "nationalist imagining . . . [has] a strong affinity with religious imagining"[14] insofar as they both deal with and transform death, fatality, and contingency into continuity and meaning; second, people are ready to die in self-sacrifice for these invented nations. For Anderson, nationalism and death are primarily linked in the nation's ability to command self-sacrifice and persuade its citizens to lay down their lives. However, the literary and public discourse of 1947 reveals that in the unofficial narratives of ethnic nationalism prevalent in this period, the nation did not demand self-sacrifice so much as it demanded and permitted killing (often in ritualistic ways) those who were deemed "other" to it according to religion. Thus, it is not the affinity of nationalist and/or religious imagining, but the complex articulation of both that engenders death through gendered violence. This articulation of nation and religion demands that we rethink contemporary understandings of the nation through its relation to gender, ethnicity, and violence.[15] In interrogating Anderson's theory of nationality, Homi Bhabha's work is especially useful. Contrary to sociological and political understandings of nationalism, Bhabha proffers an understanding of the form of the Western nation, as a form of "living the locality of culture," as "a narrative strategy," and a "form of social and textual affiliation." He therefore brings together attention to the Western nation as a process, with attention to the "incommensurability in the midst of the every-day," "the telling details that emerge as metaphors for national life."[16] Turning to the form of the postcolonial nation, we can then ask: How is "the locality of culture" lived in a violent transition to postcoloniality?

In the exigencies of Partition violence, Hari's conversion through circumcision and prayer recitation is a cultural act that becomes an everyday tactic for resisting the historical effects of Partition he might have otherwise faced: forced migration, castration, or death. Michel de Certeau's notion of everyday practice is pertinent here: For de Certeau, everyday life refers to a set of practices made up of tactics—minor, banal, unintentional modes of action that reappropriate the dominating, colonizing context to their own ends.[17] If the mob's demand (and this includes his friend Ice-Candy Man) depersonalizes social relations such that it turns Hari into "the Hindu"—thus repressing his historical identity as their friend and fellow inhabitant of Lahore—Hari's conversion enables him not just to live, but to reproduce his everyday life in Lahore. In this sense, Hari lives the locality of culture in a non-nationalist mode—in order to survive the dominating history of partitioned nations. In this sense, *Cracking India* recasts the idea of everyday practices as being banal and unintentional modes of behavior: The novel reveals how modes of behavior which are certainly not unintentional or banal can also become everyday tactics for surviving decolonization, ordinary in the extra-ordinary moment of violence.[18] This scene shows that everyday life can also become the time in which people as agents resist and survive colonial/national history (and its ethno-religious myths)—a history thrust upon them, whose official narrative is one of freedom being granted to them. *Cracking India* shows that for many ordinary people like Hari, postcolonial nationhood did not come in the form of a much-desired freedom and equal citizenship; instead, it came as a necessary religious conversion to be able to stay where you were, because partition had now named it the wrong country to be in.

The different impact on male and female sexuality of this moment becomes apparent in what follows. The mob asks, "Where's the Hindu woman? The ayah!" Imam Din tells them that she has left Lahore; to dispel their disbelief, when raucously pressed to swear upon God, Imam Din stages his Islamic faith by calling upon Allah to witness his oath that she is truly gone. Lenny says: "I study the men's faces in the silence that follows. Some of them still don't believe him. Some turn away or look at the ground. It is an oath a Muslim will not take lightly" (193). By lying under oath, Imam Din performatively deploys his Muslim identity to protect "the Hindu woman" Ayah; he acts like a good Muslim as defined by the mob, to undermine its violence in the name of Islam. This moment reveals not only how people were often actively produced as Hindu, Sikh, or Muslim ethnic subjects through everyday performative acts, but also how these gendered ethnic identities and subjectivities were often *ethically* appropriated and deployed to interrupt political violence.

In this moment of uncertainty, Lenny is approached and deceived by the familiarity and friendly demeanor of Ice-Candy Man, who is in the mob, and who had been one of Ayah's devotees: "Something strange happened then. The whole disorderly melee dissolved and consolidated into a single face. The face, amber-eyed, spread before me: hypnotic, reassuring, blotting out the ugly frightening crowd. Ice-Candy Man's versatile face transformed into a saviour's in our hour of need." Ice-Candy Man promises Lenny that he will take care of Ayah if she tells him where Ayah is. Lenny is unwittingly deceived and betrays Ayah: "And dredging from some foul truthful depth in me a fragment of overheard conversation that I had not registered at the time, I say: 'On the roof—or in one of the godowns . . .'" (194). Lenny merely tells the truth as she has been routinely taught to; in this sense, her innocent, childish "betrayal" is both everyday and banal. However, the violent outcome of her betrayal is not.

Lenny's betrayal leads to the mob swarming all through the house, until they find Ayah. What follows is not a test of Ayah's "proper" identity, like Hari's, but her systematic abduction and gang rape. Lenny describes the scene of this abduction. The present-tense narration evokes the temporality of the immediate present and recreates the visual, spectatorial experience from a child's viewpoint.

> They move forward from all points. They swarm into our bedrooms, search the servants' quarters, climb to the roofs, break locks, and enter our godowns and the small storerooms near the bathrooms.
>
> They drag Ayah out. They drag her by her arms stretched taut, and her bare feet—that want to move backwards—are forced forward instead. Her lips are drawn away from her teeth, and the resisting curve of her throat opens her mouth like the dead child's screamless

mouth. Her violet sari slips off her shoulder, and her breasts strain at her sari blouse stretching the cloth so that the white stitching at the seams shows. A sleeve tears under her arm.

The men drag her in grotesque strides to the cart and their harsh hands, supporting her with careless intimacy, lift her into it. Four men stand pressed against her, propping her body upright, their lips stretched in triumphant grimaces.

The last thing I noticed was Ayah, her mouth slack and piteously gaping, her disheveled hair flying into her kidnappers' faces, staring at us as if she wanted to leave behind her wide-open and terrified eyes. (195)

Sidhwa's account of this "intricate invasion" of history into the "recesses of the domestic sphere"[19] does not attempt to reveal Ayah's feelings—her pain—or to give her a voice. Instead, it dramatizes her abduction as a visual spectacle; its "telling details" about her lips, throat, mouth, bare feet, torn sleeve, the stitching of the blouse seams, her eyes and hair signify the material, bodily rupture of her everyday in postcolonial Pakistan. The narration creates a haunting, surreal present tense in which trust is betrayed, and Ayah is staring back at the family she has served over the years—a family which is unable to protect her from this sexual violence. This account marks the moment when sexual desire is communalized—reified through its translation into communal discourse—for its realization. For Ice-Candy Man, who desired Ayah but had been rejected by her for Masseur, identifying Ayah as "Hindu" facilitates her objectification and violation in order to fulfill his desire for her. This process not only encodes her body as symbolically "Hindu," but also suppresses the historicity of her body in order to construct it as ethnic. As a result, her body becomes a site of sexual and cultural transaction. Simultaneously, as Hortense Spillers has argued in a different context, this "*theft of the body*"[20] (italics in original) de-genders Ayah—insofar as it also robs her of privacy, personal dignity, and agency. Exploring the struggles and shifts in the meanings of citizenship in U.S. national culture, Lauren Berlant has usefully illuminated the hegemonic and banal everyday practices that participate in the reproduction of a violent, privatized citizenship through racial and sexual violence.[21] In this postcolonial scene, the conjunction of the dominant territorialization of gendered and ethnic belonging, with the banality of everyday life—the child tells the truth, the lover promises to take care of the beloved—enables an unbanal act of violence on a working-class woman's body.

Allen Feldman has suggested that "[h]istory is not lodged in the body but in the act that constructs the body and locates it in metonymy. . . . The transformation of somatic and other material domains into symbolic time and space by violence and ideology forms a closure that represses historic-ity in favor of the mimetic and the recursive."[22] Ayah's abduction and rape are historical acts of violence which were repeatedly enacted on thousands of women's bodies after they were dehistoricized as individual subjects and symbolically constructed as Hindu or Muslim. After her abduction and rape, Ice-Candy Man gives Ayah a Muslim name and turns her into a courtesan in a less reputable part of Lahore, where they live together. When India and Pakistan begin recovering abducted women, fearing he will lose Ayah, Ice-Candy Man marries her. Yet, in this violent process, as Feldman suggests, Ayah's body "acquires its own clandestine history of alterity."[23] If Hari's alterity lies in the Hindu cadence of recitation, Ayah's body acquires its history of alterity in her rejection of Ice-Candy Man's desperate overtures of love. Ayah refuses to forget her abduction and rape, and rejects his offers of love and romantic coupledom—in other words, of respectability after rape. Eventually, Lenny's grandmother and mother find Ayah, and at her expressed desire they arrange for her to be safely escorted across the border to her family in India.

Ayah probably knew that her abduction and rape might mark her as impure, polluted, and dishonored for her family and others in India. In this context, by refusing to make peace with (as often happened with abducted women) her abductor and now husband, and by choosing to return to her family in India, Ayah insists on being other to both social spaces of kinship: nation and patriarchal community. On the dominant gendered ideology about Partition violence in India, Sangeeta Ray has noted, "The inevitabil-ity of rape leaves women with the 'choice' of committing suicide so that she can be accommodated within the narrative of the nation as legitimate and pure—albeit dead—citizen. Those who survive rape are refused entry into the domestic space of the new nation."[24] It is important then, that here it is Ayah who refuses entry into the domestic space of the new nation, Pakistan, which she is offered by Ice-Candy Man's ideas about romantic coupledom. Simultaneously, through her willed return to the everyday life of her family's domestic space in India, she troubles and rejects both discourses of suicide and nationalism. In this novel, then, the figure of the urban female subaltern Ayah *does not* syntax the "patriarchal continuity" of national "territoriality and the communal mode of power" that Gayatri Chakravorty Spivak has sug-gested persistently marks the narrativization of woman by subaltern studies historians.[25] Instead, the figure of Ayah interrupts the continuity and mobi-lization of nation and patriarchal community, and marks their discontinuity through her insistent, intentional otherness to both in civil society.

Women's abduction and rape was one of the salient forms of violence that prevailed in this period of transition. Indeed, in a letter dated April 4, 1947, to Evan Jenkins (then the Governor of Punjab) regarding the March '47 riots in the Punjab and North West frontier Province, Jawaharlal Nehru said:

> There is one point, however, to which I should like to draw your attention, and this is the question of rescuing women who have been abducted or forcibly converted. You will realize that nothing adds to popular passions more than stories of abduction of women, and so long as these women are not rescued, trouble will simmer and might blaze out.[26]

This note constructs women as victims and objects of both religious communities and the colonial state; it fails to grant any voice and agency to the particular desires of the "abducted" women themselves, representing them as victims to be forcibly rescued. In the preceding chapters, I have discussed how feminist- and subaltern studies historiography over the last decade has analyzed how anti-colonial nationalist discourse in India was gendered; this research also demonstrates that while Indian nationalists supported and indeed demanded suffrage and equal political rights for Indian women, patriarchal nationalist discourse in the pre- as well as post-independence era also constructed women as embodied representatives of the nation "Mother India."[27] Anees Qidwai's memoirs reveal that Nehru's position was reflected in the official ideology and "The Recovery Operation" of 1948 in the new Indian and Pakistani states: abducted women were represented as "properties" belonging to particular national (configured as religious) communities. This determined that all abducted women should be "rescued" and "returned" to their rightful "owners" (namely, the nation, which coincided with the dominant ethnic community): "[After Independence] the Governments of India and Pakistan came to an agreement . . . that any [abducted] girl [of any community] who was in the possession of a different community should be forcibly recovered and returned to her relatives and, during such time as her relatives remain untraced, to the Government [of her country].[28] The official estimate of the number of abducted women during Partition was placed at 33,000 non-Muslim (Hindu or Sikh, predominantly) women in Pakistan, and 50,000 Muslim women in India. Mridula Sarabhai, a prominent figure in the Recovery project, placed the unofficial count of abducted women in Pakistan at ten times the 1948 official figure of 12,500.[29] About 30,000 women were "recovered" over the course of eight years by both nation-states. In this way, the patriarchal objectification that engenders and sustains sexual violence against women was reiterated in the state's objectification of women's bodies as property. In his memoir, *A Diary of Partition Days,* Ganda Singh's entry dated Monday, 29 Dec 1947, reads thus: "Smt. Shanta Kumari, president of the National Women's Conference, Jammu and Kashmir, said that 'many who were abducted were exhibited in the bazaars of Peshawar and Bannu, thereby enticing Pathans towards Kashmir."[30] This memoir bears witness to the capitalist dehumanization and circulation of women as objects of exchange, and the rescripting of the reproductive woman's body as currency yet again, for the contest over control of Kashmir as early as 1947.

As discussed earlier, feminist historiography has argued that during Partition, abducting women from the other community became a common way to dishonor the Muslim/Hindu other; the appropriation of women from the other community was a way to affect the collective honor, religious sentiment, and the physical reproduction of that community.[31] Often, these abducted women were forced to convert; in most cases, they ended up marrying their abductors. The program of the two governments to exchange women led to the continued discursive production of abducted women as objects, as religiously marked Hindu or Muslim subjects according to their family origin (and not their individual practice), and ultimately as symbols of the patriarchal nation's honor. As Ritu Menon and Kamala Bhasin have suggested, "family, community and state emerge as the three mediating and interlocking forces determining women's individual and collective destinies. . . . [Partition] once again recast them as keepers of national honour and markers of boundaries: between communities, and between communities and countries."[32] It is significant, however, that accounts from those involved in the recovery efforts reveal that many abducted women resisted this forced governmental repatriation and refused to return to their original families. Often, they had settled into new lives with children and family, and did not want upheaval and displacement again; moreover, they recognized that if they returned, they would likely be stigmatized and shunned as dishonored and impure.

In a thoughtful piece that draws out the problems of writing a "non-imperious" history of Partition, Urvashi Butalia has acknowledged the complex responsibility of the intellectual to respect the refusal of most abducted women, when interviewed, to remember and speak of their experience of abduction or sexual violence.[33] While Menon and Bhasin have located the legal and political discourse around this "recovery" of abducted women,[34] the memory of the violence of abduction remains today both an object of horrified curiosity and a site of silence unnarrativized in South Asian history. In this moment, Sidhwa's literary attempt to bring the scene-memory of that violence into being risks a patriarchal nationalist criticism haunted by the fear of its repetition in the present. Furthermore, Lenny's account of the scene of abduction and its aftermath complicates and calls into question the assimilation of sexual violence into anthropological explanatory narratives of patriarchal, communal, and national honor. Ayah's abduction, after all, is initiated by her friend and admirer who deploys his intimacy and familiarity with Lenny to inflict upon Ayah a sexual intimacy she had earlier rejected. Her abduction as a "Hindu woman" is less about her dishonor as a Hindu for Ice-Candy Man, and more about Ice-Candy Man's use of the communal narratives at hand to fulfill his desire for her (which he sees as his love for her). This literary moment, then, questions any easy explanation of sexual violence in the belated terms of national, communal, and patriarchal honor. It reveals that ethnic and national identities are produced not only through normative discourses of culture and community, but also *through violence*—to intimacy, to friendship, and to dehistoricized bodies. In the process, it eloquently shows that the issues of identity, ethnicity, and sexuality that were at play in this moment around 1947 were, as Homi Bhabha has eloquently argued in a different context, "as much issues of desire and affect as they were part of a wider political and historical discussion of rights and representations."[35] Thus, even as Sidhwa maps the loss of belonging engendered by the violent histories of postcolonial nation-formation on women's lives, she also suggests that national and feminist histories need to be rewritten through the fraught ambivalences and desiring practices which permeate everyday life, which belie conventional narratives of oppression and victimization, and which are not always centered upon discourses of nation or community.

So far, I have suggested that *Cracking India* reveals how communal identities for both men and women sometimes are not prior to, but come to be produced through, violence. The question remains as to whether these acts, which produce new ethnic identities—Hindu or Muslim—also produce them as "national" identities. While narratives of India and Pakistan as Hindu and Muslim nations prevailed in this historical moment, Sidhwa's text is interesting because it resists reading acts of violence as communal *and* therefore necessarily national; in this, she takes up the task, in Foucault's words, to "look from above and descend to seize the various perspectives, to disclose dispersions and differences, to leave things undisturbed in their own dimension and intensity."[36] In doing so, this novel opens up the possibility of rethinking the meaning of "communal violence" and the equation of the communal with the national.

Indeed, I do not deny that in many instances nationalist rhetoric by both Hindu and Muslim communalist groups motivated acts of violence. However, I want to argue, and I think *Cracking India* illustrates this rather eloquently, that the "communal" did not always map onto the "national," and that acts of violence were often rationalized variously in terms other than nationalist, such that the nation became an afterthought in this discourse of violence—in terms of counter-violence to avenge "co-religionists," in terms of economic oppression by the other community, or simply (as in the case of Hari/Himat Ali) in terms of proper membership of the proper community at hand/The disjunction between the ethnic and the national in these acts of violence enables the disavowal of this violence subsequently by the postcolonial nation-states as "madness" and "temporary insanity."/Yet, this disjunction—which the literature of Partition makes visible—opens up a space for retheorizing the relations between violence, community, and nation. Ultimately, it is in the space or gap between the communalist discourses of belonging (Hindu, Sikh, or Muslim), and the nation's commitment to a secular, national community—that is, in the performative temporality of everyday life in which identities, subjectivities and citizenships are lived and performed—that we can locate the agency that interrupts gendered and ethnic violence.

Sidhwa's attention to the spectatorial materiality of bodily violence and pain through the child's vision of heightened perception begins to address the problem of how to understand the sexualizing of bodily violence that characterized Partition, but that issue nonetheless has remained marginal in the middle-class, urban fictions of Salman Rushdie and Amitav Ghosh. *Cracking India* speaks to the history of ethnic violence, by showing how violence reproduces in everyday life the material identities and categories instituted by the colonial state. In recreating the scene of Ayah's abduction by a mob of men in the name of religion, and in tracking Ayah's life after the event, Sidhwa is the first novelist of this second generation of diasporic writers that I know of who attempts to bear testimony to the scene of violence done to abducted women, while refusing to represent the abducted woman as symbolic of national community. Indeed, in *Cracking India*, it is Lenny's disabled, minor body that is continually linked to the fragmenting national body; her birthday falls on the day India is partitioned, and her disability due to polio (blamed by Dr. Bharucha on the British who brought polio to India) is a metaphor for the birth of two nations as disabled by the British partitioning of the subcontinent. Thus, the child Lenny's minoritized, female, disabled body materially represents the legacy of British colonialism: disease and a disabled South Asia.

Furthermore, Lenny's postmodern account in the first person in this novel debanalizes the spectacle of communal violence (burning localities, dead bodies in gunny sacks and gutters, a child suspended from a spear through its body), but not through metaphor, allegory or irony. Instead, it recreates the texture of the material everyday through its detail of fragmented observations and a visual aesthetic. Elaine Scarry writes about the relationship between pain and language: "Physical pain does not simply resist language but actively destroys it."[37] *Cracking India* brings into being an aesthetic that does not attempt to represent Ayah's interiority and pain; instead, this aesthetic recreates the scene of terror as a spectacle which inhabited and emerged from the space of everyday life, and which both nations, India and Pakistan, have needed to forget in order to heal from Partition violence.

Intra-ethnic Violence: Beyond History and Honor

> Subaltern pasts are like stubborn knots that stand out and break up
> the otherwise evenly woven surface of the fabric.
>
> —Dipesh Chakrabarty[38]

In *Borders & Boundaries*, Ritu Menon and Kamala Bhasin show how Partition's gendered violence was often linked to discourses of communal and national "honor"; they argue that women were symbolically constructed as bearers of communal *and* national honor in this period. Hence, communal violence against women constituted symbolic violence to that honor, both in state discourses as well as in first-person accounts from this time. From the range of sexual violence women experienced during Partition—"stripping; parading naked; mutilating and disfiguring; tattooing or branding the breasts and genitalia with triumphal slogans; amputating breasts; knifing open the womb; raping, of course; killing fetuses"—Menon and Bhasin argue that "women's sexuality symbolizes 'manhood'; its desecration is a matter of such shame and dishonor that it has to be avenged." Further, they argue that particular acts of physical violence "engraved the division of India into India and Pakistan on the women of both religious communities in a way that they became the respective countries, indelibly imprinted by the Other."[39]

On one hand, *Borders & Boundaries* illustrates how women's bodies often bear the symbolic burden of community building—national or otherwise. However, the slippage between religious community and country in its explanatory argument bears re-examining, especially when placed against the heterogeneous aesthetic representation of Partition violence and migration in everyday life. In their concern for the production of community and for the relations of power between kinship structures and the state, historical, and anthropological studies can sometimes elide several questions: Is sexual violence against women always about communal/ethnic "honor" (understood as "masculinity" in their analysis), or do other kinds of motivations and desires (class discontent, caste conflict, gender conflict, sexual desire) manifest themselves in the form of communality? How do we address, and in what histories do we inscribe, the sexual violence against women that was intra-community, for which few official records exist in the archives? What burden does sexuality bear in the production of identity—local, national, ethnic, class—through violence? Finally, if in this historical and anthropological analysis it is violence against women's bodies that constitutes violence against masculinity and male honor (as well as against community and nation), then where can we locate the space for making visible, and in which histories do we inscribe, the violence done to male bodies and its relationship to masculinity, male honor, communality and nationality?

Contrary to the translation of "gender" as "woman" in feminist discourse, . I have shown that an understanding of Partition violence must include attention to how both male and female bodies suffered ethnic, gendered, and sexual violence; both masculinity and femininity became sites of violence for symbolizing nationality and communality in this period. Simultaneously, I have cautioned that our dominant explanatory narratives often risk problematically conflating the workings of community and nation, eliding the ambivalence and differences between them; moreover, their methodological focus on community and nation often renders invisible both violence against men and the violence against women that was intra-community, and articulated with desire, affect, class and race.

Saadat Hasan Manto's Urdu short stories from the early national period dramatize what Menon and Bhasin mention briefly: It is a little-acknowledged fact that during Partition, Hindu and Muslim men did not only violate, abduct and exchange women of the other community, but also did so to women of their own community. As Menon and Bhasin point out, "Nothing like this concern [for Hindu women abducted and converted in Pakistan] was evident with regard to the abduction of Hindu women by Hindu men, or Muslim women by Muslim men (by all accounts also very widespread), presumably because here no offense against community or religion had been committed, nor anyone's "honor" compromised."[40] The scene of women's abduction for sexual violence, then, is a more complex and diverse one, one that exceeds the historiographic explanations of ethnic nationalism. In a political discourse in which women are symbols of a community, the violence against women within communities never became a politicized issue, for both the political national community and the ethnic community shared the patriarchal ideology that constructed women as male, communal property.

For example, Manto's story "The Woman in the Red Raincoat" is about a young man who, out of boredom during the violent times of partition, decides to abduct a woman.[41] The man, S, is introduced to us by the first narrator as his friend: "He's a man of ordinary looks and build and is as much interested in getting something for nothing as most of us are. But he isn't cruel by nature. It is another matter that he became the perpetrator of a strange tragedy, though he did not quite realize at the time what was happening"(Manto, 49). S owns a bicycle shop which is one of the first to be burnt down by arsonists during Partition riots. As he has nothing else to do, he joins the roaming band of looters and arsonists—nothing extraordinary at the time. "It was really more by way of entertainment and diversion than out of a feeling of communal revenge, I would say. Those were strange times" (50). The narrative thus portends the estrangement of Partition violence that it will locate, and then shifts to S's first-person account of his decision to abduct a woman on one very rainy day: "I'm not sure I was thinking even. I was in a kind of daze, very difficult to explain. Suddenly a shiver ran down my spine and a powerful desire to run out and pick up a girl took hold of me" (50). Stripped of the veneer of communal rhetoric of revenge and honor, S represents his desire to abduct a woman as both everyday and inexplicable. S then stops a woman driving a car and, though he can't see her face, notes that she is wearing a shimmering red raincoat. He ascertains that she is not English by asking her—because, he says, "I hated Englishwomen" (51). Then he drives her to his home. It is important to note that S does not inquire about her ethnicity as Hindu, Sikh, or Muslim. Hesitant and ambivalent about his own plan, however, he does not rape her. He politely tries to persuade her to consent to sexual intercourse; twice, he interrupts these efforts by offering to let her leave his house if she likes.

In the course of their conversation in his faintly lit living room, she is seduced by him, and from her initial reaction of fear of being killed, she moves to shyness, and finally consents to sex: "I was about to get up, when she grabbed my hand and put it on her breast. Her heart was beating violently. I became excited. 'Darling,' I whispered, taking her into my arms again" (54). Just then, S's servant brings in a lamp, and he discovers that the woman he has abducted is not a young girl, but an older woman. Shocked, he says: "You may leave now if you wish" (Manto, 57). She leaves that night and dies. Whether it is suicide or not is unclear. S discovers, when he narrates this experience to his friend (our first narrator), that she was the much-acclaimed artist Miss "M," whom he had greatly admired and whose work he had attempted to imitate. She was also the principal of the local art college, who had a reputation for hating men. The story ends with his friend telling S, "That night when you let her out of your house, she died in a car accident. You are her murderer. In fact, you are the murderer of two women. One, who is known as a great artist, and the other who was born from the body of the first woman in your living room that night and whom you alone know" (57). The first narrator thus charges his friend with bringing about the literal and psychic death of Miss M: His actions led to the destruction of Miss M's body, and her newborn sexual selfhood—the part of her that was temporarily and paradoxically transformed by her abduction and seduction. This story illuminates how women's abduction and sexual violence during Partition by men might not be always motivated by ethnic hatred. Instead, the prevalence of ethnic conflict at this time made possible Miss M's abduction by S. This abduction had little to do with any intent to violate the masculinity and honor of another community. Moreover, S's sexual desire is racially, not communally marked: After all, he ascertains that she is not English before taking her home. Of course, ethnic violence during Partition does materialize the desire for and possibility of sexual gratification through violence for S. It is thus the condition of possibility of gendered violence that is, however, not ethnicized but racialized. Furthermore, while S constructs Miss M as an object to pick up, he later tries to transform her into a willing sexual partner by invoking the language of romance. When S asks her to leave, Miss M is twice abjected—from being an abducted woman to a willing but rejected sexual partner. "Woman in the Red Raincoat" makes visible the complex workings of desire, affect, and patriarchal power in this moment—the abducted victim becomes a desiring subject, the abductor becomes the polite seducer and then cruel rejector—and critiques violence against women, but from beyond the limits of conventional anthropological critiques of Partition's gendered violence as ethnic and nationalist.

Another story, "The Return,"[42] in the same collection by Manto is a modernist representation of the encounter of language and gendered intra-ethnic violence against women during Partition. "The Return" is about a Muslim refugee, Sirajuddin, his wife and 17-year-old daughter, Sakina, traveling on a special train for refugees from Amritsar in India across the border to Lahore in Pakistan. When the train reaches Lahore (which is usually two hours away) after an arduous eight-hour journey at 10 P.M., many passengers have died or been dispersed by ethnic attacks. When Sirajuddin regains consciousness the next day in a refugee camp, he cannot remember the circumstances of how he was separated from his wife and Sakina. The narrative inscribes Sirajuddin's trauma through the cinematic representation of his fragmented memory. Images from the past flash like shots before his eyes: for example, he sees "the dead body of his wife, her stomach ripped open," with her voice saying, "Leave me where I am. Take the girl away." Next, he remembers that as the two of them ran, "Sakina's *dupatta* had slipped to the ground and he had stopped to pick it up and she had said: "'Father, leave it.' He could feel a bulge in his pocket. . . . It was Sakina's *dupatta*, but where was she?" (11–12). The memory of stopping to pick up the fallen *dupatta*—a scarf that is a sartorial sign of modesty—is significant. The fall of the dupatta foreshadows the imminent rape of his daughter; in the symbolic economy of the story,

Sirajuddin attempts to forestall this by picking up the scarf. Ironically, this leads to their separation.

In the refugee camp he reaches, he meets a band of eight young Muslim men armed with guns in a truck. The gang "said they brought back women and children left behind on the other side." They promise Sirajuddin that if his daughter is alive, they will find her. Sirajuddin describes Sakina as fair and very pretty: "About seventeen. Big eyes, black hair, a mole on the left cheek. Find my daughter. May God bless you" (12). The gang members risk their lives by driving to Amritsar, and rescue many women and children, but fail to find Sakina. On their next trip out, they find a girl on the roadside, who initially flees from them out of fear. They chase her in the field, catch up with her and explain who they are, at which point she acknowledges that she is Sirajuddin's daughter Sakina. After this, "The young men were very kind to her. They had fed her, given her milk to drink, and put her in their truck. One of them had given her his jacket so that she could cover herself. It was obvious that she was ill-at-ease trying nervously to cover her breasts with her arms" (13). The narrative thus represents the Muslim men as benevolent saviors of Sakina, a Muslim woman whose honor they seemingly protect, as the young man's jacket evocatively replaces the fallen dupatta her father had picked up for her.

However, many days pass, Sakina fails to return and Sirajuddin's days are spent running from camp to camp looking for her, as many refugees did for their loved ones. One day, he sees the gang and asks them if they have found Sakina; they all reply together "we will, we will." The protection of Sakina's absent, Muslim female body constitutes the apparent relation of support between them, and Sirajuddin prays for them. Then Sakina's body reappears in the narrative: Four men find her unconscious by the railway tracks close to Sirajuddin's refugee camp. They carry her to a camp hospital, and Sirajuddin follows. He screams "Sakina" as he recognizes her lying on the stretcher. The doctor checks the pulse of her "prostrate body" to see if she is alive, and then, pointing to the window, says to Sirajuddin, "Open it." This utterance evokes a response from the unconscious Sakina which suggests Sakina's repeated rape after "rescue": "The young woman on the stretcher moved slightly. Her hands groped for the cord which kept her *shalwar* tied round her waist." Then, the narrator reveals the telling detail that undoes the preceding implied mapping of ethnic identity and gendered protection: "With painful slowness, she unfastened it, pulled the garment down and opened her thighs. 'She is alive. My daughter is alive,' Sirajuddin shouted with joy. The doctor broke into a cold sweat" (14).

The end of the story thus presents a revelation and reversal: Sakina has suffered repeated sexual violence in the days after she was found by the group of Muslim men. Thus, her rapists were the very Muslim men who had claimed to rescue her. This is signaled in the singular image of her barely conscious physical response to the utterance "open it," voiced by a man. Her response gets read in two ways: her loving father joyfully sees it as a sign of her being alive. However, we, like the doctor, 'recognize' it as her identification of the authoritative male doctor's voice with that of her rapists, and as an explanation of her absence. Her bodily gesture is both a mark of trauma, and is the estranging evidence of her body's violent history. The utterance incites her memory of being subject to repeated rape; her abject movement in response represents the history of her embodied suffering. The image of the benevolent men rescuing women of their community is overturned: from protectors of honor, they are now revealed to be abductors and rapists. Manto thus critiques the sexual violence done to women even within communities, during Partition, which remains invisible in socio-political discourses about ethnic violence—because it is intra- and not inter-communal. The Muslim refugee, Sakina, possibly escaped sexual violation at the hands of Hindu men (in the story, there is no suggestion of her having been raped prior to being found by the gang), only to be repeatedly raped by Muslim men. Here, sexual violence is not communalized for its realization; it is intra-communal and disjunct from the nationalist horizon, part of an economy of power in which women's bodies are transacted and exchanged as objects of desire and consumption.

Manto's narrative does not represent sexual violence through a chronological account of events or through first-person testimony of pain and feeling. Instead, he signals the violence by depicting its material effects on Sakina's body and consciousness. By juxtaposing the doctor's banal injunction to open the window with the abject, automatic response of a barely alive young girl undressing herself to be raped, Manto makes visible the uncanny, transformed meanings of ordinary language in everyday life during the Partition. In this ironic story Manto challenges prevailing communalist and nationalist rhetorics, and articulates a devastating critique of their patriarchal objectification and abjection of women's bodies. Manto lived in Bombay for a considerable amount of time, and his modernist writings are marked by a sense of irony and cosmopolitanism, signaling his urban cultural dislocation and rejection of nationalism. His fiction experiments with an elliptical style that explores sensory perception, bodily experience and affect, and his work is a prescient instance of what Kwame Anthony Appiah has named "postcolonial": "it is postnationalist and post-nativist, seeing through the hegemonic rhetorics of nationalism and refusing the idealization of the indigenous and ethnic community."[43] Manto's political, humanist commitment to the secular, to the contestation of human suffering, and to the critique of patriarchal communalism and nationalism all signal his unique contribution to the world of South Asian postcolonial literary modernism.

The preceding two stories appear in Manto's collection of short stories *Mottled Dawn: Fifty Sketches and Stories of Partition*; the collection also includes a series of sketches or vignettes that he published as a slim volume titled *Siyah Hashye*, or "Black Borderlines." These vignettes from the margins or borders of the 1947 Partition and Independence, in the words of C. M. Naim, "are like the 'marginal' material to some larger thing, tiny in themselves but having great defining power."[44] When *Black Borderlines* was published, Manto's oppositional and bleak voice received harsh criticism for what many called his bad taste and cynicism. One sketch, "Losing Proposition," is about two friends who "purchase" a young girl for 42 rupees, from a dozen or so shown to them. After one spends the night with her, he asks her, "What is your name?" The narrator suggests that the girl's name signals a shared ethnic identity: "When she told him, he was taken aback. 'But we were told you are the other religion.'" The narrative here deliberately does not mention the religion or ethnicity of these two men or of the girl subject to commodified sexual violence, indicating the pervasiveness of this sexual violence across ethnicities. When the raped female subject asserts, "They lied," the man's response evinces the immateriality of ethnicity in this gendered, capitalist violence: "'The bastards cheated us!' he screamed, 'selling us a girl who is one of us. I want our money refunded'" (198). This scene represents what few nationalists and communalists wanted to talk about—the persistent, dehumanizing sexual commodification of and violence against women *within* communities that exceeded the 1947 rhetorics of ethnic conflict and honor. It also reveals the capitalist articulation of patriarchal ideologies that sustains sexual violence against women. The man is outraged at being misled about the identity of the commodified body he has "purchased" and raped, because it signifies a mis-description of the body as commodity purchased. He is not concerned at all about having raped a woman of his own ethnicity—as one would assume he would be, if he was concerned about the "honor" of his own community as embodied by the girl. In showing the contradictions and hypocrisy of communalism in this period, in making visible the fantasies and capitalist ironies of acts of violence that are, or get narrativized as, communal, Manto articulates a powerful critique of sexual violence against women. Manto enunciates a critique of the articulation of gender and capital in this sexual violence but from the ground of a postcolonial humanism, by interrogating what Judith Butler has described in a different context as the "vanishing of the human."[45] Nearly fifty years later, the South Asian American writer Shauna Singh Baldwin's novel *What the Body Remembers* also reminds us of this forgotten intra-ethnic violence. While traveling to

India from Lahore in 1947, the Muslim female character Jorimon is traveling
with the Sikh protagonist Roop when she is attacked and nearly raped by a
large group of Muslim men—even though they know that she is Muslim. At
this, Roop's words also indicate how Partition's gendered violence exceeded
the explanations of ethnic dishonor: "If men treat a woman they know to be
of their quom in this cruel way, can any woman be safe?"[46]

Saadat Hasan Manto's short stories, like "The Woman in the Red
Raincoat" and "The Return," and Shauna Singh Baldwin's novel *What the
Body Remembers* thus remind us that Partition's sexual violence was not
always about nationalism or ethnicity: If "Woman in the Red Raincoat"
marks a site where it is *racialized* desire, and not nationalism or ethnic hatred
that engenders abduction, then "The Return" makes visible another silenced
history: intra-ethnic abduction and sexual violence. Such scenes of intra-ethnic and racialized sexual violence, for which there are no archival histories,
and which are enabled by this moment of ethnic and inter-national conflict,
fall through the cracks of national as well as nationalist histories. This violence remains domestic and unchallenged, individual and invisible because
it is about no one's "honor."

Above all, Manto's aesthetic representations of these forgotten scenes
or subaltern pasts illuminate how ethnic violence is not always nationalist:
the nation as a desired community rarely figures in these stories. Unlike the
stories that later diasporic writers like Salman Rushdie and Bapsi Sidhwa
tell, where the nation-form is both the subject and the determining context
for its embodied postcolonial subject, Manto's stories from those early independence years signal the contingent, arbitrary presences and absences of
national belonging in the lived relations of antagonism he depicts. They disclose the incommensurabilities of the urban everyday saturated with violence
during Partition, and reveal the local subjectivizing processes by which bodies
are symbolically encoded and violated to produce a different history of alterity—acts whose singularity and heterogeneity will be assimilated eventually
into homogenizing, historicist narratives of communal and national honor,
rather than being coded as products of patriarchal power, urban dislocation,
or poverty. The singularity of these events resists the generalizing tendency
of the social sciences, and is one whose recognition is not encouraged in the
hegemonic narratives of history and anthropology.[47]

Manto's short stories, then, are interesting not simply as documentary
evidence for Partition historiography, but as aesthetic texts that bring into
being a scene of violence that challenges contemporary equations of ethnic
community and nation, female sexuality and ethnic honor. They are narratives that destabilize our revisionist critiques of Partition and nationalism,
and problematize the efficacy of historiographical and socio-anthropological

frames in accounting for and addressing the history of everyday forms of gender violence that were made possible by the British partition of India, which inhabit the lived temporality of the nation, and yet are not nationalist.

Returning Women and Restoring Heterosexual Coupledom in Hindi Cinema

The Indian film industry's response to independence and partition in 1947 and immediately after bore certain similarities and articulated certain differences from the literary critique of Partition and secular nationalism's failures in the early national period. Film historians like Sumita Chakravarty have noted that in the period following Partition, "[n]ot only did the threat of censorship deter filmmakers from attempting communal subjects, but perhaps the events were too close in time and therefore too painful to confront. (It was not until 1975, with *Garm Hawa* . . . that an Indian filmmaker could take up the subject.)"[48] However, insofar as films as well as film trade journals and magazines like *Sound* and *Film India* from this period reveal that many films took up the historical processes of nation-formation and decolonization, the inscription of Partition in these accounts can illuminate the hegemonic rhetorics about it that prevailed at the time.[49] Partition also impacted the Bombay film industry in other ways: For one, many Hindu producers who fled Lahore, like B. R. Chopra, came to Bombay and subsequently became very successful in terms of capturing audiences for their films. Moreover, Partition created a huge displaced population of refugees that became the new, rootless urban audience that Bombay cinema could engage as modern Indian citizens who belonged not so much to the villages they had been displaced from, but to a new, imagined nation: India. As Girish Karnad has observed, the new audience of Indian cinema after 1947 was largely made up of an uprooted population that came to the cities due to Partition and its accompanying devastation of rural life. This population had the qualities that characterized the next phase of Indian cinema: "anger at being torn from its roots, and a great sentimentality for the family."[50] As such, these new citizens became key for the constitution of the postcolonial counter-publics as spectators and consumers of the films about nation and belonging after 1947.

Chakravarty has noted that in certain Indian films of the post-independence period, "nationhood" assumes a certain figurability evidenced in changes in the narrative structure. Among the historical films made around the mid-twentieth century in India, the favorite themes were early colonial conquests and resistance; and in the social films, or social melodramas, social and national consciousness was dominated by the conflict between tradition and modernity as the nation made the transition "from feudalism to industrialism, from colonialism to democracy, from economic backwardness to material advancement."[51] In this context, the lack of a strong response to the Partition experience often gets explained away by pointing to the strict laws of censorship that the Nehruvian government had imposed on public sphere representations of ethnic relations and identities that might "inflame communal passions" and exacerbate ethnic violence.

While centralized film censorship laws in Bombay in 1951 at the behest of Nehru certainly limited the autonomy of filmic representations of Partition, film production in India did extensively explore themes of nation building, independence from colonial rule, and anti-colonial struggle in documentaries, historical films, and social realist "art films"—all of which often referred to Partition if not as a central theme, certainly as an event that marked the plot and shaped the aesthetics of the filmic narrative. Many documentaries made around this time also accounted for India's transition to Independence after the anti-colonial struggle, and addressed the 1947 Partition and its violence. The Indian Motion Picture Producers' Association (IMPPA) made a documentary on Independence Day celebrations in Delhi entitled *Azadi Ka Utsav* (*The Occasion of Independence*; 1947). Footage from this was used in a Films Division documentary, *India Independent*. In addition, historical fictionalizations like Phani Mazumdar's (dir) *Andolan* (*Struggle*; 1951) were made, which traced India's freedom struggle from 1885 to 1947. Also of this genre was V. Shantaram's (dir) Hindi venture *Apna Desh* (*Our Country*; 1949), which was produced by Raj Kamal Kala Mandir, with a cast including Pushpa Hans and Umesh Sharma (I discuss this film's representation of abducted women and refugees in Chapter Four); *Azadi Ki Rah Par* (*On the Road to Freedom*; 1948), directed by Lalit Mehta, casting Prithviraj and Vanmala; and *Hindustan Hamara* (*Our Hindustan*; 1950), directed by Paul Zils, which was made by the Documentary Unit of India. This last film used extensive documentary footage while presenting a fictional story that included a cast of several prominent actors from the Bombay film industry, including Prithviraj and Dev Anand. Furthermore, Rajendra Jolly of Rajdeep Pictures in Bombay directed *Kashmir* (1951), a historical film about the Indo–Pak conflict over Kashmir in 1947–1948; Ramesh Saigal (dir) brought out *26th January/Bharti* in 1956, casting Nalini Jaywant and Ajit; and finally, this genre of historical films included one entitled *Bapu Ne Kaha Tha* (*Bapu Had Said*) in 1950, which also addressed the Kashmir war between India and Pakistan in 1947–1948. In fact, *Lahore*, a Hindi social melodrama directed by M. L. Anand, came out as early as 1949, exploring the popular theme of lovers separated by Partition and the fate of abducted women and separated families at this time. The cast included Nargis, Karan Dewan, Kuldip Kaur, and Om Parkash.

Other Hindi films about Partition in the early national period, besides those discussed in Chapter Four, include *Andolan* (1951), directed by Phani Majumdar, Manmohan Desai's *Chhalia* (1960), *Mere Apne* (1971), directed by Gulzar, and *Palanka* (1975). *Chhalia*, with Raj Kapoor as the hero, was a mainstream Hindi film about the separation of families on the eve of independence, and the abjection of women in the process. *Mere Apne* is the story of an old widow who becomes a silent witness to two kinds of violence that mark postcolonial India: first, Partition violence, and later, the criminal politics and gang warfare that marked the sixties in India. *Palanka* was an Indo-Bangladeshi international production, based in East Bengal. The story revolves around an old Hindu patriarch during Partition who stays on in what was then E. Pakistan, even as the rest of his family immigrates to Calcutta. In addition, in 1947 itself, *The Miracle of Gandhi*, the story of Gandhi's recent fast to end Hindu–Muslim riots in Calcutta as photographed by Mr. P. Mohan for the British Movietone, was released at the leading Regal Cinema in Delhi. This reveals the range of cinematic production—commercial, state-sponsored, as well as art cinema—that emerged during this early national period of upheaval, and that took up the challenge of representing nationalism and Partition's violence and migrations in the postcolonial public sphere.

In addition to these Bombay productions, the Bengali film industry, albeit much smaller, also led to the emergence of some of the most politicized films about the Partition experience. Among these are Ritwik Ghatak's directorial debut film *Nagarik (The Citizen)*, which was shot and edited in 1952–1953; *Chinnamul* (1955), a film about the traumatic separation of a married couple as they are forced to migrate from their village in East Pakistan, and their reunification in the refugee settlements of Calcutta; *Meghe Dhaka Tara (The Cloud-Capped Star;* 1960), about the experience of a refugee family that financially depends upon and so emotionally and financially exploits their eldest daughter in rural Bengal; and finally, Ghatak's *Subarnarekha (The Golden Line)*, a 1962 film about a Bengali man who migrates with his daughter from what is now Bangladesh to work in a quarry in rural Bengal. All this suggests that while censorship may have been a constraint, it by no means silenced the filmic representation of the experiences that constituted and were effects of Partition. Films like *Lahore, Chinnamul, Subarnarekha,* and *Meghe Dhaka Tara* directly address the Partition and its effects: forced migration, familial separation, abduction and sexual violence against women, displaced urban and rural refugees and their economic and socio-cultural hardships. As such, they play a very complex didactic, sometimes critical, and sometimes nation-building role in promoting the rhetorics of secular citizenship or problematizing the violence of decolonization and nation-formation in the public spheres of postcolonial India.

In particular, the Hindi film *Lahore,* directed by M. L. Anand, is an important melodramatic romance that was released in 1949 in India; it is a mainstream film that, remarkably early on, takes up Partition's ethnic violence and women's abduction. Based in Lahore in West Pakistan, it devolves upon on a popular theme at this moment (and in Bollywood cinema more generally): lovers separated by Partition. In *Lahore,* the Hindu middle-class lovers Chaman (Karan Dewan) and Neela (Nargis) are separated due to ethnic violence, Neela's subsequent abduction, and Chaman's forced migration; they are then reunited across the border in India. The film engages the issue of abducted women but in order to advocate the nationalist, state-sponsored rescue and recovery of abducted women and their social acceptance by Hindu Indian men. When it came out in 1949, it was widely praised in the trade journals in Bombay. For example, the Left, secular magazine *Sound,* the most well-written, serious, and reputed film magazine with communist leanings (whose editor, K. A. Abbas, was also a prominent member of the Progressive Writers' Movement), carried a review that reported:

> As the unfortunate lovers torn apart by the blood and thunder of the Punjab holocaust, Nargis and Karan Dewan earn new laurels by their heartwarming performances in *Lahore.* Inspired by a historic speech made by the Deputy Prime Minister, *Lahore* is one the most significant films ever produced and tells a story as tender as any ever told since the movies began to talk.[52]

This review yokes together the just-preceding Holocaust in Nazi Germany and the Partition, to critique the genocide of both. Interestingly enough, *Lahore,* despite its success at the time, and its unique place as one of the few, rare, commercial films centered upon Partition and on abducted women, has been largely forgotten in the story of the development of Indian cinema. Few scholars of Indian cinema speak of its existence, and it fails to appear even in the otherwise excellent and comprehensive *Encyclopedia of Indian Cinema.*[53] At any rate, the high praise of the contemporary review just presented is both reiterated and qualified in another, more extensive review of *Lahore* in June 1949, even as the film by now had been banned by the Pakistani Government. The review is worth quoting extensively here, both for its reproduction of the dominant language in which Partition was spoken of in urban, Left circles, and for its pointed, vivid criticism:

> When producer-director Jaimani Dewan announced *Lahore* as his fourth production, many a critic openly suggested that the amiable Jaimani was courting disaster. One couldn't blame the critics because

the embers that kindled the Lahore inferno were very much alive then. A more inauspicious moment couldn't have been chosen for a venture like Lahore. . . . *Lahore* tells a story hitherto untold—the rescue and rehabilitation of abducted women. Everyone will agree that the story of innocent women who fell prey to hoodlums during the Great Divide had to be told, as film is the most potent chronicler of day to day life.

No honest critic however, can admit that the makers of this film have succeeded in tackling this problem. The story is told with such restraint—thanks to the Censors—that it almost loses its identity as a purposeful film. . . . The hero's hair-raising adventures in Pakistan do not offer a solution to the problem of rescuing abducted women as not all such unfortunate women can be rescued by gallant bands of Don Juans. *Lahore* merely skims the fringe of this burning problem, and a golden opportunity to present something really worthwhile on the screen was thus lost.[54]

This review points out how *Lahore* is unique as one of the first and few Indian films made about the experiences of abducted women, but it also stresses in the Indian public sphere the importance of film as the *most* powerful "chronicler" of everyday life—despite draconian censorship laws. If the review is critical of *Lahore*'s lack of purposefulness and its melodramatic Don Juan-style rescues (far from the bureaucratic state-driven rescues which would have made for less entertaining fare), it still defends the film from the implicit criticism levied at it by the Pakistani ban:

Yet, none but the most debased communalist could find anything in this film that would hurt the feelings of our Sister Dominion. If the Muslim girl in India is saved by a chivalrous Indian youth, his counterpart in Pakistan is a noble Muslim. . . . Thus, Jaimani Dewan has admirably succeeded in showing that virtue and vice go hand in hand, and that it is the same on both sides of the artificial barrier which separates India and Pakistan. The scriptwriter has allowed his imagination to run riot, and the resulting photoplay is more or less like a not-so-suspenseful dime novel. Karan's entry into Pakistan in the guise of a Muslim vendor, Om's sudden transformation [into a good man], and Nargis' escape in a *burqa* appear fantastic in the face of reality and should have been omitted.

Even as it approvingly mentions the stereotypical stock figures like "the noble Muslims" and "chivalrous Indian youth" that populate the film, the ambivalent review then concludes that because of its unrealistic melodramatic elements, rather than a successful "purposeful film," *Lahore* is a "memorable romance."[55]

The film opens by introducing Partition in a scene in which rioting noise accompanies a blank black screen, and is followed by a montage of shots of the front pages of newspapers in English, Hindi, and Urdu announcing the vivisection. The opening of the film lays claim to its own veracity through this text which appears on the screen: "This film is an inspiration from a brilliant broadcast by Vallabhbhai Patel and based on press accounts fictionalized for screen purposes." The mention of Vallabhbhai Patel, who was also well known for his anti-Gandhi, Hindu-centered stance in Congress nationalist politics, prefigures the film's reproduction of the ethno-nationalist discourses that came to dominate early nationalist politics after Gandhi's sidelining in the late forties. This is followed by a shot of a distant view of Lahore city, followed by several stills of different monuments in the city, interspersed with some footage of street scenes taken from a moving vehicle. Obviously, this is the Lahore of peaceful, pre-Partition days in which the story is set; a voiceover declares in Hindi, "This is Lahore, the heart of Punjab. This is a true story, but the names are false." Thus, the film reiterates its earlier, chequered claims of veracity and realism, revealing the historical inter-articulation of media institutions—the press and cinema—and national politics.

Early in the film, Neela's mother calls off the protagonists Chaman and Neela's engagement when Chaman's father is convicted for robbery. Chaman subsequently leaves for Bombay as he wins a scholarship for higher education. After a year, Chaman procures a job and starts working, when he receives Neela's letter asking that he return to Lahore so that they can elope. Upon receiving this letter, he returns home and assures Neela that he will take her to Bombay as soon as he has settled into the job. Shouting and rioting noise are then heard, and the filmic sequence is interrupted by a montage of shots of various English and Urdu newspapers' front pages, juxtaposing headlines in various languages. Among the headlines shown are "India Partitioned" and "Dawn of Freedom"—highlighting the two-faced nature of decolonization. Again, a blank black screen follows, signifying Partition as unrepresentable darkness. A voiceover comments in Hindi, "and after that, light was lost in the darkness. . . . Lakhs of innocent people died. . . . Humanity was crying, hiding her face in shame. . . . Evil had spread everywhere. . . . Gandhi tried to spread the message of truth, but hearts were dead. There was no sign of life . . . in our own nation, unpatriotic evil started on a journey which begins with hatred and ends who knows where." Thus, ethnic violence is simultaneously visually unrepresentable, even as it is verbally described as dehumanizing, "evil," and opposed to life and truth as embodied by Gandhi. The film's vacillation between Patel and Gandhi signifies its ambivalent commitment to the secular nationalist project, even as it names ethnic violence as "unpatriotic"—the nation's other.

The heavy reliance of this story on journalistic accounts—both in the claim that it is based on press reports and in its repeated presentation of stills of the front pages of newspapers—signals the central role and power of modern institutions like the press in shaping the public, cultural narration of historical experience, and the imagining of modern Indian nationality. This voiceover is followed by documentary footage of wide columns of Partition refugees proceeding on foot across the border, in columns that often were one or two miles wide and six or seven miles long. The documentary footage is interspersed with studio shots of actors imitating this journey, as Chaman, his mother, and his crippled younger brother, Kishan, flee to Amritsar in India. When Kishan gets tired and is unable to walk, Chaman carries him on his back, as many did for their young ones; after a while, thirsty and tired, the disabled Kishan collapses and dies, as thousands did in those thirty- to forty-mile journeys. In a refugee camp in Amritsar, Chaman and his mother find out that Neela has been abducted. Chaman's elder brother Dev is a good-for-nothing who is rather fond of gambling, drinking, and stealing; after Partition, he chooses to convert to Christianity and stay on in Lahore. Eventually, Neela is "rescued" by Chaman in Lahore with some help from his maverick elder brother. Parallel to this story of Neela's rescue and recovery is the story of Chaman's friend Ramesh, who spurns his fiancée, Radha, when she returns to him pregnant after having been abducted and raped. Ramesh marries Radha in the end, after some convincing by Chaman. In the interest of brevity, my discussion will focus on the scenes in which the film's characters negotiate the place of abducted women in Indian national life, and on the ideas about heteronormative coupledom that they proffer in postcolonial India.

Earlier, when Chaman goes off to inquire after Neela in the refugee camp, the film cuts to the first scene that directly debates the issue of abducted women. The setting is a bedroom in Chaman's friend Ramesh's house, where Ramesh is confronted with the return of his formerly abducted fiancée, Radha. The scene opens with Ramesh throwing Radha's photo on the ground, and the glass frame splinters to pieces, suggesting the disintegration of her social subjectivity. Evocatively, Radha picks up the broken photo frame, and remarks: "So now you don't even like to see my face . . . today you're turning me out of the house of which I was once going to be the queen." He angrily replies, "You're not Radha. That Radha is dead." However, to Ramesh's rejection and attempt to inscribe her as socially dead after rape,

Radha replies, "Radha is not dead! If someone abducted me, it is not my fault. If fate has dishonored me, it is not my fault." Ramesh derisively asks, referring to Radha's pregnancy, "And what about 'the truth' you are carrying around with you?" She replies, "This is not my sin; it is your own brother's sin, who didn't have pity or shame in his eyes, who didn't listen to the cries of a helpless woman. . . . And now you would banish me from earth to hell?" This is a unique moment: rather than having a male protagonist urging men and families to accept abducted women back in their lives as blameless victims (as is common in Partition short stories like Rajinder Singh Bedi's "Lajwanti"[56]), the film presents its audience with an assertive, middle-class woman who—although abducted—represents herself and affirms her own blamelessness. Furthermore, she radically ascribes responsibility for her rape to Ramesh, by linking him to her rapist and abductor relationally, as his brother via their shared masculinity.

When Ramesh shouts at Radha, "Stop it! Enough! Go away! I refuse to hear any more of this," she angrily warns him:

> Fine, turn your eyes away and continue to worship old thoughts! Don't listen, don't look! Continue to make our blood, the blood of unfortunate women flow. When our blood will flow like water, only then you men will open your eyes. Then you will recognize that this [child] is of your blood, it is a part of your body too.

Here, while Radha deploys the rhetoric of victimhood to assert her blame-lessness, she simultaneously assumes a position of agency in which she challenges Ramesh's rejection. Interrogating the social and symbolic death that he inflicts on her ("Radha is dead") because of her abduction, she refuses to be interpellated into the prevailing ideology of feminine dishonoring, and exhorts him to take collective responsibility for her rape. Her name, Radha, has a special valence in Hindu religious imagery, for Radha is worshipped as the pure lover of the Lord Krishna. Further, there are two senses in which the word "khoon" (blood) functions here. On the one hand, it represents the social death Ramesh is trying to inflict upon Radha by rejecting her as a physical death—as her murder. At the same time, however, it refers in the metaphorical sense to Radha's unborn child, and links Ramesh's male body to hers; by connecting the fetus with Ramesh's body—"it is a part of your body too"—she asserts that the child is as much a man's responsibility as it is the woman's, while making a radical claim about the child's collective pater-nity and her/his rightful place in the social body of the nation.

However, Ramesh is not convinced by her arguments; he forces her to leave, and shortly thereafter we encounter the next sequence dealing with the abducted Muslim woman Salma. Chaman visits Ramesh, and finds Salma in his bedroom. When he asks Ramesh who she is, Ramesh informs him that he decided to keep her in his house with him, since she is "separated" from her parents who migrated to Pakistan. Clearly, while it is not explicitly stated, Ramesh has either bought her from the men who ran a trade of abducting and then selling women, or has abducted her himself. Chaman roundly condemns Ramesh's actions, and convinces him that he ought to look upon Salma as a sister (as Gandhi had also exhorted), and to help her to return to her parents across the border. Ramesh eventually agrees, and Salma is "returned" to a Refugee Rehabilitation Officer in Pakistan.

The third abducted woman is the protagonist Neela: Salma, in gratitude and friendship for having been "returned" to Pakistan, helps Chaman to find Neela in Lahore; Neela now lives as "Laila"—renamed, implicitly converted, and married to her abductor Yusuf. There, Chaman accidentally bumps into his now Christian brother Dev. When he inquires after Neela, Dev echoes the popular discourse about women's impurity and honor at the time, suggesting that the abducted Neela has become a pariah and Chaman had best forget about her. However, Chaman, as the representative of a modern, progressive Hindu man, refuses, saying, "It is our duty to look for her, for time has brought us this new problem." Ideologically, he echoes Gandhi's response to the question of abducted women's place in the new nation:

> Many of our women are in Pakistan. They are being molested. Those unfortunate women are made to feel ashamed. It would be gross injustice if any woman is considered worthless by society and abandoned by her brothers, parents and husband because she had been abducted by the Muslims. It is my belief that any woman who has the purity of Sita cannot be touched by anyone. But where can we find women like Sita these days? And not all women can be like Sita. Should we show contempt for the woman who had been forcibly abducted and tyrannized? She is not a woman of loose character. My daughter or wife too could be abducted and raped. But I would not hate her for that reason. Many such women had approached me in Noakhali. Many Muslim women also came. We have all become goondas. I consoled those women. It is the men who commit rape that should feel ashamed, not these poor women.[57]

Thus, both Radha and Chaman reproduce a Gandhian position on the question of nation, honor, and sexual violence against women. In the film, through the usual melodramatic plot devices of stealth and disguise, Chaman and Dev manage to rescue Neela, and aided by officers of the Ministry of

Rehabilitation in Pakistan they return together across the border to the refugee camp where their mothers are awaiting them.

The heteronormative film thus ends with the patriarchal family unit reunited and restored; this includes Ramesh, who finally marries Radha. In one shot, Radha touches Chaman's feet in traditional obeisance. He blesses her, then looks straight into the camera and didactically urges the audience:

> I just hope that all girls like Radha are reunited with their Rameshes. That these unfortunate women are not sacrificed in the name of religion. If we do not help these unfortunate women, then successive generations will heap scorn upon us. A woman is the mother of all. To honor a mother is the duty of every man.

It is interesting that here it is a pregnant Radha, and not Neela, who becomes the representative abducted Hindu woman, re-presented and celebrated as reproductive body and national mother. The film's critique of the social stigmatization of abducted women still relies on the Hindu woman's submissive performance of tradition and subjection to male patriarchal power. Chaman performs ideal Indian, masculinized citizenship as he agentively engenders the abducted woman's return to family, community, and national belonging.

In making visible and asserting the agency and citizenship of middle-class raped and abducted women, in their own voice, the film offers a radical critique for its time, of the repressive patriarchal discourses around abducted women. However, *Lahore* as a film takes a nationalist stance, in which Partition and its desirability are never challenged. In many ways, it reinforces popular ideologies of Hindu and Muslim (thus also eliding the Sikh) ethnic difference, and the idea of India and Pakistan as Hindu and Muslim nations. The film's vision of modern secularism that Chaman embodies relies on the recognition and separation of religiously determined ethnic communities and identities. The Hindu Chaman represents progressive, modern Indian masculinity in this account; witness the absence of Indian Muslim masculinity. In this film's narrative structure, ethnically normative heterosexual coupledom is valorized and sustains the narration of the postcolonial nations India and Pakistan.

Lahore reinforces patriotic sentimentality, and links nationalism with secular humanism, but can only imagine inter-ethnic social relations as those of friendship and brother-sister love as prescribed by Gandhi: Inter-ethnic romance is completely absent from the horizon of the social relations of its predominantly Hindu characters. Thus, the ethnicized woman has to be cited as a sister when she is Muslim and a mother when she is Hindu.[58] Reinserted into narratives of kinship, women as objects rightfully restored to their men ("their Rameshes") get deployed to mobilize middle-class solidarity for the nation—a nation built on the imagined, dutiful reunification of the Radhas and Rameshes, the heterosexual couples torn apart by sexual violence. The film criticizes communal violence against women by deploying the rhetoric of motherhood, such that its abducted Hindu and Muslim female characters like Neela, Radha, and Salma can only be accepted by inserting them into the paradigmatic roles of kinship: as sister and as mother. It is important to note that this film is one of the few cultural representations from this early national period that represents ethnic sexual violence as something that happened to middle-class women too, and not simply to working-class or poor women, thus undoing its elision in most middle-class accounts governed by denial and notions of respectability. However, in this patriotic melodrama, the ambivalence of secular Indian nationalism towards the communal modes of power that are a constitutive part of it, is resolved through the figure of ethnicized woman. Stereotyped and at once emptied of meaning, this ethnicized woman (Hindu, Muslim, or Sikh) becomes a hyper-embodied signifier of the nation-state's patriarchal authority and (re)productive power, a citizen-figure who mediates between the nation's anxiety about secular commitments and its ambivalence about its own ethnicized territorial formation.

(In)Conclusion: Impurity, Diaspora and the Subaltern Pasts of Partition Histories

In Krishan Chandar's Hindi short story "The Peshawar Express," when a Muslim family traveling on a train to Pakistan is mercilessly killed by Hindu and Sikh men who had ambushed the train, their young beautiful daughter, a college student, is left alive until the end. She is forced off the train and is holding a book as they walk towards the jungle. Then she says to the killers, who are debating whether they should kill her or to spare her life, "Don't kill me. Convert me to Hinduism. I'm prepared to embrace your religion. I'm also willing to marry one of you. What good will it do you to kill me?" Even while one of the men agrees, another stabs her to death. As she falls to the ground and dies, her book is "soiled with her blood." The narrator notes: "The title of the book was 'Socialism: Theory and Practice,' and the writer's name: John Strachey."[59] This incident, where the ethnicized woman attempts to survive ethnic war by voluntarily choosing conversion and marriage to her family's killer, not only counters the popular nationalist imagery of women as voluntarily choosing death over the "dishonor" of rape and conversion, but it also, through the bloody book, indicts Nehru's intellectual "Western" secular socialism as having failed the female Indian citizen.

Bhisham Sahni's Hindi novel *Tamas* has a similar scene in which a Hindu woman, when trapped by a couple of Muslim men, suggests that instead of killing her, they rape her.[60] It is to no avail, because she is killed anyway; this scene then becomes a counterpoint to the following scene in the novel where hundreds of Sikh women "voluntarily" drown themselves by jumping into wells, to escape the dishonor of rape at the hands of the Muslim men who are about to storm the gurudwara. These scenes of violence, where some female figures choose "dishonoring" over death and others don't, bear witness to the complexities of conceptualizing agency in such moments where the choice is between suffering and death. Through their testimony, these writers challenge the nationalist ideology that suggests that for a Hindu woman raped by a Muslim man or its threat, suicide is the only desirable and honorable option. Their texts articulate a critical postcolonial humanism that disavows nationalism on the basis of this violence, and constitutes a space-clearing gesture that allows visibility for women's agency when it rejects patriarchal, ethnic, and nationalist demands of women's bodies. Further, if it is through acts of violence that ethnic identity and national citizenship are produced, then it is through the narration of this violence that these urban, secular writers seek to challenge the legitimacy of discriminatory gendered ethnic and nationalist discourses.

After 1980, the second generation of South Asian writers that have taken up the Partition moment are largely diasporic, living in the U.K. or United States. The novels by writers like Bapsi Sidhwa, Salman Rushdie, and Shauna Singh Baldwin identify and address violence, especially gendered violence, in places where it is not normally seen—the home, domestic spaces, private lives. They link the apparently singular Partition violence to the parallel forms of domestic and political violence that inhabit the domesticity of national history. In Indian historiography, violence tends to be studied through riots, which usually occur in public spaces like the street or the bazaar. In contrast, South Asian diasporic literature constitutes a counter-public that uncovers the subaltern past of violent un-belongings that mark the failures of nationalism. One of the significant features of this diasporic literature is that its account of national emergence is largely the story of the urban Indian and Pakistani middle class. Thus, except for Sidhwa's *Cracking India*, these cultural texts—in their urban, middle-class narratives of metaphor and memory—attend to the circulation of acts of ethnic and sexual bodily violence that occurred in both urban and rural areas around Independence through allegory and metaphor. In addition, *Cracking India* reveals what *Midnight's Children* unwittingly reinforces: that "proper" identity—religious and national—is always already a masculinized position;

women do not evoke that anxiety of identity, for they cannot inhabit those locations of identity except by proxy and as reproducers of those who might, if sexed male, occupy it.

Significantly, unlike the few literary texts in the seventies that emerged in South Asia and represent the Partition experience, these diasporic novels do not express nostalgia for the pre-Partition land and home left behind through migration. Instead, they raise in the public sphere questions about ethnicity, citizenship, and gendered belonging that South Asian nationalist histories cannot answer. In this sense, they return to memories of Partition and the alterity of its everyday life in order to tell the story of the present. In the transnational counter-public sphere constituted by this diasporic fiction about national experience, Sidhwa, Rushdie and other writers of their generation narrate the historical emergence of the nation through the duality of formation and fragmentation that characterized it, as a living legacy of violent freedoms. Sidhwa situates the materiality of sexed bodies as a site inscribed with the violence of nationalist histories, even as she challenges the homogenizing historical and anthropological narratives of sexual and bodily violence as always linked to communality figured as nationality; as such, Sidhwa "locate[s] the site of a fleeting articulation that [Partition] discourse has obscured and finally lost."[61] This enables us to better understand and devise strategies to address the heterogeneous forces that produce the sexual violence even today that ends up being called "ethnic, nationalist violence" in national historiography. Both Sidhwa and Rushdie exemplify an anxiety about national unity and ethnic belonging that persists in popular public discourse among South Asians in the sub-continent and in the South Asian American community even today. Ultimately, these works reveal the imaginative fictionality and failure of the promises of nations and nationalisms; further, they remind us that the story of any national emergence is always already transnational.

In April 2001 a family friend, Amrit Randhir Singh, recounted her mother's and elder sister's memories of growing up in Delhi in the tumultuous days of 1947, and said, "When it was decided to Partition the country, people went mad and started harassing and attacking women. Even the British soldiers, we used to call them 'tommies,' would harass women on the street, molest them. My mother would tell me so many stories about how even the British men were misbehaving during that time." She further added that once, her grandmother was accosted on the street by a couple of "Tommies" and harassed. In a story—the story of Partition—that is always told as a story about South Asian ethnicities and communities, the memory of this British participation in gendered violence against women has remained unrecalled and unwritten. The articulation of ethnic, gendered violence with caste as well as race reveals the complexity of the enunciation of identity in this moment: Ganda Singh's *A Diary of Partition Days, 1947–48* bears witness to the premium price Muslim men paid to purchase Brahmin women for the purpose of marriage, from among the Hindu abducted women available for sale in Pakistan.[62]

In part, then, this chapter has also been about the inassimilability of sexual violence in the history and discourse of national modernity. The public sphere narrations of Partition raise questions about the publicity and permissions for what one can say about family, domesticity, community and country. At this time of crisis, the rhetorics of honor and duty in normative gender relations that dominate this period's response to sexual violence against women produce masculinity and manhood as honor, indexed by the heteronormative control of women and their sexuality. These rhetorics, and the explanations that amount to pointing to these rhetorics, can unwittingly reinforce the notions of honor that are central to the respect that people accord to communal/ethnic violence. In their conclusion in *Borders & Boundaries*, Menon and Bhasin remark that "the dispute over abducted women and who their rightful claimants were so compromised their status as to deny them every fundamental right as adult citizens. Each of their multiple identities—as women, as wives and mothers, as members of families and communities, and as citizens—was set up against the other making any honorable resolution of their predicament, impossible."[63] However, what does "honorable" mean here, from their feminist critical standpoint? If we are to challenge the unhomely domestication of sexual violence into the terms of honor and duty, then we need to move towards locating the genealogies of honor and its terrors in the transitional nation.

This chapter has attempted to make visible the forms of sexual violence whose origins are not communalistic or nationalist. Such sexual violence, sometimes intra-ethnic and sometimes racialized, is constitutively articulated with the capitalist saturation of modern subjectivity and everyday life. It remains subaltern to the official narration of nationality, even as it shapes it. The subversive narratives of women's agency and citizenship that emerge from both the subcontinental and diasporic Asian American writers constitute a minor counter-discourse that pressures the coherent accounts of Indian historiography; in mapping agency that refuses to syntax communal and patriarchal power, these transnational texts, spanning the global geographies of the late twentieth century, insist that we revisit and rethink violence against women in moments of ethnic conflict. This project is thus continuous with that of the Subaltern Studies Group, insofar as it is crucial for counter histories to ask: on behalf of whose world does history writing organize knowledge? The middle-class patriarchalism of what constitutes ethnic and national history ultimately leaves us with the problem of the singularity of sexual violence that is elided when it is middle-class, when it is intra-community, or when it is *not* ethnic and national.

4

"We Were Never Refugees"

Migrants and Citizens in the Postcolonial State

In his memoir of the turbulent times of partitioned transitions in the sub-continent, a British doctor, Lt. Col. S. H. Heard, described how British officers in north India going about their daily duties, especially at airports, were often surrounded by groups of Muslims who felt safe in their company. He added, "In Pakistan, a similar situation prevailed. Once I found myself accompanying a family of Sikhs through the streets of Lahore to the airport from which they made a safe journey to Delhi." By September 1947, Heard and the other British officers in Delhi realized that the ethnic violence against Muslims in India showed little sign of relenting. Since they had a large number of mostly Muslim servants, they formed a plan to lead their Muslim "bearers and their families" to the refugee camp in Purana Qila for Muslims who planned to transit to Pakistan. As per this plan, they arranged to meet the Muslims after dark outside the compound. Although they were breaking curfew, it was considered less risky than proceeding in daylight:

> With an officer leading and others covering the flanks, I followed in the rear as is customary for the doctor lest there should be casualties. When we were within a few hundred yards of the great gate we knew that we would be spotted by the armed guards who would certainly be trigger-happy. It was essential to identify ourselves, and therefore we turned our torches on our faces while singing "God Save the King," while the bearers sang in praise of Allah.[1]

At this, to their relief, the gates to the Qila were opened and the Muslim refugees were taken in.

In this dramatic scene, white faces flooded with the flashlight's luminous gaze, along with the tones of "God Save the King," break the enforced shadows and silences of a curfew-ridden city in order to proffer to Muslim refugees safe passage to a refugee camp (and eventually to Pakistan). This representation reveals both the precarious performance of identity—racial and ethnic—as well as the persistent power of the British in this post-independence moment. From being the undesired and routed rulers, they emerge in this memoir as glowing, white heroes in the darkness of decolonization's violent freedoms. It is also an evocative moment, for the British who had once conquered Purana Qila from India's Mughal rulers now, as defeated rulers, deployed the signs of colonial power—white skin and a song of saving the British King—to protect and lead into the Fort the fleeing Muslim subalterns performing ethnicity through songs in praise of Allah in urban, independent India. This narrative moment—at once comical and terrifying, singular and yet resonant with the tropes of colonial identity—illuminates how in one version of the story, decolonization ironically turned the British into the heroes of subcontinental history, and how the conflicts and alliances articulated by race and ethnicity in colonialism were radically refigured by the violent, ethnicized mass migrations that occurred during this transition to partitioned, independent nationhood.

In mapping a genealogy of Partition, I have so far sought to introduce some dissent in historical and anthropological accounts of Partition's communal or ethnic violence. I have suggested that we pluralize traditional accounts of this violence as being economically motivated, or as elite political manipulation, and feminist culturalist accounts of communal violence, when gendered and sexual, as engendered by discourses of masculine, communal, and national honor. This chapter now moves from gendered bodily violence to the other singular feature of Partition: the forced displacement, mass migration, or "exchange of populations" of, by unofficial counts, over sixteen million people. Out of ninety million Muslims, thirty-five million remained in India—making India the country with the biggest Muslim population outside Muslim states. While displacement has long been, as event, experience and trope, a pre-occupation of colonial and postcolonial studies, most scholarship on the subject tends to focus on migrations—legal and illegal, elite and subaltern—from South Asia to the so-called First World. But what of the constitutive migrations of 1947 and their impact on the cultural imagining of belonging—national and otherwise? The little-explored experience of the Partition's sixteen million migrants, when examined through its cultural and political articulation in South Asian public spheres, uncovers a new history of postcolonial belongings: Indian art and popular cinema, as well as newspapers and film magazines, reveal that the Partition refugee occupied a highly charged and ambivalent space in the new Indian nation following 1947, as the state struggled with its constitutional commitment to secularism in the face of the British ethnicization of territoriality that was Partition.

Article 1 of the 1951 Refugee Convention defines "refugee" as any person who,

> As a result of events occurring before 1 January 1951 and owing to well-founded fear of being persecuted for reasons of race, religion, nationality, membership of a particular social group or political opinion, is outside the country of his nationality and is unable, or owing to such fear, is unwilling to avail himself of the protection of that country; or who, not having a nationality and being outside the country of his former habitual residence as a result of such events, is unable or, owing to such fear, is unwilling to return to it. In the case of a person who has more than one nationality, the term "the country of his nationality" shall mean each of the countries of which he is a national, and a person shall not be deemed to be lacking the protection of the country of his nationality if, without any valid reason based on well-founded fear, he has not availed himself of the protection of one of the countries of which he is a national.[2]

Criticizing this exemplary international discourse about migrants and refugees, Hannah Arendt has taken up the Jewish history of forced migration and refugee experience to problematize the renaming of stateless or rightless persons as "refugees" or "Displaced Persons." "The term 'stateless,'" she argues, "at least acknowledged the fact that these persons had lost the protection of their government and required international agreements for safeguarding their status. The postwar term 'displaced persons' was invented during the war for the express purpose of liquidating statelessness once and for all by ignoring its existence."[3] Foregrounding the role of the modern nation-state in realizing access to human rights, Arendt points out that the discursive deployment of the terms "displaced persons" and "refugees" elides stateless people's loss of human rights which have today become, for all practical purposes, only guaranteed by national rights.

Engaging this important critique of the international legal discourse about the refugee with the experience of Partition refugees in 1947, we can note that the latter occupied a unique and liminal position: Ideologically, they were also simultaneously citizens in the nations to which they migrated. This considerably differentiated their experience from the stateless that Arendt describes, insofar as they were promised national rights as citizens and were in the process of "becoming citizens." Nonetheless, the dissonance between this proffered nationality and its material realization in the lives of refugees who had suddenly lost their belongings—historical, material, emotional—marks their marginality in the processes of nation-formation. In the transition or rite of passage from being colonized subjects to becoming refugees and then citizens, Partition refugees inhabit a liminal space. In Victor Turner's influential formation, it is a zone of fluidity and transformation that carries the creative potential to produce alternative structures and new meanings: "Undoing, dissolution, decomposition are accompanied by growth, transformation, and the reformulation of old elements in new patterns" in this liminal space.[4] In this sense, the liminal condition of Partition refugees/ citizens in transit mirrors the liminal state of political transition from colony to partitioned nationhood of decolonized India. This chapter explores the contours of this liminality, the kinds of cultural and political transformations it engendered, and the contradictory modes—of assimilation, resistance, oppression, exploitation, loss, and alienation—by which Partition refugees' transnational belongings and loss of belongings came to be articulated in India. Concurrently represented in the public sphere as iconic citizens as well as victims of the state, as national subjects and anti-national outsiders, Partition migrants themselves also responded ambivalently to the very identity of "refugee" in India and Pakistan. In the narration of the Partition experience in public and political discourse, then, it was around the figure of the refugee that debates about citizenship, ethnicity, and gender coalesced in the early national period in India. An examination of these representations reveals that, in addition to ethnicity, race, and gender, modern notions of capitalist property ownership became a key determinant of postcolonial citizenship in complex and contradictory ways.

My desire here is to write the specific experience of Partition refugees into the story of independent India through their representation in the public sphere. I do so in order to recast the story of Partition refugees' experience not as an anomaly, but as a constitutive part of a larger history of South Asian migration and nationalism in the twentieth century. Giorgio Agamben has argued that the refugee "is nothing less than a limit concept that radically calls into question the fundamental categories of the nation-state, from the birth-nation to the man-citizen link." As such, Agamben suggests, the refugee "makes it possible to clear the way for a long over-due renewal of categories in the service of a politics in which bare life is no longer separated and excepted, either in the state order or in the figure of human rights."[5] In what follows, I suggest that it was the figure of the gendered Partition refugee that became a site through which a range of questions about nationality, ethnicity, class, and belonging were negotiated in South Asia. The refugee-citizen's liminality both reflects and interrogates the hegemonic governmentality of these nations in transition between colonialism and postcoloniality. My aim is not to situate Partition refugees at the heart of the discourse on postcolonial national identity in India, but to reinsert Partition refugees' negotiation of national belonging—in its own dimension and intensity—into the narrative of postcolonial national modernity. This account is, by all admissions, partial, uneven and incomplete; piecing together the fragments that give us access to this subaltern past, it cannot claim for itself historical comprehensiveness. Instead, I focus on a few sites in the postcolonial public sphere—the representation of refugees in the international press, the transformation of Hindi cinema, the discourses around land and property—through which I track some of the political transformations and national implications of urban refugee life. My hope is that this will enable further inquiry into the questions of how normative citizenship has come to be culturally marked ethnically Hindu in India and Muslim in Pakistan, and of how the refugees in India today—Tibetan, Kashmiri, Bangladeshi, Sri Lankan Tamils—might lead us to better address statelessness, rights, and ethno-nationalisms.

In the early national period, from 1947 through the 1950s, journalistic accounts in both England and India represented Partition refugees not only as victims but also as agents of violence. Refugees' story telling, their oral testimony of the violence they witnessed and experienced, were seen to be acts of narration that "inflamed passions," engendered ethnic violence, and so were best suppressed. Thus, unlike the celebratory turn to oral testimony in historical and anthropological writing over the last decade or so, popular public sphere accounts from the early national moment are marked by fear and anxiety over the potential threat of violence seen to be residing in the circulation of the "stories" and "tales" of these very refugees. Moreover, the differential treatment of Partition refugees when they were Muslim or Jewish illustrates the complexities negotiated by the Indian state as it attempted, on one hand, to enact its constitutional commitment to secularism and individual rights without discrimination on the basis of religion and, on the other hand, to manage a mass migration that was ideologically based largely on ethnic difference and the two-nation theory. Finally, in literature and films that depict refugees, the refugee became the figure through which a middle-class, Left intelligentsia criticized nationalist politics and socio-economic oppression in postcolonial India. For example, focusing on the role of Partition refugees in West Bengal politics, Joya Chatterji has shown how the refugee was used in Left political discourse to debate and demand the question of rights for all Indian citizens, in order to "achieve a broader, more egalitarian definition of citizenship."[6] In the counter-public cultural narration of Partition, then, violence done to refugee bodies was represented not only as the price paid for freedom, but also as the violence of elite nationalism for which the British, Indians, and Pakistanis were all responsible. Contrary to the tendency in international policy discourses to represent the refugee as *outside* the nation, then, in postcolonial India refugees were represented simultaneously as agents, victims, and exemplary citizens in the nation.

Accordingly, the questions that preoccupy this chapter are: How were the refugees who came to India received and represented in the postcolonial public sphere? What was the place of the refugee in the public imagination, as the newly emergent nation and its discourses of citizenship were being fashioned? How do our aesthetic texts translate the history of Partition migration and its impact on national identities, urban culture, and gendered citizenship? Muslim refugees who went to Pakistan are often, even today, considered outsiders there, such that the status of "refugee" or "muhajir" has generated a "Muhajir national identity" and the Muhajir Qaumi Movement in the eighties that combats the former Partition refugees' oppression as outsiders in contemporary social and political life.[7] Indeed, the ethnic violence between Muhajirs and Pathans as recently as 1986 is exemplary of the consolidation of political community by Partition "refugees" in Pakistan.[8] In contrast, Hindu and Sikh refugees in India have been relatively unpoliticized and assimilated into the social fabric despite the initial hostility, poverty, hardship, and envy they faced. Thus if, in Pakistan, the shame and stigma associated with being refugees has been translated into a retaliatory political mobilization, in India that shame and stigma have led to a disavowal of the very identity of "refugee" by middle-class Partition migrants. This chapter thus tracks an alternative, partial, cultural history of Partition migrations through urban, public, and state discourses (locally and abroad) about refugees, citizenship, violence and minority ethnic belonging.

State Rehabilitation Practices and the Matter of Courtesy

Nearly a month after the Partition of India on August 15, 1947, the Government of India, under the Governor-Generalship of Mountbatten, set up an Emergency Committee that "launched a formidable administrative counter-offensive against the prevailing chaos." According to Alan Campbell-Johnson, it had

> requisitioned civilian transport, dispatched to provinces and states
> ready to receive them tens of thousands of non-Moslem refugees who

had come to Delhi, arranged for special trains for Moslems to go to Pakistan, provided guards, called for volunteer constables, arranged for the saving and harvesting of crops from deserted lands, given orders for the searching of passengers for arms on trains and for the stiffening of punishments for delinquent military and police guards of trains . . . [Furthermore, it] cancelled public holidays, including Sundays, helped to keep going two newspapers as well as All India Radio, arranged for government servants to be brought to their work and for the telephone system to be maintained, provided guards for hospitals [which were frequently attacked by communalists seeking to perpetrate more violence], arranged for the collecting and burying of corpses found in the streets, for the movement of food, for the broadcasting of daily official bulletins to the Provinces and for the large-scale cholera injections.[9]

Yet, these were two states in transition, with the British colonial state in withdrawal, and these efforts proved inadequate to the scale of economic and political transformation that Partition demanded. When the migrations—which Nehru and the rest of the political elite had assumed would be temporary—continued large-scale, they were caught by surprise by its sheer magnitude. Having failed to anticipate this mass migration and "exchange" of populations fleeing ethnic violence following the Partition, the two countries struggled to cope with its effects with inadequate resources. As millions of refugees moved in opposite directions, several factors—famine, starvation, diseases like cholera, flooded rivers to be crossed on the Punjab border, sheer exhaustion, and communal attacks on the refugees—left at least a million refugees dead on the journey towards a new nation and a new home.

According to the Indian Annual Report of the Ministry of Rehabilitation 1952–53, the places in India most populated with refugees were, in order, as follows: Punjab, West Bengal, Delhi, Uttar Pradesh, PEPSU and Bombay. The 1953–54 report also informs us that female refugees called (in the language of the report) "unattached women" who were "in receipt of gratuitous relief in regular homes and infirmaries" were mostly placed in Punjab, and then Bombay state.[10] Thus, in the late forties and fifties, the Indian cities of Delhi, Calcutta and Bombay were not only political, cultural and economic centers, but also became key destinations for many of the approximately eight million migrant refugees from the Partition. Yet, most studies of Partition experience have been regional studies, focusing on the states of Punjab and/ or Bengal; there has been relatively less investigation of the impact of refugees on urban cultural life.[11] In the Indian case, the official rhetoric of refugees' easy assimilation into Indian social and political life was undermined, especially in urban areas, by local competition and hostility between the refugees and previously settled city dwellers for scarce economic jobs and resources. Especially in the urban context, refugees were greeted by varied responses of pity, disdain, resentment, fear, guilt, and envy. This is also represented in literary accounts of urban experience in the early national period. For example, in Anita Desai's *Clear Light of Day*, set in the forties and fifties, when the protagonist Bim inquires after her neighbors the Misras' new real estate business, the senior Mr. Misra tells her that it has been failing, due to his son Brij's prejudices against the refugees in Delhi. He says, "Can it succeed when Brij the manager cannot go to the office because he thinks it's degrading and refuses to speak to his clients because they are Punjabis, from Pakistan, and don't belong to the old families of Delhi?"[12] Thus, the prevalence of hostile, denigrating treatment of refugees, and criticism of this treatment in other quarters on humanist grounds, is also visible in the Constituent Assembly debates. In early 1948, member Giani Gurmukh Singh Musaffar asked the Minister of Relief and Rehabilitation, "What steps have been taken to see that the West Punjab refugees are treated by the Custodian of Evacuee Property and other officials with sympathy and kindness?" Of course, this concern for refugees is also marked by regional difference: The question suggests that Giani Gurmukh Singh Musaffar, being Punjabi, cared more about refugees from West Punjab than about refugees from East Bengal. To his query, the Minister of Rehabilitation K. C. Neogy replied, "Strict instructions have been issued to ensure courteous treatment to refugees and other visitors."[13] Oddly enough, the Partition refugee is constructed here as a "visitor" to the nation. This "strict" state injunction to treat refugees with sympathy, kindness and courtesy is important, as it both suggestively indicates the ill treatment and discrimination often faced by refugees, and also signals how the Indian state's official discourse welcomed and took under its care these refugees as rightful citizens.

Stories that Cause Slaughter: The Threat of Speaking Refugees

A unique feature of the representation of Partition refugees in the public sphere during the early national period (roughly from 1947 through the sixties) was that they were often represented not only as victims, but also as agents of ethnic violence. Much of the oral testimony recently recorded by scholars like Pandey, Butalia, Menon and Bhasin refers to refugees as "outsiders" and "trouble-makers" who initiated violence in the places they were displaced to; newspaper accounts in India and England from the time told a similar story. For example, in London, the August 15, 1947 issue of the *Times* printed the following news item: "District Aflame: The trouble in the east Punjab started about a month ago in the Hoshiarpur district, where refugees from Rawalpindi spread tales of suffering and requested co-religionists to avenge them. A peaceful district was thus set aflame." This shows how refugees were blamed for Partition's ethnic violence; in the same paper, it is astonishing to see an article which claims that "in spite of reports of bloodshed which appear in the paper everyday, the fact remains that this gigantic surgical operation has been performed *with amazingly little bloodshed and violence*. For this development, Gandhi's doctrines of non-violence and the conception of non-violence which spread among millions of people has been mainly responsible" [my italics]. The editorial "The End of an Era" of the same paper, however, predicts that Hindu–Muslim relations, or Indo–Pak relations, will not be normalized for another two or three generations. Reflecting the contradictory colonialist representation of Partition, it also waxes eloquent about the benevolence of the British Empire, concluding that "Never since the heroic days of Greece has the world had such a sweet, just, boyish master."[14] Another newspaper report from Lahore on August 26, 1947 asserts, "The chief danger at the moment is that the tens of thousands of Muslim refugees who are trekking westwards with tales that are grim enough in reality, but become more lurid with every telling, will cause a wave of reprisals in West Punjab."[15] Refugees and their oral testimony in this period come to be seen as powerful enough to generate mass political violence. Narratives that bear witness to refugees' experiences—"their suffering"—are denigrated as "tales" that become "more lurid" in their re-telling. Thus, newspaper accounts represent refugees' testimonies regarding their experiences as implicitly false, exaggerated fictions, and as technologies that produce ethnic violence: the recounting of "tales of suffering" become vocal performances that produce ethnic violence. In another news item, a Sikh man waiting in the long queues for passage in Karachi via ship to Bombay in 1947 is reported to have said, "Our community is on good terms with the others. We have no fear of our neighbors but fear that feelings may be stirred up against us by the refugees from Punjab."[16] Fear of the repercussions from refugees' stories produced more refugees; ironically enough, this anxiety in the public sphere over the violent effects of refugees' oral testimony, cites the testimony of a Sikh refugee as evidence of the violence engendered by refugees' voices and their accounts of the Partition experience.

Thus, contrary to the dominant policy discourse about refugees that casts them as victims, the depiction of refugees in journalism and oral accounts from this time also cast refugees as active agents of violence through their story telling, dispossessed looting and physical aggression. The biopolitics of this discourse thus leads to the subjectification of the suffering refugee as potential threat to local communities and national peace. An editorial from the *Times* stated:

> As the refugees toil across the frontier in each direction, and make their way to the nearest center of population, the harrowing spectacle of their misfortunes inflame their co-religionists to murderous vengeance upon the rival community. Stories brought by Sikh and Hindu survivors from the Western Punjab caused the slaughter of Muslims in Paharganj and other wards of old Delhi by neighbors with whom they have dwelt in amity for centuries.[17]

The rhetoric of this news report expresses both sympathy for and a fearful anxiety about refugees. While it sympathetically describes refugees as toiling across the border, it also constructs refugees as a "harrowing spectacle" whose "misfortunes" incite ethnic violence. Instead of naming the refugees' experience as harrowing, this account turns the refugee herself into a "harrowing spectacle" for the national public, even as her "stories" cause "the slaughter of Muslims." Both as harrowing spectacle and as story teller, speaker-subject and silenced object, the refugee is simultaneously imagined as survivor and agent of violence. In this, both her bodily presence and her voice purportedly threaten to destroy peaceful rural and urban communities—communities that have apparently been dwelling in the fabled, centuries-old syncretism of India. Such great effectivity attributed to story telling, rumors, migrant voices, and tales of witness and experience in the production of violence illuminates how the narration of oral testimony itself becomes—in the media, public imagination and state discourse—a political act of public violence.

Of course, the question of ideological bias in journalistic reporting is pertinent here: It is interesting to note that while in the *Times*, a standard refrain in the reporting was "it is not possible to ascertain the exact situation" or "it is not accurately known what occurred," many Indian journalists like D. F. Karaka accuse the press, both British and Indian, of deliberately obscuring what was really going on. While Nehru accused the foreign press of deliberately exaggerating the horrors of violence and misrepresenting events, the *Times* (London) argued that Indian newspapers exaggerated reports in order to incite violence. Karaka however, referring to the Holocaust in Germany, argued, "Much the same will happen if the curtain is not lifted on the happenings in the Punjab. Our newspapers have played down the story of Punjab to a point [where] it has become inaccurate and almost untrue. What has been virtually a war of extermination—an undeclared civil war—our editors have called 'disturbances.' The places where thousands of innocent people have been butchered have been called 'dangerously disturbed areas.' On the ground that the spreading of the news would affect other areas, the Indian press has volunteered to suppress the truth."[18]

The depiction of refugees in the Indian press was similar: For example, the *Illustrated Weekly of India* also reiterated the twin tropes of refugees as both victims and agents of violence. An editorial from September 14, 1947 stated:

> The aftermath of the horror in the Punjab is sporadic outbreaks of violence in many parts of the country. Much of this trouble is undoubtedly due to the stories carried by refugees which are one-sided, often distorted and lose nothing in the telling.
>
> Refugees deserve everyone's sympathy and aid in their plight, but however pitiable their cases may be, they cannot be allowed to become a source of vengeance propaganda or the organizers of further killings. Yet it is apparent that these people have not refrained from abusing in this fashion the hospitality of other provinces.[19]

This editorial expresses a perfunctory sympathy for refugees, even as it constructs them as subjects who, through the act of narrating their experience of violence and uprooting, are de facto agents and "organizers" of violence. They are simultaneously "pitiable" and sources of "vengeance propaganda"; the stories of their experience are "one-sided" and "distorted" in their very telling, and their speech is read as abusive of a sympathetic national hospitality. This dominant hostility, in the end, paves the way for both a silencing of survivor testimonies in public culture and state censorship of the representation and remembering of Partition violence in the public sphere. Hence, for example, in 1951, newspaper censorship and centralized film censorship in the interests of state security in Bombay significantly shaped the independence of representations of Partition in public life.

The editorial just quoted further continues to describe refugees through biological metaphors, as sick and diseased presences in the body politic of the "hospitable provinces" that received them:

> Provincial governments can and must act firmly. Their own citizens must be protected against murderous communalism and refugees who carry it should be segregated in quarantine until the fever has passed. Communalism has proved to be just as fatal a disease as cholera and plague, and the private citizen, whatever his station in life, has the right to expect protection against it. Such a suggestion may seem hard on the refugees, but the peace of the whole country is at stake.[20]

In this account, citizenship and refugee-ness are opposing terms in the biopolitics of Indian nationality, even as refugees are cast as inherently communalist. Thus, in the hegemonic middle-class public sphere, refugees who were welcomed as citizens by the Indian nation-state were nonetheless seen to be distinct from other citizens: They were objects deserving of sympathy and pity, or guests benevolently granted hospitality in the provinces. Simultaneously, they were by definition communalists, and they constituted a threat from which both "private citizens" and national peace were to be protected. Implicitly, then, the refugee becomes a de-privatized, public citizen-subject who infects the national body with a "murderous communalism." Communalism is here cast in bio-political terms as a fever and a disease carried and transmitted by refugees—an infection that must be tackled in public life by the state government through the segregation of refugees. Even as non-migrant "citizens" get constructed as inherently secular, Partition refugee-citizens become, in this view, a collective primitivistic threat to the health of a sturdy and secular national modernity.[21]

The pervasive media representation of refugees as victims and yet as agents of violence through their oral story telling contrasts with fictional representations of refugees in novels and short stories from this period. Early national literature often represents the refugee as the ideal, secular, humanist subject who suffers ethnic violence and, through the experience of this suffering, determines to undermine it. In this literature by writers that often belonged to the leftist Progressive Writers' Association, the male refugee becomes the ideal secular citizen who, because of his suffering, devotes his life to preventing ethnic violence. For example, in Agyeya's Hindi story "No Revenge," a Sikh male refugee who has lost his entire family except for his son now continually enacts their displacement in everyday life; both he and his son simply live on the trains that ferry refugees between India and Pakistan. When, on such a journey, a Hindu man traveling in the same compartment attempts to incite the elderly Sikh refugee to violence against two Muslim refugees—a woman and child—traveling with them (by telling him stories about Muslim "atrocities" against Sikh women), the Sikh refugee responds by criticizing, on humanist grounds, the Hindu's desire to harm their fellow travelers. It turns out that the Sikh refugee lives on the trains between India and Pakistan to protect and escort fleeing Muslim refugees to Pakistan; shuttling around in a permanent displacement, the suffering Sikh man prevents the violence and loss that his family experienced from occurring again in other migrants' lives.[22] We also saw this gendered discursive idealization of suffering Sikh masculinity earlier; these multiple representations of heroic and suffering Sikh masculinity in the public sphere also mark the nationalist minoritization and loss of belonging for many Sikhs in postcolonial South Asia.

Similarly, in the Hindi film industry in Bombay—which was the largest center of indigenous film production—refugees were ambivalently addressed, and the discourses about ethnic difference, communalism, and national belonging were conflicted. For example, if *Sound*, one of the most prominent English film magazines, had secular, socialist leanings, then *Filmindia*, its competitor, was given a very anti-Muslim communalist slant by its editor Baburao Patel in the early national period. Like *Sound*, *Filmindia* argued that readers must recognize that Indian cinema was "an index of national life."[23] It also argued that films should be celebratory but also didactic: films should be "instructive to people as to how to behave in a free country."[24] At the same time, Patel's vitriolic editorials often centered upon propagating communalist, anti-Muslim sentiments: for example, in one editorial, he asked readers to report any information they might have about which Muslim film producers were exporting their films and profits thereof to Pakistan without paying income tax in India. In another editorial, he solicited from readers "reliable information of evacuee misappropriations in Pakistan and holdings of semi-evacuees[25] in India so that the same can be forwarded to the government."[26] By facilitating the state capture of Muslims' properties in India, Patel seeks to disenfranchise Indian Muslims already displaced during this violent time. As if foreshadowing the resurgence of BJP-led Hindu nationalist discourse in the late twentieth century that constructs the Indian Muslim as third column (indicted in Khalid Mohammad's Bollywood film *Fiza* in 2000), Patel's call in an emergent postcolonial public sphere both reproduces Rajendra Prasad's rhetoric of the Indian Muslim as a "problem" in post-1947 India and evinces the central place of property and its ethnicization in the determination of citizenship and belonging during this South Asian transition to nationhood.

In contrast to *Filmindia*, *Sound* persisted in advocating secularism and ethnic harmony, and also criticized state efforts to rehabilitate refugees as inadequate. For example, Saba, whose commentary appeared in a regular column "With Love and Irony," wrote in 1950:

> The refugees from Pakistan came to India expecting love. They received only irony. After the repeated incidence of police firings in various refugee camps, well might these unfortunates cry out, "We asked for bread and got bullets."
>
> There is surely something wrong about the whole organization of refugee relief and rehabilitation if, after nearly three years of Partition, many thousands of refugees are still living in sub-human conditions in camps and barracks, which are not fit even for cattle.
>
> The recent firing in the Koliwada Refugee camp near Bombay has once again spotlighted the discontent that is still brewing in the

hearts and minds of the refugees, as a result of the callous official indifference towards their welfare.[27]

Here, Saba vigorously criticizes the inadequacy of state processes of rehabilitation and "callous official indifference" to the continual material deprivation refugees faced in urban camps, even three years after independence. Irony is the name that Saba gives to the structural and material violence that permeates the lives of refugees in urban India: they live in abject sub-human conditions unfit even for animals, and their discontent is met by police firing. Through this critique, Saba appeals to the state government for a more sympathetic, humane and effective rehabilitation process that ensures refugees' welfare and safety.[28]

In addition to this counter-discourse about the state's efforts in the public sphere, refugee discontent against the new nation-state (rather than against a particular ethnic community) at the poor state of rehabilitation practices was also pervasive. This was evident in newspaper accounts like one about riots in Simla (India) as early as September 1947. The item reports massive looting, and again casts refugees as troublemakers: "Shops have been looted, the looters, who are mostly refugees from West Punjab making no distinction between Muslim and Hindu establishments."[29] This news item is important in that it makes visible that refugees' violent acts were not always ethnicized; in this case, they were acts of violence against the state and its perceived failure to protect its new migrant-citizens. Thus, the transnational public-sphere representations of this experience also make visible the complexities of historicizing this ethnic conflict. Scenes like the aforementioned one disarticulate violence and ethnicity, and suggestively point to a much neglected dimension of Partition: the place of property in the historical relationship between refugees and the nation-state. I return to this issue of the place of property later in this chapter.

Suffice it to say that in the hegemonic and counter-public spheres in India and England, the narration of 1947 marked a range of responses to Partition refugees: they were addressed with both fear and pity, both anxiety about their oral testimony and sympathy for inclusion and assimilation into the national community. For example, the discrimination and prejudice against refugees in India was also something that legislators urged the state to redress: many advocated government assistance for refugees (especially for those refugees who had been "government servants" or state workers), given that "it is not possible for any one coming from outside Delhi, to obtain residential accommodation in Delhi by private negotiations with the landlords."[30] This points to not only the discriminatory hostility of locals in Delhi towards renting property to migrants, but also to how the nation-state, in its attempt to manage an unprecedented, violent mass migration at the same time that it was itself coming into being, took on great responsibility for refugee rehabilitation. It offered immediate succor through services in refugee camps and train stations, gave loans and assigned land to Sindhi refugee organizations to enable resettlement, and was committed to providing jobs, financial aid, and housing to Partition refugees for a sustainable everyday life. Nonetheless, given that the postcolonial state—its arms, procedures and policies—was still in the process of being formed, in a land dispossessed by more than a century of colonial exploitation, the tremendous task of rehabilitation was often enacted through contingent, contested, and ad hoc policies and practices. This ad hoc quality, combined with the administrative, political, and financial burden of rehabilitation, sometimes engendered its own forms of structural state violence for those displaced by Partition.

Urban Transformations: Bombay Refugees and Early Bollywood Film Culture

The contribution of refugees to urban cultural life in India has been significant. In the Hindi film industry many Partition migrants came to dominate and transform the scene. Filmmakers like N. Sippy, B. R. Chopra, Yash Chopra (B. R.'s younger brother), and Ramanand Sagar, among India's most successful commercial filmmakers, were Partition migrants.[31] Once heavily dominated by Muslim filmmakers, writers, and actors, the Hindi film industry changed dramatically after Partition: many of its most successful members migrated to Pakistan between 1947 and 1950, including producers like Mehboob and Shaukat Hussein Rizvi, who went to Lahore with capital to buy Hindu-owned studios. Prominent producers in Lahore, like Dalsukh Pancholi[32] and Shorey, were forced to sell their studios and property in Lahore for a song and to flee to India after August 1947 because of unabated ethnic violence. Some Muslim film artists returned to Bombay after a few years when they realized that the Lahore film industry had largely collapsed due to the exodus of predominantly Hindu producers after Partition. Others stayed. The Indian film industry, then, becomes a very interesting site to examine the effects of Partition on Indian cultural discourses. It is one that I have tried to situate in relation to other practices of cultural representation, like literature and journalism.[33] I deliberately focus on plot and thematic content in the case of films, rather than film technique and genre, to map the ways in which the history of Partition appears in the stories they tell.

Related to the crucial role played by film in Indian public culture, is the interesting note that as a part of the relief measures in relief camps in Delhi

and elsewhere, for two hours every evening refugees were treated to enter-
tainment programs that included news broadcasts and films. As Donald F.
Ebright, Director of the Refugees and Famine Relief (1949–1952) cell of the
National Christian Council of India (NCC), reports:

> Sixteen mm sound projectors, screens, turntables, microphones,
> generators, and converters were collected and films borrowed from
> the North India Film Library of the National Christian Council.
> Recorded music, an hour of films and the All-India radio 9:00 pm
> news relayed through the public address system, was our night's
> work, if you remember to include the trip, setting up and taking
> down equipment with 2 to 10,000 people getting closer and closer
> to see it all.
> "Mickey Mouse," "Donald Duck," "Our Gang," and the "Careless
> Charley Health Film," produced by Walt Disney for Latin American
> use, were favourites. Month after month, the cinema programs were
> held, and the audiences did not diminish. Utilizing a cloth screen
> for a two-way projection, Kurukshetra crowds of 20,000 watched the
> same 16 mm film show.[34]

Thus, both in the representation of Partition and in the state practices for
relief and rehabilitation of refugees, films played a significant role in the
postcolonial public sphere. While it is beyond the scope of this chapter to
explore spectatorship and cinematic practices, it is important to note the
increasing relevance of film and cinematic culture in the state and individual
negotiation of Partition and its effects. I return to this question of film in the
public sphere later.

The heterogeneous, critical, and ambivalent responses to refugees, well
exemplified in popular film discourse from the time that ranged from communalist to secularist, were also uniquely gendered. Witness, for example,
Filmindia's Judas' curious suggestions regarding female refugees in his
"Bombay Calling" column: "Bombay has over 15,000 refugees already from
Sind and the Punjab. Among these refugees, there are beautiful young
women, completely helpless and destitute. Many of them have education,
and many more have good figures and features [sic]. Almost all of them
speak good Hindustani." Judas recommends therefore, that these women be
approached and guaranteed "respectable conditions of work" as film artistes.
He further argues,

> All these refugees are our own people and they have to be helped to
> settle down one day or another. They cannot go back now. We can't

go on feeding idle refugees. We must give them work so that they become useful members of society. . . . And film work is good work. It often needs less brains than other jobs, and can be made acceptable to anyone from the idiot to the intellectual. [sic][35]

The ambivalence towards refugees in this piece is striking: on one hand, refugees are claimed as "our own people." Yet, simultaneously, they are seen as parasitical "idle refugees" being fed by Indians; they are depicted as citizens who have to be trained and pedagogically transformed into "useful members of society." This usefulness, achieved primarily through their productive labor, lies for female refugees in their objectification: in their beauty, shapeliness, and linguistic ability. Judas thus advocates female refugees' bodily exploitation through film work as a technique by which they might be transformed into useful citizens.

The schemes suggested in *Filmindia* all originate in a patriarchal nationalism that is, more often than not, a pro-Hindu, anti-Muslim nationalism.[36] Furthermore, the representation of Muslims in the paranoid, vicious rhetoric of Judas in *Filmindia* is worth attending to: Muslims are described as "greedy wolves" and unpatriotic Indians who should be assumed to be Pakistanis until proven otherwise. Furthermore, Judas argues that Muslims, who largely control the powerful medium of cinema, should be carefully watched because they will likely use their power in cinema for propaganda to promote Islam under the instruction of Jinnah, targeting especially the eight crore untouchables in India. For all of *Filmindia*'s anti-Muslim spleen however, it did recognize that the film industry was largely united in its anti-communalist, secular impulse. For example, on October 2, 1947 several members of the film industry, including prominent artists like Durga Khote and Prithviraj Kapoor, organized a rally in Bombay. For a good six hours, loaded onto several trucks, they drove around the streets of Bombay shouting slogans in English and Hindi like "Mahatma Gandhi Ki Jai" (Long Live Mahatma Gandhi), "Hindu-Muslim Ek Hai" (The Hindu and Muslim are One), "Jawaharlal Nehru Ki Jai" (Long Live Jawaharlal Nehru), and "We shall not allow riots in Bombay." They also gave speeches at select points affirming their determination to maintain Hindu-Muslim unity and peace in the city of Bombay; ethnic violence had disrupted the film industry (both film shootings and screenings), and "they preferred peace to starvation."[37] Later in 1950, when the migrations from East Bengal (West Pakistan) were at their most violent peak, many prominent members of the film industry, like the singer Lata Mangeshkar and actress Madhubala, organized and contributed to charity shows to raise funds for those refugees.[38]

"Refugees Have Paid The True Price of Freedom": Women, Patriotism, Citizenship

In exploring the gendered responses to refugees and their national belonging in the early national period, the controversy around the mainstream Hindi film *Apna Desh* (*Our Country*) is also instructive about popular sentiment towards refugees in general, as well as towards women refugees in particular. Made by V. Shantaram and released in 1949, the melodrama *Apna Desh* was advertised as being about a Hindu Indian "refugee girl who sells her nation's honor and fools the Indian Police Force by her seductive charm."[39] The film was widely distributed across India and even abroad: it was translated into several South Indian languages, and also exported to Sri Lanka. Although no copies of the film have survived for viewing to my knowledge, it was at the time an important text that generated much discourse and debate in the post-colonial public sphere regarding the gendered Partition refugee and national belonging. As such, the film's reception illuminates the popular discursive negotiation of nationalist patriarchy and patriotic expectations of gendered refugees and non-refugees at this time. Film reviews and letters in contemporary film magazines reveal that the film's plot revolves around Mohini, a Punjabi Hindu woman who is abducted and raped by Muslims in Pakistan, and who subsequently returns to her family in India only to be rejected by her parents and ostracized by society. In vengeance for this social rejection in the new Indian nation, she turns into a smuggler, and traffics cloth and arms to Pakistan in exchange for gold and money. She eventually confesses to her crimes when her lover, Satish, is about to be mistakenly indicted for them. The film drew much criticism for being a sensationalist misrepresentation and an unpatriotic film, but most of all for proffering an unsympathetic view of the refugee experience. For example, a letter to the editor of *Filmindia* in November chastises V. Shantaram for his depiction of refugees. The writer asserts, "Refugees have paid the true price of freedom":

> Does Shantaram think that all refugees are traitors? These people, whom we call refugees, are the real martyrs. Having lost their all in Pakistan and suffered beyond description at the hands of merciless goondas, they still have not uttered a word of complaint. To call them traitors, or even to depict them in a bad light, is extremely unjust and amounts to a heinous crime.[40]

The representation of Partition refugees as "the real martyrs" of the nationalist struggle, and as people whose violent uprooting and loss had been the "true price of freedom" was popular during this period: It insists that we recognize and value the collective, cultural marginalization of the refugees' trauma and loss. Several other letters in subsequent issues also condemn *Apna Desh* as an anti-refugee film. Among these is a unique letter from a Punjabi refugee, Krishen Chandra Paul, himself—for in this melee, where refugees are spoken for and about, the refugee's own speech is often silenced for its potential threat of violence. Paul, now residing in Bombay, expresses outrage as well as hurt at the vilification of refugees:

> I was very much hurt when I saw Shantaram's *Apna Desh*. . . . According to Shantaram's *Apna Desh*, a Hindu refugee girl from West Punjab betrays the so-called Azad Hindustan but has this fellow Shantaram studied the life of these unfortunate Punjabi refugees? If not, how the fellow dared to show such things on the screen. [sic] The people who have chanced to study the life of Punjabi refugee men and women can judge from their hard work for a living. These refugee men can be seen sitting in the hot sun on the footpaths of each and every city of East Punjab, U.P. and Delhi itself . . . refugee women are working in camps on 8 annas to 1/- per day [50 paise to Rs. 1 per day].
>
> I being a Punjabi cannot tolerate such blame for my own province. The fellow Shantaram has hurt our hearts by producing *Apna Desh* for filling his boxes with money and winning popularity from the so-called National Government due to whose mistake we have become and are named "refugees."[41]

This self-representation of a Partition refugee is important and unique for two reasons: first, because it challenges the exploitation of refugee experience for commercial gain; second, because it criticizes the nation-state whose very existence has made many Punjabis refugees. Contrary to the official nationalist rhetoric about how the nation-state magnanimously offered shelter and solace to refugees, Paul argues that it is the very existence of the Indian nation and its government that are responsible for engendering his displacement as a "refugee." By calling the nation and the state "so-called Azad Hindustan" and "so-called National Government," he interrogates the claim that India is free, and indeed, the very existence and authority of both nation and government. The marking off of the word "refugee" in quotes also suggests Paul's distance from the political identity that this history has inscribed on his displaced body; he remains alienated from the political languages of the state and his ascribed place within it. He holds the postcolonial state responsible—it is due to the nation-state's "mistake"—for his becoming a refugee, even as he implicitly criticizes the Partition as the government's "mistake." Thus, Paul expresses hurt and anger both at being displaced and at the elision of refugees' hard work and suffering in vilifying, fictional portraits of their supposed unpatriotism in the hegemonic public sphere.

The response to *Apna Desh* in the magazine *Filmindia* takes a different route that echoes dominant, gendered nationalist ideology. In his review, Baburao Patel demands, "Find us a woman among the six million Hindu refugees—thrown by destiny and distress into our laps, raped and molested by Muslims of Pakistan—so perverse as to be a traitor to her own people and country merely [sic] because she was disowned by her people."[42] The misogyny of this statement, where the raped female subject is expected to perform her patriotic loyalty towards "her people" even as the latter disown her, is astonishing for its blinded hypocrisy. In Patel's view, perversity does not lie in the family and community that rejects the woman because of sexual violence done to her; instead, it lies in the choices and actions of the raped female subject if she betrays "her people" and patrie "merely" because they disown her. The attribution of perversity to Mohini is based on the assumption that patriotism is a form of feeling that is natural, inevitable and good, regardless of the experience of violence, rape, uprooting and loss that accompanied nationality and that was the lot of its female refugees.

Generally, then, popular sentimental sympathy for refugees and criticism of *Apna Desh* had two dimensions. Firstly, it criticized the representation of Mohini as "an outrageous slander on Indian womanhood"[43] by citing the "honorable" sacrifices and "suicides" of thousands of women to escape rape, as examples that give the lie to an unpatriotic figure like Mohini. Secondly, it abstracted the gendered representation of "national betrayal" as "an insult to six million refugees" who are helpless, hardworking victims and martyrs of the nation. None of the reviews or letters problematizes the circumstances of Mohini's life—her abduction, multiple rapes, rejection by family, ostracism and marginalization. Their common occurrence is neither contested as untrue nor criticized; unlike its contemporary *Lahore* (which I discussed in Chapter Three), *Apna Desh* and its critics do not criticize the multiple forms of bodily and psychic violence inflicted upon women like Mohini. They simply foreclose the imaginative possibility of retaliation, resistance, and rejection of nation and nationalism by the liminal female refugee-citizen who has suffered ethnicized sexual violence and patriarchal psychic violence during Partition. In the process, these multiple voices in the public sphere mark a space of anxiety about the threat of anger and retaliatory violence from refugees, especially women, towards a largely unwanted partitioned nation.

In her discussion of the genre of "avenging women" films in Indian cinema in the 1980s, Lalitha Gopalan has shown that these narratives with

powerful female protagonists avenging their rape stage the anxious relationship "between patriarchy and the state," even as they always end "by revealing the avenging woman's own overwhelming investment in the restoration
of the social imaginary." From this perspective, then, *Apna Desh* can be
usefully read as a precursor of the later avenging-women films that explore
what Gopalan has called the "patriarchal abandonment"[44] by nation, community, and family of the raped female refugee-citizen. The film resolves the
conflict between Mohini and the patriarchal Indian nation-state through the
denouement of heterosexual romance as redeeming Mohini and transform-
ing her from an avenging woman-refugee into a repentant, compliant citizen.
Thus, heterosexual coupledom subverts the liminal potential of Mohini and
reinvigorates the authority of the new, patriarchal postcolonial nation-state.
In the process, *Apna Desh* stands apart from other literary and film narratives that construct the raped female refugee as suffering victim and the male
refugee as heroic, suffering citizen.

Migrant Rights and the Fantasy
of the Postcolonial State

Often described as "exchange or transfer of populations" in political discourse, this Partition's mass migration—one of the largest involuntary
migrations in modern history—was not planned or anticipated, but came to
be recognized, by many but not all, as inevitable around August 1947. For
example, by August 22, 1947, the 300,000 strong population of Hindus and
Sikhs in Lahore in Pakistan had dwindled to a mere 10,000 following a mass
exodus to escape violence. In India, the Ministry of Relief and Rehabilitation,
which became the Ministry of Rehabilitation, was set up in August 1947. It
was, in the words of its Annual Report (1952–53),

> faced with the gigantic task of evacuation, relief, and rehabilitation of
> millions of people who were suddenly—and irretrievably—torn from
> their moorings. During these five years [1947–1952] every effort has
> been made to secure the integration of these uprooted people in the
> social and economic life of the country.[45]

Under The Displaced Persons (Compensation and Rehabilitation) Act of
1954, the term "displaced person" refers to

> any person who, on account of the setting up of the Dominions of
> India and Pakistan, or on account of civil disturbances or the fear of

such disturbances in any area now forming part of West Pakistan, has after the first day of March 1947, left, or been displaced from, his place of residence in such area and who has been subsequently residing in India, and includes any person who is resident in any place now forming part of India and who for that reason is unable or has been rendered unable to manage, supervise or control any immovable property belonging to him in West Pakistan, and also includes the successors-interest of any such person.[46]

This definition of a displaced person not only fails to include those displaced from East Pakistan, but it also articulates displacement and property ownership: an articulation that was critical in the violence and displacement of 1947 and after. As per this definition, the status of "displaced person" can be retroactively applied to those displaced even before the independent national existence of India and Pakistan in August 1947. Furthermore, ownership of immovable property in West Pakistan confers upon even a person residing in India the status of "displaced person," often used interchangeably with the term "refugee." As a result, belonging becomes disarticulated with the sense of living, residing and inhabiting a territorialized space as home; being displaced is reconfigured as being divested of managerial control over private property. Losing one's place thus also becomes about literally losing property; conversely, a privileged class position with the power to own property entitles one to the title of refugee/displaced person and access to the state protection offered to such groups, when that property is lost. Property ownership, then, in critical ways, impacts the production and realization of postcolonial citizenship.

It is interesting to note here the recurrent assumption of intimacy and responsibility that marks the relationship between refugees and the nation-state as embodied in its political representatives. The voices of refugees during the early national period—evident in memoirs, oral accounts, letters to editors of newspapers and magazines—reveal that Partition refugees envisioned the newly formed states as directly responsible to and for them. Thus, the critique of the nation-state emerges not in the form of a general critique of nationalism, which stood for a hard-won freedom from British subjection, but in holding accountable the state for its failure to ensure a peaceful transition and migration. For example, when the Prime Ministers of the two countries, Jawaharlal Nehru and Liaquat Ali Khan, toured refugee camps in east and west Punjab after 1947, they heard from the refugees on both sides similar criticisms of the failure of the police and army to be neutral protectors. Furthermore, "East Punjab Muslims seemed to think that they were having to pay the price of Pakistan. If Punjab had to be divided, they said, why could they not have been informed in advance, so that they could have evacuated the area in time, with their possessions."[47] The *Illustrated Weekly of India*, a left secular magazine, also documents similar sentiments, though in harsher tones: An editorial states, "Certainly, the attitude of many refugees to touring ministers of both dominions suggests disgust rather than admiration."[48]

An unpublished memoir by Amar Devi Gupta, a Kashmiri Hindu from the Poonch area, who fled to a refugee camp in Srinagar when Pathans from Pakistan attacked Kashmir in 1948, recounts her violent anger at the elite Indian nationalist politicians. When the Indian Prime Minister Jawaharlal Nehru visited the refugee camp in which Gupta was living, she angrily slapped Nehru for the failure of the Indian nation-state to protect Kashmir, which led to thousands dying in the Pathan attack.[49] This violent criticism of nationalist politics and politicians in the public sphere signifies both a hope that the nation-state is an agent and space of protection and safety of its citizens, and a view that Partition violence and displacement was, in part, eloquent evidence of state failure. The accusation directed at Nehru is based upon a fantasy of the nation-state as a site that resolved ethnic conflict and sheltered familial belongings, as well as on a notion of political and personal accountability of politicians like Nehru towards the populace. Amar Devi Gupta subsequently decided, having lost much of her family, to leave the new Indian nation and migrate with her brother first to Kenya in 1948, and then to the U.K. in 1955, even though Sheikh Abdullah had reportedly offered her the headship of the Red Cross in Kashmir. This decision evinces how many refugees rejected this new partitioned nationality—a choice of non-belonging over assimilation in independent but partitioned India. Such migrations by Partition refugees, primarily to North America and England, thus suture Euro-American immigration histories with the history of Partition.[50] They reveal the transnational effects of this sub-continental partition, and how Indian nationality came to be disavowed by these citizens-in-transition.

The history of state practices of rehabilitation in India is remarkable and rife with contradictions. According to the Deputy Minister of Rehabilitation, J. K. Bhosle, refugees or "destitute displaced persons" were first taken to camps where doles for maintenance were paid. Later they were dispersed to rehabilitation or work sites, as the case may be, and provided with work against wages instead of doles. Displaced persons who remained outside camps were also given rehabilitation facilities according to various schemes.[51] As per such schemes, shops were constructed for displaced persons in Delhi, and loans (including agricultural loans) were disbursed by the government to enable refugees to develop land, resettle communities, and rebuild their lives and livelihoods.[52] Those who were government employees had a certain amount deducted from their salaries every month towards refugee rehabilitation funds. Yet, despite state efforts, the scale of rehabilitation required meant that as late as 1952, relief measures, and especially the attendant procedures for determining citizenship and domicile, were still in flux and marked by ad hoc arrangements that often simply responded to immediate needs.

This is evident, for instance, in the arrangements for enabling the migration of Hindu and Sikh refugees from Pakistan. "Intending immigrants to India from Pakistan," especially those who were assembled at border stations in Pakistan in order to come to India, were required from 1948 onwards, to have migration certificates from Indian diplomatic missions. The Government of India decreed that until October 31, 1952, those migrants who had already passed the Pakistani check posts and reached the Indian border were allowed entry without travel documents.[53] The proposal to introduce the passport system between the two nations was made by the government of Pakistan in 1952. According to Anil K. Chanda, then Deputy Minister of External Affairs,

> The Government of India were [sic] not in favor of it and did not wish to impose any restrictions on travel between East Pakistan and India. On Pakistan's insistence however, the matter was discussed at considerable length. . . . These discussions were carried out with a view to facilitate travel and minimise hardship.[54]

Although the passport and visa system was established, the Indian government offered to abolish passport and visa requirements between the two countries. However, perhaps to consolidate its own precarious nationality, the Pakistani state insisted upon a passport and visa system that concretized its national borders and consolidated its territorial integrity.

The ad hoc nature of state policy and practices was also played out in the vastly different histories of rehabilitation of East Bengal and West Punjab refugees. Khushwant Singh's polemical and patriotic critique of refugee rehabilitation in *The Unending Trail*, based on interviews with Partition's East Bengal refugees, illuminates the material complexities of refugee rehabilitation in the newly formed Indian nation-state.[55] The East Pakistan migrations were relatively less violent and spread out over a longer period of time than the west Punjab migrations. *The Unending Trail* opens with a scene on a railway platform in Calcutta where Singh interviews refugees from East Pakistan who have made a home at the station. Among them is Sarvamangala Devi, who has just migrated to India in 1957 and, eager to speak to Singh, has "edged her way through the crowd, thrust her migration papers into my hand, and rapidly narrated her tale of woe." Singh summarizes her account thus: "How her widowed daughter had been killed in the riots eleven years ago—one year before Pakistan had been formed; how she had brought up her two year old orphaned grandson." Anxious about her grandson's future as a minoritized Hindu in East Pakistan, Devi becomes desperate. She "made a false declaration before the Indian High Commissioner in Dacca, stating that she had relatives in India and would require no relief from the government." As a result, she now "found herself stranded at the first railway station on the Indian side, barely 100 yards from the Pakistan border—with no friends or relatives to look after her and no money to proceed anywhere." That the abjection of ethnic minoritization is only compounded by their stark poverty and helplessness as refugees in India is evident in her summation of their dilemma: "The platform of Petrapole railway station had been their home since they had come to India and her grandson's earnings from beggary their only means of livelihood. They could not go back because they had renounced Pakistani nationality. They could go no further because they did not have the money to pay for their fares, nor strength in their limbs to walk long distances."[56] Refugees like Sarvamangala Devi, then, are truly stateless: As Hannah Arendt suggests, statelessness is not "the loss of specific rights, then, but the loss of a community willing and able to guarantee any rights whatsoever."[57] In this sense, Sarvamangala's loss of community and country is absolute: She has not only lost the protection of Pakistan as an ethnicized, minor Hindu subject, but is also allowed to become a refugee in India only when she promises to not expect the realization of her rights as a refugee and a share of the state's aid for refugees.

In the East Pakistan she has fled, she tells Singh that while her Muslim neighbors were very kind and had even given her money to come to India,

> "It was the outsiders and small officials who kept bothering us. They took whatever they wanted from our homes, and no one listened to our complaints. When we went to the police station, they said, 'You go to India. There is no room for Hindus in Pakistan.'"

Singh then writes, "She looked up at me and added bitterly, "It seems there is no room for Hindus in India either!"[58] Sarvamangala Devi's ethnicized body is thus twice minoritized—first by the Pakistani state in which she is a part of an ethnic minority and hence subject to state discrimination, harassment and eventually expulsion, and later by the Indian nation where she is allowed entrance as a "refugee" only if she officially agrees not to exercise her rights as one. At her cry about the lack of place for Hindu refugees in India, "there were murmurs of assent from the crowd. They were all in the same predicament, having left Pakistan with permits from the Indian High Commissioner after making false declarations that they would not ask for relief."[59] The state already overburdened with the task of refugee rehabilitation is here desired as a site of care, protection and belonging. Instead, it becomes a site of erasure: the stateless female subject is granted legal identity only on the condition that that she misrepresents herself as not needing state protection. Through her angry comment, "It seems there is no room for Hindus in India either," Sarvamangala Devi and refugees like her criticize their double ethnicized and economic exclusion from the human rights accruing to national citizenship and refugee status. Caught in a violent liminality, they assert themselves as critics of the state and take on the work, if temporarily, of subjectification—what Foucault has called the "way a human being turns him- or herself into a subject."[60]

In Khushwant Singh's account, the "false declarations" refugees are required to make in order to attain the status of "refugee" entail an abdication of the rights (including the right to ask for relief) that normally accrue to that status. These false declarations of the *need* for relief become inevitable given that their need for state assistance was obviously secondary to the need to escape ethnic violence that prompted their migration. While the Indian government did take on great responsibility for the relief and rehabilitation of refugees in this period, there were also thus several such contradictions in state practices of rehabilitation—contradictions that mark the discrimination and limitations of the incipient state apparatus, and bear witness to a subaltern past of violent unbelongings in the history of postcolonial nation-formation.

Muslims, Jews, and Kashmiris: Secularism and its Failures

Another anomalous moment in the history of rehabilitating Partition refugees in India was the differential treatment of Muslim and Jewish refugees in the distribution of aid. Despite being a secular nation-state, the Indian Ministry of Rehabilitation Reports until 1954 refer to government aid as being for "non-Muslim refugees." Given that the partition of India and the creation of Pakistan was based upon ethnic difference, such that the mass migration or "exchange of populations" largely entailed the migration of Muslims to Pakistan and Hindus and Sikhs to India, it is not surprising that the state assumed that all refugees coming to India were non-Muslims; yet the fact that it is made explicit that refugees of all other denominations other than Muslim were to be aided is problematic in the light of the secularist commitments of the Indian constitution. In the 1953–54 Annual Report, for the purposes of enumeration, there are new categories added to the list of displaced Hindus and Sikhs, and refugees are differentiated on the basis of health, gender, age, and caste: "displaced TB patients," "displaced unattached women and children" and "Displaced Harijans." In the 1954–55 Annual Report, a new category emerges in the governmentality of rehabilitation: "relief and rehabilitation of Muslim migrants, displaced Muslims, etc." This category for Muslim migrants is taken to include Muslims who migrated to Pakistan in 1947 and then returned to India shortly thereafter, as well as internally displaced Muslims who were unable to return to their original residence due to the threat of violence. In a partition largely based on the two-nation theory, then, the Indian nation-state not only attempts to take care of Hindu and Sikh refugees, but also comes to recognize, accommodate and aid the unprecedented case of Muslim refugees to India—albeit belatedly. This could include Muslims who chose to live in secular India and migrated to India from Pakistan, Muslims who left for Pakistan temporarily only to return to India, and internally displaced Muslims—all migrations that countered the official, intended, ethnicized exchange of populations. Given conflicting and imprecise reports from this period of upheaval and flux, reliable exact numbers of such returning Muslims have been difficult to ascertain, though historians like Gyan Pandey have also noticed the difficulties faced by Muslims who initially opted for Pakistan, and then changed their minds.[61] However, what is interesting is that by including internally displaced Muslims in the category of Muslim refugees, and arranging for state assistance for them as displaced persons along with those who had crossed national borders as refugees, the Indian nation-state thus, unlike its Pakistani counterpart, eventually came to a commitment to aid and protect its Muslim political minority: "Financial assistance in the shape of business loans up to Rs. 500 per family and ad hoc relief grant up to Rs. 200 per family is given to Muslim migrants who left the country and subsequently came back, and also to displaced Muslims who did not leave India."[62] While this aid was not on par with that given to Hindu and Sikh migrants, these transformations illustrate the unfinished, contradictory processes during the transition to independence that both enacted secularism and undermined it. They also draw attention to the privileges and pains of being named "refugee," "Muslim," and "citizen" simultaneously in early postcolonial India— complexities that also haunt the "Indian Muslim" today.

Now, while the Indian state belatedly did acknowledge the existence of Muslim refugees, Jewish refugees fleeing Muslim persecution in Pakistan offered a new challenge to an India that was already overburdened with the demands of rehabilitation and resettlement of over eight million migrants. The Maharashtra State Government Archives regarding refugee rehabilitation reveal an important anomaly of this transition: the case of Jews settled in India as subjects of the British Empire. A significant number of Jews were settled in what became West Pakistan, and were engaged in the cotton and wool trades. According to Adil Najam, "Various Jewish websites suggest that there were about 2,500 Jews living in Karachi at the beginning of the twentieth century and a few hundred lived in Peshawar. There were synagogues in both cities." Najam describes a vibrant Jewish community in Pakistan, evident in its "various Jewish social organisations, including the Young Men's Jewish Association (founded 1903), the Karachi Bene Israel Relief Fund, and the Karachi Jewish Syndicate formed to provide affordable homes to poor Jews." Najam notes that in 1947 some Jews migrated to India, but reportedly some 2,000 remained.[63] In late 1948, with increasing religious persecution at the hands of Muslims, including the burning of the Karachi synagogue, many Jews, along with Hindus and Sikhs, fled to India. They came mostly to Bombay via steamer from Karachi. The Jewish community in India is over 2,000 years old with many different groups of Jews, from the Bene Israel to the Baghdadi Jews, arriving as migrants on Indian shores. Many scholars have noted that the history of Jewish presence in India is a remarkable one, for Jews have never faced anti-Semitism in India from Indians (except at the hands of the colonizing Portuguese and British), and Indian Jews, although a small minority, have historically played a prominent role in the commercial, cultural, and political life of major cities like Bombay and Calcutta.[64] In fact, during the Holocaust, India provided harbor to many Jewish refugees that were unable to gain asylum in North America and some European countries, where the doors to Jewish immigration had been closed. In India, they were aided by Indian Jews as well: for example, the Jewish Relief Association of Bombay helped hundreds of European Jews fleeing from the Nazis, even establishing hostels and homes for them to live in.[65]

Given this remarkable syncretism in India's long history of Jewish settlement, the experience of the mostly Baghdadi Jews who unwittingly became Partition refugees in Bombay is surprising. The Central Jewish Board of Bombay attempted to assist the motley group of Russian, Afghani and Iranian Jews when they landed in Bombay, and mediated between the government of Bombay province and the refugees. On December 20, 1947, for example, the Central Jewish Board of Bombay reported their arrival to the Deputy Commissioner of Police in Bombay and certified the refugees' ethnicity: "The persons mentioned below are Jews and they have arrived in Bombay from Peshawar via Karachi due to the anti-Jewish tension there." The Board proceeded to list and describe ten people, out of whom several were registered residents of Peshawar from 1941 onwards and who, having arrived in Bombay, intended to stay there.[66] The Political and Service department of the

Bombay province, however, responded to their request for residence by saying that while they are allowed to land in India temporarily, they "cannot be put in the category of 'refugees' and hence their cases will have to be normally treated as of alien."[67] A letter from the Commissioner of Police on January 8, 1948 to the Political and Services department reveals that the Secretary of the Central Jewish Board of Bombay had until then been able to secure immigration visas for Palestine "for only 50 out of the 300 Jewish refugees who came to Bombay." The Commissioner suggests that the refugees should not be granted refugee status because, among other reasons, they were not technicians:

> None of these persons are technicians nor will their residence in India be demonstrably to this country's advantage. The Government of India desires the early departure of Jewish refugees from Afghanistan and elsewhere. Fresh arrivals therefore would not only aggravate the refugee problem but also be an added strain on the overbounded resources of this country.[68]

In this arbitrary and contradictory response, the ethnicization of Indian citizenship is combined with the biopolitics of modern governmentality. The letter reproduces the official Nehruvian emphasis on national growth through technological and industrial advance, and this functions as the grounds for considering the "usefulness" of refugees for the country. Mostly traders and not technicians, these Jewish Partition refugees were then denied the status of "refugees"; this was justified by the state through a claim that they were Jewish and should therefore go to Israel, which had just been formed. The common ideological construction on the basis of which both India and Palestine were divided by British design in 1947—namely, the ethnic territorialization of geographical space and nationality—thus now gets reproduced and deployed by the postcolonial state.

While the Commissioner's letter cited earlier reveals that this decision emerged not from any anti-Semitism, but from a strategic, bureaucratic deployment of ethnicity to ease the state's enormous burden of refugee rehabilitation, it nonetheless stands as yet another stunning moment of crisis in counterpoint to the state's commitment to secularism. Despite much political lobbying testified to in these Government records, the Jewish refugees were eventually sent to Israel. Thus, both Muslim and Jewish refugees became, as Jacqueline Bhabha says in a different context, "limit cases for the ethics of [the Indian] state"—making visible the fluid, contradictory processes that produced discourses of ethnicized nationality.[69] Similarly, the abjection of internally displaced Hindus and Christians in Pakistan has received little attention in South Asian histories, their numbers being too few to constitute a politically important constituency in Pakistan. C. M. Naim is one of the few scholars who notes this marginalization of minorities in Pakistan: "Pakistan, a Muslim majority nation, has miniscule Christian and Hindu minorities, but they must lead precarious lives. Innocent Pakistani Hindus are attacked whenever there is a major anti-Muslim incident in India, while Pakistani Christians are frequently accused—quite falsely—of blasphemy against Islam and its Prophet." [70] I uncover these anomalies and contradictions not only as constitutive parts of the silenced history of Indian secularism and South Asian ethnicities, but also as the exemplary roots of contemporary, global discourses of ethnicized nationality. They remind us of the urgency to rethink today the historical construction and deployment of categories and communities like "refugee," "migrant" and "citizen" as well as their transnational constitution in global politics.

(Un)Homely States: Citizenship as a Technology of Displacement

In colonial and pre-colonial times in India, when communal riots occurred between Hindus/Sikhs and Muslims, those involved and affected usually left the town or village (the local site of conflict) for some time—usually a few days or a couple of weeks. After some time, when the tension had abated, they would return to their original homes. However, the difference between Partition and previous moments of communal conflicts is as follows:

1. Previously, only one of the communities gathered up and moved away; this time the displacement involved all three communities.
2. The magnitude of this migration was unprecedented: As Campbell-Johnson says, "the numbers on the move are incomparably greater than ever before, and this time, there is no return." [71]
3. Finally, the communal violence during Partition involved large-scale violence against women—their abduction, rape, disfiguring, forced conversion—hitherto largely uncommon in mostly male-centered forms of communal violence.

It is interesting that while Campbell-Johnson, writing in his diary on September 21, 1947, is able to assert that in this crisis, return to the original home will be impossible, most migrants, as most of the literature and oral testimonies indicate, still saw themselves as moving away temporarily, until things quieted down and they could return to their homes and livelihoods.

Most left their assets and the keys to their homes with trusted friends in their locality, who promised to take care of their property until they returned home. For example, in the summer of 2000, I interviewed a couple, Mr. and Mrs. Malhotra, in Pune, India, who came from Rawalpindi to Bombay in September 1947.[72] When I asked them why they didn't migrate before August 1947, they explained that they had wanted to continue staying in Rawalpindi. Even though they left in September 1947 because the violence had escalated, they thought at the time that they would return in ten or fifteen days when everything quieted down. The Malhotras, like many other Punjabi refugees, have done well for themselves: They own a leading ice-cream company, and they hobnob with the South Asian elite, Pakistani and Indian. Mr. Malhotra mentioned that when he went to Pakistan for Benazir Bhutto's wedding in December 1987, he also stopped by his ancestral house in Rawalpindi where he once lived, to have a look at it "after 40 years and 3 months." He met the Muslim family from Bareilly that now lived there, and he was full of sentimental praise about them: He said that when they learned that he had lived in that house until 1947, they welcomed him into the home, insisted that he stay for a meal and hospitably cooked up a sumptuous dinner of over twenty dishes.

But what made the permanent return home impossible? In political and historical discourse, this impossibility often tends to be attributed to the memory of ethnic violence and the scars left by its pain. However, there is another dimension to this impossible return that has been rarely acknowledged: the new nation-states' boundaries in new, critical and indelible ways positioned displaced people within new spatial geographies of nationality, thus subjecting them to the governmental apparatus of the state within whose territory they happened to be displaced temporarily (at least in their own eyes). The attendant confusion and sense of temporary displacement is also testified to in Gandhi's speech on October 3, 1947. He exhorts refugees in camps that they "must clean their places themselves." Acknowledging that "there is not enough food or water for them," he argues that this is not reason enough for them to "start refusing to do any work." This, he says, will lead them to "fall a prey to vices." Finally, and most significantly, he notes, "*No one can say when they will able to return to their homes.* We shall certainly provide food for them; but let them at least do some work to earn it. . . . And if we get absorbed in our work our anger will subside. The desire for revenge in our hearts will also die out"[73] (italics mine). Gandhi's words reflect the popular assumption that the Partition migrants' displacement was temporary, and their return to their original homes was not yet foreclosed as impossible in October 1947. However, in the eyes of the newly constituted South Asian states, once you had been displaced to a particular area, and that area was announced as being either in India or in Pakistan, you were automatically seen to be a citizen of that country (provided you were Hindu or Sikh if in India, and Muslim if in Pakistan). This ethnicized conferring of citizenship in either India or Pakistan now ironically meant being simultaneously constructed as an alien in one's original home located in the nation-state from which one had been displaced. *Citizenship, then, in the new nation-state, became one of the technologies by which the migrants during Partition became refugees and were permanently displaced from their homes.*

The Indian Legislative Assembly debates from 1952 reveal how state procedures of determining citizenship and nationality were still in flux, five years after the 1947 Partition. In 1948, when asked by a member about the plans of the Indian government for addressing the concerns of non-Muslims in Pakistan who were "being treated as non-Pakistanis," "as aliens" and "as not the subjects of Pakistan," Vallabhbhai Patel replied, "It is rather a difficult matter, because the present position is not quite settled, but the non-Muslims coming from Pakistan here are treated as our nationals, as they have left Pakistan with the intention of settling down here."[74] Thus, in the midst of the instability and uncertainty of determining state processes of citizenship, Patel's comment reveals that movement across the border itself was institutionally interpreted by the state as a sign of the intention of permanent residence in India, *if* the migrant was "non-Muslim." This assumption not only linked ethnicity to nationality but, more importantly, also consolidated the migrant's displacement into permanent alienation from their original homes through their production as "nationals." As Rajeswari Sunder Rajan has also reminded us in a different context, the state is both a totalizing project and "an *individualizing* project that produces citizens in specific ways and specific roles."[75] India came into being as a nation-state under the Indian Independence Act of 1947. Between 1947 and 1950, the Constitution of India was drafted, debated, framed, and finally passed on August 26, 1950. However, it was only in 1955 that the Indian Parliament passed the Citizenship Act. Until then, the Drafting Committee that drafted the constitution of India also addressed the question of citizenship; it took up this question by giving special consideration to the case of refugees from Pakistan that it was assumed were Hindu or Sikh. Those who had migrated from Pakistan to India were put into two categories: (a) those who had come before July 19, 1948, and (b) those who had come after July 19, 1948. Those who had come before July 19, 1948 would automatically become citizens of India, and those who had come after July 19, 1948 would be entitled to citizenship at the date of commencement of the new Constitution, namely, January 26, 1950, if certain procedures were followed. Those who fell into the latter category (b) had to be residing in India for at least six months, following which they had to apply to be registered as citizens by the designated government officer.[76] Muslims who had left India for Pakistan and subsequently returned to India were allowed to settle in India under a permit system which was introduced on July 19, 1948.[77] It is interesting to note that Indian citizenship could also legally be determined by one's location or place in South Asia prior to nation formation on August 15, 1947. Hence, a person who had migrated from the territory of India after March 1, 1947, to the territory now included in Pakistan, was now no longer deemed a citizen of India (although India and Pakistan did not exist at the time as two distinct nations); she could only be considered an Indian citizen if she had returned to Indian territory with a resettlement permit for permanent return.[78] Thus, nationality became retroactive and prior to the nation-state.

Shyam Benegal's film *Mammo* (1994) offers a poignant representation of minor women's experience of gendered subjection and ethnicized citizenship in postcolonial South Asia. The film is co-produced with the National Film Development Corporation (NFDC) of India, and thus stands apart from mainstream Bollywood cinema is its social and political project of the critique of modern citizenship. In 1995, the film was screened at several international film festivals and won National Awards for Best Feature Film in Hindi and Best Supporting Actress, 1995. Its protagonist is a middle-aged Muslim woman, Mehmooda Begum, nicknamed Mammo (Farida Jalal), who lives in Lahore with her husband. Both of them automatically become Pakistani citizens in 1947. When her husband dies, disputes over property matters lead to her being thrown out of her house by her in-laws, and she comes to the land of her pre-Partition birth India. Mammo procures a temporary visa to live with her elder sister and her 13-year-old grandson in Bombay. Reluctant to return to her widowed isolation and destitution in Pakistan, Mammo goes to the police station to extend her stay every month, and even bribes the officer in charge to have her name removed from the records of the Foreigners Registration Office. Much of the action takes place within their middle-class house in India, and the film uncovers Partition history's disfiguring and grotesque invasion of the minor home. Benegal's social realism invokes a common Indo–Pakistani culture through the background musical score of the ghazals of Iqbal Bano and Faiz Ahmed Faiz, even as he lays bare the doubling of private and public, domestic and state abjection lived by the minor female subject in South Asia. Mammo's gendered financial and familial exploitation, articulated with the modern violence of South Asia's ethnicized citizenships, turns her into a liminal subject shuttling between India and Pakistan, disallowed the belongings desired by her.

The film's depiction of Mammo's failed negotiations of free India's bureaucracy signals the violence of governmentality and Partition to the emotional and material everyday lives of South Asian Muslims. When the officer she bribed is transferred and replaced by a new one, the latter refuses to extend her stay and has her deported. A moving scene dramatizes her brutally forced departure, as police suddenly arrive at her house and forcibly take her without any of her possessions or her burqa to put her on the train to Pakistan—evoking the 1947 forced migrations of other Muslims from India. However, Mammo returns to her sister's house in India after a few months with another temporary visa. Then, in order to stay on in India with her widowed sister and her grandson, free from the oppressions of state modernity and the constraints of nationality, she procures her own "death certificate." The death certificate is deposited with the authorities in Bombay, who remove her name from their record as a political subject, freeing Mammo from the state apparatus. Mammo stages her legal death in the nation as a strategy of social survival in everyday life. Rendered subaltern by Partition and an oppressive patriarchal society in a modern nation-state, she must effectively disavow the abstract promises of both Pakistani and Indian citizenships in order to survive Partition and its new nationalities. The film thus represents that rather than being an enabling form that granted access to human rights, citizenship as a technology of the postcolonial state engenders abjection in everyday life for many women displaced by Partition. As such, it constitutes a critical counter-memory in the postcolonial counter-publics that signals a subaltern history of modern citizenship.

Postcolonial Governmentality: Managing Private Property and Minority Citizens

An important dimension of the production of Partition migrants as refugees through the technology of citizenship was its imbrication with the state production of "evacuee property." Migrants' property and assets were appropriated not only by local thieves, incoming refugees, neighbors and others, but also by the postcolonial state apparatus which cited the urgent demands of refugee rehabilitation to justify the appropriation. Although the Administration of Evacuee Property Act was passed only in 1950, abandoned properties were being requisitioned and reassigned by the government as "evacuee property" as early as February 1948. An exception to this was the case of the refugees from Muzaffarabad, who were refused settlement in Jammu and Kashmir because the land and property were reserved, even in 1952, for Muslims who might come back from Pakistan.[79] By requisitioning migrants' properties as "evacuee property," and by then constructing these properties as permanently abandoned and therefore to be assigned to incoming refugees who had lost their property across the border, the state apparatus effectively ensured that many who chose to return after the violence had abated would no longer have a home to return to. Indeed, there are many stories of those who left their homes during Partition hoping, and indeed assuming, that they would return in a few weeks once the violence abated, only to discover after several months that their homes had been taken over by refugees or by the government and reallocated to other migrants. For example, the Partition migrants Mr. and Mrs. Malhotra from Pune, mentioned previously, told me that in their experience, once you had left your house, the Pakistani government took over the property and sealed it off as "evacuee property." In fact, as one of Gandhi's speeches points out, Partition became a time in which the desire for property was realized by using the prevailing ethnic conflict permeating the moment to strategically, forcibly displace people of a different ethnicity from their homes: "I begin to think that there are some among us who are really murderers. I do not quite know who they are, but they are definitely there, and are working to carry out pre-planned murders, arson and forcible occupation of buildings."[80]

To address the loss of property by refugees, and to compensate them with evacuee property, the governments of both India and Pakistan established mechanisms by which one could appeal to the government for compensation of land lost due to forced displacement, provided one had documents that corroborated or authenticated one's claims of previous ownership. Hence, both nation-states tied together citizenship rights and wealth, and worked towards maintaining the prior class-status of individual refugees by guaranteeing the right to property in the new nation—if one owned similar property of equivalent value in the nation which one had fled. As early as February 25, 1948, Constituent Assembly debates reveal that refugees were being allotted land evacuated by Muslims who had left for Pakistan. For example, the allotment of abandoned factories and industrial concerns left behind by Muslims in Delhi amounted to 420, and was started on February 24, 1948; these concerns were allotted to both "refugees from West Pakistan" and "the local residents of Delhi," already suggesting corruption in the works.[81] By March 1948, there were 12,512 houses sealed by the state as evacuee property; out of these, 2,000 were still vacant, but Neogy said that those would not be allotted to refugees;[82] thus, even as property was ethnicized to enable state power, it was questionably deployed towards ends other than the ostensible ones of refugee rehabilitation.

This articulation of state violence, corruption and ethnicized property led to interesting forms of resistance: in Ferozepur, sometimes, Muslims set fire to their own homes before "evacuating" them, thus effectively destroying their value for the state.[83] Thus, property, both in the form of private homes and as commodities bearing value, became a critical and contested site in the production of the new nation. In 1947–1948, many Muslims often turned to Gandhi and complained of their forced displacement from their homes by state officials. Gandhi addressed these complaints in a prayer meeting one day: "Complaints are being repeatedly made that Muslims are being forced to leave their ancestral homes in the Union and migrate to Pakistan. Thus it is said that in a variety of ways they are being made to vacate their houses and live in camps to await dispatch by train or even on foot." He responded to these complaints of forced displacement from ancestral properties by turning to the question of state policy: "I am quite sure that such is not the policy of the Cabinet. When I tell the complainants about this they laugh at it and tell me in reply that either my information is incorrect or the [Armed] Services do not carry out the policy. I know that my information is quite correct." This speech indicates that in the experience of these Muslims complaining to Gandhi, their displacement was initiated by Army officials; Gandhi's assertion that the possession of their homes was not state policy was mocked in its dissonance with the reality of their experience. Gandhi then stated, "Are the Services then disloyal? I hope not. Yet the complaint is universal. Various reasons are given for the alleged disloyalty. The most plausible one is that the military and the police are largely divided on a communal basis and that their members are carried away by the prevalent prejudice."[84] Here, Gandhi both acknowledged and disavowed that Muslims in India were forced to vacate their homes, often by or with the support of state functionaries like the military and the police. Muslims complained about the variety of ways in which they were being forced to leave their own homes and go to refugee camps, and from there, forced to go on to Pakistan against their own wishes. Gandhi first took up this complaint about a forced, ethnicized migration for the acquisition of property by asserting that this "alleged" practice was not endorsed by Cabinet policy. Then, he responded to this widespread complaint and the various explanations proffered for it (including the communalist prejudices of members of the Armed Services), by expressing a hope that it was not true—producing instability in the truth claims of these accounts of state-supported forcible displacement to Pakistan. In other words, he hoped that these reports of both the forced migration of Muslims and the state's participation in this economic ethnic violence "have no basis:" "and that if they have, the superior authority will satisfactorily deal with them *in so far as they have any justification*" (my italics). Even as this moment revealed the use of property acquisition as a state technology of ethno-nationalism, it also reinforced state authority as Gandhi reiterated his doubt about the veracity of refugee voices about this state-initiated ethnic dispossession.

Gandhi further argued that if the Services were communalist and had a hand in engineering such ethnic displacement, then they were being disloyal towards the Indian nation-state. He invoked the law and turned to the state as the means for addressing such forcible displacement. Arguing that since "there are no written orders issued to anyone," Gandhi suggested that Muslims faced with the "alleged verbal orders" should not comply with them: "There is no helping those who will be frightened into submission to any order given by a person in uniform. My emphatic advice to all such persons is that they should ask for written orders whose validity in case of doubt should be tested in a court of justice, if appeal to the final executive fails to give satisfaction."[85] Of course, in the face of death threats the luxury of time, resources, and personal safety necessary to challenge in the courts such ethnicized, forced displacement was available to few Muslims in India, or Hindus and Sikhs in Pakistan, in the early national period.

Things Fall Apart: Minoritization and Muslims in the Postcolonial Art Film

M. S. Sathyu's 1973 Hindi film *Garam Hawa* (*Hot Winds*), based on an unpublished short story by Ismat Chughtai, is a poignant account of the transformations wrought by the state practice of appropriating properties owned or inhabited by Muslims. *Garam Hawa* makes visible how the strategic state deployment of the concept of private property enabled the deliberate if uneven state-initiated displacement of Muslims in India. The film illuminates not only the increasing discriminatory socio-economic marginalization of Muslims in India, but also the injustices perpetrated in the name of refugee rehabilitation upon Indian Muslims; as such, it uncannily foreshadows the contemporary condition of disenfranchisement that marks Muslim life in India.

Because it was about ethnic difference and the discriminations wrought by Partition, the film was held up at the censors for eight months before it was finally released. Although many anticipated that it would incite ethnic conflict, it was well received and a commercial success, and it even won the National Award for Best Film on Integration and Best Screenplay in India in 1974. The plot revolves around a Muslim joint family, the Mirzas, in Agra in the late forties and fifties in post-Partition India. When the older of two brothers living there—Halim Mirza, an opportunistic politician—migrates to Pakistan, his younger brother, Salim Mirza (Balraj Sahni), chooses to stay on in India with his family and his elderly mother. Because the property has been legally titled in the name of the elder brother, as was common, the state now deploys that technicality to designate the house inhabited by this Muslim family as "evacuee property," and to forcibly move them out. Subsequently, this once-affluent family living in a large *haveli*[86] is forced to move out into a rented, smaller home. The film thus reveals how state institutions targeted Indian Muslims living in homes whose legal title happened to be held by a family member who had migrated to Pakistan, to acquire property.

Garam Hawa links elite nationalist politics with the Mirzas' everyday life in small-town Agra. It opens with photographs of Gandhi, Mountbatten, Jinnah, Maulana Azad, and Nehru following rapidly in quick succession. These are followed by successive shots (a technique also used in *Lahore*) of iconic journalistic photographs of the Partition experience, a technique that exemplifies how the modern technologies of photography, the press, and film transformed representation in the public sphere. There are shots of press photographs of city ruins burnt and destroyed, trains crammed with refugees inside and on top, gigantic kafilas[87] stretching across the landscape, people eating in refugee camps and, lastly, a picture of Gandhi which tilts to the right three times synchronized to the sound of three gunshots. These photographs occupy the space of chronological history and thus situate the story after Gandhi's murder in January 1948. The first scene is located at a railway station, as Salim Mirza waves goodbye to his sister and her three children. He is sending her on the train to Pakistan, where her husband has already gone and arranged for resettlement. Close-up shots of Mirza's face evoke the grief of this family's separation. The train station scene recurs multiple times throughout the film, each scene marking the reiterative, ongoing fragmentation of Indian Muslim families as its members give up hope of being able to live in an unprejudiced society, and leave: After his sister and her children, Salim bids goodbye to his elder brother Halim and his family, and finally his own eldest son and his family. If the train is mostly depicted as a sign of industrialized modernity in much Indian cinema from this period (for example, in Satyajit Ray's films), here it functions as a symbolic agent of political, national and familial estrangement. As if inaugurated symbolically with the death of Gandhi, the film begins to intricately map the "unhousing" of the Indian Muslim, through both the exodus of reluctant Indian Muslims to Pakistan and increasing economic, social and political discrimination in India.

In an important scene, a government officer appears at the haveli to inform Salim Mirza that the state has decreed their home "evacuee property" because Halim Mirza has gone to Pakistan, and they should vacate it. This conversation occurs in the haveli's courtyard; Salim Mirza's aged mother, who has been listening to this conversation sitting behind a purdah in the courtyard, then says loudly, "This haveli is ours. I had given birth to only two sons. Where did this third *haqdar* (claimant) come from?" In this wonderful and ironic moment, by asserting a notion of collective, familial ownership, the grandmother's voice denaturalizes capitalist state modernity and rationality: her interrogation throws into relief the violence of the concept of private property ownership deployed by discriminatory actors of the modern nation-state to simultaneously displace some, and rehabilitate others, based on ethnic difference. The Mirza family's displacement and attendant minoritization is effectively suggested through the framing of shots; a large number of shots are framed by doors and windows, which enclose increasingly smaller spaces. Forced out of their spacious haveli, the Mirzas move to a much smaller, rented home. The ever-narrowing spaces we witness through the frames of doors and windows evoke the material and psychic processes of minoritization, and the forced squeezing into ever-smaller livable spaces of being that the Mirzas experience in their everyday life—at work, among friends, in the city. In their new home, the small roof with bars across it—through which the spectator witnesses the conflicted conversations about migrating to Pakistan between Salim Mirza and his wife—reinforce the sense of their entrapment and victimization.

The gendered effects of Partition, and particularly the place of Muslim women in the new nations, are critical to any discussion of *Garam Hawa*. Salim Mirza's wife continually urges him to leave for Pakistan, as she witnesses the ethnic discrimination faced by her husband and son: their ancestral business in leather shoe making fails, their factory is burned down, and her son is denied all the jobs for which he interviews. Her pleas are ignored, and she becomes a mute spectator to the multiple forms of disenfranchisement experienced by them. Further, Salim Mirza's daughter Amina is heartbroken when her cousin and fiancée Kazim is taken to Pakistan by his father. Kazim manages to steal back to Agra to marry Amina; however, just as the wedding festivities are on, he is arrested and escorted back to the border because he unknowingly fails to register with the police when he arrives. Those coming from Pakistan were legally required to register their presence with the police in India within 24 hours of their arrival (following the enforcement of similar policies in Pakistan for Indians from 1948 onwards). Thus, although he had been an Indian resident and citizen all his life, his few months across the border in Pakistan transform him into a Pakistani citizen and an illegal alien in his own, ancestral home. Amina's dreams of marriage are thwarted; though she gives in, after much grief, to another arduous suitor, Shamshad's, proposal of marriage, Shamshad too is forced to go to Pakistan. As C. M. Naim and others have pointed out, during this period many Muslim men, young and older, migrated with and without their families and in large numbers to Pakistan in search of opportunity.[88] For the second time, Amina's hopes for marital intimacy are foreclosed, and she sees Shamshad off at the train station, much as her father had seen others off. When she finds out later that in spite of his promises to return, he has married someone else in Pakistan, she is devastated and commits suicide. In this filmic narrative, both of these Muslim female characters cannot constitute national and familial belongings as Indians. Further, Amina's grandmother's death reinforces this generational, gendered loss of female agency: in a very moving scene, the matriarch is taken to her ancestral home, the large haveli, for one last time as she is dying. The sequence shows Salim carrying her into the haveli from a *tonga* (carriage), thus underscoring her physical frailty and helplessness. He is assisted by the sympathetic refugee Advani, who now owns the haveli but has humanely accommodated this last visit from the dying mother.

As she is taken to the central courtyard, the camera pans the surrounding walls, and the background score is accompanied by echoing sounds of laughter and conversation, suggesting the happy remembrance of things past. After looking around, as if in a different time of the past in which this was still her home, she dies. The representation of her death in the physical space of the haveli—and the family's displacement from it after many

Figure 4.1. Salim Mirza's mother being taken to her former home, seized as "evacuee property," before she dies in *Garam Hawa*. (Garam Hawa. Dir. M.S. Sathyu. Unit 3 mm, 1973.)

generations—becomes an allegory for the loss of homeliness and belonging in (and at the hands of) the new postcolonial nation.

The loss of Amina, compounded by her brother's inability to find a job because he is Muslim, Salim Mirza's own failing business and his arrest when he is framed as Pakistani spy, all eventually lead to a broken Salim Mirza's decision to migrate to Pakistan. However, on the way to the station to take the train to Pakistan he has resisted many times before, he sees his son Sikander in a procession of Leftist protesters shouting slogans against injustice, poverty, and unemployment. At this, he too joins the procession as if symbolically throwing in his lot with the Indian national polity. Articulating his own ethnic minoritization with the collective socialist struggle, he says to his wife, "I cannot live alone anymore." Thus, challenging his minoritization as ethnicized citizen, Salim Mirza chooses to remain in India and become a resisting, political subject. His wife remains helplessly seated in the tonga and watches him join the march. *Garam Hawa* thus assimilates Muslim masculinity into the performance of a left secular citizenship; yet, the filmic narrative does not posit a similar subject-position for Muslim women. For instance, disappointed twice in love, stigmatized as being unmarried, and devastated by grief, Amina commits suicide. The last shot of her, taken from above her, depicts her passively sprawled across her single bed, in her red and gold wedding saree with blood on her wrists—connoting the articulation of socially sanctioned marriage and death by suicide for the female subject. Unlike the dominant representation of Partition violence against women as marked by abduction and rape, this depiction of Amina's unheroicized suicide bears witness to another cultural, invisible violence also engendered by Partition. In one reading, Amina's death is both a counter-point and the price that Salim Mirza pays in order to stay in his home and become a national subject. Although Salim Mirza, as the middle-aged Muslim male protagonist, transforms himself into a resisting yet patriotic, secular, national subject, his wife and daughter are increasingly rendered mute spectators as Partition's social transformations invade their home. Like Mammo, Amina as a Muslim woman in India resists the cultural effects of Partition and the violence of the postcolonial nation-state through her own death—but if Mammo's death was legal, Amina's is material.

The lack of a cultural-ideological space to access political, secular nationality for the Muslim women in this film constitutes the ideological limit of this text about minority belongings. It stands as an interesting counter-point to recent representations of Muslim female citizenship in Bollywood cinema, in which it is the agentive Muslim woman, and not man, who performs a normative, secular citizenship. Witness the blind Kashmiri Muslim woman Zooni (Kajol) who kills her own Muslim husband Rehan (Aamir Khan) when she finds out he is a Jehadi terrorist in Kunal Kohli's *Fanaa* (2006). Yet, *Garam Hawa* uncovers how Salim Mirza's family, stigmatized as Muslim in post-Partition India, inhabits a world that is, as Lauren Berlant has written in a different context, "saturated with a history of ordinary violence, violence so prosaic it would be possible to wield without knowing it, violence that feels like a fact of life."[89] *Garam Hawa* is as much a film about Partition refugees and their relationship to minoritized Muslim citizenships in middle-class Agra, as it is a story of those who refused to become refugees, and those South Asian women whose quotidian lives and domestic futures were radically altered by those refugees across the national border.

The Indian state was avowedly secular in its constitution. Yet, the problem I have discussed so far is not "politicized religion,"[90] as Dipankar Gupta has suggested, but the scope, intensity, and continuity of the power of the secular nation-state to enact its central project—namely, as Talal Asad enumerates, "to establish fixed boundaries between populations, to reform and standardize their beliefs and practices, to secure their loyalties, and to define their community membership."[91] By deploying the modern concept of individual property ownership, the "secular" postcolonial state seized properties inhabited by Muslims, displaced its own Muslim citizens, and ethnicized nationality. Designating Muslim-owned and Muslim-inhabited properties first as "evacuee property" and then as "national property" to be reassigned to Hindu and Sikh refugees, the Indian nation-state consolidates itself—as *Garam Hawa* illuminates—through the production of ethnicized property and territory. Similar state practices of seizing property owned by Hindu and Sikh minorities also prevailed in Pakistan during this period. In 1960, the Indian government formally recognized the injustices of the 1954 Act regarding evacuee properties, and the act was amended:

> Instances have come to notice where some properties were wrongly declared to be evacuee property and they were also acquired. In such cases, the Custodian general is empowered under section 27 of the Administration of Evacuee Property Act, 1951, to restore such property to the non-evacuee owner. Similarly, comptent [sic] officer has also power under the Evacuee Interest Separation Act, 1951, to declare a share in a property to be non-evacuee after the whole of it has been declared to be evacuee property and been acquired. It is not sometimes possible to restore the original property to the non-evacuee owner because of its transfer to a displaced person.[92]

This amendment thus formally acknowledged the state-led discriminatory practices around property and the complex dispossession of Muslim citizens in India immediately following Partition that narratives like *Garam Hawa* reveal and critique. However, this is small consolation, appearing as it does more than a decade after the institutionalized forced, internal displacement of Muslim families by the concept of "evacuee property" and the state's problematic deployment of the capitalist construction of individual private property ownership in a context where the joint family as a dominant mode of familial organization called for a different conception of "individual" and "collective." Given that these so-called evacuee homes were now occupied by Partition migrants from Pakistan, redress and re-displacement to address the injustices of ethnic discrimination and the ethnicization of property became a gargantuan, if not impossible, task. That this issue of the Partition's ethnicization of property remains a contemporary concern is revealed by the protest organized by the BJP in Jammu in 2005 to demand the scrapping of the Resettlement Act. The act enables those who migrated to Pakistan during the Partition to still claim their properties left behind in Jammu and Kashmir. The BJP protest was organized after it discovered "a PoK woman staking claim over three properties in the state when she came to Srinagar in the inaugural bus between Srinagar and Muzaffarabad. Addressing BJP activists, Dr Nirmal Singh, president of the state unit of the BJP, demanded that the Resettlement Act should be withdrawn as it had created an uncertain situation for over 3 lakh families that were allotted properties left behind by those who migrated to Pakistan during the Partition."[93] The Kashmiri woman's claim challenges the normative, ethnic nationalization of property ownership that marks Partitioned state modernity in South Asia; as such, it also potentially signals a silenced history of the forced acquisition of properties and the displacement of Indian Muslims.

Marxist Melodrama: Woman, Capital and Refugee Suffering in Bengali Cinema

Taking up the gendered dimension of Partition's effects differently, Ritwik Ghatak's Bengali film *Meghe Dhaka Tara* (*The Cloud-Clapped Star*) was the first film of a trilogy (including *Subarnarekha*) that indexes the failure of postcolonial nationalism through the representation of the gendered violence that saturates the female refugee's life in urban India. B. D. Garga has remarked, "The Partition of Bengal, the division of a culture, was something that Ghatak was never able to accept and that scarred him forever."[94] *Meghe Dhaka Tara* offers a Marxist critique of women's commodified exploitation, whose melodramatic excess highlights the economic and familial abjection of the urban, working-class, Hindu female refugee Nita (Supriya Choudhury) in post-Partition India. Released in 1960 and considered a landmark in the history of cinema, *Meghe Dhaka Tara* is a melodramatic text that articulates a feminist critique of nationalism through the representation of the minor female refugee in urban India. Ghatak was a member of the Indian People's Theatre Association, a Marxist group that was linked to but had broken off from the Progressive Writer's Association in 1942.[95] He wrote plays and produced adaptations from Russian and Chinese theatres. Deeply influenced by Eisenstein and Kracauer, and inspired by the first International Film Festival held in Calcutta in 1942, Ghatak and his fellow members of IPTA, like Balraj Sahni (who made *Garam Hawa*) and the writer K. A. Abbas, now began to turn to the New Cinema Movement (inaugurated in 1949 with the production of *Dharti Ke Lal*[96]) and to film as a powerful pedagogic medium for the masses.

Film critics like Ashish Rajadhyaksha have focused on the relation between mythology and modernity in their discussion of *Meghe Dhaka Tara*.[97] While critics acknowledge that the film uncovers the unfulfilled "hopes and passions for life ending in a merciless annihilation of countless modern Nitas at the altar of mythic glorification of Gauri and Uma,"[98] the specific historical location of Nita and her family as refugees has remained marginal in their analyses. However, I am interested in this production as a feminist, counter-public and materialist memorialization of the working-class, female Partition refugee's complex dispossessions in the postcolonial city. In contrast to the popular heroicization of the suffering male refugee as citizen in literature and film discussed earlier in this book, *Meghe Dhaka Tara* revolves around a suffering female refugee Nita as the protagonist. Nita is a schoolteacher in a Calcutta suburb and the sole breadwinner in her six-member refugee family. The family lives in a house allotted to refugees from East Bengal, and the burden of ensuring the survival of the family on a daily basis rests on Nita's shoulders: her father becomes an invalid in an accident, her elder brother Sankar is an aspiring and unemployed musician, her spoiled and vain younger sister Gita only cares about new clothes, and her younger brother Montu works temporarily in a factory but becomes disabled in an accident at work.

Meghe Dhaka Tara turns on eight movements that follow Nita returning home at the end of the day from her work. In the first scene, Nita is returning home from school when she stumbles because her slippers are torn. She fixes them temporarily and carries on. Shortly thereafter we learn that, with her meager salary, she has purchased not new *chappals* (slippers) for herself, but instead shoes for her elder brother, a *saree* for her younger sister Gita, and a shirt for her youngest brother. Nita's self-sacrificing labor sustains the others' consumption practices, and is contrasted to her cruel mother and self-centered siblings. Through emotional blackmail and connivance, they plot and pressure her to support her family through her earnings. Hoping to buy a home of their own, the refugee family connives to keep Nita single so as to have access to her income, even as, one by one, its members leave the house for a better life. The fantasy of home relies on Nita's productive labor, and eventually leads to her physical depletion and fatal illness. Nita's own choice to sacrifice herself for her family is also inscribed in the film: She even postpones marriage to a researcher Sarat, despite his protests, out of a sense of responsibility for her family's survival. Finally, her mother encourages Gita to seduce and marry Sarat, effectively destroying Nita's potential marital intimacy, so that they can have access to Nita's income.

By the end of the film, Nita is emaciated, exhausted, and sick. As in *Garam Hawa*, the visual representation of the physical space of the home, and the framing of several shots through windows and doors, signifies the increasing minoritization of the female refugee in postcolonial India. Contrary to the idealization of the "home" as the site of the production of national culture in much patriarchal nationalist discourse, the home in Ghatak's film marks Nita's loss of normative coupledom and her increasing domestic physical and emotional oppression. The camerawork repeatedly represents Nita inside her hut in cramped, dark, claustrophobic, and smoky conditions, often with the sound of water boiling in the background. When her father orders her to leave her home in the middle of a storm, as she is sick and no longer earning, her displacement and abjection is complete. Dispossessed by her relations, literally unhoused, she dies of tertiary tuberculosis in a sanatorium in the Shillong hills where her brother Sankar, now a successful musician, has moved her after Gita's marriage to Sarat. Saving in the hope for a two-story home, her family had refused to spend any money on Nita's treatment. In the last few scenes, she realizes that she is dying so terribly young, and she cries out to her visiting brother Sankar: "But Dada, I want to live! I love life. Dada, tell me once that I will live. Dada, I want to go home. I want to live!" After this desperate cry the camera pans to shots of the surrounding hilly landscape, forests and sky, even as on the soundtrack we hear Nita's disembodied wails turning into gasps as she struggles to speak. This loss of speech, along with the shots of the vast hills around her in which we can no longer see her, foreshadows her death and disappearance as a speaking subject in her struggle to enable her refugee family's aspirations to a middle-class home and life.

Turning away from an idealization of refugees' suffering or of the family as an institution at a time when families were being torn apart by ethnic violence, Ghatak lays bare how heteronormative, patriarchal familial belongings engender psychic and material dispossession for the female refugee-citizen. Erin O'Donnell has also noted Ghatak's refusal—even in his extensive use of Rabindrasangeet—to romanticize the representation of women and refugee experience in Calcutta: "Ghatak uses Tagore songs at climactic moments to express the joy and sorrow of the post-Independence Bengali woman, who must bear the burden of rebuilding the family in the aftermath of Partition."[99] In the denouement, it is clear that the material and imagined reproduction of homeliness in this refugee family's life relies on the destructive, even deadly exploitation of Nita as surrogate, nurturing mother. Here, the patriarchal family forecloses the realization of Nita's desire for heterosexual coupledom in order to sustain itself; Nita dies in the sacrificial exploitation of her body as labor power, denuded of health, desired love and marital intimacy.

The film had opened with Nita getting a letter from her lover, Sanat, that said, "At first, I thought you were ordinary. But I realize that you are a star. You're subdued due to circumstances, but you are a cloud-capped star." In this way, the film heoricizes Nita as a suffering citizen, toward a critique of capitalist modernity. In many of the cultural texts this book takes up, the liminal figure of the suffering refugee represents the failure of the nation as imagined community. However, in Ghatak's film, national belonging is an absent concern, and Nita's liminality as a refugee is overlaid with her subalternity, born of the modern articulation of capital, colonial partition, patriarchy and nationalism. She does not represent the nation in transition; she marks its violent effectivity. Thus, Ghatak uses melodramatic conventions to challenge hegemonic narratives of nation, family and community in post-Partition India.

Further, refusing to cast Nita's story as unique, the film deliberately ends with a sequence in which another young woman resembling Nita, walks down the same road, only to stumble and cheerfully fix her broken slipper in the same way. This re-iteration inscribes Nita's story as a pervasive modern condition; it signals the structural and continual exploitation of young women like Nita in these families displaced by Partition.[100] About *Meghe Dhaka Tara*, Ghatak himself wrote, "I wanted to say that today we are all refugees, as we have lost the roots of our life. I sought to raise the word 'refugee' from a particular geographical level to a generalized one."[101] In Chapter Two I discussed Deepa Mehta as an "exilic" filmmaker and her problematic representation of Muslim masculinity and the Hindu woman's abduction. Challenging Mehta's reception as 'exilic,' I am suggesting that, in contrast, it is Ghatak's oeuvre that marks him as an exilic filmmaker. In this film's humanist impulse to historicize gendered, material displacement and dispossession, it stands at a distance from the hegemonic idealization of nationalism and (ethnic) community in the public sphere. This cinema is the eye that bears witness to the female refugee's laboring body and voice, in order to index the violence of both Partition and modern capitalism that saturate everyday life in decolonization.

Conclusion: "We Were Never Refugees"

I begin this inconclusive conclusion by signaling a problem in telling this story as a story about Partition "refugees." On one hand, fifty years after 1947, as the Sharanarthi [Refugee] Action Committee in India reported, post-Partition Hindu and Sikh refugees from Pakistan that are in Kashmir continue to be denied citizenship rights in the name of Kashmir's "permanent residents." Further, a recent report by the IDP Project (Internally Displaced Peoples Project) states that as many as 350,000 Kashmiris, mostly Hindu Pandits, have been displaced since 1989 due to cross-border terrorism and militancy. South Asia Terrorism Portal (SATP) estimates over 400,000 displaced. Some 250,000 displaced Kashmiris are living in or near the city of Jammu while an estimated 100,000 Kashmiris are displaced elsewhere in India, primarily in the New Delhi area.[102] Largely ignored by the Indian nation-state already burdened with overpopulation and ethnic refugees from Bangladesh, Afghanistan, Myanmar, and Sri Lanka, without access to the rights and privileges of equal citizenship and state redress, today over 100,000 Kashmiri Hindus languish in seventeen refugee camps in Delhi, Jammu and elsewhere, with few education or employment prospects. They are the embodied legacies of the ill-fated British division of India. As Kidar Nath Sahani, a former Mayor of Delhi, says, "We had thought the ghosts that had raised [sic] following the country's partition in 1947 had been laid to rest long ago. But we were wrong."[103] Yet, how do we write this subaltern history of the Partition that persists into the present, where so many such refugees no longer have access to the realization of national belonging and citizenship rights?

And finally, another dimension of this fraught history: As I mentioned earlier, the case of South Asian refugees was unique (and, importantly, unlike that of Holocaust refugees immediately after the Second World War) because they were not placeless like most refugees. The state's official rhetoric offered them a place—a new nation—to come to. This sense of having a nation as home—in political and state discourse—is crucial; it might explain why, in interviews conducted with many Partition migrants from 1947 in Mumbai and Pune in the period spanning 1997 to 1999, several middle-class and upper-middle-class Sindhis who migrated at the time of Partition to Bombay Presidency emphatically disavowed the status and title of "refugee." "We were never refugees," asserted Mr. Mansukhani; "we did not get a single *pie* (paisa) from the government."[104] For people like Mr. Mansukhani, you were a refugee if you received government aid for refugees; unlike in Pakistan, migrants in India firmly rejected the naming of their experience as that of refugees. Instead, it was people who lived in refugee camps and availed themselves of government help through the Ministry of Rehabilitation that were seen as "refugees." Thus, in the Indian context, or at least in Bombay Presidency, class difference often became the organizing marker of the status of refugees; in the middle-class imagination and memory of Partition, refugees were migrants of lower classes, and the very category of refugee thus also became a designation of class belonging. This poses an important ethical problem for writing the history of Partition mass migration and the refugee experience. Our vision and account of this historical experience must needs change, when a section of its agents and subjects refuse the terms in which we seek to cast it. The recognition and recording of the differential history of displacement that marked Partition migrants' lives must, then, take into account this critique of the inadequate languages and violent governmentality of the modern nation-state system.

5

War and Peace

Pakistan and Ethnic Citizenship in Bollywood Cinema

Not all Muslims are terrorists, but all terrorists are Muslim.
—SMS message circulating in India, 2006[1]

The fragmentary text of an average popular film is a serial
eruption of variously distributed affective intensities whose
individual effects are not subsumed in the overarching
narrative framework. As an effective medium of propagation
of consumer culture, popular [Hindi] cinema has managed
to combine a reassuring moral conservatism with fragments
of utopian ideology and enactments of the pleasures of
commodity culture. The very familiarity of the narrative
makes it a useful non-interfering grid within which to
elaborate the new.

—M. Madhava Prasad[2]

I have deliberately juxtaposed the two very different statements above;
the first violently enacts the Islamicization of terror that marks public-sphere discourses about violence and religion in India as well as in
the "West." The second argues for the recognition of utopian desire and
newness within the familiarity of dominant popular cinema. This chapter
examines the articulation of religion/ethnicity, citizenship and gender in
contemporary Bollywood cinema, in order to uncover how Partition history shapes the stories this cinema tells about India, Pakistan and national
belonging. Resonating with Prasad's words, Lalitha Gopalan asserts that
cinema "is inextricably linked to our Utopian imaginings, it stages the most
anxious impulses of our psychic and social life, it gives us hope for a better
world."[3] Taking this suggestion to recent popular Hindi cinema, this chapter
explores the specificity of Bollywood's utopian imaginings for nationality.
It does so by uncovering how Partition marks, inflects, and circulates in

these contemporary texts about consumption and citizenship, international war and ethnic coupledom in some recent Bollywood films: Farah Khan's *Main Hoon Na/I'm Here for You* (2004), Farhan Akhtar's *Lakshya/Objective* (2004), Chandraprakash Dwivedi's *Pinjar/Skeleton* (2003) and Yash Chopra's *Veer Zaara* (2005). Since the Hindi films produced in Bombay are in India's national language, and tend to be the biggest national box-office hits, they have come to represent national cinema, though the term "Bollywood cinema" has gained international currency and so prevails in contemporary discourse. Given their global reach, as Bollywood films have long been exported to popular audiences across Asia, Africa, Europe and North America, they constitute a transnational public culture in which Indian nationalism is often central.[4] Large diasporic Indian communities in the United States, Canada, U.K., and Europe (numbering over three million) have also become key consumers of Bollywood films, such that many Hindi films now routinely are released simultaneously in India and in the U.S. and the U.K. As Vijay Mishra argues, "diaspora consciousness is now internal to spectatorial desire within India and essential too to Bombay cinema's new global aesthetics."[5] The films I focus on reflect an important historical turn in South Asian popular cultural discourses towards peace, insofar as they attempt to unravel and rearticulate the complex, gendered entanglement of ethnicity and citizenship that Partition instituted as a persistent feature of postcolonial South Asian life. As the SMS message appearing at the beginning of this chapter (reported as having popular currency in the leading magazine *Outlook*) indicates, the ethnicization of "terror" and its discursive identification with Islam dominates public culture not only in North America but also in India. This reflects a new turn in the ethnicization of identity uncovered in the early national period in the preceding chapters. It raises troubling questions about what has been, since the mid-eighties, an increasingly popular discriminatory minoritization of Indian Muslims in contemporary national discourse. As Yoginder Sikand observes, "The growing power of aggressively anti-Muslim Hindu fascist terror groups in the country and the coming to power of the militant Hindu Bharatiya Janata Party (BJP) at the head of a coalition government at the center have led to a growing persecution of Muslims in India. In pogrom after pogrom, organized by militant Hindu groups often in collusion with agencies of the state, vast numbers of Muslims have been killed, and the toll continues to mount."[6] Radical Hindu nationalist organizations like Rashtriya Swayamsevak Sangh (RSS) and Vishwa Hindu Parishad (VHP) through the BJP in the political scene have played a key role in this violence. The rise to power of this BJP-RSS-VHP combine and its ideology of Hindutva since the mid-eighties has regenerated the dangerous discourse that ethnicizes Indian citizenship and national belonging—a discourse that the Partition had enabled, and that had been marginalized in the socialist Nehruvian years because of regional and language conflicts.

Gyan Pandey has noted the enduring shape and new form of the contemporary focus on Partition in the Indian public sphere for the negotiation of national belonging and ethnicity: "Journalists and other commentators in India invoke Partition whenever there is a major instance of inter-community strife; and local administrators have been known to describe pre-dominantly Muslim localities as 'little Pakistans' . . . On the state's side, the question of minorities in India—Sikh, Muslim and at times even Christian—has continued to be handled in the light of the 'lessons' of Partition."[7] How, then, does Partition appear in contemporary Bollywood cinema? Having taken up exilic and early national cinema in earlier chapters, I now turn to the aesthetic narrativization of these issues in popular Hindi cinema. Many Bollywood films today explore questions about national belonging by taking up Partition as gendered violence and as generative of Indo–Pakistan war and peace. I read these films as cultural texts that constitute a dominant public sphere account which inscribes, mediates, and prescribes particular normative conceptions of ethnic coupledom, gendered citizenship, nationalism and secularism. Hence, the issues of spectatorship and reception have remained beyond the scope of this discussion; I have focused instead on how particular Bollywood films in the postcolonial public sphere both produce and contest a hegemonic discourse about Partition, and mediate the "utopian imaginings" of peace and non-violent belongings. Insofar as the 1947 Partition recently appears in this cinema in historical period films, on one hand, and in the form of its legacy of conflict-ridden India–Pakistan relations, on the other hand, a closer look at its contemporary inscription as event and discourse reveals the Partition's continuing impact on the cultural politics of citizenship in South Asia. The films I take up interrogate particular dominant ideological ethno-nationalist rhetorics, towards a space-clearing gesture that de-ethnicizes citizenship and that can accommodate both patriotism and peace in the subcontinent. Ultimately, however, these films do so with varying degrees of success; their reliance on the heteronormative, patriarchal production of modern couple-dom to consolidate the story of national peace becomes the limit frame of these melodramas.

If the preceding chapters uncovered how early national constructions of secular citizenship come to be complexly gendered in post-Partition literature, they also showed how the ethnic mass migrations of 1947 led to both the erasure and the silencing of Partition refugees in India, and to the ethnicization of citizenship and property in Indian state discourse as well as urban public culture in 1947 and after. Subsequently, wars with Pakistan and China in the sixties and seventies, combined with regional, class, and language conflicts, drew attention away from the trauma of Partition in the public sphere. Paralleling the diasporic return to the memory of Partition in the writings of historians like Gyan Pandey and Dipesh Chakrabarty and of novelists like Salman Rushdie and Shauna Singh Baldwin in the subcontinent, it is in Bollywood cinema that the history and effects of the Partition are being reworked in the present. Thus, the inscription of the Partition in contemporary cinematic culture emerges from India itself, and not the diaspora; it both memorializes the 1947 experience, and, more provocatively, situates it in relationship to the current urban politics of Hindu nationalism and geopolitical conflict in South Asia. Recent Bollywood melodramas often take up the ethnicization of citizenship enabled by Partition, but they do so contradictorily—they reflect, as well as problematize, its manifestation in the cultural and political inscription of the Indian Muslim as third column/enemy, of Pakistan as "Other," and of the ascendancy of Hindu fundamentalism over secular nationalism in modern India.

The Early History of National Cinema, Before and After 1947

The Indian film industry generates, on an average, 700 to 800 films a year, and in some years more than 900—much more than Hollywood, which produces about 200. While most of these films are in regional languages such as Bengali, Tamil, Malayalam, the Bombay film industry produces about 200 films a year in Hindi, which, as mentioned earlier, have had a global presence since the fifties, in places as far flung as Russia and the Caribbean, Japan and Nigeria. The first Indian feature film, Dadasaheb Phalke's *Raja Harishchandra*, was made in 1913 in Bombay. Yet the genre of what is known today as Bollywood cinema, complete with song-and-dance sequences, was born in 1931. In spite of the presence of regional cinema, between 1940 and 1960 it was Hindi cinema that dominated Indian film culture and, in the process, helped propagate the national language Hindi as well as the notion of a collective Indian national identity. In the thirties, three producers (Prabhat, Bombay Talkies, New Theatres) dominated Hindi cinema with their socially critical but commercially successful films. In the forties, profiteering during World War II produced 600 new film producers and financiers, with whose funds some remarkable films were made during this decade. This influx of funds—some originating in questionable businesses—subsequently had profound effects on the modes and content of filmmaking in India and led to the breakdown of the studio system in favor of the "star system." Thus, Hindi cinema's earlier emphasis on social realism, in the work of Guru Dutt, Raj Kapoor, Bimal Roy, and Mehboob Khan (whose *Mother India* was nominated for an Oscar in 1957) came to be somewhat marginalized as the commercial value of films as profitable mass entertainment became apparent. At this point, as Yves Thoraval observes, "the dividing line between popular cinema and auteur ('New') cinema was quite blurred."[8] Even though the lines between popular and auteur cinema were initially blurred in the early national period, with Italian neorealism influencing not only the internationally renowned Bengali filmmaker Satyajit Ray but also Hindi filmmakers like Bimal Roy and Raj Kapoor, the state's Film Enquiry Committee Report in 1951 condemned cinema as a source of moral degeneration, and argued that the pleasures of film viewing bordered on sinful. Simultaneous to this state denigration of the institution of cinema, there emerged in Indian cinema in the fifties a new political consciousness as filmmakers began to see cinema as a pedagogic technology for the enlightenment of the illiterate masses; this was most exemplified in Ritwik Ghatak's Bengali film *Nagarik (Citizen)*. Made in 1952, it critiqued the postcolonial nation-state, illuminating the failures of nationalism and independence for the lived experience of most Indians.

That the Partition transformed the Bombay film industry not only materially, but also in terms of genres in Hindi film production is borne out by a closer look at the popularity of the "lost and found" theme in Hindi films of the early national period. Tejaswini Ganti has suggestively argued that the popularity of the "lost and found" genre—in which a nuclear family or a subset such as siblings are "separated ('lost') in childhood due to traumatic circumstances" only to be reunited in the end—from the fifties onwards through the seventies lies in its reference to the traumas of Partition "where thousands of families were separated, and many not so successfully united."[9] For example, *Afsana* (1951) was directed by B. R. Chopra (a Partition refugee from Lahore) and is about identical twin brothers separated in childhood, while Yash Chopra's *Waqt* (1965) is about three brothers separated from their parents and each other; these are only a couple of examples of the allegories of the Partition refugees' experience that dominated the cinematic public sphere in the early national years. Unlike these allegories, *Nastik (Atheist)* by I. S. Johar came out in 1954, and was a social film that dealt with the experiences of a refugee family displaced by Partition. Another film that took up the question of ethnic identity, home and belonging in popular melodrama is Yash Chopra's *Dharamputra (Son of the Faith)*, which came out in 1961. The film is set in the period immediately following Partition, and centers upon an illegitimate Muslim boy who is raised in post-Partition India by Hindu parents. Based on Acharya Chatursen Shastri's Hindi novel, it explores how this boy grows up to be a bigoted Hindu, and in fact leads a violent mob to set fire to a Muslim's ancestral home—which coincidentally turns out to be his birth mother's home. Right as he is about to succeed, his parents reveal the truth of his Muslim origins to him, and the film thus predictably ends by preaching secularism and communal harmony.[10]

While the Hindi film industry has been extremely diverse since its emergence, drawing Parsis, Jews, Hindus, Muslims, and even Germans to work together, both before and after 1947 mainstream Hindi cinema has had an ambivalent relationship to religion and secularism in the Indian nation. Ravi Vasudevan has noted how, even prior to decolonization, institutions like the All India League of Censorship (set up in 1937) explicitly worked to eradicate what it perceived as "non-Hindu" people and ideas from the Hindi film industry. The organization's communalist anti-Muslim agenda significantly affected the industry in the forties and fifties, and likely influenced how many Muslim actors and actresses took on Hindu screen names during this period.[11] From roughly the mid-sixties onwards, with the rise to power of Indira Gandhi, the Indian state initiated a series of efforts aimed at creating a "national" cinema that would disseminate progressive values and provide cultural support for the socialist government.[12] In the turbulent sixties and seventies, a range of movements, from urban working-class militancy to regionalist and Communist rural peasant-based struggles, emerged to make up a volatile political scene. In this moment, the Film Finance Corporation (later the National Film Development Corporation) was a state institution that actively sought to intervene in and shape national culture through cinematic production of socially progressive films, leading to the emergence of what Madhava Prasad has called the "middle-class cinema" of Hrishikesh Mukherjee and Basu Chatterji. Alongside these economic and political changes engendered by the politicization and democratic mobilization of the population, cinema as an institution also underwent transformations: The "social" as a genre declined and gave way to the popularity of middle-class cinema that turned around the entry of the postcolonial middle-class into national modernity. Prasad has well demonstrated these changes in cinematic production in terms of genre, narrative and economics, and has shown how they emerged in the early national period through a complex and often conflicted negotiation between film producers and directors on one hand, and the institutions of the nation-state on the other, over Hindi cinema's perceived role and responsibility in the production of nation, normative citizenship and national culture.[13]

It should come as no surprise, then, that especially since the nineties, the politics of nationalism have become almost a regular feature of Bollywood films. Even in films that are family dramas and love stories, epics about coming of age and individual growth, or what Rachel Dwyer calls the "Hindu social," very often, nationality and Indo–Pakistan relations are indexed in the plot or symbolic economy.[14] These films take up the ongoing ethnic conflict, war and violence in the Indian subcontinent in two ways: through the historical representation of Partition, on one hand, and its inscription as generative of present-day international conflict between India and Pakistan on the other. In doing so, they attempt to reconfigure, globalize and historicize contemporary questions about violent belongings, about the relation between ethnicity and citizenship in Indian national culture in the transnational postcolonial public sphere. Through an analysis of recent films like Farah Khan's *Main Hoon Na*, Yash Chopra's *Veer Zaara*, Farhan Akhtar's *Lakshya* and Chandraprakash Dwivedi's *Pinjar*, this chapter explores the production of Partition and patriotism in popular culture. It is my argument that rather than displacing religious ethnicity as a hegemonic ground for determining identity and belonging, these melodramas ambivalently reproduce the power of ethnicity as a defining category for postcolonial identity, even as their utopian imaginings seek to problematize its impact on the lived experience of minoritized citizenship and national belonging. In the process, except for *Pinjar*, these films represent heterosexual, Hindu masculinity as normative Indian citizenship that engenders geopolitical peace and invents a fantasy of the humane postcolonial state. The trope of inter-ethnic romance figured as national secularism, which we tracked earlier in early national literature, also appears re-fashioned in this cinema. Whether or not these films represent heteronormative romantic coupledom as sustaining or interrogating the nation, these films are hegemonic cultural texts which emblematize, as Lauren Berlant suggests in a different context, "the ways attachments make worlds and world-changing fantasies, bribe people to live what should be unlivable relations of domination and violence."[15]

New National Masculinity: Ram Produces Indo-Pak Peace

The popular Bollywood film *Main Hoon Na*, written and directed by Farah Khan, was released in 2004 and is considered a box-office success. It was also nominated for ten Filmfare Awards, among them Best Actor, Best Comedian, Best Supporting Actress, Best Supporting Actor, Best Director, Best Villain and Best Film. The film turns on the conflict between the hero, Major Ram (Shahrukh Khan), and the villain, Raghavan (Suneil Shetty), as the former seeks to foil the latter's plan to sabotage an Indo–Pak peace initiative, "Project Milaap," to exchange prisoners. Its representation of Indo–Pak political relations and normative citizenship is important in its commercial success in India and abroad, and is suggestive in its articulation of geo-political peace. Although its masculinist valorization of the nation-state and the military is problematic, *Main Hoon Na* is an important public sphere text insofar as it deploys the Hindu epic *Ramayana* as allegory to produce a national story that attempts to shift the discourse about terror and violence in India from the register of being coded Muslim, and in the process, to de-ethnicize national belonging.

On one hand, the film instantiates the hegemony of the nation-state and its representatives through its valorizing representation of the Indian military. On the other hand however, it critically argues for secular, de-ethnicized citizenship and international peace. It opens with a scene in which the Commander-in-Chief of the Indian Army, General Bakshi (Kabir Bedi), is being interviewed in a television studio. The interview presents the conflict of the film: a government peace initiative called Project Milaap which seeks to free fifty Pakistani prisoners who are in Indian custody, some since 1971, on August 15, India's Independence Day. When the interviewer asks if this will create friendship between India and Pakistan, the general says in English, "It's not so simple." He explains in Hindi, "There is a distance of a 55-year-old enmity, it cannot be resolved with the release of fifty people. . . . [But] no matter how far the distance, a step constitutes a beginning." "Milaap" roughly translates as "coming together"; thus, from the beginning, *Main Hoon Na* endorses Indo–Pak amity and a desire for friendship. As Bakshi speaks, black-and-white photographs of unidentified villagers, presumably the prisoners, abstractly flash in the background, creating a sentimental montage that suggestively represents the villagers as innocent victims of international politics. Bakshi makes the case for the initiative on humanist grounds, pointing out that many of these prisoners are innocent villagers who were not even aware that they had crossed a national border, as "after all, our border is not completely sealed." They have been languishing in Indian prisons for years, so, Bakshi says, "we feel it is now time to send them home." In this discourse, the home maps onto the nation, even as the Indian state is implicitly represented as a humane and peaceful agent. A murderous attack on the general by Raghavan ensues, as Raghavan swears to prevent Project Milaap's success. Before his failed attempt to shoot and kill him, Raghavan challenges Bakshi: "Is Pakistan going to release Indian prisoners to reciprocate?" When Bakshi reluctantly concedes that Pakistan has not yet offered to do so, Raghavan asks, "Then, why should we?" Bakshi replies that India has decided to release the prisoners even though Pakistan has not reciprocated: "Well, because someone has to take the first step. If we all behave like you, there will never be peace." Raghavan, another name of the mischievious Hindu god Krishna, is thus the villain and terrorist in the film's narrative structure, a foil to the protagonist Ram. As he shoots Bakshi, his security-in-charge Brigadier Shekhar Sharma (Nasseruddin Shah) steps in the way and dies. This opening sequence sets the tone for the rest of the film which turns around the conflict between secular, patriotic and pro-peace state officials like Bakshi and Shekhar Sharma's illegitimate son, Major Ram Prasad Sharma, on one hand, and on the other hand, the threat to the nation from within of anti-Pakistan forces like Raghavan—who incidentally, is an ex-Army man—determined to sabotage the Indo–Pakistan peace process. Eventually, Pakistan is shown to reciprocate, and Project Milaap succeeds.

Resisting the stereotypical discourse about the Muslim criminal and terrorist as a threat to the Indian nation that marks much Hindi cinema, this film has a Hindu villain at center stage. Moreover, its pacificist endorsement of a peace initiative constitutes a significant break from a popular political rhetoric of Indo–Pakistani mutual suspicion and animosity. The film articulates, early in the narrative, a utopian desire for geo-political peace between the two nations created by Partition. Later in *Main Hoon Na*, we learn Raghavan's "rationale" (if one can call it that) for his hatred of Pakistan; he says in his court-martial, "We have been in a state of war with Pakistan since 1947." Significantly, the 1947 Partition is therefore inscribed in the film as contingently generative of inter-national conflict and anti-Pakistan sentiment in present-day India. By making the villain of the film espouse this militantly anti-Pakistan nationalism, the film implicitly critiques it, endorsing the more centrist position voiced by Bakshi and Major Ram, of choosing inter-national peace and friendship by making the goodwill gesture first. In a flashback in the film, we learn that Raghavan's militant politics had led to his dismissal as an Indian Army officer. He was court-martialed for shooting, at point-blank range, ten Pakistani male villagers who had accidentally crossed over the Indian border in their search for water in the desert area.

Main Hoon Na also explicitly allegorizes the popular Hindu religious epic *Ramayana*; the protagonist is named Ram after the Hindu god Ram, and the character of Ram's brother is named Lakshman, as in the epic. Ram is "exiled" from his home, like the God, by a step-mother who rejects him—though in this modern version, it is because he is the illegitimate product of an extra-marital affair. Modernizing the story, the film's narrative replaces the kingdom with the nation. In exile, Lord Ram lived in the forest; the exiled Major Ram finds a home in the nation-state and its institution the Indian Army. The Indian nation-state offers Ram a sense of belonging; in turn, the state is sustained and protected by Ram. Insofar as Ram is then both a citizen and a state representative, the film's allegorical reproduction of the *Ramayana* can be read as the legitimation of the postcolonial state as hegemonic power. In tracking the revival of Ayodhya and Ram in the political imaginary of India through Bollywood cinema, Vijay Mishra has argued that "the Rama myth begins to inform the political imaginary of India when the nation finds itself threatened or when its self-projecting apparatus requires the construction of the demonic Other."[16] In the films that Mishra discusses, this demonic other contrasted to the heroic and democratic Ram is usually Muslim. In contrast, what is interesting about *Main Hoon Na*, made by a Muslim director (Farah Khan) and producer (Shahrukh Khan) is that it deploys this Hindu epic allegorically to represent the threat to the nation-state as the Hindu fanatic within. It thus recasts the dominant Islamicization of "terror" and the RSS's ideological rhetoric of the Muslim citizen as the third column that threatens national security and inter-national peace. Instead, the militant Hindu nationalist is the demonic Other who will eventually be routed by the state's institutions towards the triumph of secularism. It is worth noting that Raghavan's Muslim accomplice, Khan (Murli Sharma), is also an ex-Army man who joins Raghavan, as he misguid-edly believes that Raghavan is engaged in a nationalist war to protect India. However, the film's narrative folds his negative Muslim masculinity back into nationalist discourse through his reform and redemption: when he discovers Raghavan's personal motivations for his anti-Pakistan stance (Raghavan's son was killed by terrorists in Kashmir, who Raghavan believes were Pakistani), he switches sides and helps Ram to foil Raghavan's plans. Thus, the conflict between centrist politics and the more extremist Hindu nationalist politics of terrorists like Raghavan provides the action in the film. In the process, the film insists, in Ram's words, that there should be, and "there will be peace (aman), there will be friendship (dosti) too" between India and Pakistan. The film optimistically ends with the destruction of Raghavan after a battle with Ram; the battle concurs with the national exchange of innocent prisoners on the Wagah border by India and Pakistan.

I have suggested earlier that *Main Hoon Na* as a mainstream Bollywood production is also unique because, unlike many of its contemporaries like John Mathew Mathan's *Sarfarosh* (1999), Vidhu Vinod Chopra's *Mission Kashmir* (2000), and Farhan Akhtar's *Lakshya* (2004), it does not posit the Pakistani, the Afghani Taliban, or the Indian Muslim as the militant villain or as enemy of the Indian state. As Amit Rai has pointed out, a new wave of "cinepatriotism" in 1990s Bollywood cinema ties the filmic representation of the Muslim as terrorist "to the construction of the abnormal monster in contemporary discourses of counter-terrorism both in the West and in India." Taking up films like *Mission Kashmir* and *Fiza/Air*, Rai argues that "these films show the many strategies—complex and contradictory—at work in contemporary Hindi films aimed to manage that infection known today in

Hindu India as the Muslim 'other.'"[17] Instead, in *Main Hoon Na*, the main villain Raghavan is Hindu, is an ex-Army officer, and is a jingoistic nationalist. *Main Hoon Na* promotes an alternative discourse of nationalism as a positive sentiment, and delinks it with being marked ethnically as a Hindu or Muslim citizen. As such, it differentiates its valorized secular nationalism, from a violent nationalism driven by a hatred of the other that also emerged in, and was the legacy of, the 1947 Partition. The film politically mobilizes the *Ramayana* and the concept of Ram Rajya—used by the RSS and BJP to foment anti-Muslim violence, from the destruction of the Babri Masjid to the Godhra riots—to reinvent it as a modern allegory of international peace. Towards the end of the film, the climax involves cross-cutting between a fight sequence in which Ram and Raghavan battle it out, and scenes of the villagers/prisoners being "exchanged"—an "exchange" that repeats and reinvents the original "exchange" of populations that Partition generated. The cross-cutting metaphorically links the two scenes, suggesting that Ram and Raghavan's battle enables the return to nation as "home" of the imprisoned subaltern subjects. The scenes depict villagers that are united with anxious kin gathered behind barricades on each side: the freed men kiss their family members and the earth in several juxtaposed shots. The representation of these voiceless, subaltern, exchanged citizens stands not as a critique of the postcolonial nation-state (as in much early Partition literature and film), but serves to reinstate and authorize its power and fantasy. Thus, the film assumes and valorizes nationalism and patriotism—both Indian and Pakistani. In the scene when a gun-wielding Raghavan finally tells Ram that he should prepare to die, Ram chides him for forgetting his *Ramayana*, in which, "In the end, it is the evil Ravan who dies." As Ram waves a grenade pin in the air, the camera cuts to a close-up of Raghavan's face as realization dawns on him. The scene ends with Raghavan exploding with fire, as Ravan does in the epic, while Ram escapes unhurt and jumps to safety.

Main Hoon Na thus reproduces the imagery and authority of a traditional Hindu religious epic, but in order to create a discursive political space for a peaceful politics between the two poles of jingoistic nationalism and a non-nationalist peace activism. It embraces a hegemonic nationalism that entails sentimental investment in the nation as an idealized form of community, but rejects an extremist Hindu nationalism which entails an automatic enmity with Pakistan.

Of course, it is important to note that this narrative is deeply gendered and heteronormative: None of the female characters plays an important role in this national story about two kinds of Hindu, Indian masculinities and patriotisms. Ram Sharma's secular and strategic heroic masculinity is a Hindu, upper caste and statist one as well, and this reinvention of a patriarchal Hindu masculine

Figure 5.1. Ram and Raghavan battling it out in *Main Hoon Na*'s modern allegory of the Ramayana. *(Main Hoon Na. Dir. Farah Khan. Red Chillies Entertainment, 2004. Shahrukh Khan as Ram, Sunil Shetty as Raghavan.)*

hero and his contiguity with the nation remains problematic. In the denouement, it triumphs over Raghavan's militant Hindu masculinity—which is suggestively linked to the new, dominant Hindu nationalist discourse of the RSS-BJP bloc, and depicted as ultimately anti-national in its anti-Pakistan stance. Vijay Mishra has argued that "these symbolic restitutions of the fiction of the Hindu hero (which in a sense normalizes readings of the nation as Hindu) do not get around the psychology of mourning that is at the heart of the heritage of *batvara* [Partition]"[18]—a Partition that is described by Gen. Bakshi as a distance that after 55 years, needs to be bridged.

Inter-ethnic Coupledom, Feminism and Secularism in the Indo-Pak Romance

The promotional materials of Yash Chopra's film *Veer-Zaara* (2004) claim that the film is about a "love legend": "*Veer-Zaara* recounts the epic tale of an Indian man, Veer Pratap Singh (Shahrukh Khan) and a Pakistani woman, Zaara Hayaat Khan (Preity Zinta)—a story of a love so great that it knows no boundaries. It is also the story of Saamiya Siddiqui (Rani Mukherji), a Pakistani lawyer who tries to break the barriers separating the two."[19] The film was an international box office success, not only in India but also in the

U.K., the United States, Germany, and South Africa. In the United States, it had a record-breaking run in 2004 on eighty-eight screens, speaking to its popularity in the South Asian American diaspora. It also won several Filmfare awards in 2005, as well as the National Film Award for Best Popular Film Providing Wholesome Entertainment. It centers upon the love story between an Indian Hindu Squadron Leader, Veer Pratap Singh, who is a rescue pilot with the Indian Air Force, and a Pakistani Muslim woman, Zaara Hayaat Khan (Preity Zinta), who comes to India to fulfill her surrogate Sikh grandmother's dying wish. We learn early on that this Sikh nanny (Zohra Sehgal), a grandmotherly figure for Zaara, came to newly formed Pakistan in Zaara's grandfather's care in 1947. On her death bed, she requests Zaara to disperse her ashes in Tirathpur in India. On her way to do so, when Zaara is stranded in a bus accident on a precarious cliff, she is heroically rescued by Veer, and is subsequently taken on a tour of the Punjab countryside that is Veer's home. In the process of showing Zaara his idyllic village community, which symbolizes the nation in the narrative, Veer falls in love with her, and follows her to Pakistan. But Zaara is already betrothed in an arranged marriage by her father in what promises to be a productive alliance for his political ambitions. When Veer is requested by Zaara's mother to honorably leave them alone for the sake of Zaara and her family's reputation, he respectfully agrees. However, on his way back to India, he is arrested by Zaara's fiancé and imprisoned on false charges as an Indian spy, Rajesh Rathore. Bound by his promise to protect Zaara's reputation, Veer is unable to defend himself and explain his presence in Pakistan. Having been forced to sign a "confession," he languishes in a Pakistani jail for 22 years until a Pakistani lawyer, Saamiya Siddiqui, takes up his case.

This is the moment when the film begins: in the encounter between Saamiya, who is assigned by the International Human Rights Commission to investigate the rights of prisoners, especially those who have been languishing in jails for years without getting a fair trial like Veer ("Prisoner No. 786, alias Rajesh Rathore"). The assignment of the number 786 is significant: People in South Asia write this number to avoid writing the name of Allah on ordinary paper. Thus, although evocative of the idealized, suffering Sikh/Punjabi masculinity of early national literature, Veer's contemporary, suffering, Hindu masculinity is simultaneously overlaid with this Islamic resonance, evoking South Asian syncretism and estranging his narrativization as Hindu citizen-subject. Saamiya uncovers Veer's past, and Veer and Zaara's love story unfolds in a flashback. Saamiya takes up Veer's case and begins the effort to get him justice—to return to him his identity. The film turns upon an inter-ethnic as well as inter-national romance between a Hindu Indian man and a Muslim Pakistani woman; both appropriately perform model secular citizenship in normative prescribed ways, even as their potential heteronormative coupledom signifies inter-national peace in the family of nations in South Asia.

There are two important moments where the film takes up the history of Partition: one is when Zaara's surrogate nanny is dying. Bebe is a Sikh grandmotherly figure who has raised her and who is like a family member in their household. Now on her death bed, Bebe tells Zaara of her last wishes:

> Did you know, I am as old as Pakistan is? I was sixteen years old when your grandfather left India after the 1947 Partition to come here, and brought me with him. Your family, and this country, have given me a lot, and I have also taken much from you, with a full heart. Now I have a last wish. Will you fulfill it? Disperse my ashes only in my Hindustan, my daughter. I may be an orphan, but I am at least a Hindustani. This is my only identity. I had told you about Tirathpur once, didn't I? That is a big pilgrimage center for all Sikhs. All the generations from my side come from there. Just leave me there. There, I will find refuge.

Bebe here articulates her identity with her national origin; when she asserts that although she is an orphan, she is Indian, the nation replaces the family as locus of community and belonging, and symbolizes home and a refuge from the world for this orphaned domestic worker. Zaara reassures her that their visas to Delhi have come through, and so they can all now go to Tirathpur on pilgrimage together. But Bebe passes away. Thus, early on, the film deploys Bebe as the minoritized working-class Sikh woman in Pakistan to naturalize national origin as the basis of identity and belonging. Moreover, like many other Sikh figures in Bollywood cinema and postcolonial Indian literature, she mediates Hindu and Muslim relations, becoming the catalyst for Zaara to meet Veer. Earlier, I have noted the similar mobilization of the Sikh man as hyper-masculine national subject who mediates among different ethnicities and represents the nation; such discursive, ethnic mobilizations elide the violence that attends their minoritization in India, as became evident in the riots of 1984 in which over 2,000 Sikhs died. Also, as Rachel Dwyer notes, "Although their community was devastated by the Partition, with many of their sacred places being difficult for them to access in Pakistan, the Sikhs [in Hindi films] are shown as having no bitterness or anger."[20] A similar point must be made with respect to the now transnational Hindu Sindhi community, which lost their homeland, Sindh, when it was assimilated into Pakistan and was forced to disperse across different parts of the world after a mass exodus in 1947. Often mockingly stereotyped as marginal comic figures in Hindi cinema, their minoritized, differential history remains subaltern to the historical discourse of Partition suffering in the postcolonial public sphere.

The character of Zaara functions in contradictory ways in the statist narrative of *Veer Zaara*. On one hand, Zaara is drawn as a modern proto-feminist ethnic subject, perfectly articulating tradition and modernity, secularism and faith. On the other hand however, insofar as she marries the man her father has chosen for her and later subordinates herself to Veer's parents, she performatively reproduces hegemonic relations of gendered patriarchal power. Early on, when Zaara goes to the gurudwara in Tirathpur, the Sikh priest commends her for her devotion in conducting Bebe's Sikh death ceremony: "I have not seen such faith in the thirty years I have been practicing as a priest. Yes, I will conduct the last rites for her [Bebe]." Zaara thus performs a very particular, hybrid Muslim femininity in this narrative: She is a modern, feminist, culturally flexible subject who is a Pakistani Muslim, and who defies patriarchal authority to independently cross national and ethnic borders. Performing multiple traditions, she embodies a Pakistani secularism unavailable within the frame of the film to the Pakistani Muslim men—from Zaara's father to her fiancé. The Pakistani men uniformly reproduce stereotypes of conservative traditionalism and an oppressive, patriarchal ethno-nationalism that treats the Muslim woman as property and as an object of transaction. Zaara's feminist modernity is also signaled in her critique of the sexist Indian Hindu patriarch, Veer's uncle (Amitabh Bachchan). In one scene, while discussing female education with Zaara, the uncle says that it is unnecessary because women have to take care of the home. At this, Zaara indignantly pronounces: "This is injustice!" She proceeds to urge him to allow and enable female education, thus performing a pedagogic feminism. Enlightened by this conversation, he later announces that the land initially designated for the boy's cricket pitch in the village will now be used for a girl's high school. The first brick for the school is then ceremonially laid by Zaara, symbolizing the instantiation of gender justice and women's rights as embodied in the modern educational institution *for girls* via the agency of a Pakistani Muslim woman. When she leaves to return to Pakistan, Mr. Singh asks Zaara to tell her parents that she has instilled positive values in a sixty-year-old India. By depicting Zaara as an agent of Indian feminism and justice, the film works against dominant stereotypical discourses about the Muslim/Pakistani woman in the third world as always already oppressed victim of Islam/Pakistan; here, she is an agent of feminist transformation in patriarchal rural India. The film returns to the trope of "justice," which is engendered eventually through the trial, defense and release of Veer at the hands of another Pakistani Muslim woman: the lawyer Saamiya. Thus, even as Pakistani men are represented in negative ways, Pakistani women instantiate justice—both feminist and national—in this film.

The question of justice in *Veer-Zaara* is tied to a discourse of geo-political peace between India and Pakistan in important ways: For example, in Veer's recounting to Saamiya of how he met Zaara, there is no animosity towards Zaara or her family members as Pakistani, nor is there any anti-India senti-ment expressed by members of Zaara's household. When Veer takes Zaara to see his village in Punjab, he sings a song whose refrain is "My country is like this." The song lyrics describe India through idealizing poetic images of the rural landscape and life: It has blue skies and golden earth; every season is colorful; grandmothers tell stories every night to their grandchildren; and such other tropes of elite India's romanticization of rural life. This is the romanticized, syncretic Indian village we also see in early national literature like Khushwant Singh's *Train to Pakistan*. The song is accompanied by a juxtaposition of different scenes that invoke urban stereotypes of the rural Indian "folk": panoramic shots of picturesque green fields suggestive of Punjab, of colorfully dressed village women walking in line with earthen pots on their heads, of rural fairs and men on tractors harvesting their crops.

This is the fantasy, as Ashis Nandy has suggested about the middle-class representation of peasant life in Indian cinema, of the rural as "pastoral paradise."[21] In the style of the 1971 film *Mera Gaon Mera Desh/My Village My Country*, most contemporary Bollywood films have thus continued to ideal-ize the village as the heart of authentic India: from Subhash Ghai's *Pardes/A Foreign Country* (1997) to *Veer-Zaara*, the Punjabi village has become rep-resentative of "real" India—with one crucial difference: In *Veer-Zaara*, this romantic, ahistorical representation of an authentic, pure folk culture in a rural India, free of ethnic conflict, is suggestively transnational as well. As Zaara responds in the song, "This sounds a lot like my country/the same morning and evening are in my country too/my country is just like yours." In this refrain, a fragmentary utopian affiliation emerges in the likeness of everyday life, only to be subsumed later in the ideological respect granted to nationality in the narrative.

This rhetoric—of asserting national likeness rather than national differ-ence—permeates the ideological message of the film; however, it does not function to erase or undermine the idea of the nation-state as imagined com-munity in favor of the transnational. Instead of subverting the hegemony of the nation-state, it calls for peace, dialogue and mutual recognition between India and Pakistan on the basis of a shared humanity. It thus leaves unchal-lenged the ideological dominance of the nation as the primary basis of iden-tity and community: For example, Saamiya says in the court in her defense of Veer, "I want to return to this man his name, his identity, his nation."

Thus, identity is contiguous with nationality, and belonging is nationalized. Although Veer—which means brave—represents the Indian nation, his Indian masculinity is heroicized not through his militant action but through his chivalrous sacrificial suffering (much like Jugga in Khushwant Singh's novel *Train to Pakistan* nearly fifty years earlier). As the judge presiding over his case in the court of law proclaims, "This man, to protect the honor of a Pakistani girl, sacrificed his life." This is both an old and a new face of popular secularism, in which inter-ethnic coupledom is not realized due to Hindu–Muslim and Indo–Pakistani conflict, yet the performance of model secular citizenship is indexed by the sacrifice and suffering of the heterosexual Indian masculine body (ethnically always marked Hindu or Sikh)—for a Pakistani or Muslim woman.

The problem of how to deal with religious and national difference is resolved in the film through two moments: Veer reciting a poem he has written in court, and the statement of Pakistani lawyer Zakir Ahmed (Anupam Kher), who initially fought the case on behalf of the state. Veer's poem challenges the construction of differences between India and Pakistan: "People say, this is not your country? / Then, why does it feel like my country?/ People say she[Saamiya] is not like me? / Then why does she feel just like me?" In the repetition of the refrain "Why does she/it/the nation feel like me/mine," the narrative proffers a resemblance and identity between the Indian and Pakistani: both nation and citizen. This radical assertion of sameness embodies the utopian imagining of shared identity and community that Yash Chopra has been known to assert in interviews as well—a vision of non-antagonistic inter-ethnic relations and Indo–Pak peace. Zaara enacts this in the denouement, which shows her as having divorced her fiancé after a short marriage, only to end up living in Veer's village in India where she cares for his aged parents and runs a girl's school for the next few decades. The Pakistani prosecution lawyer, Zakir, is also reformed by the feminist Saamiya, and says didactically, "The future of these two nations is in the hands of their youth, who don't judge people unfairly on the grounds of gender, class or ethnic difference, and who don't keep rubbing salt into the wounds of '47, '65, '99 [years marking the Partition and Indo-Pakistani wars]. . . . Thank you [Saamiya] for teaching me the value of truth and justice." The film returns us to neoliberalism and the principle of justice through the Pakistani feminist woman-lawyer-citizen. Implicitly, the authority and ideology of modern institutions of law in the nation-state are upheld, and the problematic rhetorics of honor around the female figure as ethnic patriarchal property and national symbol are reinforced. Veer and Zaara's inter-ethnic romance remains unrealized until the end, when they are both aged, because Veer promises to obey Zaara's mother's request that he leave Zaara: She says Zaara is her "amanat." In Urdu, "amanat" means property, or something valuable that belongs to another, and that is in one's safekeeping. Thus, Zaara's mother both owns and disowns her, signifying Zaara's status as property—but property of the patriarchal father and fiancé. Veer's aged, interned, suffering masculine body, in contrast, bears witness to the routine violence of the ethnicized postcolonial state.

In writing about the ideological invention of the couple in Indian cinema, Madhava Prasad has noted that "in the dominant filmic narrative [in Hindi cinema] the drive towards the affirmation of conjugality is reined in by the restoration of the clan to its position of splendour and power; the couple, in other words, is repeatedly reabsorbed into the parental patriarchal family and is committed to its maintenance."[22] In the case of *Veer-Zaara*, what is interesting is that it does, as Prasad suggests, reproduce patriarchal and parental authority; however, this is done through the deferral of conjugality and the suppression of desire. Moreover, in its denouement, in which Veer and Zaara are reunited and live happily ever after in the Punjabi village, inter-ethnic romantic coupledom is realized, albeit now as aged, non-reproductive and desexualized. It could be argued that insofar as Veer and Zaara end up realizing their romance and living together in the end, albeit belatedly, the film represents a move forward from earlier representations. Like Mani Ratnam's *Bombay* (1995), it allows the realization of inter-ethnic coupledom—something unimaginable for early national cinema. However, this inter-ethnic coupledom is possible only when the female subject is ethnically Muslim and the male subject is Hindu; the reversal of this gendering has yet to find a space in the hegemonic public sphere, and this remains the ethnicist, heteronormative limit of *Veer-Zaara's* utopian imaginary.

The Bollywood War Film: Individualism, Romance and the Critique of the Middle-Class

In contrast to *Main Hoon Na*, films like J. P. Dutta's *LoC Kargil* (*Line of Control Kargil*; 2003) and Farhan Akhtar's *Lakshya* (*Objective*; 2004) are historical films that focus on the India–Pakistan Kargil War in 1999. In April 1999, Pakistan-backed infiltrators and members of the Pakistani army, disguised as militants, crossed the Line of Control that marks the boundary between India and Pakistan and captured some Indian territory in Jammu and Kashmir. The Indian Army fought for over four months to reclaim the territory, and 450 Indian soldiers lost their lives in the ensuing battle. Both films are Bollywood war films based on the Kargil war. They represent how India was forced to retaliate to this undeclared war and reclaim its territory from Pakistanis, at a great loss of lives for the Indian Army. However, unlike

Dutta's *LOC,* which articulates a patriotic tribute to those who fought the Kargil war and their bereaved families, *Lakshya* is considerably different from previous Hindi war films: It is both a war epic and a film about the protagonist Karan Shergill (Hrithik Roshan) coming of age in a modern bourgeois India. Directed by Farhan Akhtar and written by Javed Akhtar, *Lakshya's* promotional materials about the film declare, "It took him 24 years and 18000 ft to find about himself." The film thus foregrounds its bildungsroman-style account of the protagonist's search for selfhood and identity, in which the "backdrop" (namely, the Kargil war) is "an event that occurred in India in 1999" (according to a textual disclaimer before the film begins). Billed to become one of the biggest hits of 2004, it actually had little success at the box office.

An intensely individualist film, *Lakshya* follows Karan as he changes from being an aimless, upper middle-class, college-going youth into a model, hyper-masculine national subject after he joins the Indian Army. This transformation parallels his changing romantic relationship with his college friend and television journalist Romi (Preity Zinta). Through his training in the Indian Military Academy in Dehradun and his subsequent wartime experiences as Lieutenant Shergill, Karan discovers his purpose in life—the protection of the Indian nation. *Lakshya's* assertion of the positivity of national belonging is evident throughout the film: Much cinematic space is given over to the representation of the state's military institutions, especially the Indian Army and the Indian Military Academy, and the dramatic background score that accompanies these scenes only underscores their valorization. As if subtly addressing the question "Can a Muslim Be an Indian?"[23] one of the few Muslim characters—Capt. Jalal Akbar (Sushant Singh)—is shown in one scene as affirming his secular national identity as an Indian during a battle. In a Pakistani bunker Jalal and Karan have recently captured, a Pakistani army officer asks him on the phone, when he hears him say "Allah," "Are you a Muslim?" Jalal replies, "For you, I am only an Indian." Significantly, Jalal does not disavow his ethnic identity as Muslim, but instead signals its contingent positionality: in relation to the Pakistani, he avows his Indian nationality, thus subordinating the ethnic to the national in the prescribed performance of Indian secularism. This is Akhtar's nod to the languages of secularism, a gesture that seeks to, like *Main Hoon Na*, disaggregate the equations of ethnicity and citizenship that Partition instituted in 1947, and that continue to haunt Indian Muslims today.

Lakshya's inscription of the value and importance of nationality and citizenship appears earlier in the film as well. It opens in the present with a scene showing Lt. Shergill reporting to his regiment's office in Kashmir, close to the Indo–Pak border. Shortly thereafter, Karan and Jalal drive through the landscape of Kashmir to an Army outpost. Jalal pulls over at one spot to

Figure 5.2. Karan's emotional recognition of nationalist belonging in *Lakshya*.
(Lakshya. Dir. Farhan Akhtar. Excel Entertainment, 2004. Hrithik Roshan as Karan.)

point out to Karan the Pakistani Army check post and the lonely tall stone in the valley's no-man's-land that marks out the Line of Control drawn by the British in 1947 to divide India and Pakistan. The camera presents a medium shot of Karan and Jalal as they stare at the stone outside the frame; then it moves to a long shot of the landscape with the pillar that marks the border at which Karan is supposedly looking; returning to a medium shot of Karan looking astonished and exhilarated. He says, "It's amazing. I mean, [then in Hindi] I've always known, but somehow hadn't thought earlier that I'm Hindustani. [Then, in English] I'm an Indian." This is followed by a close-up of Karan's face that reinforces his emotional and psychic investment in this nationalist identification.

This dialogue deliberately enjoins English and Hindi in the recognition of nationality; thus, the film instantiates early on the hegemony of national territoriality and urban, multi-lingual middle-class citizenship. In spite of the potential in this moment to interrogate the territoriality of the nation, the film marks the border as productive of national belonging and as generative of the pleasurable identification of self and nation for Karan. Jalal also confesses to a similar recognition.

The original emergence of this present moment of sentimental national feeling is narrated by a jump cut to a flashback of Karan's youth. He is shown to be a dissolute, affluent, college-going young man whose everyday life revolves around movies, college, and DVDs. Both Romi and his parents repeatedly note that he does not have a *lakshya*—a goal—in his life: Unlike his friends, he does not know what he will do after college. The turning point for Karan appears in a scene which shows him waking up in his bed one morning and, still sleepy, switching on his television. The camera cuts to a close-up the television screen, which shows a clip of the Hollywood block-buster *Terminator* in which Arnold Schwarzenegger swaggers around with a machine gun, killing several presumable villains. The point of view then cuts back and forth, and the camera zooms in gradually, closer and closer to Karan's face as he sits in his bed, a spectator of the violence with increasing fascination and pleasure. The scene ends with a shot of Karan's face turn-ing into an inspired smile, and calling his college friend Parvesh, who had earlier mentioned his intention to join the army. Thus, the inspiration for Karan's initial turn to joining the Army is humorously shown to be an Arnold Schwarzenegger film, although in the next scene he informs Romi that he has applied to the Army because, "My country needs me." Of course, Romi does not know that this was Parvesh's explanatory statement that Karan has merely plagiarized. Here, and elsewhere, *Lakshya* critically suggests that patriotism is alien to this upper middle-class milieu; in fact, Karan's father forbids him from taking the admissions exam for entering the IMA, clearly uninterested in any national service or patriotism.

Two forces in the plot structurally contribute to Karan's transformation: his angst at his dominating and largely absent patriarchal father, who is constantly criticizing him and who asserts that Karan will fail; and his love for Romi, who breaks off their relationship when he quits the difficult IMA course after a few days and returns home. It is not patriotism, but alienation from his father as patriarch, and the loss of Romi as his love, that generate Karan's determination to prove himself through the Army. The scenes that follow track Karan's return to the IMA, followed by his training there and his transformation into a disciplined, purposeful man. These scenes of his training are accompanied by a background song whose refrain underscores that it is not patriotism, but the desire to prove himself as having a goal that transforms Karan:

> Yes, this is your path now
> You know it now
> Yes this is your dream now
> You have recognized it
> Now you have to prove
> Nothing can hinder you or stop you
> You will achieve your objective.

The repetition of the word "now" signals the personal transformation under-way, and the song as a whole contributes to the positivity attributed to the film's construction of national masculinity. Moreover, the gendered intertwin-ing of public and private, political and romantic in this film's representation is worth noting: for instance, on the day that Romi gets engaged to a friend, Rajeev, India is invaded by Pakistani intruders. Karan, now a Lieutenant, is called to the border to defend it. The loss of romantic intimacy mirrors the loss of national territory; in the end, when Karan and his regiment have heroically routed the intruders and won the battle, he returns and wins Romi back. The analogy between national victory and heterosexual coupledom, between the preservation of the state's territorial integrity and the realization of coupledom thus in part reproduces the nationalist discursive linking of woman and nation that I have discussed in earlier chapters.

The camerawork features many wide-angle panoramic shots of Kashmir and Ladakh's spectacular landscape, and of the ruins of monuments from the Mughal era in Delhi. Akhtar hired the German cinematographer Christopher Popp, and his camerawork metaphorically connects Karan's emotional geog-raphy with the national topography. For example, in one medium shot of Karan looking into the distance (at Romi, who is outside the frame, driving away from him), the smoldering walls of the one-storey buildings on fire behind him seem to echo his interior anguish at the repeated loss of Romi. Both *LOC Kargil* and *Lakshya* reproduce, at one level, essentialized repre-sentations of India and Pakistan as "enemies," as is typically the case in war films. Both have as their primary protagonists, Hindu and Sikh Indian men who end up performing masculine citizenship in normative modes compat-ible with the discourse of Indian nationalism. However, *Lakshya* is interest-ing for our purposes because it avoids the jingoistic tone of many of Dutta's films; it is a film about Indo–Pakistan war that also calls for peace, even as it critiques the apathetic Indian middle class' contemporary preoccupation with globalized consumption, with career advancement that precludes national service in the Army, and with the valorization of migration to the West for upward mobility. It also criticizes the hypocrisies of middle-class men who overtly profess women's rights but reject egalitarianism in their private lives—thus attempting a limited feminist gesture as well. The film is thus a critique of both Pakistani aggression and the corporate globalization of the Indian middle class towards an investment in nationality.

Lakshya's espousal of geopolitical peace marks both its inscription of how an unspeakable Partition haunts contemporary Indian life, as well its own ambiva-lence about its status as a "war epic." For example, fifteen minutes into the film, a scene shows Romi reading a news report about Vajpayee's famous visit to meet then Pakistani Prime Minister Nawaz Sharif in Lahore. The camera focuses on a close-up of a television monitor with two screens depicting live footage of the press conference given by Vajpayee in Lahore after talks which included the issue of Jammu and Kashmir. The camera then cuts to Romi, a newsreader at "Global News" who reports, "This is a historic day. Today, crores of citizens of India and Pakistan can hope that that this step will reduce the distances that have endured between these two nations to this day." The subtitles, however, translate the last part of that sentence as "the distance that has long divided us." An oblique reference to the antagonisms that have marked relations between these countries since Partition, and to the preceding scene depicting the no-man's-land on the border, the news report seems to foreshadow the impending failure of this hope.

Lakshya's utopian desire for peace is repeated at many other points in the film. In one scene, Romi arrives at the Army Hospital, apparently in Srinagar, to report on the shelling and bombardment on the border. When she recognizes one of the badly wounded soldiers, Abeer Saxena, being rushed into the hospital, she is shocked. The scene with Romi subsequently sitting in the hospital's reception area with her cameraman encapsulates Akhtar's ideological account of the war. A close-up of Romi—the elite, globalized, feminist citizen-subject—emphasizes her anguish. She says, "I don't understand. Why do wars happen? Why are people killed like this? When will people understand, that the solution to human problems is not war—it is peace?" During this dialogue, the camera cuts back and forth, from a medium shot of Romi to a frontal close-up shot of a soldier sitting near them, showing his increasingly taut emotional face as he overhears this speech. He has just heard news of his fellow soldier Abeer's death in the shelling on the Srinagar Leh highway. When she stops, the camera cuts to a medium shot of the soldier, who starts shouting at her, "Just shut up. Just shut up." Then, he walks over to her table, and says:

> Go give this lecture somewhere else. Get out. You want peace? We want peace too. What should we do? Stand by with folded hands and gift them our country on a platter? Peace! Capt. Abeer Saxena also wanted peace. He did not go and attack someone's country. It was his country that was attacked. The road that he lay dying on is a part of India, is Indian land. First go and have a look at his dead body. Then give these lectures. Go look at him!

The narrative here juxtaposes two different responses to Abeer's death: the perspective of the Indian soldier on the ground and that of an urban, alienated middle class. The male soldier's voice undercuts the female journalist's critique of war on humanist grounds, by foregrounding external aggression on India as the cause of war. His articulation lays the groundwork for the

representation of the Kargil war as inevitable self-defense to maintain territorial integrity, even as it is the soldier's voice that most earnestly and
movingly voices a desire for peace. Later in the film, after the first battle
in which many Indian soldiers have died, a scene depicts a conversation
between Brigadier Pritam Singh (Om Puri) and Karan, in which Singh says,
"Sometimes people explain to us that war is bad. I ask them, who knows this
better than a soldier?" Thus, in the midst of war, the call for geo-political
peace is reiterated in another soldier's voice.

Although the repetition of the call for peace between India and Pakistan
in *Lakshya* is part of its oblique discursive engagement with Partition, the
most explicit mention of Partition appears in the representation of Pakistani
Army officers discussing their plan to take control of the Siachen glacier, and
eventually, of Kashmir from India. The Pakistani Major Shabaaz Hamdani
(Parmeet Sethi) says, "That's what happened in 1948." He is referring to his
plan to stay for three to four days in the territory he has currently managed
to capture, as he has heard that "Western powers will broker a ceasefire"—
then, both sides will have to stay in their current positions and Pakistan will
have gained some territory. Shabaaz's comment historicizes the Kargil war
as a repetition of the 1947–48 war when Pakistan-backed intruders invaded
Kashmir as they were unhappy about Radcliffe's decision to include Kashmir
in India during Partition. Partition and the subsequent conflict around
Kashmir are here inscribed as a conflict between nation-states for power and
territory, rather than a Hindu–Muslim ethnic conflict.

Near the end, and before the penultimate battle, the film turns the globalized feminist subject, Romi of Global News, into a model nationalist subject
and, as happens in the conventional war film, a stereotypical woman waiting
at home for the returning soldier. Patriarchal authority is restored, the nation
is rescued and Karan reconciles with his father by admitting his earlier lack of
gratitude for all that his father gave him. The latter, now reformed himself, in
turn tells Karan how proud he is that his son is on the front. Thus, he represents Akhtar's critique of the un-patriotism of the "great Indian middle class"
when he asserts, "None of my business associates or friends has a son or a
brother out there. These people are all talk!" *Lakshya,* then, is an incitement
to perform a gendered, patriotic but de-ethnicized citizenship for the apolitical
Indian middle-class male; like Major Ram in *Main Hoon Na,* Karan performs
a Hindu, nationalized masculinity that represents the state's military power.
This is a different articulation of national masculinity than the suffering masculinity of Khushwant Singh's *Train to Pakistan,* or the later corrupt, militant
Hindu masculinity of Shiva in Rushdie's *Midnight's Children* discussed earlier.
This national masculinity is middle class, Hindu, wholesome, and invested in
the sincere performance of patriotic citizenship. Ashis Nandy has argued that,

in one sense, Indian popular cinema can be seen "as a struggle against the mas-
sified" and "as a battle over categories." This struggle emerges from the contest
between those who represent official state ideology and the global market, and
"those who by default represent the culturally confident but low brow multiculturalism in which the country has invested an important part of its genius
during the last hundred years or so, both as a means of survival in our times
and as a technology of self creation with an extended range of options."[24] This
understanding of the conflicted and contradictory nature of Indian popular
cinema resonates with Madhava Prasad and Lalitha Gopalan's suggestion,
mentioned earlier, to locate the fragments of utopian imaginings that inhabit
the popular cinematic text. *Lakshya's* critique of mass culture as it initially
saturates the everyday life of the dissolute, upper middle-class Karan and his
college friends, and its subsequent valorization of Karan's choice to become a
soldier in a multicultural Army—rather than immigrate to a comfortable diasporic life in the United States, as his brother Udesh and his friend Parvesh
choose—along with the film's problematization of the new Indian man's sexism
and patriarchal hypocrisy, marks this battle over categories and life practices in
the contemporary postcolonial public sphere.

Eventually, Karan's regiment wins the battle, and he successfully plants
the Indian flag on the peak. In the film's last scene, after the nation has been
protected and the battle has been won, the patriarchal authority of the heteronormative family is restored: Karan is shown as the prodigal son who now
returns to and is reconciled with his parents. His father then gestures him
towards Romi, who is waiting for him at a distance. When Romi asks him, "You
have achieved your goal, now what?" he replies, "Now I have one more goal:
you." By ending in this way, the film subsumes the story of the Kargil war into
the narrative of normative coupledom. The feminist citizen-subject remains
first the catalyst (as global) and then object(ive) as nation. The state's military
space becomes the site of masculine self-discovery and transformation into
purposeful citizen and desirable partner, even as it also facilitates the realization of middle-class and modern, global and national romantic coupledom.

Partition and its Abducted Women
in the Period Hindi Film

> I am the fruit of that season
> When the berries of Independence came into blossom.
> —Amrita Pritam, "The Scar"[25]

Thus far, this chapter has traced how the 1947 Partition reappears in
contemporary Bollywood cinema as both a past and also as generative of

contemporary conflict and war in India and South Asia. In the process, I have suggested that even as mainstream Bollywood cinema often reproduces dominant gendered and heteronormative discourses of Hindu–Muslim difference, citizenship and patriotism in the Indian public sphere, the heterogeneous cinematic texts I have taken up here across the genres mark an effort, albeit not always successful, to de-ethnicize citizenship and reinvent a way of being secular and national—a way of transcending the Hindu nationalist production of Hindu–Muslim ethnic difference as always already a site of conflict. In that sense, these films attempt to re-narrate and transcend Partition as national trauma and its legacy of Hindu–Muslim ethnic conflict, even though they leave unchallenged heteronormative rhetorics about gender identity and the privileging of masculine agency. I now turn to Chandra Prakash Dwivedi's *Pinjar* (The Skeleton; 2003) which, unlike previously discussed films, is a period film that recreates life in Punjab, India, between 1946 and 1948. *Pinjar* is based on the well-known Indian writer Amrita Pritam's Punjabi novel of the same name, originally written in 1950. Like Bapsi Sidhwa's *Cracking India*, it focuses on women's experience and questions about female subjectivity and agency during the 1947 Partition. In 2004, *Pinjar* was awarded a National Film Award, the Nargis Dutt Award for Best Feature Film on National Integration.

Pinjar is about the experience of a young woman, Puro (Urmila Matondkar), during the Partition. Born into a Sikh family at Gujranwala in Pakistan in 1919, Amrita Pritam was herself a Partition refugee who came to New Delhi in 1947 and lived there until she died in 2005. A prolific feminist writer until 2002, she wrote 24 novels, 15 collections of short stories and 23 volumes of poems, while also editing the monthly Punjabi magazine *Nagmani* for 35 years. She was the first woman to have received prestigious national awards like the Sahitya Akademi Award in 1956 and the Padma Shri (1969), as well as the Jnapith Award (1982) and the second highest national award, the Padma Vibhushan. Pritam is well known for her prolific writings from a feminist perspective about the violence of the 1947 Partition that she witnessed first-hand: her anguish over the human tragedy and, in particular, the suffering of Hindu, Muslim, and Sikh women marks much of her work in Hindi and Punjabi.

Set in Amritsar in August 1946, before the creation of Pakistan, the film *Pinjar* devolves upon the experiences of its protagonist, Puro, who is the daughter of the wealthy Mohanlal (Kulbushan Kharbanda) and his wife (Lillette Dubey) and is engaged to Ramchand (Sanjay Suri). When Puro is abducted by a Muslim farmer, Rashid (Manoj Bajpai), her life is transformed forever. Rashid falls in love with Puro and decides to marry her. At this, a desperate Puro escapes to her family, only to be told by her parents that she has been dishonored by her abduction and they cannot take her back. She tries to commit suicide but is rescued by and married to Rashid. Unhappy with this, she refuses to eat and becomes a pinjar (skeleton)— thus embodying the film's title and signifying her social and psychic loss of identity and belonging, as she is cast out of her family and community. Puro cannot forget Ramchand and her family, and she fantasizes of being re-united with them; she secretly wanders the area in search of them, and when Partition is announced, Puro and Ramchand end up meeting in a refugee camp, as he and his family are fleeing to India. In her conversation with Ramchand, she discovers that his sister Lajjo was married to her own brother, Trilok, and, currently pregnant, has been abducted by Muslims. Ramchand begs Puro to help find Lajjo, and a repentant Rashid promises to help Puro find her sister-in-law in order to redeem himself. Puro eventually finds and rescues the kidnapped Lajjo. When she escorts Lajjo to a Hindu camp in Lahore, Puro's brother urges her to return to India: He says that Ramchand is willing to accept and marry her, unlike many men of the time who rejected the abducted woman as dishonored. At this crucial juncture, faced with a choice between staying with Rashid and regaining her family, community, and identity, between going to India to marry the progressive Hindu Indian man Ramchand, and staying in Pakistan as a forcibly con-verted and renamed Muslim Hamida with Rashid, Puro realizes that she has been transformed. She has developed feelings for Rashid, and refuses to join her brother. But a dejected Rashid assumes she would choose to leave him and rejoin her family in India, and walks away from her. In the end, they are reunited, and *Pinjar* ends on a positive note that affirms Puro's agency as a proto-feminist subject to live with her Muslim abductor/hus-band in spite of their violent past.

This period melodrama thus focuses on the historical experience of the ethnicized abduction of women during Partition discussed earlier, in Chapter Three. However, *Pinjar's* feminist critique of the somatic and psychological violence suffered by women at the hands of men—both their abductors and in their own families—suggests that this ethnic violence emerges from the generalized patriarchal inequalities that saturate women's lives. It privileges Puro's point of view, and uses it to criticize the violence and oppression of women in colonial India. The melodramatic use of close-ups of her face serves to heighten the emotional effect of her suffering during Partition, as do the lyrics of the film songs filled with pathos. The film importantly represents Puro as subject to gendered ethnic violence due to a familial his-tory that goes back two generations. Rashid explains that he abducted her because he fell in love with her at first sight, but also because he had been goaded into doing so by his elders, in revenge for her uncle's abduction and rape of Rashid's aunt over three days, many years ago. *Pinjar* thus critically unveils in the hegemonic public sphere the subaltern history of suffering of Partition's abducted women, as a part of a longer history of sexual violence against women. Early on, when Puro escapes her captor after a few days and returns to her home, her parents reject her and ask her to leave. She begs her parents to take her back, but refusing, her weeping mother says, "If only you had died at birth." This is a critique of the violence of family that deconstructs the desirability of communal and familial belongings in which women are objectified as symbols of honor and exchange. As Puro notes in another scene, "It is a crime being born a girl in this country." Partition's specific forms of gendered and sexual ethnic violence are made visible in *Pinjar*, but they are tied to the systematic, patriarchal, everyday violence of women's social and political inequality and exploitation.

Of course, the film remains problematic insofar as it represents only the Muslim characters as agents of violence; unlike Bapsi Sidhwa's novel *Cracking India*, in which Hindus, Muslims and Sikhs are all depicted as agents of violence, in *Pinjar* for the most part the Hindu and Sikh characters are depicted as helpless victims of ethnic violence. The film's utopian space-clearing gesture, however, lies in the last scene. In the camp for Hindus in Lahore where Lajjo is being reunited with her husband and brother, Puro's brother urges her to join them: "If you want, Ramchand is ready to marry you. He understands your pain. You can start life anew. No one will know." Close-ups of Puro's face reveal her surprise at the suggestion, and then a close-up shot of her hand loosening his grip on her arm indicates her decision. She tells him, "Brother, Lajjo is coming back home. Assume Puro also came with her." Then she turns around and, finding Rashid absent, panics. Screaming "Rashid, Rashid," she runs helter-skelter in the crowded neighborhood in desperate search of him. This search is filmed in slow motion and emphasizes her anguish. When she finds him, he is weeping and says, "Puro, go back to your country. Go back to your people." The film ends with her refusal of this articulation of nationality and belonging: "This is my home now, Rashid, your home is my home." The film thus ends with a frontal shot of Puro and Rashid standing together as a reunited couple, watching the bus take her relatives away to India. This scene emphasizes their togetherness and foregrounds their deep intimacy through a close-up of the two standing together with Rashid's arm around Puro, thus legitimating their inter-ethnic coupledom.

Thus Puro, as an agentive subject, makes the non-normative choice to refuse the offer of inclusion and interpellation into family, community and nation that was once denied to her. Refusing the nation—both Indian and Pakistani—*Pinjar*'s once Hindu, feminist protagonist embodies and asserts

her choice of the abductor/Pakistani Muslim man as life partner. Its denouement overturns the title's suggestion that abduction, rape or ethnic violence
constitutes death for the female social subject. By uncovering the violence of
the institution of family and the ambivalences of human attachments in the
everyday life of abducted women, *Pinjar* legitimizes the choice of inter-ethnic
coupledom that originated in ethnic violence. Rashid and Puro/Hamida's
inter-ethnic love is not heroicized or sentimentalized in *Pinjar*'s account as
an ideal performance of sentimental secularism: It is, however, materialized,
made visible and legitimated in this non-nationalist effort to memorialize a
traumatic South Asian history of Partition violence against women.

Another important period melodrama about the Partition that became a
huge box-office success when it was released in 2001 is Anil Sharma's *Gadar:
Ek Prem Katha* (*Revolt: A Love Story*). Like *Pinjar*, it is set in 1947 and recreates the by-now legendary story of Buta Singh mentioned in Chapter Two.
The legend is based in the reportedly true story—also described by Urvashi
Butalia—of a Sikh man who rescues a Muslim woman from imminent rape,
when she is separated from her family in ethnic riots in 1947.[26] They are
eventually married, only to be separated when India and Pakistan start repa-
triating abducted women based on ethnicity. In *Gadar*, this is narrativized as
a love story between a Sikh working-class truck driver, Tara Singh (Sunny
Deol), who rescues the aristocratic Muslim woman Sakina (Amisha Patel)
from a mob of Hindu and Sikh men, who are about to abduct and rape her,
after she is separated from her family fleeing anti-Muslim riots in Amritsar.
Over time, Tara and Sakina fall in love, marry and have a son. However, a few
years later, they are separated when Sakina accidentally discovers that her
parents, who fled India, are alive and goes to Pakistan to meet her father—
now the mayor of Lahore, Pakistan. Her parents attempt to erase her life with
Tara Singh and to reintegrate her into their family by arranging her marriage
with a Pakistani Muslim man. Unlike the story of Buta Singh, who dies pin-
ing for his beloved, *Gadar* ends with the heroic rescue of Sakina from her
family of origin, with her father represented as the archvillain of the plot.

In *Gadar*, Tara Singh's heroicized Sikh Indian masculinity is consis-
tently coded as patriotic, honorable, and faultless. Reproducing the popular
representation of Sikh men as the hyper-masculine, militant arm of Hindu
India, Tara Singh is simplistically contrasted with the always already violent,
brutal, sword- and gun-wielding Pakistani masculinity of Sakina's father and
brothers. The latter spout much anti-Indian rhetoric, and constantly attempt
to humiliate and kill Tara Singh and forcibly keep Sakina in Pakistan. Also
a melodramatic period film like *Pinjar*, *Gadar* unfortunately reinscribes the
most dangerous, essentialized, and jingoistic representations of Pakistanis
and Muslims as the evil and inferior "other" in the Indian public sphere.

As one of India's leading newspapers, *The Hindu,* reported in its review, "A more incendiary film about relations between the two countries has probably never been made before in India." It further asserted that a "more nauseating film that stokes contempt among Indians for all things Pakistani (and in very thinly veiled terms for all things Islamic as well) has probably never before been screened in India. And this is a huge success at the box office."[27] Many Islamic groups as well as Muslim politicians in India protested and criticized *Gadar* when it was released for its stereotypical, negative and offensive representation of Muslim men and women. Simultaneously, *Gadar's* representation of heroic Sikh masculinity needs to be problematized. In her ethnography of Govind Nihalani's popular Partition-based television series *Tamas/Darkness* (based on Bhisham Sahni's eponymous novel), telecast on Indian national television in the late eighties, Purnima Mankekar has pointed to the elision of anti-Sikh violence in 1984 in the narratives about Partition and ethnic violence constructed by the Hindu viewers she interviewed.[28] This elision of ethnic violence against Sikhs in popular accounts of national history and ethnic belonging, which contradictorily accompanies the hegemonic deployment of the Sikh male body as virile, national masculinity in Indian nationalist discourse, marks one of the subaltern histories of Sikh subjectivity that bears re-examining in the narration of nation and belonging in India.

Both *Pinjar* and *Gadar* are period films that return to the gendered experience of Partition violence and displacement, and evince what Ashis Nandy has called "memories of a peasant or rural past serving as a 'pastoral' paradise from which it [the Indian lower middle-class] has been banished."[29] However, while *Pinjar* attempts to track from a humanist perspective the everyday ambivalences and the historical complexities of those who suffered and survived Partition violence, *Gadar* deploys the trope of inter-ethnic romance in stereotypical and troubling ways. For one, it relies on a binary opposition between the Indian and Pakistani, according to which all Pakistani male characters are homogenously and negatively represented as villains, comics or cowards. In contrast, the Muslim female protagonist, Sakina, represents an idealized minority femininity insofar as she voluntarily performs a prescribed hegemonic "secularism" through the assimilationist repetition of both Muslim and Sikh religious practices. For example, Sakina often does namaaz (prays) with sindhoor in her hair; the sindhoor or red powder marked in her hair symbolizes her status as a Sikh wife while she performs her Islamic ethnicity. In contrast, the dominant stereotypical representation of militant Sikh masculinity in the working-class Sikh Tara is mobilized to embody and instigate a jingoistic, hyper-masculinist Indian nationalism. This nationalism is based on the demonization of Muslims and Pakistanis as the menacing, unregenerate and mercenary "other" that threatens the Indian state from within and without—a demonization that also resonates with contemporary post-September 11 discourses about Islam that increasingly mark Euro-American public spheres.

In *Pinjar*, as in other Partition representations like Khushwant Singh's *Train to Pakistan* and Bapsi Sidhwa's *Cracking India* discussed in previous chapters, inter-ethnic romance often represents national secularism. However, inter-ethnic love is not posited in *Gadar* as an imagined solution to the problem of ethnic difference and international conflict, unlike many of the literary and film texts discussed earlier. Instead, it is used to reproduce a dominant, heterosexual, Hindu, Indian masculine power into which the both Muslim and Sikh difference is assimilated, and to assert a vitriolic anti-Pakistan discourse about the superiority of India and Indians over Pakistan and its citizens. For example, dialogues like this one abound in the second half of the film which stages the fight between the super-heroic Tara Singh and Pakistani policemen and army men over Sakina: "A son is the creation of his father. Thus, India is the father of Pakistan." Later, when Sakina's father, who is also the mayor of Lahore, falls to his knees and begs forgiveness from Tara Singh, his humiliation as patriarch and state representative symbolizes the complete subjugation of Pakistan, both intimately familial and political-national. The word "gadar" means "revolution," but it can also mean "rebellion"; the film claims for its dangerous, masculinist, nationalist war-mongering a positivity that must be challenged and critiqued, especially given its popularity in the Indian public sphere.

(In)Conclusion: Partition and Mass Media

My discussion of the emergence of Partition in contemporary Bollywood cinema here is by no means exhaustive; for example, I have not discussed other films that refract the tragedy of Partition and ethnic nationalism through the trials of inter-ethnic romance, like J. P. Dutta's *Refugee* (2000) or Mani Ratnam's *Bombay* (1995). Like *Veer Zaara*, *Refugee* is also about the tribulations of two lovers, Indian and Pakistani, separated by the Indo–Pak border. However, in Dutta's much-criticized plot, the two lovers manage, through an unlikely series of character transformations of the villains, to get united on the border. The Pakistani Muslim heroine Naaz (Kareena Kapoor) gives birth to their hybrid child on the no-man's-land between India and Pakistan. Parallel to this popular figuring of tragic inter-ethnic coupledom in Hindi cinema is the proliferation of films in which Muslim masculinity constitutes an ambivalently charged sign through which a range of post-Partition questions about gender, ethnicity and equal citizenship are negotiated. Although not discussed in detail here, it bears examining further how Hindi cinema often depicts the Muslim male subject as a villain or terrorist alienated from national belonging. In most such films, the non-Indian Muslim male is destroyed, while the Indian Muslim male figure is always redeemed, reformed and returned to the nation—albeit often as a dead citizen. For example, Kunal Kohli's *Fanaa* (*Destruction*; 2006) is a box-office hit about a Kashmiri Muslim, Rehan (Aamir Khan), who executes terrorist attacks in India but is reformed in the end through his love for the blind Kashmiri Muslim woman, Zooni (Kajol). However, in spite of his redemption, his potent Muslim masculinity coded as terrorist must be destroyed in the end to save the nation-state, and it is Zooni who performs patriotic citizenship when she kills him—thus sacrificing love and coupledom for the nation. Shoojit Sircar's Kashmir-based inter-ethnic romance *Yahaan* (*Here*; 2005) is a rare contemporary representation that realizes on screen the inter-ethnic coupledom of its protagonists. It represents the hero as a Hindu Indian Army soldier in love with the Kashmiri Muslim heroine Adaa. Adaa's brother, however, is a discontent, anti-state terrorist who is only reformed when he realizes the error of his ways in the end. Another cinematic inscription of the Partition as screen-memory that addresses the question of Muslim minoritization and nationality in postcolonial India is John Mathew Mathan's film *Sarfarosh* (*Fervour*). *Sarfarosh* (1999) deals with cross-border terrorism in India and dramatizes Partition's effects on contemporary minority national belonging. It represents good Muslim masculinity in the character Inspector Salim (Mukesh Rishi) who critiques the popular demonization of Muslims as third column in India. He is contrasted to the evil Pakistani Muslim masculinity of the villain, Gulfam Hasan (Naseeruddin Shah), who is a Partition refugee who migrated to India from Pakistan. A poet and ghazal singer, Hasan foments terrorism in India as an undercover ISI agent, but is ultimately betrayed by his own country because he is only a "Mohajir." Through the heroic agency of the Hindu hero ACP Ajay (Aamir Khan), Gulfam is killed while Salim is folded back into nationalist belonging in the narrative's space of multicultural India.

I have sought to uncover here the shape of mainstream filmic imagining of de-ethnicized citizenship, of Partition as a discourse about gendered ethnic belongings, and of normative, nationalized coupledom in the postcolonial public sphere. The preceding chapters chapters showed how the literary and cinematic representations of the early national period deploy the ordinary citizen—as suffering Sikh peasant, self-sacrificing refugee, and abducted woman—to figure the violence of Partition in an agonistic critique of the nation-state and its political elite. In contrast, in contemporary Bollywood films, the protagonist who battles Partition's legacy of ethnic conflict, terror, and war is often identified with the nation-state, as a representative of its institutions: the Army (*Lakshya* and *Main Hoon Na*), the Air Force (*Veer-Zaara*), the police (*Sarfarosh*). Insofar as the films I have discussed here are part of a national cinema that is global in reach, they evince dominant re-imaginings of the meanings of secularism and national belonging. Their frag-mentary, utopian fantasies of peace and gender equality in the postcolonial state, insofar as they are articulated with heterosexual coupledom and nor-mative citizenship, must be complicated if we are to interrogate the violence of nationalism in the formation of belonging. Bollywood cinema has narrativ-ized the 1947 Partition both as a violent historical event to be remembered, recreated and memorialized in the public sphere, and as a metaphor for the divisions around ethnic identity and national belonging that increasingly violently mark political life in the subcontinent. Of course, this return to the history of partition in Bollywood cinema is not isolated; if the diaspora has seen the re-emergence of Partition in literary and historiographical discourse since the eighties, in the subcontinent this has occurred not only in film but also in mass media.

Thus, what I leave unfinished here is the conversation about the link-ages between the aesthetic negotiation of partition and ethnic citizenship in Bollywood cinema with its global circulation, on one hand, and its rep-resentation in (now also globalized) Indian television on the other. After all, it was in the eighties that Doordarshan, the national and only television channel in India at the time, telecast Govind Nihalani's three-part televi-sion series *Tamas* and Ramesh Sippy's popular and ground-breaking serial drama *Buniyaad*. *Tamas* was about four days of ethnic riots among Hindus, Muslims and Sikhs in 1947 Pakistan, while *Buniyaad* was about the experi-ences of Hindu Partition refugees in Delhi from Lahore. From the 1980s onwards, official state policy that conceived of television as a technology to promote socialist development was changed; Anjali Monteiro has noted how the state's introduction of commercial sponsorship of Doordarshan serials in 1980 renewed entertainment programming which "made possible the entry of the state into the familial space."[30] Nihalani's five-hour film—telecast as a serial—was based on Bhisham Sahni's novel *Tamas*, which won Sahni the national Sahitya Akademi award in 1975. Bhisham Sahni was the younger brother of the esteemed actor Balraj Sahni, who played the protagonist Salim Mirza in M. S. Sathyu's film *Garam Hawa*. From a Lahore-based family that was forced to migrate to India following the Partition, both Balraj and Bhisham Sahni went on to create powerful socialist texts in lit-erature and cinema that challenged the politics of nationalism and critiqued ethnic discrimination in India. It is notable that Bhisham Sahni wrote the novel about Partition violence after witnessing the Hindu–Muslim riots of Bhiwandi in Bombay in 1970 in which 142 Muslims and 20 Hindus were killed.[31] Ravikant has already mapped the conflicted reception of *Tamas*—its popular viewership of 3.5 crore people, and the protests by right-wing Hindu organizations like the VHP, Bajrang Dal and RSS following the telecast. He points out that it was "widely acclaimed by critics as a landmark . . . and an eye-opening account that helped understand what had hitherto remained by and large comprehensible."[32] Yet, uncovering how Bhisham Sahni and Govind Nihalani received death threats at this time, Ravikant notes that "[t]he BJP, together with its mass fronts, carried out violent demonstrations at various Doordarshan Centers in Punjab, Delhi, and Bombay, demanding the serial to be taken off air." This conflict-ridden popular reception illuminates the politics of the aesthetic narration of the Partition for contemporary India; even as the serial was telecast by a state institution as a pedagogical vehicle for ethnic harmony, it was challenged in court by political parties like the Shiv Sena for "distorting history."[33]

Similarly, *Buniyaad*, now called India's first soap opera, focused on the lives of a Hindu family rendered refugees in Delhi by the Partition and was a landmark TV serial that ran for 104 episodes at a stretch in the late eighties. Produced by G. P. Sippy, himself a Sindhi migrant from Pakistan displaced by the Partition, and directed by his son Ramesh Sippy, *Buniyaad* made Indian television history in its sheer popularity. Its run ended only because Doordarshan refused to renew its contract for another 104 episodes, claiming it was against policy. *Buniyaad* recently enjoyed a brief revival in 2006, when it was re-telecast in the subcontinent and internationally (including the United States) via Dish Network on the privately owned cable channel Sahara-One. That these TV serials like *Tamas* and *Buniyaad* about the Partition experience of violence and displacement had the tremendous mass popularity they had, and were telecast on the state-controlled channel Doordarshan alongside the immensely successful serializations of Hindu mythological epic texts like *Mahabharat* and *Ramayana* suggestively indicates the contradictory pulls and popular imperatives of representing religion, history and/in the Indian nation in the late national public sphere.

Mahabharat was produced by B. R. Chopra, and was immensely popular not only in India from 1988–1990, but also in the diaspora: for example, it was shown with subtitles on BBC in the U.K. to a record afternoon audience of five million. The tremendously popular weekly serial *Ramayana* was made by Ramanand Sagar, who, like Chopra and Sippy, was from Lahore and fled to India during the Partition period. Also a writer—his 1948 novel *Aur Insaan Mar Gaya* (And Humanity Died) was about the violence and suffering of Partition—Sagar launched *Ramayana* in January 1987, and managed to capture forty million viewers until it ended in 1990. The state-sponsored televising of these religious narratives played into the project of "Hindutva"

or Hindu nationalism; indeed, as Arvind Rajagopal has shown in his study of
the impact of the serial *Ramayana* on Indian society in the late eighties, the
epic serial contributed to the mass mobilization of support for Hindu nationalism, which culminated in the 1992 demolition of the Babri Masjid in India
by the BJP-RSS combine, and country-wide ethnic violence between Hindus
and Muslims thereafter that took thousands of lives.[34] Vijay Mishra has
analyzed the global reach of this serial, and its contribution to the emergent
political culture of Hindutva. He argues that the "Ramayana, in all its forms,
signified the return of the repressed notion of *batvara* or partition for the
Hindu, not as a Freudian negation but as a projection of a dangerously fascist
idealism."[35] That Chopra's serial *Mahabharat*—with English subtitles—is
now available for consumption in the subcontinent and diaspora through
Rajshri's website for free streaming and paid downloads on PCs and other
broadband-enabled devices, signals the ethnic mobilization of new media
in the transnational public sphere. Clearly, then, in the Indian context, the
state's popular humanist memorialization of partition's suffering—its gendered ethnic violence, its displacement and its refugees—through popular
television serials like *Tamas* and *Buniyaad* could not abet the repetition of
Hindu–Muslim ethnic violence, cultural and physical, unleashed by Hindu
nationalist politics in the nineties. But its mass-media memorialization, when
taken with the increasing narrative space given to the role of mass media in
the Bollywood films I have discussed here, speaks to the utopian potentialities as well as the dangers of the Internet and the vehicles of visual culture in
the material, discursive production of nations, violence, and belongings.

6

Provincializing the Nation

State Violence and Transnational Belongings in the Diaspora

also pre-parithion

T he preceding chapters have noted how the heterogeneous and contradictory history of Partition reveals the violence of postcolonial
nations and nationalisms and the limits of modern mappings of
nationality, citizenship and belonging. While the journey back to their
homes that Partition refugees thought they would make once the ethnic violence of Partition abated never materialized, the idea or fantasy of "returning
home" dominates the representation of migrants and refugees in transnational public spheres today. In the U.S. national public sphere for example,
journalistic accounts of diverse global scenes of displacement evince this
focus in their representations. A *New York Times* report on Sri Lankan
tsunami refugees asserts about one, "Mr. Selvam, for one, had made up his
mind: There was no place like home, even if home no longer existed."[1] This
report simultaneously recognizes the disappearance of material and psychic
home-liness, and reproduces the fetishization of the migrant's "return home"
in popular discourse. Another news investigation about a Congolese refugee
of ethnic violence reiterates this production of the migrant/refugee's desire
to "return home": "Going back one day is necessary, Ms. Dhikpala . . . said,
to ensure proper burials for the dead. Another woman who fled with Ms.
Dhikpala is returning right away."[2] As these accounts show, in the dominant
public sphere, refugees from diverse historical and geopolitical contexts are
often described as desiring the return "home." Home is represented as the
original physical location of their huts/houses, and the national territory in
which those huts/houses were located. This chapter is a meditation on the

possibilities and violence of nationalist notions of "home" and belonging, through the cultural representation of transnational migrations. Moving from a consideration of the aesthetics and politics of Partition in South Asia, this concluding chapter takes the journey of this book to a broad reconsideration of the hegemony of the nation in an era of globalization, and ends at the particular location of the imperial United States, or what Inderpal Grewal calls "Transnational America."[3] Through a range of postcolonial and diasporic voices—on Partition, state violence and racial dispossession—I will show that the forms of gendered migrations they depict articulate a postcolonial critique of citizenship and the hegemony of the nation-state, in the context of both anti-colonial nationalism and globalization. Scholars across the humanities and social sciences, like Gayatri Chakravorty Spivak, Jacqueline Bhabha and Saskia Sassen, have problematized the feminization of globalization and the transnational circuits of economic and political displacements for women and children in the contemporary era.[4] My desire is that this chapter will contribute to nascent conversations between the fields of Postcolonial Studies and Asian American Studies, by examining Partition in relation to other contemporary scenes of violence and displacement, through South Asian and South Asian American voices in the diaspora.

This chapter thus develops the engagement of postcolonial studies, diaspora and ethnic American studies implied in earlier chapters of the book by taking Dipesh Chrakrabarty's urgent call to provincialize Europe to the problem of the hegemony of nationalism. I am suggesting that the history of Partition reverberates and resonates today for both the contemporary national life of the Indian subcontinent, in which violence around ethnicity and belonging has become a fact of daily life, as well as for diasporic and immigrant South Asians in North America, for whom the experience of migration also raises questions about ethnic identity, history, racial discrimination, and gendered citizenship—especially after the terrorist attacks of September 11, 2001. Through diverse diasporic South Asian literary texts like Amitav Ghosh's *The Shadow Lines*, Jhumpa Lahiri's *The Interpreter of Maladies*, Salman Rushdie's *Shalimar, the Clown*, and Michael Ondaatje's *Anil's Ghost* and cinematic inscriptions of post-September 11 minority experiences, I propose, among other things, that the violent emergence and ascendancy of ethnicity as a dominant and gendered technology of nationality is not only a feature of Indian history, or indeed of postcolonial histories, but of national modernities across the world. Yet, in the diasporic inflections of ethnic (im)migrant experience, we can locate the minor voices that struggle to articulate new, non-oppressive and non-national modes of belonging and community. Lisa Lowe and Kandice Chuh have pointed out how Asian American studies, for a long time, have tended to devolve upon Asian

American claims of American national belonging, upon a desire for America as "home."[5] As the imperial reach of the United States continues to grow globally, what would it mean to rethink this dominant discourse of the nation as home—in America and elsewhere? This chapter engages the specific articulation of America as home in ethnic American cultural representations. Simultaneously, it maps the persistent critique of the nation-state's violent agency in contemporary formations of belonging that join diaspora and sub-continent, in order to provincialize the nation-form, and indeed to provincial-ize America. Dipesh Chakrabarty has suggested that to provincialize Europe "is to see the modern as inevitably contested, to write over the given and privileged narratives of citizenship other narratives of human connections that draw sustenance from dreamed-up pasts and futures where collectivi-ties are defined neither by the rituals of citizenship, nor by the nightmare of 'tradition' that 'modernity' creates." Chakrabarty admits that "there are of course, no (infra)structural sites where such dreams could lodge themselves." Yet, he argues, "they will recur, so long as the dreams of citizenship and the nation-state dominate our narratives of historical transition, for these dreams are what the modern represses in order to be."[6] What I am suggesting here is that in the contemporary moment, where the United States has replaced Europe as an imperial power, engaging this postcolonial project of interrogat-ing the hegemonic national modern with the production of the "American" in ethnic American Studies is both imperative and urgent. It can enable us to provincialize America and the pervasive discriminatory narratives of raced citizenship that underlie its global-imperial rhetorics of "democracy." In an age of globalization, it is through such an engagement of postcolonial thought and Asian American studies that we can locate a critical, transnational poli-tics of optimistic struggle in the face of the violences that ravage our present and possible futures.

I take "globalization" to refer, as Saskia Sassen and Arjun Appadurai have suggested, to the expansion of economic globalization beyond the boundaries of nation-states, and the attendant intensification and reorganization of the "flows" of people, commodities, cultural texts and capital across the globe in the last twenty to thirty years.[7] As Sassen recently also wrote, "Globalization has not only facilitated the global flows of capital, goods, information, and business people. It has also facilitated a variety of other entanglements."[8] September 11, 2001, in New York, increasing ethnic violence in South Asia and Africa, and the rhetoric and politics of terror are only some of these entanglements. At this time, it also bears remembering that the globaliza-tion of culture is racially marked; racial or ethnic identities are engendered, sustained, affected by, and performed not simply through the local, but also by the transnational flows of goods, capital, and ideas. This is important because the resurgence of ethnic nationalisms and ethnic violence around the world at a time when it is increasingly becoming globalized is no coincidence. Fundamentalism, grounded in the rhetorics of authenticity, is as much a product of European modernity as of globalization. Given these intensified, global cultural, economic, and political flows, given this transformation of transnational topographies and communities through immigration and new spatial formations, how do we limn the intricate relationships among gender, ethnicity and nationality? How do we come to unravel what Tom Holt has called the "narratives of contradiction and incoherence"[9] that mark contemporary ethnic/racial formations, and in more complex ways—in relation to other forms of social difference and discrimination? Toward provincializing the nation through an interrogation of American national modernity and its discourses of citizenship for the raced minority subject, I see postcolonial critique as an analytic that illuminates the transnational, historical production of racial, ethnic, and gendered belonging; it makes imperative a self-reflexive reconsideration of the nationalist investments of Asian American and race studies more generally, in thinking political belonging and change.

Amritjit Singh and Peter Schmidt have similarly suggested that both U.S. ethnic studies and postcolonial studies have much to teach other, and indeed, "are best engaged together" insofar as they share a new emphasis on borders paradigms, the transnational or diasporic, "whiteness" studies and feminist analysis.[10] In particular, they call for the resituating of U.S. minority politics "within the context of the new cultural politics of difference operating globalization theory," especially in its determination of "discourses defining 'human rights' and 'the global economy.'" Arguing for a critique of how U.S. elites seek "to dominate not just narratives of the proper forms of ethnicity in 'American' but also the proper forms of world citizenship for both individuals and nations," Singh and Schmidt remind us that "[w]hatever the counter-narratives to dominant current globalization theories are called— Spivak's 'transnational cultural studies,' Appadurai's 'diasporic public spheres' and 'disjunctive cultural flows,' San Juan's 'new dialogic alliances,' Jan Mohamed's 'specular border intellectuals,' Lowe's 'immigrant acts,' etc.—the contributions of both the U.S. borders studies and the postcolonial studies fields should prove central."[11] The literature and film addressed here represent transnational migration and the violence of the nation-state through the experience of raced and gendered minor subjects in the decolonized nation and its displaced diasporas. In the process, they illuminate the contours of gendered and racialized citizenship and the limits of transnational rhetorics of human rights and national "homeliness." This chapter begins with exploring the postcolonial literary representations that provincialize the hegemony of nationalist imaginings, unveil the violence of the postcolonial state in refugee experience, and posit alternative modes of envisioning community, belonging and politics. It concludes with the diasporic project of North American ethnic literatures—through South Asian voices—to provincialize America through the uncovering of national violence and its failures for those who are minoritized by class, race, ethnicity and gender, and through the affirmation of transnational solidarities.

Women, Exile, and National Belonging

In the face of the ubiquity of the nation as a way of imagining community in the world today, Ghosh's second novel, *The Shadow Lines,* brings to the fore two generations of migrant women—the narrator's grandmother, Tha'ama, and cousin, Ila—who become the figures through which different kinds of promises of nationality and migration rendered common by nationalism and globalization are belied.[12] *The Shadow Lines* focuses on the unnamed middle-class, Bengali Hindu narrator's family in Calcutta and Dhaka, and on their connection with an English family in London, spanning the period from the thirties to the present. The relationship between Tha'ama (who is very fond of the narrator), and her grand-niece Ila (with whom the narrator is in love) figures the conflict between anti-colonial nationalism and migrant cosmopolitanism, even as it makes visible the limits and failures of both for these middle-class, female citizens of India and the U.K. Tha'ama grows up in the tumultuous days of the Indian freedom struggle in Dhaka and is fiercely nationalist: She reveals to the narrator that she had once dreamed of joining the Bengali revolutionaries who struggled to overthrow the mantle of colonial oppression, and she would have readily killed a British officer for freedom. Having grown up in Dhaka and living in Burma where her husband works, she migrates to Calcutta in the thirties, when he suddenly dies. A relative arranges a job for her to teach in a school there, and she single-handedly raises her children, proudly refusing all help from family and friends. Fervently patriotic, she has ideologically embraced the anti-colonial nationalism in whose revolutionary activities she could not directly participate because she is a woman.

Ila is the privileged daughter of a diplomat and has grown up in different parts of the world; she self-consciously performs an elite cosmopolitanism that dismisses the "importance" of third-world places like India in world history. Brought up in international schools, having visited India in the summer holidays, she decides to study and live in England. Her reason for migrating to England becomes evident to the narrator one summer, when there is a confrontation between Ila and her cousin Robi (with the narrator looking on) at a discotheque in Calcutta. Having cajoled them into going to the disco, Ila is horrified when Robi tells her that she cannot dance with any men there. As she defiantly begins to dance on the dance floor with a stranger, Robi hits the stranger and drags Ila out of the disco, saying that "girls don't behave like that here. . . . [I]t's our culture." Furious and crying, Ila shouts at the narrator, "Do you see now why I've chosen to live in London? Do you see? It's only because I want to be free. . . . Free of your bloody culture and free of all of you" (87). If the narrator understands and sympathizes with Ila's desire to be free of the violent machismo and oppression of Indian patriarchal gender relations that restrict her, his grandmother doesn't. Tha'ama's fierce patriotism, born from a desire to be free of British colonial subjection, scoffs at Ila's desire: "It's not freedom she wants. . . . She wants to be left alone to do what she pleases; that's all any whore would want. She'll find it easily enough over there; that's what those places have to offer. But that is not what it means to be free" (88). As the narrator realizes, his grandmother has nothing but contempt for "freedom that could be bought for the price of an air ticket. For she too had once wanted to be free: she had dreamt of killing for her freedom" (87). This contestation over the legitimacy of conceptions of freedom—the grandmother's notion of freedom as liberty from colonial subjection, which refuses Ila's internal criticism of gendered oppression—reveals that for both, freedom is imagined as accessed through the nation or migration. In this contest over the meaning of freedom, Ghosh signals to us the translational and transnational space in which, as Homi Bhabha has suggested, "culture becomes a problem": This is "the point at which there is a loss of meaning in the contestation and articulation of everyday life, between classes, genders, races, nations" and generations, one might add.[13]

In the novel, neither Tha'ama's dreams of a middle-class citizenship and national belonging nor Ila's dreams of being free of patriarchal "culture" are realized. Ila escapes Robi's machismo, only to end up marrying her English childhood crush, Nick Price, who is unemployed and depends on her father's wealth financially, and who (shortly after their honeymoon) openly admits to her that he is unfaithful. He tells her that he is simultaneously involved with her, an Indonesian, and a woman from Martinique, because "he just likes a bit of variety . . . it's his way of traveling" (185). Treated as an embodiment of the country and culture she sought to escape by the orientalist Nick, she realizes that the squalor of Robi's patriarchal behavior is mirrored in Nick's sexist and racist exoticization, infidelity and exploitation of her: It is "part too of the free world she had tried to build for herself" (187). The freedom from patriarchal oppression that Ila had imagined for herself when she fled India and migrated to the First World is never realized. Exoticized and sexually objectified as the racial "other," desperate for the love of a man who abuses her, Ila accepts Nick's psychic, physical, and economic exploitation and refuses to leave him, ostensibly because she loves him. Thus, Ila is unable to make either nation—India or England—a home in the world for herself. Other in her desire—to be uncontrolled by men in the name of culture or race and to be respected as an equal in both patriarchal nations—she remains minor to both nation-spaces, embodying a middle-class cosmopolitanism in exile, limited by her racial and gender difference.

Similarly, Tha'ama's desire for a national community free from British subjection culminates in the failure of the middle-class life she had envisioned for herself, because of the Partition of 1947: Now her place of birth had come to be "so messily at odds" with her nationality. Separated from her home and family in Dhaka, which is now in East Pakistan, displaced to Calcutta through the Partition that brought the postcolonial freedom she had fervently hoped for, Tha'ama has "no home but in memory" (190). When she tells the narrator that Ila has no right to live in England, for she has not earned the right to be there with blood, as others who had lived there over the generations had, the narrator insists that "she was not a fascist [as Ila had interpreted her remarks to be], she was only a modern middle-class woman—though not wholly, for she would not permit herself the deceptions that make up the fantasy world of that kind of person" (77). Tha'ama's middle-class fantasy of the postcolonial state as a source of respect, unified community, and belonging falls apart: "All she wanted was a middle-class life in which, like middle classes the world over, she would thrive believing in the unity of nationhood and territory, of self-respect and national power; that was all she wanted—a modern middle-class life, a small thing, that history had denied her in its fullness and for which she could never forgive it" (77). For Tha'ama, her forced migration from her place of birth Dhaka by Partition, the internal religious and regional conflicts between "Muslim or Hindu, Bengali or Punjabi" that fracture the fabric of her free country and, finally, the ethnic violence that claims her nephew Tridib's life in Dhaka all embody the violent failure of her dream of freedom.

Tha'ama's vision of freedom from colonial rule also included a vision of a national citizenship that articulated homeliness and a sense of belonging. Postcolonial nationality in South Asia, riven as it was by ethnic hostility and regionalist movements after Partition, fails to realize the promise of national citizenship and unity. The 1947 Partition not only separates Tha'ama from her family and her childhood home, but its legacy of violence fails to replace that loss with national unity and belonging that might transcend communal and regional identity. Bishnupriya Ghosh argues that "Women often find themselves in contextually marginal positions which distance them from investments in national interests, and enable them to critique or interrogate both conceptions of nation and the power of the nation-state."[14] However, in *The Shadow Lines*, female marginality is intimately linked to migrant investments in the nation form. It is precisely Tha'ama's wholehearted invest-ment in nationality, and Ghosh's skillful depiction of its disjunction from her middle-class everyday life, that becomes a powerful indictment of the politics and power of nationalism. Tha'ama's migrant nationalism is thus mir-rored in Ila's migration to England; both emerge from a desire for freedom. Simultaneously, the class-marked conception of "refugee" that circulated in the early national period in India, identified in Chapter Four, is evinced: When the narrator's father reminds Th'ama that as migrants from Dhaka they were once refugees in India, she refuses the appellation "refugee"—for her, the refugee is the "other" who is poor and who lives in filthy hutments and shanty towns that scar the Calcutta landscape.

Ghosh's fiction illuminates the urgency of provincializing the univer-sality of the nation as ideal community, through the representations of its material and psychological abjection of women's bodies and women's lives. Thus, he criticizes the failures of nationalism and global migration for minor subjects. Tha'ama and Ila's middle-class migrant desires for national belong-ing are belied by the realities of gender oppression and ethnic conflict in postcolonial history. For Ghosh, there are no easy answers to the different kinds of violence endured by these women who leave their homes in search of newness—where that newness named "freedom" is variously defined as middle-class community or as racial and gender equality. What he does insist on, however, is the need to question the myths of both nationalism and glo-balization and to witness their violence.

If Salman Rushdie's *Midnight's Children* allegorizes national fragmenta-tion through the violence inflicted upon the masculine citizen's body, *The Shadow Lines* interrogates nationalism not only through Tha'ama, but also through the testimony of riot violence suffered by the Bengali middle-class male body. The novel underscores the fragility of Partition's borders between nations as etched out in maps, and of the frontiers policed by nation-states that separate people, communities, and families; it does so to suggest that communities are transnational through the work of historical memory. Ghosh's narrator acknowledges that, initially, he had faith in the myths of nationality; he "believed that distance separates": "I believed in the reality of nations and borders; I believed that across the border there existed another reality" (214). But, as he researches newspaper accounts of a communal riot in Calcutta in 1962 he remembered from his childhood, he realizes that South Asia is "a land of looking-glass events" (219). The looking-glass event he is referring to is the concurrence of ethnic violence in two different cities in two different nations: Hindu–Muslim riots in Calcutta and in Dhaka on the same day on which his young cousin, Tridib, dies. What becomes evident

to the narrator as he researches the two distant and mysteriously simultaneous riots is that, beyond the logic of nation-states, an "indivisible sanity binds
people to each other independently of their governments" (225). Implicitly
critiquing the 1947 Partition, *The Shadow Lines* ascribes an irrationality to
the postcolonial nation-state, and Tridib's violent death becomes both sign
and effect of the identity of memories and people across Partition's border.
The sacrifice of his masculine body bears witness to the transnational affiliations that survive Partition. The narrative thus suggests that the nature of
boundaries can be understood through the metaphor of the looking glass:
Partition's border between the people of India and West Pakistan resembles
the mirror's boundary, in which self and other are identical.

The Shadow Lines shows how Partition bloodies a common historical
memory and displaces whole populations as refugees. Simultaneously, it suggests that ethnic violence can make visible the continuity of intimacy and
community that nation-states seek to efface. Critiquing the elite political
production of Partition, the narrator asserts: "They had drawn their borders,
believing in that pattern, in the enchantment of lines, hoping perhaps that
once they had etched their borders upon the map, the two bits of land would
sail away from each other" (228). Yet, in the uncanny, identical temporality
of the Hindu–Muslim violence in both places in which Tridib loses his life
(in Dhaka), the nation as home is undone, and another, intimate, transnational community emerges. Partition, for him, "had created not a separation,
but a yet-undiscovered irony—the irony that killed Tridib: the simple fact
that there had never been a moment in the 4000-year-old history of that
map when the places we know as Dhaka and Calcutta were more closely
bound to each other than after they had drawn their lines." This assertion
that Partition intensified intimacy and generated identity between those it
divided is unique: " . . . that I, in Calcutta, had only to look into the mirror to
be in Dhaka; a moment when each city was the inverted image of the other,
locked into an irreversible symmetry by the line that was to set us free—our
looking-glass border" (228). Partition has thus failed, and ethno-religious
violence in the city space signals the continuity of community in spite of
nation-states. For the narrator and his cousins, Robi and Ila, a different kind
of freedom—freedom from memory—becomes impossible. Robi then ironically links the Partition to the postcolonial separatist movements that have
marked South Asia since: "You know, if you look at the pictures on the front
pages of the newspapers at home now, all those pictures of dead people—in
Assam, the North-east, Punjab, Sri Lanka, Tripura—people shot by terrorists
and separatists and the army and the police, you'll find somewhere behind it
all that single word; everyone's doing it to be free" (251). The unraveling of
the signifier "freedom" in Tha'ama and Ila's lives represented earlier thus now

reappears articulated to the rhetorics of "freedom" and the resulting violence that marks ethno-nationalist movements in the postcolonial space. Ghosh's critique of Partition and its postcolonial repetitions, then, emerges in a question: "How can anyone divide a memory?" (251).

By affirming the power of memory as the basis of community, Robi challenges the politics of "freedom" of regional and religious nationalisms. He shows how Partition and nationalism annihilate community in the name of myths of freedom and newness. In this, he reminds us of Rushdie's account of the failure of the nation in the face of a shared mythic and historical memory in *Shame*.[15] Ghosh points to the transnationality of community and memory (not quite national or global) by disclosing the gendered violence effected on minor bodies and minor lives by the structures and politics of both nationalism and globalization. Brinda Bose and Bishnupriya Ghosh have usefully defined "intervention" as both "an active negotiation of oppressive configurations and the practices, discourse and institutions that generate them"and "the redefinition of one configuration by another."[16] Ghosh's fiction constitutes an intervention that urges us to provincialize national modernity and problematize the failures of postcolonial citizenship for women—"first world" immigrants and "third world" middle-class citizens.

Becoming South Asian American: Myopic Histories and Transnational Solidarities

I now turn to the disjunctive diasporic articulation of Partition and American belongings in the South Asian American writer Jhumpa Lahiri's short story entitled "When Mr. Pirzada Came to Dine" in her Pulitzer prize-winning collection of short stories *The Interpreter of Maladies*.[17] Lahiri's collection is often included in both postcolonial and Asian American literature lists; the intersection of both in Lahiri's stories enables us to take the critique of nationality articulated thus far to the U.S. nation-space in order to provincialize America. "When Mr. Pirzada Came to Dine" is a wonderful short story about the disparate meanings that being "American" takes in the lives of first- and second-generation South Asian Americans. It is also about how the history of decolonization in South Asia in 1947 reverberates across nations and across generations, in the life of a ten-year-old South Asian American girl, Lilia, growing up in an area north of Boston in 1971. The story focuses on a visiting researcher, Mr. Pirzada, from Dacca in what was then East Pakistan (now Bangladesh). Through the encounter with the migrant Mr. Pirzada, Lilia discovers and negotiates the colonial and postcolonial history of partition in the sub-continent; in the process, the story maps how this encounter affects her negotiation of ethnic and national belonging as an Asian American.

Mr. Pirzada dines with Lilia's Indian family every evening, where they together follow the television news of the civil war raging between East and West Pakistan in 1971. Because Mr. Pirzada's wife and seven daughters are still in East Pakistan, the nightly news-watching is marked by intense anxiety and fear for their safety and well-being. The specter of potential sexual violence and death thus haunts these anxious evenings in suburban Boston. When Lilia one day refers to Mr. Pirzada as "that Indian man," Lilia's father insists that she understand the difference between them and Mr. Pirzada—namely, that while they are Indian, Mr. Pirzada is Pakistani (and he might be insulted if she calls him Indian). He says, "Mr. Pirzada is no longer considered Indian. Not since Partition. Our country was divided. 1947 . . . Mr. Pirzada *is* Bengali [like Lilia's family], but he is a Muslim. . . . Therefore he lives in East Pakistan, not India" (24, emphasis added). Ethnic difference, as religious difference, and not linguistic commonality, thus determines national-cultural identity in this diaspora's pre-history, explains Lilia's father. Her mother attempts to silence this transmission of historical knowledge, because, as she puts it, Lilia does not need it: "Lilia has plenty to learn at school. We live here now. She was born here" (26). This is a significant moment: For a first-generation immigrant like Lilia's mother, American nationality promises freedom, both for self and for future generations, from a violent sub-continental history; the privilege of American citizenship is the forgetting of an Indian past. Kandice Chuh has pointed out that "the master narrative of the nation, according to which 'America' is a destined, natural result, relies on citizenship as its primary trope for conceptualizing who Americans are." Chuh notes the dehistoricization of American immigrant belonging: "The abstract citizen—she or he who successfully assimilates into and is assimilated by the national master plot—is the legitimate owner of the political space of the nation, whose past is (should be) irrelevant in light of the naturalized present."[18] The internalization of this ideology of American nationality is represented through Lilia's mother's response to her husband: The subaltern past of Partition is best forgotten.

Lilia attempts to understand the difference between Indian and Pakistani that her father presents through a map of South Asia, but she fails: "It made no sense to me. Mr. Pirzada and my parents spoke the same language, laughed at the same jokes, looked more or less the same." Noting the likeness of Mr. Pirzada and her parents' material everyday lives, the recognition of their difference eludes her: "They ate pickled mangoes with their meals, ate rice every night for supper with their hands. Like my parents, Mr. Pirzada took off his shoes before entering a room, chewed fennel seeds after meals as a digestive, drank no alcohol, for dessert dipped austere biscuits into successive cups of tea." Then, Lilia's minor knowledge of everyday life is subordinated to the chronological knowledge of partitioned nation-formation: "Nevertheless my father insisted that I understand the difference and he led me to a map of the world taped to the wall over his desk" (25).

For Lilia, the banal commonalities of language, cuisine, humor, and habit affirm the likeness of Mr. Pirzada and her own family. Through this intimate, shared everydayness, Lilia interrogates the differences produced by the cartographies of ethnicized nationalities engendered by the British decolonization of South Asia. If Lilia uneasily inhabits her hyphenated American and ethnicized Indian nationalities, she also challenges the political construction of ethnic nationality through her affirmation of common cross-national South Asian domestic practices. It is within the space of home, then, that Lilia both learns of her divided history and simultaneously finds a basis for an incipient South Asian identity that will articulate the terms "Indian," "Pakistani" and "American" across national boundaries. This scene illustrates how a South Asian American diaspora, despite the myths of American assimilation, is still haunted by the tattered history of violence and nationalism in Asia. In this diasporic family, a war in the subcontinent, watched on TV, emerges also as a catalyst of transnational belongings and solidarities, of this American family's investments in another culture and continent, nation and history. This story illuminates, as Chuh has suggested in a different context, "the limitations of a territorial imagination that cannot account for the transnational dimensions of nationalized subjectivities."[19] Rajini Srikanth has argued that another story, "Third and Final Continent" in the same collection, celebrates the immigrant's journey and represents America as "the ultimate destination—beyond which there is no need to go, for one has arrived at the best of all possible locations."[20] In contrast, in "When Mr. Pirzada Came to Dine," the United States becomes a more problematized national context: It becomes the site of both freedom and historical erasure, with which the protagonist forges an agonist relation.

Furthermore, this story criticizes the disjunction between the histories of the South Asian diaspora that mark Lilia's home, and the public world of American education where she is taught history not as world history, but as a provincial American history. Her father's questions, "But what does she learn about the world [in school]?" are answered by the narrator in this way: "We learned American history of course, and American geography. That year, and every year, it seemed we began by studying the Revolutionary War" (27). The obviousness implied in her "of course" signals the distance between Lilia's domestic everyday life and her history class at school, from which the war in the subcontinent, which she watches every evening on TV, is completely absent: "No one at school talked about the war followed so faithfully in my living room. We continued to study the American Revolution, and learned about the injustices of taxation without representation, and memorized passages from the Declaration of Independence" (32). Lilia's ironic juxtaposition here of one ongoing war of independence and its violence in Bangladesh, with the American Declaration of independence and its "injustice" of taxation without representation, illuminates the disjunction between diasporic domesticity and the national public. In articulating both in an antagonistic relation, the narrative destabilizes the historiographic nationalism that dominates American education, and pluralizes history. It illuminates the elision of an ongoing war by an earlier, American war, and constitutes a counterpublic critique of a provincial America. One day, to do a class report about the surrender at Yorktown, Lilia is sent to the school's library. When Lilia seeks out the "Asia" section instead of focusing on her Yorktown report, and starts reading a book on Pakistan, she is tracked down by the teacher, Mrs. Kenyon, who asks, "Is this a part of your report Lilia?" When Lilia replies no, the history teacher takes the book out of her hands and puts it back on the shelf, pronouncing, "Then I see no reason to consult it. Do you?" (Lahiri, 33). The violence of that question and gesture emblematizes a myopic American educational system that deliberately elides global histories. "History" remains the province of an unprovincialized United States.

"When Mr. Pirzada Came to Dine" is not only about how the 1947 Partition and its legacies in the subcontinent emerge in everyday ways in South Asian Americans lives, but also how these disjunctive and diverse histories of ethnicity can come to be learned and challenged by South Asian Americans. As Lisa Lowe has suggested, Asian American cultural forms, "rather than dictating that subjects be constituted through identification with the liberal citizen-formation of American national culture," actually "offer the possibility of subjects and practices constituted through dialectics of difference and disidentification."[21] Moreover, it is in Lilia's generation, and in her female Asian American subjectivity, that Lahiri locates the potential and agency for recasting South Asian ethnic and nationalist belongings—the dreams for which, as Chakrabarty points out, there are no sites. Lahiri's work, like many other Asian American texts, makes visible how, for a raced diasporic community, "America" (and what it means to be "American") is always complex and under contestation. For some, like Lilia's mother, it embodies an American nationalist freedom from a violent Asian history. However, for others, like Lilia, "America" becomes an ambivalently charged nation-space, which needs to be provincialized and which also *enables* her to dream of a transnational, non-nationalist South Asian American politics.

Furthermore, this story reveals the impossibility of disengaging a critique of colonialism from the articulation of a progressive Asian American politics. It shows that such an Asian American politics must needs challenge the erasure of global realities in the United States in the name of American national assimilation, in the name of a discourse based on the raced subject's desire for America as "home." As mentioned earlier, Chuh and others have called for a re-examination of how Asian American studies have historically targeted national subjectivity as an objective to counter the often juridically imposed exclusions of Asian-raced peoples in the United States. Towards decolonizing this formation of belongingness and the coupling of "home" and "nation," Chuh has proposed that Asian Americanists must "conceptually 'disown' America, the ideal, to further the work of creating home as a space relieved of states of domination."[22] Accompanying this disowning of America, I believe, must be its *provincializing;* and towards this, postcolonial thought not only makes visible how national identities are produced within global nexuses of power, but it also complicates and pluralizes the political as a modern category to challenge intimate and gendered, national and globalized inequalities. Raced minority politics, based on the struggle for inclusionary nationalist belonging in the United States, can therefore be productively rethought through the postcolonial critiques of contemporary economic and political globalization. The insistent attention to the historical specificity of colonialism and U.S. imperialism (given its history of imported slave and contract labor, continental expansion and overseas occupation and imperialism), and the uncoupling of racial and religious ethnicity and nationality, is essential if we are to interrogate contemporary political violence and discrimination, most recently visited upon those who have an Islamic background or look South Asian/Middle-Eastern in the United States.

Globalizing Race Through the Postcolonial

What is suggested here, and (I hope) demonstrated thus far in this chapter, is that the field of postcolonial studies has important contributions to make to critically rethinking and rearticulating the culture and politics of color in the United States. This chapter, then, contributes to a growing body of recent work by Homi Bhabha, Jenny Sharpe, Kandice Chuh, Inderpal Grewal, Amy Kaplan and others that has begun to engage postcolonial critique and American studies. Such an engagement opens up possibilities for understanding the complexities of national racial formations as transnationally constituted, in their specific histories and in an increasingly globalized world. This is not to homogenize race as a mythic global category that is always already present and unchanging across different times, cultures, and nations. Instead, this is about situating the constitution and contestation of U.S. racial identities and oppressions in relation to a wider set of unequal power relations across and among nations—in terms of regions like "the Americas" and the United States as an empire—and in relation to the colonial and neo-colonial histories of migration that have often generated U.S. national minorities. Consider, for example, recent attention to the United States as an empire, the case of Hawa'iian nationalism and the specificities of the Filipino American experience, the discriminatory racialization of Islam (and those of us from South Asia and the Middle East) following September 11, 2001, and the attempt to think of indigenous resistance in terms of a project for native North America. New initiatives in many U.S. universities to think of "Race in the Americas," as well as the new cartographies drawn by Asian/Pacific/American programs—such as the one at NYU—indicate both the need for, and the illuminating possibility contained in, a transnational examination of race and ethnicity.

While the questions about race and postcoloniality are not identical, the engagement of American studies in general, and ethnic studies like Asian American studies in particular, with postcolonial thought enable what Michel Foucault calls "the work of reciprocal elucidation."[23] This reciprocal elucidation is not merely the end, but should serve as a point of departure for pluralizing and re-articulating the meanings of concepts like justice, citizenship and belonging for minority politics in an age of American imperialism. It is from this perspective of articulating postcolonial studies and Asian American studies that I read the phrase "globalizing race": as a commitment to examining how U.S. national racial identities and discourses are contingently, transnationally constituted; how they emerge from linked global histories of domination and displacement; and how they are often implicated in contemporary, unequal global relations of U.S. imperialism.

But why the postcolonial? Because in the critique of the Enlightenment's totalizing narratives articulated in postcolonial thought, we can locate and appropriate the critique of the national modern and its rationality. Furthermore, in problematizing both nationalism and globalization, postcolonial thought can enable the project of provincializing the Euro-American modern and denaturalizing the contemporary mapping of ethnicity/race onto national citizenship that marks the twentieth century and continues to define the twenty-first. Finally, postcolonial thought bears witness to the instability and heterogeneity of the hegemonic, transnationally circulating languages of "justice," "freedom," and "democracy" in the public sphere—languages that historically ground minority struggles(Asian American and others), even as they are simultaneously deployed towards neo-imperialist politics. Homi Bhabha has illuminated how, in contemporary postcolonial writings, "there is an attempt to interrupt the Western discourses of modernity through these displacing interrogative subaltern or postslavery narratives and the critical theoretical perspectives they engender."[24] For the raced minority subject in the U.S. national context, postcolonial critique is an analytic that goes beyond the nationalist assumptions of multiculturalism to problematize the modern, historical production of racial, ethnic, and national belonging (American and others). Moreover, it makes imperative a critique of nationalist investments in the articulation of political subjectivity, citizenship and resistance in order to situate our struggles within a larger and increasingly violent history of American imperialism and globalization.

Terrorism, September 11, 2001, and the Racialization of Religion

I now turn briefly to the terrorist attack on September 11, 2001, in New York. I remember that when the full impact of the terrorist attacks on September 11 had sunk in, a deep and unequivocal sympathy and support for the United States, for Americans, and for the victims of this attack dominated its narrativization in the postcolonial Indian public sphere. Both politicians and the general public in India expressed support for America and for Americans. Having experienced the violent effects of cross-border militancy and terrorism in Kashmir for over two decades, many Indians immediately responded with understanding—this was a violence, a fear they were familiar with in some ways. As just one example of this, let me quote the September 13, 2001, editorial from the newspaper *The Hindu*: "To empathise with the United States and its people and Government in their worst hour of crisis since the Pearl Harbour bombing during the Second World War is to pay the minimal civilised homage to mankind."[25] September 11 thus became a moment of identification, of international and transnational solidarity in the face of this unnecessary, senseless, tragic loss of life. There were other similarities in the experiences of the United States and India. After September 11, there was a terrorist attack on the Indian Parliament on December 12, 2001, a bomb attack in Delhi on October 29, 2005, a series of seven coordinated bombings that left over five hundred dead in Mumbai on July 11, 2006, and the bombing of Samjhauta Express on February 18, 2007. That the sympathy over September 11 continued in the public sphere is evident in the editorial of the leading Indian newspaper, *The Times of India*, on its first anniversary, September 11, 2002: "Commemoration exercises are rarely proportionate; quite the opposite, in fact, as tributes by nature border on the hyperbolic. Nonetheless, one year after September 11, the worst overstatement would seem inadequate to capture the full meaning and impact of what happened to the United States, and by implication the world, on that day."[26] More recently, the leading Indian actor Nasseruddin Shah has directed a 2006 Bollywood film, *Yun Hota To Kya Hota* (*What If*), about September 11, 2001. The film is written by the Gujarati short story writer Uttam Gada, and it represents the diverse migrant hopes of five Indians, old and young, male and female, from diverse class locations who seek to escape different kinds of dispossessions and violence when they migrate to America. Except for one, they all die when their plane from Boston crashes into the World Trade Center in the terrorist attack on September 11. In memorializing the transnational hopes and dreams of these raced immigrant subjects who also were victims of the violence on September 11, and who remain marginal to the nationalist narrativization in the hegemonic U.S. public sphere, this film instantiates a counter-public memorialization and mourning of 9/11.

Yet, let me turn to another interesting dimension of this relationship between South Asia and the United States. Like earlier moments in American history when Asian Americans have been demonized in times of geopolitical conflict, South Asians in the United States became demonized as threatening Others in America after September 11, 2001. Before September 11, South Asians in the United States had, as a group, often been a self-constructed and racist model minority, as Vijay Prashad has also pointed out.[27] Believing they are "almost white" given the myths of Aryan origins, many have sometimes clung to racist attitudes towards other U.S. minorities. The terrorist attacks of September 11 changed that forever. From model minority, they became potential terrorists. Hindus, Muslims, and especially Sikhs indiscriminately became targets of racist "revenge" violence and state discrimination. A report commissioned by the National Asian Pacific American Legal Consortium says there were 243 attacks on Sikhs (many of them deadly, like the murder of Balbir Singh Sodhi in Arizona) and other South Asian Americans in the three months after September 11, 2001. Human Rights Watch and the American Civil Liberties Union said in a report released in 2006 that since September 11, 2001, Muslim men have been subject to extreme state violence and discrimination in the United States. They have often been arrested for little more than attending the same mosque as a September 11 hijacker or owning a box cutter. Simultaneously, Sikh men who wear turbans have been subject to racial violence that constructs them as being associated with the Taliban; thus, one kind of discourse about September 11 has created new modes of minoritization through the racialization of gendered ethnicity, which engenders state as well as individual violence. Spike Lee's film *Inside Man* (2006) quietly marks the complexities of the diasporic racisms that inhabit everyday life in the United States. The film is about hostages taken during a bank robbery in Manhattan. When one of the hostages, a Sikh man, Vikram (Waris Ahluwalia), comes out of the bank with a black box tied to him, one of the policemen who have surrounded the building's entrance shouts out "He's an Arab!" Even as he responds "I'm a Sikh," he is shoved to the ground by the ignorant and racist policemen, and his turban is removed. The scene underscores the cultural violence of this racist de-turbaning, which humiliates and violates Vikram's Sikhism; his submissive posture as he is forced to the ground and falls down, with the policeman towering over him, emphasizes his abjection at the hands of the state.

The implicit identification of "Arab" is "terrorist," and its attendant violence is evident here. The camera then cuts to a scene in which he is sitting in a diner with three police officers, voicing his frustration at the regular harassment he faces from the police, airport security workers, and others for his "misrecognition" as Arab. Even as the African American detective Keith Frazier (Denzel Washington) sympathizes with his criticism of such post-September 11 racism, he humorously and ironically notes, "I'll bet you can get a cab, though." Vikram nods in acknowledgement, implicitly recognizing the reference to the common South Asian American cab drivers' racism against African Americans in New York. *Inside Man* thus ironically inscribes and enjoins, without the erasure of their difference, the persistent and multiple forms of racism that mark minor lives in post-September 11 United States.

Discussing this issue of racialization and discriminated nationalities in the classroom in late 2001, one of my South Asian American students, a woman, remarked, "You know, so far, I have always seen myself as Indian American. But after September 11, I have realized how *American* I am." This affirmation of national belonging, and the erasure of "Indian" in that identity, can be read as a rejection of the dominant negative racialized representation of the self as a threatening Other. But it might also be an impossible articulation born out of the coercion of performing national allegiance even as one is denied national belonging because of one's race. This comment was challenged by another female student in class: "It's interesting to me that you say that, as an Indian, because I'm Italian American, but I am so disgusted by the jingoistic patriotism after September 11 that I don't want to identify myself as an American. I see myself as more Italian, as *European*." And so I note that to be able to disavow national belonging becomes a raced privilege of unmarked citizenship in this post-September 11 America. The institutionalized state violence enacted upon racialized citizenship in the United States is also eloquently commented on by Rajini Srikanth in the context of Asian American history: "[R]egardless of how deep their roots may be in this country, there is always some doubt about the strength of their allegiance. Being Asian American is no guarantee of being American. Certain groups are always seen to have transnational alliances, and this forced transnationality is sometimes deployed to de-nationalize them." Srikanth has also noted that such was the case with the Japanese Americans during World War II, and such is the case now with South Asian Americans and Arab Americans who have been indefinitely and secretly detained in connection with America's "War on Terror."[28] If September 11, 2001 initiated a new wave of Islamophobia and the demonization of Muslims in much of North America and Europe, it also inspired a re-investment in ethnic identities in troubling ways. For example, a recent report revealed that 80 percent of the Hindus in Britain would prefer to be called British Indian or British Hindus, rather than be identified as British Asian, primarily because of the dominant anti-Muslim sentiment in the public sphere.[29] The BBC Asian Network aired a recent documentary titled "Don't Call Me Asian," which suggested that most of its interviewees who rejected the bureaucratic and political nomenclature of "British Asian" were members of the Hindu Forum of Britain, Hindu Youth and Sikh Federation.

Vijay Prashad has called for a revival of the category "people of color" in the articulation of political struggles, because "[t]here can be no radical politics of South Asian America that does not deny the model minority stereotype and that does not ally itself with elements of the black and Latino Liberation Movement as well as with currents of American socialism." According to him, "[t]his is the minimum contribution that Asian communities must make to a political project against the racial formation that is embedded in capitalism."[30] This necessary inter-racial articulation, however, needs to be recast today to account for how the racialization of religion that saturates the United States following September 11, 2001, has created new modes of nationalist minoritization and discrimination. In yet another interesting twist, many South Asians (thought not all, of course) who have been victims of racial profiling at airports in the United States since September 11, 2001, have responded, "Its okay, I understand." Such complex and ambivalent transnational solidarities across races and nations, these diverse negotiations of racial violence, ethnic belonging, and national unbelonging, suggest to me that now, more than ever, we need to provincialize America and recast normative American belongings transnationally. Sustained by an agonistic humanism, such a project would emancipate the minor subject from the tyranny of national power.

"I Cannot Pack the Moments Spent in This House": Refugee States and Globalized Terror

Salman Rushdie's latest novel, *Shalimar, the Clown* (2005), is a postmodern critique of the violence that has marked and divided Kashmir since the 1947

Partition. This state of Kashmir in the novel becomes emblematic of the persistent and globalized production of war and conflict in violent nation-states. *Shalimar, the Clown* interrogates the rhetorics of "freedom" put forth by terrorist movements, even as it provincializes the nation-state—from the United States to Pakistan and India—to reveal the intimate link between state power and the historical emergence of terror in remote parts of the world. The novel's plot begins with the representation of Kashmir as an idyllic, rural, communally harmonious paradise. As the protagonist Max Ophuls' Kashmiri-American daughter India muses, "Her mother had been Kashmiri, and was lost to her, like paradise, like Kashmir, in a time before memory."[31] Although Kashmir and India are here problematically feminized, embodied respectively by the Kashmiri Hindu Boonyi and by her racially hybrid American daughter India, Rushdie deploys this image to criticize the nation-state system. Reminiscent of the earlier discourses of pre-Partition communal harmony tracked in early national writings, Kashmir's peaceful syncretism in *Shalimar the Clown* is manifest in the locally celebrated inter-ethnic romance of the initially secular protagonists, a Hindu dancer named Boonyi Kaul and her childhood sweetheart, Shalimar the clown, the son of a Muslim family. Their marriage, solemnized by both Hindu and Muslim rites, falls apart when Max Ophuls, a "terrorism" expert in a post 9/11 world who is the American ambassador to India, and whose own personal history marks him as a Holocaust survivor who lost his parents to the Nazi extermination of Jews, seduces Boonyi. This seduction ruins both her life and the fragile, idealized inter-ethnic love that Boonyi and Shalimar's coupledom represented. As their marriage falls apart, so does the syncretic paradise of Kashmir. Like many other South Asian representations discussed earlier, inter-ethnic coupledom remains unrealized, and its failure is a symbolic indictment of Indian secularism. Devastated at Boonyi's betrayal with Ophuls, Shalimar is transformed into a "terrorist" and inducted into the euphemistically named, self-proclaimed "world of the liberation front," even as Kashmir is destroyed by the violent conflict between the Indian Army and Pakistan-sponsored cross-border terrorists (256).

In making visible the historical complicity of the United States and Al Qaeda, and the Islamist-jihadist activities in Pakistan, Philippines, Afghanistan and India in the reinvention of Shalimar as terrorist, the novel underscores the complicity of the system of nation-states in the production of violence that is ultimately named terrorist, ethnic, religious, or fundamentalist (269). The narrator critiques the partition of Kashmir after the Indo–Pakistan war of 1948 by calling it a "mistake" that the Kashmiris disregarded (97), and he simultaneously bears witness to the "ethnic cleansing" of Hindus and the mass exodus of 350,000 Kashmiri Pandits that began in Kashmir from the late eighties onwards: "Kill one, scare ten, the Muslim mobs chanted . . . almost the entire Pandit population of Kashmir, fled from their homes and headed south to the refugee camps where they would rot, like bitter, fallen apples, like the unloved, undead, dead they had become" (296). This representation enjoins the documentary history of contemporary ethnic violence in Kashmir, with the recognition of the lack of "love" and national protection that marks their unrecognized lives. By calling the refugees the "undead, dead," Rushdie reiterates and extends Judith Butler's call to re-examine our state-dominated ways of constructing particular lives as human, and therefore valuable, grievable and, Rushdie says, "protectable".[32]

Since 1989, the systematic targeting of this 5,000-year-old community in the Kashmir valley has left thousands dead, and over 300,000 languishing in refugee camps in Jammu and Delhi. Their properties have been looted, temples and cultural artifacts looted and razed to the ground, books and sacred texts destroyed, women and children raped and killed. One Pandit female survivor's words to her son, as she recognizes her imminent forced displacement, resonate with the critical assertion of non-nationalist belonging, located in the everyday, that also emerged in earlier South Asian literary texts:

> I came to this house as a young bride. This house has been a witness to all my good times and bad times and even when your father left us forever, this house protected me against all outsiders and evils. Today I am leaving the security of my house and don't know where I am going. I cannot pack the moments spent in this house. I cannot pack my memories, why am I being forced to leave my homeland, I have not committed any crime, why am I paying the price for the mistakes of others.[33]

This refugee's eloquent testimony of the irreparable loss of homeliness inhabits not what Chakrabarty calls a "subaltern past" suppressed in the dominant public sphere, but a stubborn "subaltern present" made visible in the counter-publics articulated transnationally today—in literature, in online communities and film. It resonates with the displaced, diasporic perspective that writers like Lahiri, Ghosh and Rushdie attempt to write into narrative: These voices interrogate the normative narration of nationalist histories, and make visible the material human displacements they engender as well as make disappear from the public sphere.

Shalimar, the Clown criticizes not only the mass ethnic cleansing and forced migration of Hindus from Kashmir, but also the failure of the Indian state to prevent the violence and assist the displaced citizens: "There were six hundred thousand Indian troops in Kashmir but the pogrom of the Pandits was not prevented, why was that. Three and a half lakhs of human beings arrived in Jammu as displaced persons and for many months the government did not provide shelters or relief or even register their names, why was that" (297). Through the reiteration of the phrase "why was that," the narrator demands national accountability and state responsibility towards its citizens, reminiscent of cultural representations from the early national period, as the state failed to protect the Pandits in spite of its heavily militarized presence in Kashmir. The state's refusal to recognize the Pandits' displacement renders them, as Arendt suggests, "stateless": "When the government finally built camps it only allowed for six thousand families to remain [in] the state, dispersing the others around the country, where they would be invisible and impotent, why was that." Relentlessly, the narrative thus catalogues the multiple forms of state failure for these citizens-refugees, revealing the disjunction between the elite political and public recognition of the "ethnic cleansing" and its disavowal in the state's institutions: "The ministers of the government made speeches about ethnic cleansing but the civil servants wrote one another memos saying that the Pandits were simply internal migrants whose displacement had been self-imposed, why was that" (297). This narration uncovers the political hypocrisy and juridical violence of the state's erasure of contemporary Kashmiri refugee experience—mirroring 1947. That the phrase "why was that" is followed not by a question mark, but by a period, bleakly suggests that the narrator does not expect an answer. Written from the diaspora, Shalimar, the Clown is an evocative postmodern archive of migration and the globalized production of modern terrorism, which articulates the present with a counter-public, minor perspective of the 1947 Partition. The novel reiterates the tropes of inter-ethnic romance, syncretism, state failure and secularism that mark postcolonial Indian representations of Partition. Simultaneously, it is also Rushdie's most politicized work that denounces state power and its production of terrorism, the violent experience of "stateless citizens," and the imperial American nation-state in the contemporary moment. It unmasks how globalization also enables the violent empire of nation-states, and how states can generate unbelonging.

"Unhistorical Lives": International State Violence and the Critique of Human Rights

In tracking the postcolonial critique of nationality, Michael Ondaatje's novel *Anil's Ghost* (2000) is important: It illuminates the globalized production of what gets narrated in the hegemonic, global public sphere as nationalist, Tamil-Sinhala ethnic conflict in Sri Lanka. While contemporary ethnic conflict in South Asia has recently received considerable attention in the social sciences, its literary exploration has been comparatively limited.[34] Although not about the Partition, *Anil's Ghost* takes up the problem of ethnic violence and mass displacement in South Asia that this book focuses on, and insofar as it re-situates this "ethnic violence" within the global economy of terror and state violence, it complicates the criticism of postcolonial nationalism as well as contemporary terrorism. Like Rushdie's *Shalimar the Clown* and *Midnight's Children*, Ondaatje represents the violence generated by the postcolonial nation-state through the representation of the male body. *Anil's Ghost* is set in a war-ravaged Sri Lankan landscape littered with dead bodies that is produced by the legacies of colonialism and the globalized circulation of mass weaponry from first-world nations to the East. The plot turns on the return to Sri Lanka of the well-heeled and globe-trotting female forensic specialist, Anil Tissera. An elite diasporic subject with a sexually ambiguous name, Anil is born in Sri Lanka, and later moves to England and America; she now travels around the world with a British passport working for the United Nations on investigations into human rights abuses across the world. Anil is selected by the Center for Human Rights in Geneva to go to Sri Lanka as part of a team conducting a seven-week Human Rights investigation in conjunction with the Sri Lankan government into organized extrajudicial killings going on since the late eighties. The narrative follows her arrival and subsequent work on a dead male body to identify it and to locate the killers of the victim they have provisionally named "Sailor." Early on, her Sri Lankan colleague—the archaeologist, Sarath—informs her, "The bodies turn up weekly now. The height of the terror was 'eighty-eight and eighty-nine,' but of course it was going on long before that. Every side was killing and hiding the evidence. Every side." Emphasizing the complicity of all constituencies in this violence, Sarath illuminates why this is "an unofficial war": "No one wants to alienate the foreign powers. So it's secret gangs and squads. . . . A couple of years ago people just started disappearing. Or bodies kept being found burned beyond recognition. There's no hope of affixing blame. And no one can tell who the victims are."[35] This insistence that every one is responsible for the "unofficial" devastating violence reappears elsewhere in the novel; it recognizes the modernity of this saturating violence, even as it notes it's global, official erasure. Ondaatje thus makes visible in the postcolonial public sphere what I have earlier called a "subaltern present"—a relatively marginalized scene of postcolonial violence and suffering in Sri Lanka where, in addition to the terrifying death toll, at least one million people have become internally displaced refugees, and hundreds of thousands of Tamils have fled abroad as refugees to India, North America, and Europe.

In his analysis of the difference between the postcolonial and the post-modern, Kwame Anthony Appiah argues that the postcolonial work is also necessarily post-nationalist; it refuses both the nativist celebration of indigenous "culture" and the bourgeois nationalist endorsement of the postcolonial state. Instead, Appiah suggests, a work of art can be properly named postcolonial when it evinces a non-nationalist and humanist political commitment to the witnessing of and struggle against the human suffering that inhabits the late postcolonial world.[36] Ondaatje articulates just such a post-national critique, like Rushdie, of the failure of both the protection symbolized by citizenship, and the postcolonial nation-state as it engenders violence. The narrator of *Anil's Ghost* unravels the economic and political complicity between East and West in the production of terror and postcolonial violence: "There had been continual emergency from 1983 onwards, racial attacks and political killings. The terrorism of the separatist guerilla groups, who were fighting for a homeland in the north. The insurrection of the insurgents in the south, against the government. The counterterrorism of the special forces, against both of them" (42–43). Thus, all parties are culpable for the violence, including diasporic Sri Lankans: "It was a Hundred Years' War with modern weaponry, and backers on the sidelines in safe countries, a war sponsored by gun and drug runners. It became evident that political enemies were secretly joined in financial arms deals. 'The reason for war was war.'" This is a politicized critique that ironically notes the capitalist rationality and global sustenance—in the form of diasporic financing and the military-industrial complex in the West—of the 'casual sense of massacre' that pervades contemporary Sri Lankan everyday life (283). Rejecting the ideological claims of both Tamil nationalists and Sinhala-dominated state government, *Anil's Ghost* likens them by naming them all agents of "terror." It illuminates their normalization of everyday violence by repeatedly presenting images, as if in cinematic flashes, of mutilated and dead bodies, and skeletons—these are images of "the unhistorical dead" (56), "all those lost voices" (56), "beheaded bodies" (187) who are the casualties of this war. In doing so, the subaltern unidentifiable bodies Ondaatje writes into his narrative get historicized, even as his protagonist, Anil, notes the impossibility of making intelligible this death of those whose names and identities cannot be recovered because of the extreme violence done to them: "[I]n the midst of such events, she realized, there could never be any logic to the human violence without the distance of time. For now it would be reported, filed in Geneva, but no one could ever give meaning to it" (55). This loss of meaning, and so a loss of history for the lives destroyed by violence that saturates everyday life in Sri Lanka, then, cannot be repaired by its documentation in Europe. Now Europe is provincialized, no longer the site of the production of history, but only generative—as part of the "foreign powers" and in its spectacular silence about the violence—of the dead, disfigured beyond recognition.

Although Ondaatje criticizes the Sri Lankan government's state-sponsored killings and massacres, he also eschews locating hope for transformation in the diasporic female subject Anil or in international human rights organizations and movements. Indeed, the novel problematizes Western intervention represented by Anil's human rights mission; as Sarath tells Anil, "[i]nternational investigations don't mean a lot" (45). Instead, the investigation of the dead, male body enables the diasporic cosmopolitan subject to realize a transnational political identification with Sri Lankan nationality as opposed to the Sri Lankan state, through the critique of state violence. The novel's postmodern form constantly interrupts the chronological account about Anil's ongoing investigation by moving back and forth in time, and juxtaposing it with scenes describing her at work on human rights investigations in different parts of the world, her remembrances of her past, journalistic descriptions of acts of murder and somatic violence, and documentary information about the victims of this civil war. The politicized formal disruption that is enacted in these diverse scenes placed as contiguous fragments only serves to underscore the lack of logic and coherence in a violent Sri Lanka, and signals the limits of diverse discourses and modes for the representation of violence. It also refuses colonialist rhetorics of Sri Lanka's exemplarity, linking its violence to other topographies of brutal violence and lost human rights across the world. Finally, placed thus, the narrative underlines the futility of documentary history, and the failure of rhetorics of human rights in the face of the annihilating violence. The novel ends with the government-organized murder of Sarath, with Anil's investigation into the state's role in the killings sabotaged and failed, and the reconstruction of a Buddha statue in a beautiful forest where victims who were picked up were brought in trucks and burned. This reconstruction suggests a desperate hope for peace in and through the recognition of Buddha's values, despite "the harsh political events of the twentieth century" (300).

Postscript

In exploring the experiences and effects of South Asian migration in Chapter Four, I discussed the rejection of postcolonial Indian nationality by many Partition refugees, and the decision to migrate to other continents and countries like the U.K. and Africa, thus in part contributing to the formations of diaspora that pre-occupy ethnic American studies today. Immigration of workers into England from many of the former British colonies (including the Indian subcontinent) started after 1945 and grew during the fifties.

Recruitment of workers by London Transport, and other labor demands, enabled the immigration of many South Asians to England. By 1951, there were 218,000 people originally from Britain's ex-colonies, and by 1961 this figure had risen to 541,000. However, around 1962, immigration from these locations almost stopped, partly due to economic stagnation, but mostly due to the severe restrictions placed by the racist Commonwealth Immigrants Act of 1962.[37] Today, the United States is by far the largest recipient of international migrants, including South Asians, with about twenty-five million foreign-born residents at the end of the 1990s. As many studies have noted, the momentous numbers of legal and illegal migrants in the world today point to the centrality of ethnic conflict as a leading cause of displacement and migration; thus, attention to international migration must address the problem of ethnic conflict and violence from a transnational perspective, as well as to the cultural production of belonging and community in this globalized world. In his tribute to Edward Said, Homi Bhabha has reminded us of Said's call to recognize the "worldliness" of knowledge, towards the struggle to change the conditions of "communities who live in the shadow lines of everyday conflict—beset, day by day, with the problems of death and mourning, diaspora and resettlement, racial discrimination and human rights abuses, the immiseration of civic life and the militarization of citizenship." The knowledges that we produce in the public sphere, about ethnic belongings and economic oppressions, about gendered migration and modern minoritization, must constitute an agonistic secularism that can be non-Eurocentric. As Bhabha suggests, "Secularism is an interpretational, hermeneutic kind of humanism, open to dialogue and dispute; its values are relational and aspectival; its principles are to be found not in norms but in processes, in modes of making or in poesis."[38]

I began this chapter by considering how Ghosh's fiction inscribes a relation between Partition and both contemporary Hindu–Muslim conflict in South Asia and the post-1950 South Asian migrations to the West. Both Ghosh and Lahiri mark the failure of the nation-state and popular, public-sphere ideologies of national homeliness when seen through the lens of migrant and diasporic women's experiences. Like them, Ondaatje and Rushdie refuse to celebrate the hybridity and heterogeneity born of global migrations. Instead, the diasporic texts I consider reveal a dystopic nationalism, challenge the hegemonic state, and uncover the failures of migration through the experiences of women as citizens and migrants—acknowledging what Spivak has called "the failure of decolonization at home and abroad."[39] This chapter does not seek to valorize or privilege diasporic critique over the indigenous, or to construct the diaspora as an exemplary site of suffering or critique. Indeed, it is salutary to remember that even as diasporic experience is often marked by discrimination, racial minoritization, and un-belonging, diasporas can shore up particular ethno-nationalist agendas for political and cultural self-representation in their countries of origin or residence—witness the Hindu diasporic support from the U.K. and North America for Hindu nationalist agendas. What I have been interested in is the textual strategy that emerges as a counter-discourse to the current celebratory discourses of globalization and ideologies of the nation as "home." This ideology has a long colonial history; as Timothy Brennan has noted, "[t]he markets made possible by European imperial penetration motivated the construction of the nation-state as home . . . the 'nation idea,' in other words, flourished in the soil of foreign conquest."[40] The cultural texts—literary and filmic—explored here criticize both globalization and postcolonial nationalism, by depicting the experiences of migrants caught violently in-between nation-states, those going back and forth as travelers and migrants in search of lost homes and better lives. They also problematize the ideologies and abstract promises of national citizenship in the context of capitalist dispossessions marked by gender, poverty, and race. These postcolonial representations of the minor migrant—as decolonized subject, diasporic cosmopolitan, unloved dead, or Asian American youth—unveil the diverse geographies of capitalist and ethnic politics in which abject subjects emerge. As such, they urgently direct us to interrogate liberal languages of citizenship and globalization, and posit a secular and contingent, transnational and inter-ethnic affiliation as an alternative.

Conclusion

Like Jews, Yehudis, Palestinians,
Alienated,
I'm a Sindhi
Everywhere in the world,
Wanted nowhere.

      —Ishwar Anchal, "Exile"[1]

The Sindhi poet and Partition refugee Anchal here inscribes the kind of humanist, transnational form of affiliation that I have hoped to uncover in this book—a mode of agonistic identification that emerges from the liminality that the loss of belonging Partition generated, and that lies in what Homi Bhabha has named "an inassimilable place outside history."[2] Articulating community with other minoritized and displaced groups in world history, this is a transnational practice of identity rooted in the recognition of historical violence and shared human-ness, even as it is also an inscription of the violence of un-belonging experienced by refugees in a system of nation-states. This book began with the exploration of how cultural and national belongings were transformed in and through the gendered violence and mass migrations engendered by the 1947 Partition of India. Along the way, the chapters uncovered some of the fragmentary scenes and the subaltern spaces in which we can glimpse the transformation of belonging, the emergence of citizenship and its violence, and the hegemonic production of nationalized intimacies during Partition. One of the arguments of this book is that both capitalist citizenship and gendered ethnicity emerged in 1947 as contingent categories that were deployed *by* state governmentality and *in* everyday life, as technologies to engender the displacement of minor subjects in the new nations India and Pakistan. In the process of uncovering the mode and effects of this deployment in contemporary South Asian cultures, and in other globalized scenes of violence, I have attempted to track the formations that mark the postcolonial public sphere and to locate the hegemonic as well as counter-discourses that mark the collective negotiation, translation and contestation of violence and violent belongings. In part, I have sought to historicize this violence around ethnic belongings by exploring how the Partition as a fragmentary, "subaltern past" contributed not only to the territorialization of ethnicity, but also to the ambivalent discursive and political production of the ethnic citizen, of normative masculinities and femininities, and of national coupledom. The texts and voices that are a part of this book's archive uncover the numerous ways in which gendered ethnicity has functioned, since World War II, to transform subjects into citizens and refugees, into "unhistorical bodies" and the "undead, dead." As such, these voices incite us to continue the interrogation of the violence of governmentality and gendered ethnicities that persist into the contemporary moment.

In another sense, what I hope has emerged from the chapters is a sense of how "Partition" marks not only a historical event in 1947, but also a discourse—a *contemporary* discourse about the ethnicization of gendered belonging and citizenship in South Asia, and its territorialization through the nation-state/ I have interrogated Partition's discursive inscription as an exceptional moment already over, to signal how Partition is also a "subaltern present" that informs and reappears in the contemporary violence of Hindu nationalism/ in the destruction of Babri Masjid, the Godhra riots, the Samjhauta Express bombings. That this discourse, this way of speaking about ethnicity, nation, gender and belonging continues to be mobilized by the Hindu Right as a transnational formation sustained by and in the North American diaspora, points to the urgency of re-appropriating the Partition towards fashioning both transnational alliances and a differently hegemonic citizenship. My journey to understand the twin axes of the transnational memory of my own familial past and the violent present of Hindu nationalism in 1990s Bombay took me to the 1947 Partition; my location as a diasporic raced feminist subject in the United States has enjoined my inquiry into the meanings, effects, and discourses of Partition with not only the contemporary ethnicization of identity and rise of fundamentalism in India, but also the exclusions and minoritization that mark the racialization of religion and citizenship in the United States. I found the story of South Asia's Partition that I wanted to tell, could not be fully described without the story about violent gendered and racialized belongings in North America as well.

In the years during which this book has taken shape, there has emerged a new field called Partition Studies, as many scholars—unknown to me at the time, I have gratefully discovered—have also been simultaneously committed to the re-examination of the Partition experience. Taking up the question of the valence of the literary critic's work of reading and writing, Henry Schwartz and Henry Dienst have suggested that we "read the shape of the world as if the world can be shaped by reading, as if the world can be put in better shape when people become attentive to, cautious about, and answerable for the shaping force of words and images."[3] My humble hope is that in some measure, this book enacts that suggestion and contributes to the voices and struggles against the transnational hegemony of ethno-nationalist rhetorics in India as well as the imperial United States. The desire of this book is that this exploration of Partition as an event, as a field of transition to postcoloniality and as a discourse about gendered ethnicity will contribute to what this book began with: Judith Butler's call for the performance of a "sensate democracy." This investigation is a mode of speaking for the struggle against contemporary Hindu–Muslim conflict in South Asia, and against the diverse forms of minoritizing violence—state and civil—that inhabit the everyday lives of so many around the world, from India, to Sri Lanka, Iraq and the United States.

Across the diverse and discontinuous scenes encountered in this book, I have sought to reveal the disjunction between citizenship and the everyday experience of (un)belonging for postcolonial, minor subjects of the modern nation, both in India and its diaspora. In mapping the postcolonial counter-public critique of the nation-state and the failures of citizenship engendered by state violence, gendered discrimination, and migration upon historically minoritized bodies during Partition and later, I am not suggesting that we disavow the desire for and assertion of legal citizenship. As Rajeswari Sunder Rajan has observed, "Law and the rights of citizenship, deeply, even constitutively, flawed though they may be as structures of egalitarianism and justice, are nevertheless an *option* available to those who have been traditionally denied them under long-standing conditions of oppression."[4] The cultural texts taken up here signal a subaltern past in which the state deploys both citizenship and "refugee" status as a modern technology of displacing and disenfranchising ethnically minor populations. They also disclose the loss of human rights for those who lack citizenship or for those whose citizenship is violently marked minor by the technologies of ethnicity, racialized religion, gender, or poverty. This is then, I hope, a different look at the checkered, historical unfolding of gendered citizenship cultures and their promises of national belonging and state protection, in decolonization in 1947 India, and in globalization now. The turn to what I have theorized as the postcolonial public sphere is crucial: the counter-public contestation of state violence and migrant re-imagining of national belonging illuminates, albeit fragmentarily, some of the political languages and practices by which people survive partitioned postcoloniality. Gayatri Spivak has usefully reminded us that "however transnationalized or globalized today's world might be, the boundaries of a civil society still mark out the individual state and are still nationally defined."[5] In the struggle for the material realization of justice and human rights, the scene of the national gets rewritten in the transnational counter-public sphere; this counter-public evinces that the effects of colonialism, globalization and imperialism in Asia and elsewhere demand that we denaturalize state power and violence that gendered ideologies of nationality as homeliness often consolidate. Misha Kavka has also pointed out that "the ongoing history of doing/thinking feminism is precisely that which keeps the possibility of justice in place as a promise."[6] The genealogical impulse of this book's feminist project not only identifies the accidents and errors that produced the nations and minor identities that dominate the public imagination of South Asians today, but also insists on a new look at the ambivalent gendered embodiments and normative intimate attachments that mar nationalist histories.

My desire here has been to locate and theorize the alternative forms of ethical belonging, cultural community and political alliance in the postcolonial public sphere that "unmatter race" (to use Toni Morrison's phrase) and refuse a politics of nation as home. This can enable us to formulate a fuller account of what Foucault has called the project of "freedom and liberation" that dominates the political imagination in the United States. Our alternative or counter-narratives of transnational identities and communities can not only challenge the dominance of the nation form in narratives of belonging, but can also forge counter-geographies that interrogate the impact of gendered economic and ethnic violence, mass migration and minoritized politics in a more transnational, less nationalist form. The poem with which this conclusion began enacts the humanist mode of non-normative belongings that this book wishes to imagine into hegemony: it embodies a minor culture that, to appropriate Bhabha's words, "prefigures a kind of solidarity between ethnicities that meet in the tryst of colonial history."[7]

Notes

CHAPTER 1

1. M. K. Gandhi, *Non-Violence in Peace and War* vol. II (Ahmedabad: Navajivan Publishing House, 1948) 55.

2. Walter Benjamin, *Reflections*, ed. Peter Demetz, trans. Edmund Jephcott (New York: Schocken Books, 1978) 277.

3. Judith Butler, *Precarious Life: The Power of Mourning and Violence* (New York: Verso Books, 2004) 151.

4. Muzamil Jaleel, "Kashmir's Bus Ride to Peace," April 8, 2005, February 5, 2006, <http://www.opendemocracy.net>

5. David Ludden, *Making India Hindu: Religion, Community and the Politics of Democracy in India* (Delhi, Oxford University Press, 1996) 16.

6. Daya Gamage, "United States Issues Country Report on Terrorism: *Asian Tribune* presents South/Central Asia Assessment," May 1, 2007 <www.asiantribune.com>

7. H. V. Hodson, *The Great Divide* (London: Heinemann, 1969) 236.

8. See Sumit Sarkar, *Modern India 1885–1947* (New Delhi: Macmillan India, 1983).

9. This is the unofficial count, culled from the accounts of journalists and military officers who witnessed Partition in 1947. See Patrick French, *Liberty or Death: India's Journey to Independence and Division* (London: Harper Collins Publishers, 1997). By official counts, ten million people migrated and approximately 180,000 were killed. While this communal violence was unprecedented, a structural antagonism between Hindus and Muslims (where those religious affiliations were slowly translated into political identities) had been initiated first by British colonial political discourse and policy, and changes in colonial economic relations, and later by the growing Hinduization of nationalism. For a good account of this development, see, among others, Achin Vanaik, *The Painful Transition: Bourgeois Democracy in India* (London: Verso, 1990) 139–145.

10. Amitav Ghosh, *The Shadow Lines* (New York: Viking, 1988) 190.

11. Urvashi Butalia, *The Other Side of Silence: Voices from the Partition of India* (New Delhi: Viking, 1998) 272.

12. For an excellent account of these socio-political transitions, see Sunil Khilnani, *The Idea of India* (London: Penguin, 1997).

13. Jawaharlal Nehru, "Speech on the Granting of Indian Independence, August 14, 1947," *Penguin Book of Twentieth Century Speeches*, ed. Brian McArthur (London: Penguin Viking, 1992) 234–237.

14. Vallabhbhai Patel, *Speeches of Patel: For a United India* (Delhi: Publications Division, Old Secretariat, 1950) 135.

15. Vallabhbhai Patel, *Speeches of Patel*, 137.

16. Rajendra Prasad, "Introduction," *The Way to Communal Harmony*, ed. U R Rao (Ahmedabad: Navjivan, 1992) xi–xii.

17. "Partition Still Remains a Curse: Advani," *The Economic Times* [Bombay] June 9, 1997.

18. Gyan Pandey, "The Prose of Otherness," *Subaltern Studies VIII*, eds. David Arnold and David Hardiman (Delhi: Oxford University Press, 1994) 189.

19. Urvashi Butalia "Community, State and Gender: On Women's Agency During Partition," *Economic and Political Weekly* (April 24, 1993): 13.

20. Purnima Mankekar, *Screening Culture, Viewing Politics: An Ethnography of Television, Womanhood and Nation in Postcolonial India* (Durham: Duke University Press, 1999) 332.

21. See Christopher Alan Bayly, *Indian Society and the Making of the British Empire* (Cambridge: Cambridge University Press, 1988); Ajit Bhattacharjea, *Countdown to Partition: The Final Days* (New Delhi: HarperCollins Publishers India, 1997); Sumit Sarkar, *Modern India 1885–1947* (New Delhi: Macmillan India 1983); Alan Campbell- Johnson, *Mission with Mountbatten* (Pennsylvania: Atheneum, 1951); Walter Wallbank, ed., *The Partition of India: Causes and Responsibilities* (Boston: D. C. Heath & Company, 1966); H. V. Seshadri, *Tragic Story of Partition* (Bangalore, 1982) and Mushirul Hasan, ed., *India's Partition: Process, Strategy and Mobilization* (Delhi; Oxford: Oxford University Press, 1994 [1993]).

22. For example, see Soumitra De, *Nationalism and Separatism in Bengal: A Study of India's Partition* (Delhi: Vikas and Har Anand Publications, 1992); Joya Chatterji, *Bengal Divided: Hindu Communalism and Partition, 1932–47* (Cambridge: Cambridge University Press, 1994); Penderel Moon, *Divide and Quit* (London: Chatto & Windus, 1961); J. Nanda, *Punjab Uprooted: A Survey of the Punjab Riots and Rehabilitation Problems* (Bombay: Hind Kitab Publishers, April 1948).

23. See among others, Paul R. Brass, *The Politics of India Since Independence* (Cambridge [England]; New York: Cambridge University Press, 1990); Achin Vanaik, *The Painful Transition: Bourgeois Democracy in India* (London: Verso, 1990); Asghar Ali Engineer, ed. *Communal Riots in Post-Independence India* (Hyderabad: Sangam Books, 1984).

24. Mushirul Hasan, ed., *India Partitioned: The Other Face of Freedom volumes I & II* (New Delhi: Roli Books, 1995); Alok Bhalla, ed., *Stories About the Partition of India* 3 vols (New Delhi: HarperCollins, 1994); Alok Bhalla, ed., *The Life and Works of Saadat Hasan Manto* (Simla: Indian Institute of Advanced Study, 1997). See also Ravikant and Tarun K. Saint, eds., *Translating Partition* (Delhi: Katha, 2001); Sukrita

Paul Kumar and Muhammad Ali Siddiqui, eds., *Mapping Memories: Urdu Stories from India and Pakistan* (Delhi: Katha, 1998).

25. Gyan Pandey, *Remembering Partition: Violence, Nationalism and History in India* (Cambridge: Cambridge University Press, 2002); Dipesh Chakrabarty, *Habitations of Modernity: Essays in the Wake of Subaltern Studies* (Chicago: University of Chicago Press, 2002); Veena Das, *Critical Events, An Anthropological Perspective on Contemporary India* (Delhi; New York: Oxford University Press, 1995) and *Life and Words: Violence and the Descent into the Ordinary* (Berkeley: University of California Press, 2007). See also Veena Das, ed., *Mirrors of Violence: Communities, Riots and Survivors in South Asia* (Delhi, New York: Oxford University Press, 1990); Urvashi Butalia, "Community, State, and Gender" and *The Other Side of Silence*; Ritu Menon and Kamla Bhasin, "Abducted Women, the State and Questions of Honour: Three Perspectives on the Recovery of Operation in Post-Partition India," *Embodied Violence: Communalising Women's Sexuality in South Asia*, eds. Kumari Jayawardena and Malathi de Alwis (Delhi: Kali for Women, 1996) 1–31. Also by Menon and Bhasin, *Borders & Boundaries: Women in India's Partition* (New Delhi: Kali for Women, 1998). Other recent writings that focus on the issues of trauma and recovering the memory of 1947 are Sukeshi Karma, *Bearing Witness: Partition, Independence, End of the Raj* (Calgary: University of Calgary Press, 2002); Suvir Kaul, ed., *Partitions of Memory: Afterlife of the Division of India* (Delhi: Permanent Black, 2001).

26. Pandey, *Remembering Partition*, 48.

27. Mankekar, *Screening Culture, Viewing Politics*, 332.

28. Pandey, *Remembering Partition*, 16.

29. Oskar Negt and Alexander Kluge, *Public Sphere and Experience: Toward an Analysis of the Bourgeois and Proletarian Public Sphere* trans. Peter Labanyi, Jamie Owen Daniel, and Assenka Oksiloff, Foreword by Miriam Hansen (Minneapolis: University of Minnesota Press, 1993) ix.

30. Jurgen Habermas, *The Structural Transformation of the Public Sphere* (Cambridge, MA: MIT Press, 1989).

31. Negt and Kluge, *Public Sphere*, xiv.

32. Miriam Hansen, *Babel and Babylon: Spectatorship in American Silent Film* (Cambridge: Harvard University Press, 1991) 13.

33. Rita Felski, *Beyond Feminist Aesthetics: Feminist Literature and Social Change* (Cambridge: Harvard University Press, 1989) 167.

34. Dietrich Reetz, *Islam in the Public Sphere: Religious Groups in India, 1900–1947* (New York: Oxford University Press, 2006).

35. Francesca Orsini, *The Hindi Public Sphere 1920–1940: Language and Literature in the Age of Nationalism* (New York: Oxford University Press, 2002).

36. Michel Foucault, *Power/Knowledge: Selected Interviews & Other Writings 1972–1977* (New York: Pantheon Books, 1980) 82.

37. Homi K. Bhabha, "Making Difference" *Artforum International* 41.8 (Apr 2003): 73.

38. See Partha Chatterjee, *The Nation and Its Fragments: Colonial and Postcolonial Histories* (Delhi; New York: Oxford University Press, 1994); Kumkum Sangari and Sudesh Vaid, eds., *Recasting Women: Essays in Colonial History* (Delhi: Kali for Women, 1989); Ravi Vasudevan, "Dislocations: The Cinematic Imagining of a new Society in 1950s in India," *Oxford Literary Review* 16 (1994): 93–124. For

an illuminating discussion of this transformation of gender relations in the colonial context, see Lata Mani, *Contentious Traditions: The Debate on Sati in Colonial India* (Berkeley and Los Angeles: University of California Press, 1998). See also Gayatri Chakravorty Spivak, "Can the Subaltern Speak?" *Marxism and the Interpretation of Culture*, eds. Cary Nelson and Lawrence Grossberg (Urbana, IL: University of Illinois Press, 1988); Ashish Nandy, *The Intimate Enemy: Loss and Recovery of Self Under Colonialism* (Delhi: Oxford, 1983).

39. Benedict Anderson, *Imagined Communities* (London, New York: Verso, 1983).

40. Recently, a rich debate has emerged, through the efforts of Rajeev Bhargav and Helmut Reifeld, about the valence of the concept of the public sphere as "Western" and its relationship to civil society and the production of citizenship in colonial and postcolonial India. See Rajeev Bhargava and Helmut Reifeld, eds., *Civil Society, Public Sphere and Citizenship: Dialogues and Perceptions* (London: Sage Publications, 2005).

41. Michel Foucault, *Power/Knowledge*, 85.

42. Arjun Appadurai, *Modernity at Large: Cultural Dimensions of Globalization.* Minneapolis: University of Minnesota Press, 1995; Saskia Sassen, *Guests and Aliens* (New York: The New Press, 1999) and *Globalization and Its Discontents* (New York: The New Press, 1998).

43. Jacqueline Bhabha, "Embodied Rights: Gender Persecution, State Sovereignty and Refugees," *Public Culture* 9 (1996): 65–87. See also Liisa H. Malkki, *Purity and Exile: Violence, Memory, and National Cosmology Among Hutu Refugees in Tanzania* (Chicago: University of Chicago Press, 1995); Susan Forbes-Martin, *Refugee Women*, Women and World Development Series (London: Zed Books, 1992).

44. Recent scholarship by Roberta Cohen, Francis Mading Deng and others has explored the causes and consequences of displacement, including its devastating impact both within and beyond the borders of affected countries. See Roberta Cohen and Francis Mading Deng, *Masses in Flight: The Global Crisis of Internal Displacement* (Brookings Institute, 1998). See also Doreen Marie Indra, ed., *Engendering Forced Migration: Theory and Practice*, Refugee and Forced Migration Studies, Vol. 5 (Berghahn Books: 1999).

45. Hannah Arendt, *Imperialism* (San Diego, New York, London: Harcourt Brace Jovanovich, Publishers 1968[1951]) 159.

46. Arendt, *Imperialism*, 175.

47. Victor Turner, *The Ritual Process: Structure and Anti-Structure* (Chicago: Aldine, 1969) 95.

48. Victor Turner, *The Forest of Symbols: Aspects of Ndembu Ritual* (Ithaca, NY: Cornell University Press, 1967) 97.

49. Malkki, *Purity and Exile*, 9.

50. Malkki, *Purity and Exile*, 13.

51. Rajeswari Sunder Rajan, *The Scandal of the State: Women, Law and Citizenship in India* (Durham and London: Duke University Press, 2003) 42.

52. Sangeeta Ray, *En-gendering India: Woman and Nation in Colonial and Postcolonial Narratives* (Durham: Duke University Press, 2000); Partha Chatterjee, *The Nation and Its Fragments*; Anne McClintock, *Imperial Leather: Race, Gender, and Sexuality in the Colonial Conquest* (New York: Routledge, 1995).

53. Sunder Rajan, *The Scandal of the State.*

54. Ray, *En-gendering India*, 155.

55. Mrinalini Sinha, *Colonial Masculinity: The "Manly Englishman" and the "Effeminate Bengali" in the Late 19th Century* (Manchester: Manchester University Press, 1995); Rosalind O'Hanlon, "Issues of Masculinity in North Indian History: The Bangash Nawabs of Farrukhabad," *Indian Journal of Gender Studies* 4 (1997): 1–19; Sikata Banerjee, *Make Me a Man!: Masculinity, Hinduism and Nationalism in India* (Albany: State University of New York Press, 2005). See also the volume of essays edited by Sanjay Srivastava, ed., *Sexual Sites, Seminal Attitudes Sexualities, Masculinities and Culture* (New Delhi: Sage Publications, 2004).

56. Lauren Berlant and Michael Warner, "Sex in Public," *Critical Inquiry* 24.2 (Winter 1998): 547–566. 554.

57. Berlant and Warner, "Sex in Public," 553.

58. Laura Kipnis, "Adultery" *Critical Inquiry* 24. 2 (Winter 1998): 289–327. 323.

59. Lauren Berlant, *The Queen of America Goes to Washington City* (Durham and London: Duke University Press, 1997) 18.

60. Amritjit Singh and Peter Schmidt, eds., *Postcolonial Theory and the United States: Race, Ethnicity and Literature* (Jackson: University Press of Mississippi, 2000) viii.

61. Sugata Bose and Ayesha Jalal, *Modern South Asia; History, Culture, Political Economy* (New York: Routledge, 2004) 162.

62. Henry Schwarz, "Mission Impossible: Introducing Postcolonial Studies in the U.S. Academy," *A Companion to Postcolonial Studies*, eds. Henry Schwarz and Sangeeta Ray (Oxford, U.K.: Blackwell Publishers, 2000) 9.

63. Rajini Srikanth, *The World Next Door: South Asian American Literature and the Idea of America* (Philadelphia: Temple University Press, 2004) 44.

64. Robert Stam and Ella Shohat, *Flagging Patriotism: Crises of Narcissism and Anti-Americanism* (New York: Routledge, 2007) 245.

65. Chatterjee, *The Nation and Its Fragments*, 134.

66. "Migration Facts and Figures," The International Organization for Migration, 2007, February 20, 2007 <http://www.iom.int/>

67. Hillary Mayel, "World Refugees Number 35 Million," *National Geographic News*, 2003, June 16, 2003 <http://news.nationalgeographic.com>

68. Bruce Robbins and Pheng Cheah, eds., *Cosmopolitics: Thinking and Feeling Beyond the Nation* (Minneapolis: University of Minnesota Press, 1998).

69. Benedict Anderson, qtd. in Bruce Robbins, "Introduction Part I: Actually Existing Cosmopolitanism," *Cosmopolitics: Thinking and Feeling Beyond the Nation*, eds. Pheng Cheah and Bruce Robbins (Minneapolis: University of Minnesota Press, 1998) 11.

70. Sucheta Mazumdar, "The Politics of Religion and National Origin: Rediscovering Hindu Indian Identity in the United States," *Antinomies of Modernity: Essays on Race, Orient, Nation*, eds. Vasant Kaiwar and Sucheta Mazumdar (Durham: Duke University Press, 2003) 236.

71. Mazumdar, "The Politics of Religion," 251.

72. Gayatri Chakravorty Spivak, *A Critique of Postcolonial Reason* (Durham and London: Duke University Press, 1999) 363.

73. Homi Bhabha, "Democracy De-Realized," *Diógenes* 50.1 (2003): 27–35.

74. Dipesh Chakrabarty, *Provincializing Europe* (Princeton: Princeton University Press, 2000).

75. Shahid Amin, *Event, Metaphor, Memory: Chauri Chaura, 1922–1992* (Berkeley, University of California Press, 1995).

76. David L. Eng, *Racial Castration: Managing Masculinity in Asian America* (Durham: Duke University Press, 2001) 21.

77. Michel Foucault, *Language, Counter-Memory, Practice*, ed. Donald F. Bouchard (Ithaca, NY: Cornell University Press, 1988 [1977]) 146.

78. Chakrabarty, *Habitations of Modernity*, 148.

79. S. Shankar, "Passage to North America," *Contours of the Heart: South Asians Map North America*, eds. Sunaina Maira and Rajini Srikanth (New York: The Asian American Writers' Workshop, 1996) 113.

CHAPTER 2

1. Khushwant Singh, *Train to Pakistan* (New Delhi: Ravi Dayal Publisher, 1956) 201.

2. Sumit Sarkar, *Modern India 1885–1947* (Delhi: Macmillan, 1983) 79.

3. Bernard Cohn, *An Anthropologist Among the Historians and Other Essays* (Delhi: Oxford University Press, 1987). Lloyd and Susanne Rudolph, *The Pursuit of Lakshmi: The Political Economy of the Indian State* (Chicago: University of Chicago Press, 1987) 55. The Rudolphs have pointed out that even the "Hindu majority" in India "is an artifact of categorization." See also Dipesh Chakrabarty, "Modernity and Ethnicity in India," *Politics of Violence*, eds. John McGuire, Peter Reeves and Howard Brasted (London: Sage Publications, 1996).

4. See Dipesh Chakrabarty, "Modernity and Ethnicity in India," *Recasting Women: Essays in Colonial History*, eds. Kumkum Sangari and Sudesh Vaid (New Delhi: Kali for Women, 1993); Partha Chatterjee, *The Nation and Its Fragments: Colonial and Postcolonial Histories* (Delhi; New York: Oxford University Press, 1994).

5. The Hindu cow-protection movement sought to ban the slaughter of cows in Muslim slaughter-houses (and especially on the annual Muslim festival of the Bakr-Id sacrifice), and the consumption of beef in Muslim kabab-houses. The cow was seen as sacred, a religious symbol of Hinduism, and was also, apart from land, the most valuable economic asset for the peasant. This issue thus united elite as well as popular communalist sentiment, as J. R. McLane suggests in *Indian Nationalism and the Early Congress* (Princeton, 1977).

6. Sarkar, *Modern India*, 233–234.

7. Ayesha Jalal, "Exploding Communalism," *Nationalism, Democracy and Development*, eds. Sugata Bose and Ayesha Jalal (Delhi: Oxford University Press, 1998) 76–104.

8. Sarkar, *Modern India*, 234.

9. Jawaharlal Nehru, *Selected Works*, vol. 7 (Delhi: Orient Longman, 1975) 175–190.

10. The rule of Ram, the legendary Hindu god and one-time ruler of India in Hindu mythology.

11. Asghar Ali Engineer, *Communalism in India: A Historical and Empirical Study* (New Delhi: Vikas Publishing House, 1995). See also Mushirul Hasan, ed., *India's Partition: Process, Strategy and Mobilization* (Delhi; Oxford: Oxford University Press, 1993).

12. Ayesha Jalal, *The Sole Spokesman: Jinnah, the Muslim League and the Demand for Pakistan* (New York: Cambridge University Press, 1985), 2. Quoted in Ritu Menon and Kamala Bhasin, *Borders & Boundaries: Women in India's Partition* (New Delhi: Kali for Women, 1998) 4.

13. Bipan Chandra, *Selected Writings on Communalism* (Delhi: People's Publishing House, 1994) 31.

14. Asghar Ali Engineer, *Communal Riots in Post-Independence India* (Hyderabad: Sangam Books, 1984) xvi. See also Mushirul Hasan, ed., *India's Partition*.

15. Sarkar, *Modern India*. See also Mushirul Hasan, ed., *India's Partition*.

16. See Veena Das, ed., *Mirrors of Violence: Communities, Riots and Survivors in South Asia* (Oxford: Oxford University Press, 1990) 5.

17. Louis Dumont, "Nationalism and Communalism," *Contributions to Indian Sociology*, vol 7 (March 1964): 30–70.

18. Jawaharlal Nehru, "Presidential Address at Lucknow Congress, April 12, 1936," *Selected Works of Jawaharlal Nehru* vol. 7 (Delhi: Orient Longman, 1975) 190.

19. See, among others, Kumkum Sangari and Sudesh Vaid, eds., *Recasting Women: Essays in Colonial History* (Delhi: Kali for Women, 1989); Partha Chatterjee, *The Nation and Its Fragments*; Dipesh Chakrabarty, *Habitations of Modernity: Essays in the Wake of Subaltern Studies* (Chicago: University of Chicago Press, 2002).

20. Ayesha Jalal, "Exploding Communalism," *Nationalism, Democracy and Development*, eds. Sugata Bose and Ayesha Jalal (Delhi: Oxford University Press, 1998) 101–102.

21. Jalal, "Exploding Communalism," 102.

22. Aamir R. Mufti, "Auerbach in Istanbul: Edward Said, Secular Criticism, and the Question of Minority Culture," *Edward Said and the Work of the Critic: Speaking Truth to Power*, ed. Paul A. Bove (Durham: Duke University Press, 2000) 250.

23. Dipesh Chakrabarty, "Modernity and Ethnicity in India," 94.

24. Gyan Pandey, *Remembering Partition: Violence, Nationalism and History in India* (Cambridge: Cambridge University Press, 2001) 3.

25. Gyan Pandey, *Memory, History and Political Violence: Recollections of India's Partition* (unpublished paper, 1999).

26. Ritu Menon and Kamala Bhasin, *Borders & Boundaries: Women in India's Partition*; Veena Das, *Critical Events: An Anthropological Perspective on Contemporary India* (Delhi; New York: Oxford University Press, 1995). See also Veena Das, ed., *Mirrors of Violence* and Urvashi Butalia, *The Other Side of Silence: Voices from the Partition of India* (New Delhi: Viking, 1998). Butalia has suggested that we take these stories as personal histories of Partition that supplement received, nationalist political histories; in the stories collected in her book, many men confess having killed people of the "other" community, in what now seems to them an incomprehensible nightmare that continues to haunt them until today. Many of these oral narratives describe communal violence as that which was inevitable given the disparaging ways in which Hindus treated Muslims, and given the class conflicts between largely Muslim peasants and workers, and their wealthier Hindu bosses. Communal violence thus gets alternately constructed as Muslim "rebellion" or "temporary madness" in many of these oral remembered accounts.

27. Allen Feldman, *Formations of Violence: The Narrative of the Body and Political Terror in Northern Ireland* (Chicago: University of Chicago Press, 1991).

28. Urvashi Butalia, *The Other Side of Silence: Voices from the Partition of India* (New Delhi: Viking, 1998).

29. Butalia, *The Other Side of Silence*, 265.

30. Shahid Amin, *Event, Metaphor, Memory: Chauri Chaura, 1922–1992* (Berkeley: University of California Press, 1995).

31. Sangeeta Ray, *En-Gendering India: Woman and Nation in Colonial and Postcolonial Narratives* (Duke University Press, 2000); Henry Schwarz, "Sexing the Pundits: Gender, Romance and Realism in the Cultural Politics of Colonial Bengal," *Reading the Shape of the World*, eds. Henry Schwarz and Richard Dienst (Boulder: Westview Press, 1996); Partha Chatterjee, *The Nation and Its Fragments: Colonial and Postcolonial Histories* (Delhi; New York: Oxford University Press, 1994). See also Partha Chatterjee, "The Nationalist Resolution of the Women's Question," *Recasting Women: Essays in Colonial History*, eds. Kumkum Sangari and Sudesh Vaid (New Delhi: Kali for Women, 1989); Lata Mani, "Contentious Traditions: The Debate on Sati in Colonial India," *Recasting Women: Essays in Colonial History*, eds. Kumkum Sangari and Sudesh Vaid (Delhi: Kali for Women, 1989).

32. Sangeeta Ray, *En-gendering India: Woman and Nation in Colonial and Postcolonial Narratives* (Durham: Duke University Press, 2000) 52.

33. Partha Chatterjee, *The Nation and Its Fragments*, 134.

34. Frantz Fanon, *Black Skin, White Masks* (London: Paladin, 1970).

35. Judith Kegan Gardiner, ed., *Masculinity Studies and Feminist Theory* (New York: Columbia University Press, 2001); Peter J. Murphy, ed., *Feminism and Masculinities* (Oxford: Oxford University Press, 2004); David L. Eng, *Racial Castration: Managing Masculinity in Asian America* (Durham & London: Duke University Press, 2001); Stephen M. Whitehead and Frank J. Barrett, eds., *The Masculinities Reader* (New York: Polity Press, 2001).

36. Rachel Adams and David Savran, eds., *The Masculinity Studies Reader* (Oxford: Blackwell Publishers, 2002) 12. On war and masculinity, see Leo Brady, *From Chivalry to Terrorism: War and the Changing Nature of Masculinity* (New York: Knopf, 2003).

37. Mrinalini Sinha, *Colonial Masculinity: The "Manly Englishman" and the "Effeminate Bengali" in the Late 19th Century* (Manchester: Manchester University Press, 1995).

38. Rosalind O'Hanlon, "Issues of Masculinity in North Indian History: The Bangash Nawabs of Farrukhabad," *Indian Journal of Gender Studies* 4 (1997): 1–19.

39. David Eng, *Racial Castration*, 21.

40. Anne McClintock, "'No Longer in a Future Heaven:' Gender, Race and Nationalism," *Dangerous Liaisons: Gender, Nation and Postcolonial Perspectives*, eds. Anne McClintock, Aamir Mufti, and Ella Shohat (Minneapolis; London: University of Minnesota Press, 1997) 92.

41. Gayatri Gopinath, *Impossible Desires: Queer Diasporas and South Asian Public Cultures* (Durham: Duke University Press, 2005) 72.

42. Michael Gorra, *After Empire: Scott, Naipaul, Rushdie* (Chicago: University of Chicago Press, 1997) 133.

43. Gorra, *After Empire*, 140.

44. Amy Kaplan, "Romancing the Empire: The Embodiment of American Masculinity in the Popular Historical Novel of the 1890s," *Postcolonial Theory and the*

United States: Race, Ethnicity and Literature, eds. Amritjit Singh and Peter Schmidt (Jackson: University of Mississippi Press, 2000) 224.

45. *Times* (London), September 26, 1947.

46. See Mohandas K. Gandhi, "Speech at a Prayer Meeting—September, 18, 1947," *Gandhi on Women,* ed. Pushpa Joshi (Ahmedabad: Centre for Women's Development Studies and Navajivan Trust, 1988). See also Sangeeta Ray for an extended discussion about this ideology of suicide in *En-Gendering India: Woman and Nation in Colonial and Postcolonial Narratives* (Durham: Duke University Press, 2000).

47. Brian Keith Axel, *The Nation's Tortured Body: Violence, Representation, and the Formation of a Sikh "Diaspora"* (Durham: Duke University Press, 2001) 40.

48. Judith Butler, *Bodies that Matter* (New York and London: Routledge, 1993) 23.

49. Arjun Appadurai has suggested that ethnic violence is engendered by the very anxiety and lack of certainty about identity: one's own and that of others, in "Dead Certainty: Ethnic Violence in the Era of Globalization," *Public Culture* 10.2 (Winter 1998): 225–247.

50. A similar and melodramatic narrative is offered by a contemporary Punjabi film *Shahid-e-Mohabbat* (Martyr of Love), which was popular in the U.K. and U.S. and has been regularly broadcast on television in India since 1998. It is based on a true story, widely reported in Indian newspapers in the early 1950s.

51. Both Gandhi as well as Nehru contributed to this dominant construction of the rural as folk, as "authentic" and representative of true India. For the most articulate vision of this, see Jawaharlal Nehru's *Discovery of India* (Garden City, New York: Doubleday & Company, 1960) and M. K. Gandhi's *Autobiography: Story of My Experiments with Truth* (Beacon Press, [1927] 1993).

52. S. H. Manto, *Kingdom's End and Other Stories,* trans. Khalid Hasan (Delhi: Penguin, 1989) and S. H. Manto, *The Best of Manto: A Collection of His Stories,* trans. J. Rattan (Delhi: Sterling, 1991). Some of his stories have also been translated by Tahira Naqvi and included in L. Flemming, ed., *The Life and Works of Saadat Hasan Manto* (Lahore: Vanguard, 1985).

53. For example, there is a three-volume set of stories translated into English and edited by Alok Bhalla, *Stories About the Partition of India* (Delhi: Indus, 1994); see also a recent two-volume set of literary texts compiled by Mushirul Hasan, ed., *India Partitioned: The Other Face of Freedom vols. 1 and 2* (Delhi: Lotus: 1995).

54. While I disagree with Rushdie's claim that there is very little of worth in vernacular literatures apart from Manto, it is interesting to note that Rushdie's essay is part of this international movement that has renewed attention to Manto as a great writer. See his piece "Damme, This is the Oriental Scene For You!" *The New Yorker,* June 23–30 1997: 52.

55. Khalid Hasan, "Introduction," *Mottled Dawn: Fifty Sketches and Stories of Partition,* by S. H. Manto, trans. Khalid Hasan (Delhi: Penguin India, 1997) 2.

56. See Gyan Pandey, "The Prose of Otherness," *Subaltern Studies,* Volume VIII, eds. D. Arnold and D. Hardiman (Delhi: Oxford University Press, 1992) 188–221. See also Pandey's "In Defense of the Fragment: Writing About Hindu–Muslim Riots in India Today," *Representations* 37 (Winter 1992): 27–55. Some other examples (though there are many more) are Susie Tharu, "Rendering Account of the Nation: Partition Narratives and Other Genres of the Passive Revolution," *Oxford Literature Review,* vol. 16, nos. 1–2 (1994): 69–92; Urvashi Butalia, "Partition and Its Texts," *The Hindu,*

September 21 (1997) 37a; Ian Talbot, "Literature and the Human Drama of the 1947 Partition," *South Asia*, Special Issue, Vol. xviii (1995): 37–56; Ashish Nandy, "Too Painful for Words," *The Sunday Times of India*, July 20, 1997, 1, 3.

57. Khalid Ḥasan, "Introduction," 2.

58. Saadat Hasan Manto, "Colder Than Ice," *Mottled Dawn*, 23–29.

59. Bapsi Sidhwa, *Cracking India* (Minneapolis: Milkweed Editions, 1991). *Cracking India* was originally published in the U.K. as *Ice-Candy Man* (London: Heinemann. 1988).

60. Stephen Holden, "India Torn Apart, as a Child Sees It," *The New York Times* September 10, 1999.

61. Roger Ebert, "Earth," *Chicago Sun-Times*, October 15, 1999.

62. Dorothy Barenscott, ""This is our Holocaust": Deepa Mehta's *Earth* and the Question of Partition Trauma," *Mediascape* 1.2 (Spring 2006), July 5, 2007 <www.tft.ucla.edu/mediascape>

63. Hamid Naficy, *An Accented Cinema: Exilic and Diasporic Filmmaking* (Princeton: Princeton University Press, 2001) 13.

64. Jessica Winter, "Across the Great Divide 'Earth'," *The Village Voice* September 8–14, 1999.

65. Jigna Desai, *Beyond Bollywood: The Cultural Politics of South Asian American Film* (New York: Routledge, 2004) 185.

66. Terry Eagleton, *Rape of Clarissa: Writing, Sexuality and Class Struggle in Samuel Richardson* (Oxford: Blackwell, 1982) 61.

67. Kavita Daiya, "'Honourable Resolutions:' Gendered Violence, Ethnicity and the Nation," *Alternatives: Global Local Political* 27. 2 (April–June 2002): 72–86.

CHAPTER 3

1. Ganda Singh, "A Diary of Partition Days," *India Partitioned: The Other Face of Freedom* vol. 2, ed. Mushirul Hasan (Delhi: Roli International, 1997) 79.

2. Judith Butler, *Precarious Life: The Powers of Mourning and Violence* (London, New York: Verso, 2004) 24.

3. Anita Desai, *Clear Light of Day* (London: Heinemann, 1980).

4. Urvashi Butalia, *The Other Side of Silence: Voices from the Partition of India* (New Delhi: Viking, 1998) 208.

5. Butalia, *The Other Side of Silence,* 143.

6. Butalia, *The Other Side of Silence,* 145.

7. Ritu Menon and Kamala Bhasin, *Borders & Boundaries: Women in India's Partition* (New Delhi: Kali for Women, 1998) 41.

8. Bapsi Sidhwa, *Cracking India* (Milkweed Editions, 1991). All subsequent references appear in parentheses in the text.

9. Interestingly, the child narrator has a special place in Hindi and Urdu literature: As a figure of innocence and heightened non-verbal awareness, the child narrator is understood as presenting the most honest, direct apprehension of reality. Moreover, the innocence attributed to children enables the child narrator to (a) access and be privy to the secret knowledge of house members, and (b) mediate between the sharp, gendered separation of inner and outer (female and male) spaces of the home, as well

as the split between public and private—both within the home, and as it appears in the split between the home and the world in Indian social life.

10. Jill Didur, *Unsettling Partition: Literature, Gender and Memory* (Toronto: University of Toronto Press, 2006) 71.

11. "Co-religionist" was the common term in public and political discourse at the time for those belonging to the same religion.

12. Of course, this raises the question of agency, and to what extent conversions such as Hari's can be described as "voluntary" or "forced." In the face of death, forced displacement, mutilation, rape and torture, the "choice" to convert is only an appearance whose form is a violent one. The conditions of possibility of such "voluntary" conversion make the conversion—inflicted in the name of religion and/or the nation—a historical form of violence upon the other.

13. Unlike Islam, Hinduism and Sikhism are not proselytizing religions, and therefore they do not have official rituals that mark someone as a convert. This posed several problems for Hindus and Sikhs who wanted to retaliate against the forced conversions of Hindus and Sikhs to Islam, and began to re-invent particular cultural practices as "conversion" rituals.

14. Benedict Anderson, *Imagined Communities: Reflections on the Origin and Spread of Nationalism* (London, New York: Verso, 1983) 71.

15. In the Indian context, Bernard Cohn has brilliantly shown how "caste" and "religion" became established by the colonial regime as the "sociological keys" (as instruments and concepts) to the numerical description of society. This in turn contributed to their (the categories') mobilization by those groups seeking representation in the state. See Bernard Cohn, *An Anthropologist Among the Historians and Other Essays* (Delhi: Oxford University Press, 1987) 224–254.

16. Homi Bhabha, *Location of Culture* (London: Routledge, 1994) 140–142.

17. Michel de Certeau, *The Practice of Everyday Life*, trans. Steven Rendall (Berkeley: University of California Press, 1984).

18. Agnes Heller, *Everyday Life* (London: Routledge and Kegan Paul, 1984).

19. Homi Bhabha, *Location of Culture*, 9.

20. Hortense J. Spillers, "Mama's Baby, Papa's Maybe: An American Grammar Book," *Diacritics* 17.2 (Summer 1987): 67.

21. Lauren Berlant, *The Queen of America Goes to Washington City* (Durham and London: Duke University Press, 1997).

22. Allen Feldman, *Formations of Violence* (Chicago: University of Chicago Press, 1991) 80.

23. Alan Feldman, *Formations of Violence*, 80.

24. Sangeeta Ray, *En-Gendering India: Woman and Nation in Colonial and Postcolonial Narratives* (Durham: Duke University Press, 2000) 135–136.

25. Gayatri Chakravarty Spivak, "Introduction," *Selected Subaltern Studies*, eds. Ranajit Guha and Gayatri Chakravarty Spivak (New York, Oxford: Oxford University Press, 1988) 31.

26. Evan Jenkins, *Confidential Reports, April 1947*, Oriental and India Office Collection, British Library R13/1/176.

27. See also Chatterjee, *The Nation and Its Fragments: Colonial and Postcolonial Histories* (Delhi; New York: Oxford University Press, 1994); Kumkum Sangari and

Sudesh Vaid, eds., *Recasting Women: Essays in Colonial History* (New Delhi: Kali for Women, [1989] 1993); Ravi Vasudevan, "Dislocations: The Cinematic Imagining of a New Society in 1950s in India," *Oxford Literary Review* 16 (1994): 93–124.

28. Begum Anees Qidwai, *Azadi ki Chhaon Mein*, qt. in Gyan Pandey, "The Prose of Otherness," *Subaltern Studies* VIII, eds. David Arnold and David Hardiman (Delhi: Oxford University Press, 1994) 188.

29. Aparna Basu, *Rebel With a Cause: Mridula Sarabhai, A Biography* (Delhi: Oxford University Press, 1995).

30. Ganda Singh, *India Partitioned*, 81.

31. Ritu Menon and Kamala Bhasin, *Borders & Boundaries: Women in India's Partition* (New Delhi: Kali for Women, 1998); Urvashi Butalia, "Muslims and Hindus, Men and Women," *Women and the Hindu Right*, eds. Urvashi Butalia and Tanika Sarkar (Delhi: Kali for Women, 1995); Veena Das, *Critical Events* (Delhi: Oxford University Press, 1995).

32. Menon and Bhasin, *Borders & Boundaries*, 215.

33. Urvashi Butalia, "Community, State and Gender: On Women's Agency During Partition," *Economic and Political Weekly* 28.17 (April 24, 1993): 13–24.

34. Ritu Menon and Kamala Bhasin, "Abducted Women, the State and Questions of Honour: Three Perspectives on the Recovery of Operation in Post-Partition India," *Embodied Violence: Communalising Women's Sexuality in South Asia*, eds. Kumari Jayawardena and Malathi de Alwis (Delhi: Kali for Women, 1996) 1–31; see also, by these authors, *Borders & Boundaries: Women in India's Partition.*

35. Homi Bhabha, "Surviving Theory: A Conversation with Homi Bhabha," interview by Kalpana Seshadri Crooks, *The Pre-Occupation of Postcolonial Studies*, eds. Kalpana Seshadri Crooks and Fawzia Afzal-Khan (Durham and London: Duke University Press, 2000) 378b.

36. Michel Foucault, *The Foucault Reader*, ed. Paul Rabinow (New York: Random House, 1984) 89.

37. Elaine Scarry, *The Body in Pain* (Oxford: Oxford University Press, 1985) 4.

38. Dipesh Chakrabarty, *Provincializing Europe: Postcolonial Thought and Historical Difference* (Princeton: Princeton University Press, 2000) 106.

39. Menon and Bhasin, *Borders & Boundaries*, 43.

40. Menon and Bhasin, *Borders & Boundaries*, 116.

41. Saadat Hasan Manto, *Mottled Dawn*, 49–57.

42. Saadat Hasan Manto, *Mottled Dawn*, 11–14.

43. Kwame Anthony Appiah, "Is the Post- in 'Postmodern the Post- in Postcolonial?" *Critical Inquiry* 17 (Winter, 1991): 336–357.

44. C. M. Naim, Correspondence, March 12, 2000.

45. Judith Butler, *Precarious Life: The Powers of Mourning and Violence* (London: Verso, 2004) 151.

46. Shauna Singh Baldwin, *What the Body Remembers* (Doubleday: New York, 1999).

47. Sumathi Ramaswamy, "Catastrophic Cartographies: Mapping the Lost Continent of Lemuria," *Representations* 67 (Summer 1999): 115–142.

48. Sumita S. Chakravarty, *National Identity in Indian Popular Cinema* (New Delhi, Oxford: Oxford University Press, 1996) 197.

49. I am grateful to Mr. Buddhikot at the National Film Archives of India, Pune, for facilitating my access to these rare journals and films.

50. Girish Karnad, "Comments from the Gallery," *India International Centre Quarterly* 8, 1(1981): 104.

51. Sumita Chakravarty, *National Identity in Indian Popular Cinema*, 129.

52. *Sound*, May 1949, 19.

53. Ashish Rajadhyaksha and Paul Willemen, *Encyclopedia of Indian Cinema* (New Delhi, New York: Oxford University Press, 1994).

54. *Sound*, June 1949, 52–53.

55. *Sound*, June 1949, 52–53.

56. Rajinder Singh Bedi, "Lajwanti," *Stories About the Partition of India* vol I, II, III, ed. Alok Bhalla (New Delhi: Indus, 1994) 25–33.

57. Mohandas K. Gandhi, "Speech at a Prayer Meeting, November 26, 1947," *The Collected Works of Mahatma Gandhi* XC (New Delhi: Publications Division: Ministry of Information and Broadcasting, Government of India, 1984)111–113. 112.

58. Gandhi had a similar perspective on inter-communal relations: When asked whether he encouraged inter-communal marriage between Hindus and Muslims to promote better relations and understanding between them, he asserted that it was not necessary for Hindus and Muslims to marry into each other's communities, but only necessary to maintain relations of friendship and fraternal love: The Hindu man must see the Muslim woman as his sister, and the Muslim man must see the Hindu woman as a sister.

59. Krishan Chandar, "The Peshawar Express," *Writings on India's Partition,* eds. Ramesh Mathur and Mahendra Kulasrestha (Delhi: Simant Publications, 1976) 69–77.

60. Bhisham Sahni, *Tamas*, trans. Jai Rattan (New Delhi: Penguin, 1988). It is worth mentioning that this woman who chooses rape over death is supposed to be low-caste; thus, this characterization articulates discourses of women's honor with hierarchies of caste superiority.

61. Foucault, *The Foucault Reader*, 79.

62. Ganda Singh, "A Diary of Partition Days, 1947–48," *Journal of Indian History* 112.1 (April–August 1960): 55–78.

63. Menon and Bhasin, *Borders & Boundaries*, 253.

CHAPTER 4

1. S. H. Heard, *A Doctor Remembers: I.M.S. Days* (Mss Eur C475, OIOC Collection, British Library) 4–5. .

2. This is stated in the "Convention relating to the Status of Refugees" that was adopted on July 28, 1951 by the United Nations Conference of Plenipotentiaries on the Status of Refugees and Stateless Persons convened under General Assembly resolution 429 (V) of December 14, 1950 < http://www.unhchr.ch/>

3. Hannah Arendt, *Imperialism* (San Diego, New York, London: Harcourt Brace Jovanovich, Publishers, 1968[1951]) 159.

4. Victor Turner, *The Forest of Symbols: Aspects of Ndembu Ritual* (Ithaca, NY: Cornell University Press, 1967) 99.

5. Giorgio Agamben, *Homo Sacer: Sovereign Power and Bare Life* (Stanford: Stanford University Press, 1998) 134.

6. Joya Chatterji, "Right or Charity: The Debate Over Relief and Rehabilitation West Bengal, 1947–1950," *The Partitions of Memory: The Afterlife of the Division of India*, ed. Suvir Kaul (Bloomington: Indiana University Press, 2002) 101.

7. C. M. Naim, *Ambiguities of Heritage: Fictions and Polemics* (Karachi: City Press, 1999) 177.

8. See Akmal Hussain, "The Karachi Riots of December 1986: Crisis of State and Civil Society in Pakistan" and Farida Shaheed, "The Pathan-Muhajir Conflicts, 1985–6: A National Perspective," *Mirrors of Violence: Communities, Riots and Survivors in South Asia*, ed. Veena Das (Delhi: Oxford University Press, 1990).

9. Alan Campbell-Johnson, *Mission with Mountbatten* (Pennsylvania: Atheneum, 1951) 188–189.

10. Government of India, *Annual Report of Ministry of Rehabilitation 1953–54*, 47–49. In Bombay Presidency, these homes are listed as being located in Ulhasnagar, Sardarnagar, and Kolhapur. The term "unattached women" referred not to abducted women (the other category in which women who were outside of traditional familial and community structures were placed by the state), but to women who were separated from their families, left alone and destitute, or widowed, and as a result were placed in the care of the Indian state.

11. Some exceptions to this are V. K. R. V. Rao and P. B. Desai, *Greater Delhi: A Study in Urbanization 1940–1957* (Bombay, New York: Asia Publication House, 1965) and V. N. Datta, "Punjabi Refugees and the Urban Development of Greater Delhi," *Delhi Through the Ages: Selected Essays in Urban History, Culture and Society*, ed. R. E. Frykenberg (Delhi: Oxford University Press, 1993) 287–306. Datta's primarily sociological study offers a useful account of the efforts of the state government to rehabilitate refugees, as well as offers a celebratory narrative of the hardiness of Punjabi identity that enabled Punjabi Partition refugees to assimilate successfully into, and indeed expand and grow, Delhi's urban life. Its striking reinforcement of a collective regional Punjabi identity that is recast in a postcolonial urban mode also challenges discursive claims about refugees' national assimilation.

12. Anita Desai, *Clear Light of Day* (Middlesex, England: Penguin, with William Heinmann Ltd., 1980) 33.

13. *Constituent Assembly of India (Legislative) Debates*, v. ii no. 7, February 25, 1948, 208. The question itself was inspired by a letter in the *Indian News Chronicle* dated October 11, 1947 under the caption "Is it people's rule?"

14. *Times* (London), August 15, 1947, 4–5.

15. *Times* (London), August 26, 1947.

16. *Times* (London), August 30, 1947.

17. *Times* (London), September 13, 1947.

18. See D. F. Karaka, *Freedom Must Not Stink* (Delhi: Kutub, 1948). IOR P/T 5030, OIOC Collection, British Library.

19. *Illustrated Weekly of India*, September 14, 1947.

20. *Illustrated Weekly of India*, September 14, 1947.

21. It is interesting that an exception to this representation of refugees as agents of ethnic violence in the British and Indian press is Peter Green's retrospective article, 40 years later, "Eye-Witness to the End of an Empire," *Canberra Times*, August 15, 1987.

Here, Green mentions that once Hindu and Sikh refugees had arrived in India, "their morale and conduct were exemplary, including their treatment of refugees of both communities." MSS Eur C 416, OIOC Collection, British Library.

22. Agyeya, "No Revenge," *Writings on India's Partition,* eds. Ramesh Mathur and Mahendra Kulasrestha (Calcutta: Simant Publications, 1976) 58–63.

23. *Filmindia,* March 1949, 43–45.

24. *Filmindia,* March 1949, 45. In another instance, Patel's editorial from January 1948 accuses Jinnah of having the blood of millions on his hands, and argues that the greatest price for Pakistan was paid by the film industry, in which many went bankrupt due to the instability caused by ethnic violence. In the same editorial, he also protests the Pakistan government's policy of not allowing their Hindu state employees in Sind to migrate to India, or even to send the women in their family to India for safety (as many Hindu men desired, in the face of the threat of sexual violence against women). This dimension of the transition is very interesting: the Pakistani state, in an attempt to prevent the complete breakdown of the state machinery, made it very difficult—if not impossible—for Hindu state employees to migrate to India: they had to get several "clearance" certificates from various government agencies, certifying things like they did not owe any money to the state, before they were granted permission to dispose of their properties and leave.

25. Those who had migrated to Pakistan, but not permanently, for they had held on to their properties in India.

26. *Filmindia,* October 1949, 3. Earlier, in the November 1947 issue, the "Bombay Calling" column, authored by one "Judas" (probably Patel's pseudonym), expressed similar communal nationalist sentiments. For example, Judas writes, "Muslim producers have become so many Pakistani shovels to lift and throw Indian wealth into the Pakistani territory. . . . A few years ago when we had asked the Hindu and the Muslim producers to vote against communalism in film art, quite a number of fanatic Pakistanis had desisted from voting" (9–11).

27. *Sound,* September 1950, 8.

28. A conference of representatives of displaced persons staying in refugee townships and colonies was held in Bombay on August 31, 1952. These representatives passed a resolution demanding an economic and social survey of displaced persons in the Bombay State and communicated this resolution to the Minister of Rehabilitation. Government of India, *Parliamentary Debates,* November 10, 1952, 188.

29. *Times* (London), September 12, 1947.

30. *Constituent Assembly of India Debates,* February 23, 1948, 1083.

31. B. R. Chopra's house in Lahore had been set on fire and reduced to rubble during the violent period following Partition; he had to flee Lahore with his family in the thick of ethnic violence.

32. Dalsukh Pancholi was known as the king of the Punjab film industry; due to Partition and ethnic violence in Lahore, he migrated first to Delhi in 1947, and then, two years later, to Bombay where he made the film *Meena Bazaar*—a big hit. Before this, he had made *Khazanchi,* which popularized on a national scale the "Punjabi dress" and *Khandaan,* which started the vogue of "socials" on Muslim society. Kuldip Sehgal was another "refugee producer" from this time, who made the Hindi film *Naach* in 1950.

33. Although it is beyond the scope of this project to explore this in detail, it is important to note that Partition also critically impacted the development of modern

Indian art; many prominent contemporary Indian artists today were among those originally displaced to India during or because of Partition, and their work bears the traces of the trauma of the Partition experience. For example, Ganesh Haloi was born in Jamalpur, Mymensingh, now in Bangladesh, in 1936. He moved to Calcutta after the Partition in 1950. The trauma of the uprooting left its mark on his work as it did on some other painters of his generation. He graduated from the Government College of Art and Craft, Calcutta, in 1956. The next year he joined the Archaeological Survey of India to make copies of the Ajanta murals. After seven years' involvement in the work, Haloi returned to work in Calcutta. He taught at the Government College of Art and Craft from 1963 until his retirement. Since 1971, he has been a member of the Society of Contemporary Artists. Similarly, Satish Gujral, a leading artist in India, is originally from Lahore; Gujral came to Bombay in 1944 to study at the J. J. School of Art, and ended up staying on in free India after Partition—he lived in Delhi in and after 1947.

34. Donald F. Ebright, *Free India: The First Five Years, An Account of the 1947 Riots, Refugees, Relief and Rehabilitation* (Nashville, Tennessee: Parthenon Press, 1954), 63.

35. *Filmindia,* November 1947, 11.

36. *Filmindia,* December 1947, 11.

37. *Filmindia,* November 1947, 12.

38. *Sound,* June 1950, 45. This continued through July, August, and September 1950.

39. *Filmindia,* November 1949, 3.

40. *Filmindia,* November 1949, 4.

41. *Filmindia,* September 1949, 3.

42. *Filmindia,* February 1951, 15.

43. *Filmindia,* September 1949, 15.

44. Lalitha Gopalan, *Cinema of Interruptions: Action Genres in Contemporary Indian Cinema* (London: BFI, 2002) 49.

45. *Report of Ministry of Rehabilitation 1952–53,* 2, IOL:V/24/3615, OIOC Collection, British Library.

46. Dina Nath Nijhawan and R. D. Chopra, *Exhaustive Commentary on The Displaced Persons (Compensation and Rehabilitation) Act 1954 and The Displaced Persons (Compensation and Rehabilitation) Rules 1955* (Delhi: Federal Law Depot, Law Publishers [1955] 1980), 3.

47. *Times* (London), September 5, 1947, 4.

48. *Illustrated Weekly of India,* September 14, 1947, 21.

49. Amar Devi Gupta, *A 1947 Tragedy of Jammu and Kashmir State: The Cleansing of Mirpur,* unpublished memoirs manuscript. IOR: Mss Eur C705, OIOC Collection, British Library. This is a fascinating memoir and account of the violent upheavals that the author experienced as her family was scattered, separated, and lost as they fled the Pathan attack. It describes the sexual violence that Muslim, Hindu and American Christian women in the area suffered at the hands of the Pathans, and the complex interweaving of this destruction of domesticity and property with local ethnic and class politics.

50. See Stephen Castles and Mark J. Miller, *The Age of Migration: International Population Movements in the Modern World* (London: Macmillan Press, [1993] 1998).

73. In contrast, the migration to the United States significantly increased with the revised immigration laws of 1965.

51. *Parliamentary Debates: House of the People*, November 18, 1952, 516.

52. In Bombay in 1952, displaced Sindhis also asked the provincial government (which put the matter under further consideration) for a market to be built especially for Sindhis.

53. *Parliamentary Debates: House of the People*, November 21, 1952, 664. Included in this forced migration, or "exchange of populations" in this process of transition, were prisoners: In 1948, Pakistan and India agreed to exchange "an equal number" of prisoners in east and west Punjab jails, some of which contained well-known public workers, primarily because, as Nehru said, Hindu and Sikh prisoners in west Punjab jails must be "undergoing physical and mental suffering." *Constituent Assembly of India Debates*, February 23, 1948, 1083.

54. *Parliamentary Debates: House of the People*, November 13, 1952, 329.

55. Khushwant Singh, *The Unending Trail* (Delhi: Rajkamal Publications, 1957) 1.

56. Singh, *The Unending Trail*, 3.

57. Hannah Arendt, *The Origins of Totalitarianism* (New York: Harcourt Brace and Company, 1979) 298.

58. Singh, *The Unending Trail*, 2.

59. Singh, *The Unending Trail*, 4.

60. Michel Foucault, "The Subject and Power," *Michel Foucault: Beyond Structuralism and Hermeneutics*, eds. Hubert Dreyfus and Paul Rabinow (Chicago: University of Chicago Press, 1982) 208.

61. Gyan Pandey, *Remembering Partition: Violence, Nationalism and History in India* (Cambridge: Cambridge University Press, 2001) 171–172.

62. Government of India, *Annual Report of the Ministry for Rehabilitation 1954–55*, 5.

63. Adil Najam, "Where have Pakistan's Jews gone?" *The Daily Times* (Pakistan) September 16, 2005.

64. For example, see Joan Roland, *The Jewish Communities of India: Identity in a Colonial Era* (New Brunswick: Transaction Publishers, 1998); see also Orpa Slapak, ed., *The Jews of India: A Story of Three Communities* (Jerusalem: The Israel Museum, 1995).

65. Nathan Katz, ed., *Studies of Indian Jewish Identity* (Delhi: Rajkamal Electric Press, 1995).

66. P&S 17/F/2101 (R), Maharashtra State Government Archives, Bombay, India.

67. P&S 3146/46, Maharashtra State Government Archives, Bombay, India.

68. P&S 3146/46/9–11, Maharashtra State Government Archives, Bombay, India.

69. Jacqueline Bhabha, "Embodied Rights: Gender Persecution, State Sovereignty and Refugees," *Public Culture* 9 (1996): 3–32.

70. Naim, *Ambiguities of Heritage*, 152.

71. Campbell-Johnson, *Mission with Mountbatten*, 200.

72. Names changed to protect privacy. Mr. and Mrs. Malhotra, interview by Kavita Daiya, July 25, 1998, Pune, India.

73. Mahatma Gandhi, "Speech at a Prayer Meeting, New Delhi, October 3, 1947," *The Collected Works of Mahatma Gandhi* LXXXIX (New Delhi: Ministry of Information and Broadcasting, Government of India, 1983).

74. *Constituent Assembly of India (Legislative) Debates* vol. ii, no. 5, February 23, 1948, 1048.

75. Rajeswari Sunder Rajan, *The Scandal of the State: Women, Law and Citizenship in Postcolonial India* (Durham and London: Duke University Press, 2003) 6.

76. Pratap Kumar Ghosh, *The Constitution of India: How It Has Been Framed* (Calcutta: The World Press Private Ltd, 1966) 270–271.

77. *Constituent Assembly of India (Legislative) Debates*, August 10, 1949, 349.

78. Pratap Kumar Ghosh, *The Constitution of India,* 269. See also Raj Narain Gupta, *Indian Constitution and Civic Life* (Bombay: Kitab Mahal, Allahabad 1963).

79. *Parliamentary Debates*, 21 Nov 1952, 632.

80. Gandhi, "Speech at a Prayer Meeting, October 1, 1947," *The Collected Works of Mahatma Gandhi* LXXXIX (New Delhi: Ministry of Information and Broadcasting, Government of India, 1983) 268–272. 271.

81. *Constituent Assembly of India (Legislative) Debates*, February 25, 1948, 208.

82. *Constituent Assembly of India (Legislative) Debates*, March 3, 1948, 1509.

83. Eur Mss D/807. OIOC Collection, British Library. Papers of Evan Jenkins. "Report on the Punjab Boundary Force 1 August–1 September 1947," prepared by Major General T. W. Rees in New Delhi on November 15, 1947, 31.

84. Gandhi, "Speech at a Prayer Meeting October 27, 1947," *The Collected Works of Mahatma Gandhi* LXXXIX (New Delhi: Ministry of Information and Broadcasting, Government of India, 1983) 422.

85. Gandhi, "Speech at a Prayer Meeting October 27, 1947," 423.

86. Large sprawling home, usually two storyed and with a terrace, with an inner courtyard around which the various rooms of a house are organized.

87. Convoy of travelers.

88. Naim, *Ambiguities of Heritage*, 55.

89. Lauren Berlant, *The Queen of America Goes to Washington City: Essays on Sex and Citizenship* (Durham and London: Duke University Press, 1997) 212.

90. Dipankar Gupta, "Communalism and Fundamentalism: Some Notes on the Nature of Ethnic Politics in India," *Economic and Political Weekly*, Annual Number (March 1991): 573.

91. Talal Asad, "Religion and Politics: An Introduction," *Social Research*, 59.1(1992): 11.

92. Dina Nath Nijhawan and R. D. Chopra, *Exhaustive Commentary on The Displaced Persons (Compensation and Rehabilitation) Act, 1954, Act. No. 44 and The Displaced Persons (Compensation and Rehabilitation) Rules, 1955* (New Delhi: Federal Law Depot: Law Publishers, 1955.

93. "BJP for Scrapping Resettlement Act," *The Tribune India*, April 30, 2005.

94. Garga, *So Many Cinemas,* 228.

95. The Progressive Writers' Association (PWA) was committed to a self-consciously realist aesthetics and practice in which narrative became the staging ground for a vision (often socialist) of national life as a secular social landscape—an aesthetics that dominated much of the breakaway IPTA filmic production, too. For an excellent account of the history of IPTA, see Nandi Bhatia, "Staging Resistance: The Indian People's Theatre Association," *The Politics of Culture in the Shadow of Capital*, eds. Lisa Lowe and David Lloyd (Durham and London: Duke University Press, 1997) 432–460.

96. Partly based on Krishan Chandar's novelette *Anndata*.

97. Ashish Rajadhyaksha, *A Return to the Epic* (Bombay: Screen Unit, 1982) 72. For other relevant critical excerpts and commentary, see Haimanti Banerjee, *Ritwik Kumar Ghatak* (Pune, India: National Film Archive, 1985).

98. Gurudas Bhattacharya, "Ritwik Ghatak: Ganga to Subarnarekha to Titas," qt. in Haimanti Banerjee, *Ritwik Kumar Ghatak*, 58–59.

99. Erin O'Donnell, "'Woman' and 'homeland' in Ritwik Ghatak's Films: Constructing Post-Independence Bengali Cultural Identity," *Jump Cut: A Review of Contemporary Media* 47 (2004), December 15, 2006 <http://www.ejumpcut.org/>

100. This also illustrates that the prospect of working outside the home, for women in the so-called third world, as also suggested by Gayatri Chakravorty Spivak in a different context, can often be less a privilege or a source of independence and individual fulfillment and realization, and more a form of women's continued exploitation—less a right, and more an unavoidable necessity. Spivak, *In Other Worlds: Essays in Cultural Politics* (New York: Methuen, 1987).

101. Ritwik Ghatak, qt in Garga, *So Many Cinemas*, 230.

102. See http://www.db.idpproject.org/

103. B. M. Sinha, "New Delhi Camps Filled With Hindu Refugees," October 1992, October 25, 2006 <www.hinduismtoday.org>

104. Mr. Gul Mansukhani, interview by Kavita Daiya, August 7, 1999, Pune, India.

CHAPTER 5

1. SMS message circulating on Indian mobile phone networks, as cited by Saba Naqvi Bhaumik, "Bearded and Tagged," *Outlook* July 31, 2006 (India) 36.

2. M. Madhava Prasad, *Ideology of the Hindi Film: A Historical Construction* (Delhi: Oxford University Press, 1998) 109.

3. Lalitha Gopalan, *Cinema of Interruptions: Action Genres in Contemporary Indian Cinema* (London: BFI, 2002) 29.

4. For excellent historical accounts of the development of Indian cinema, see Sumita Chakravarty, *National Identity in Indian Popular Cinema* (New Delhi, Oxford: Oxford University Press, 1996); B. D. Garga, *So Many Cinemas: The Motion Picture in India* (Mumbai: Eminence Designs, 1996); Yves Thoraval, *The Cinemas of India (1896–2000)* (Delhi: Macmillan India, 2000). On the development of Bombay cinema, see Vijay Mishra, *Bollywood Cinema: Temples of Desire* (London and New York: Routledge, 2002).

5. Vijay Mishra, *Bollywood Cinema*, 269.

6. Yoginder Sikand, *Muslims in India Since 1947: Islamic Perspectives on Inter-Faith Relations* (London: Routledge, 2004) 6.

7. Gyan Pandey, *Remembering Partition: Violence, Nationalism and History in India* (Cambridge: Cambridge University Press, 2001) 16–17.

8. Yves Thoraval, *The Cinemas of India*, 51.

9. Tejaswini Ganti, *Bollywood: A Guide to Popular Hindi Cinema* (New York, London: Routledge, 2004) 33.

10. See B. D. Garga, *So Many Cinemas*, 166.

11. Ravi Vasudevan, "Addressing the Spectator of a 'Third World' National Cinema: The Bombay 'Social' Film of the 1940s and 1950s," *Screen* 36.4: 305–324.

12. Ravi Vasudevan, "Addressing the Spectator," 121.

13. See Madhava Prasad, *Ideology of the Hindi Film.*

14. Rachel Dwyer, *Filming the Gods: Religion and Indian Cinema* (New Delhi, Routledge, 2007).

15. Lauren Berlant, "Introduction," *Critical Inquiry* 24.2 (Winter 1988): 288.

16. Vijay Mishra, *Bollywood Cinema,* 216.

17. Amit Rai, "Patriotism and the Muslim Citizen in Hindi Films," *Harvard Asia Quarterly,* vii.3 (Summer 2003).

18. Vijay Mishra, *Bollywood Cinema,* 232–233.

19. Promotional Synopsis. December 10, 2006 <www.yashrajfilms.com>

20. Rachel Dwyer, *Filming the Gods: Religion and Indian Cinema* (London and New York: Routledge, 2006) 129.

21. Ashis Nandy, "Introduction: Indian Popular Cinema as a Slum's Eye View of Politics," *The Secret Politics of our Desires: Innocence, Culpability and Indian Popular Cinema,* ed. Ashis Nandy (London: Zed Books, 1999) 5.

22. M. Madhava Prasad, *Ideology of the Hindi Film,* 95.

23. Gyan Pandey, *Remembering Partition: Violence, Nationalism and History in India* (Cambridge: Cambridge University Press, 2001).

24. Ashis Nandy, "Introduction," 13–14.

25. Amrita Pritam, *A Slice of Life—Selected Works* (New Delhi: UBS Publishers, 1996).

26. Urvashi Butalia, *The Other Side of Silence: Voices from the Partition of India* (New Delhi: Viking, 1998).

27. "'Gadar' at Agra," *The Hindu,* Sunday July 15, 2001.

28. Purnima Mankekar, *Screening Culture, Viewing Politics: An Ethnography of Television, Womanhood and Nation in Postcolonial India* (Durham: Duke University Press, 1999) 331–332.

29. Ashis Nandy, "Introduction," 5.

30. Anjali Monteiro, "Official television and unofficial fabrications of the self," *The Secret Politics of Our Desires: Innocence, Culpability and Indian Popular Cinema,* ed. Ashis Nandy (London: Zed Books, 1999) 162.

31. Alok Bhalla, *Partition Dialogues: Memories of a Lost Home* (Delhi: Oxford University Press, 2006).

32. Ravikant, "Partition: Strategies of Oblivion, Ways of Remembering," *Translating Partition,* eds. Ravikant and Tarun K. Saint (Delhi: Katha, 2001) 162–163.

33. Ravikant, "Partition," 163.

34. Arvind Rajagopal, *Politics After Television: Hindu Nationalism and the Reshaping of the Indian Public* (New York: Cambridge University Press, 2001).

35. Vijay Mishra, *Bollywood Cinema,* 221–222.

CHAPTER 6

1. Amy Waldman, "Torn from Moorings, Villagers Grasp for Past," *The New York Times,* March 6, 2005: 1, 22.

2. Marc Lacey, "Congo Tribal Killings Create a New Wave of Refugees," *The New York Times*, March 6, 2005: 3.

3. Inderpal Grewal, *Transnational America: Feminisms, Diasporas, Neoliberalisms* (Durham: Duke University Press, 2005).

4. See Jacqueline Bhabha, "Border Rights and Rites: Generalizations, Stereotypes and Gendered Migration," *Women and Immigration Law: New Variations on Classical Feminist Themes*, eds. Sarah Van Walsum and Thomas Spijkerboer (Routledge-Cavendish, 2006) and "The Child—What Sort of Human?," *PMLA* 121.5 (October 2006). Also by Bhabha, "'Not a Sack of Potatoes': Moving and Removing Children Across Borders," *Boston University Public Interest Law Journal* 15.2 (Spring 2006): 197. Saskia Sassen, *Globalization and Its Discontents* (New York: The New Press, 1998); Gayatri Chakravorty Spivak, *A Critique of Postcolonial Reason: Toward a History of the Vanishing Present* (Cambridge: Harvard University Press, 1999).

5. Lisa Lowe, *Immigrant Acts: On Asian American Politics* (Durham, London; Duke University Press, 1996); Kandice Chuh, *Imagine Otherwise: On Asian Americanist Critique* (Durham: Duke University Press 2003).

6. Dipesh Chakrabarty, *Provincializing Europe: Postcolonial Thought and Historical Difference* (Princeton: Princeton University Press, 2000) 46.

7. Saskia Sassen, *Globalization and Its Discontents: Selected Essays 1984–1998* (New York: The New Press, 1998). See also Arjun Appadurai, *Modernity at Large: Cultural Dimensions of Globalization* (Minneapolis: University of Minnesota Press, 1996).

8. Saskia Sassen, "Entrapments Rich Countries Cannot Escape: Governance Hotspots," August 1, 2002. <http://ontology.buffalo.edu/>

9. Thomas C. Holt, *The Problem of Race in the 21st Century* (Cambridge, MA: Harvard University Press, 2002) 7.

10. Amritjit Singh and Peter Schmidt, eds., *Postcolonial Theory and the United States: Race, Ethnicity and Literature* (Jackson: University Press of Mississippi, 2000) 4.

11. Singh and Schmidt, *Postcolonial Theory and the United States,* 41.

12. Amitav Ghosh, *The Shadow Lines* (New York: Penguin, 1988). All subsequent references appear in parentheses in the chapter.

13. Homi Bhabha, *Location of Culture* (New York: Routledge, 1994) 34.

14. Bishnupriya Ghosh, "Feminist Critiques of Nationalism and Communalism from Bangladesh and India: A Transnational Reading," *Interventions: Feminist Dialogues on Third World Literature and Film*, eds. Bishnupriya Ghosh and Brinda Bose (New York: Garland Publishing, 1997) 135.

15. Salman Rushdie, *Shame* (New York, Knopf, 1983).

16. Brinda Bose and Bishnupriya Ghosh, "Introduction," *Interventions*, xxiii.

17. Jhumpa Lahiri, *The Interpreter of Maladies* (New York: Mariner, 1999). All subsequent references appear in parentheses in the chapter.

18. Kandice Chuh, "Imaginary Borders," *Orientations: Mapping Studies in the Asian Diaspora*, eds. Kandice Chuh and Karen Shimakawa (Durham: Duke University Press, 2001) 277.

19. Chuh, *Imagine Otherwise,* 15.

20. Rajini Srikanth, *The World Next Door: South Asian American Literature and the Idea of America* (Philadelphia: Temple, 2004) 233.

21. Lowe, *Immigrant Acts,* 167.

22. Chuh, *Imagine Otherwise,* 124.

23. Michel Foucault, *Ethics: Essential Works of Foucault, 1954–1984, Volume 1* (New York: New Press, 2006) 111.

24. Homi Bhabha, *Location of Culture* (New York: Routledge, 1994) 241.

25. "An Attack on the Civilised World," *The Hindu* September 13, 2001.

26. "9/11/2002," *The Times of India,* September 11, 2002 <www.Indiatimes.com>

27. Vijay Prashad, *The Karma of Brown Folk* (Minneapolis: University of Minnesota Press, 2000).

28. Rajini Srikanth, *The World Next Door,* 54.

29. "Britain's Hindus Have Had Enough of 'Asian' Label," July 1, 2006, December 13, 2006 <www.wwrn.org>

30. Vijay Prashad, "Crafting Solidarities," *Apart, Yet Apart: South Asians in Asian America,* eds. Lavina Dhingra Shankar and Rajini Srikanth (Philadelphia: Temple University Press, 1998) 121.

31. Salman Rushdie, *Shalimar, the Clown* (New York: Random House, 2005). All references appear in parentheses in the chapter.

32. Judith Butler, *Precarious Life: The Powers of Mourning and Violence* (London: Verso, 2004).

33. Her son goes on to recount the events following their forced migration in 1990 thus, revealing the problematics of the state response, as well as underscoring the traumatic nature of this ethnic cleansing: "The moment we left our house we were branded as 'MIGRANTS' by the Government and so called 'ALREADY SETTLED' Pandits living outside valley. For the first time I realized how tough it was to survive in this harsh world. We lived in a rented apartment in Faridabad, near Delhi. The house we lived in had no windows and no fans. For first couple of weeks we didn't even have a refrigerator. We had to battle against a lot of things outside valley, heat of plains being one of them. God somehow gave us, and many families like us, a lot of strength. We survived and took everything as a challenge. My mother found a job for herself. We started gathering the threads of our life with time. But strangely enough, the scars have only become bigger with time. My grandfather literally went insane. He could not bear the fact that he was being forcibly made to leave his house. He could not bear that he had left his palatial bungalow and was living in a rented home in Jammu with absolutely no amenities. He soon stopped recognizing people and stopped eating. We lost him soon and the tragedy was that we could not even mourn for him properly. Many more such tragedies happened. Many people have been languishing ever since in the migrant camps and normal life has never been restored for them." "January 20, 1990—A survivor's story," July 5, 2006, October 20, 2006 <http://www.kashmiri-pandit.org>

34. See, among others, Valentine E. Daniel, *Charred Lullabies: Chapters in an Anthropology of Violence* (Princeton: Princeton University Press, 1996); Stanley. J Tambiah, *Leveling Crowds: Ethnonationalist Conflicts and Collective Violence in South Asia* (Berkeley: University of California Press, 1996).

35. Michael Ondaatje, *Anil's Ghost* (New York: Vintage Books, 2000) 17. All subsequent references appear in parentheses in the chapter.

36. Kwame Anthony Appiah, "Is the Post- in Postmodern the Post- in Postcolonial?" *Critical Inquiry* 17 (1991): 336–357.

37. See Stephen Castles and Mark J. Miller, *The Age of Migration: International Population Movements in the Modern World* (London: Macmillan Press, [1993] 1998).

38. Homi Bhabha, "Untimely Ends: Homi K. Bhabha on Edward Said," *Artforum International* v. 42 no. February 6, 2004, 19.

39. Gayatri Spivak, *A Critique of Postcolonial Reason*, 401.

40. Timothy Brennan, "The National Longing for Form," *Nation and Narration: Post-Structuralism and the Culture of National Identity*, ed. Homi Bhabha (London: Routledge, 1990) 59.

CONCLUSION

1. Ishwar Anchal, "Exile," *Freedom and Fissures: An Anthology of Sindhi Partition Poetry*, trans. Anju Makhija and Menka Shivdasani (New Delhi: Sahitya Akademi, 1998), 40.

2. Homi Bhabha, *Location of Culture* (London: Routledge, 1993), 250.

3. Henry Schwarz and Richard Dienst, "Introduction: Warning! Cautious Readers!" *Reading the Shape of the World*, eds. Henry Schwarz and Richard Dienst (Boulder: Westview Press, 1996), 2.

4. Rajeswari Sunder Rajan, *The Scandal of the State: Women, Law and Citizenship in Postcolonial India* (Durham and London: Duke University Press, 2003), 234.

5. Gayatri Chakravorty Spivak, *A Critique of Postcolonial Reason: Toward a History of the Vanishing Present* (Cambridge and London: Harvard University Press, 1999), 399.

6. Misha Kavka, "Introduction," *Feminist Consequences: Theory for a New Century*, eds. Elisabeth Bronfen and Misha Kavka (New York: Columbia University Press, 2001), xxiv.

7. Homi Bhabha, *Location of Culture*, 231.

Bibliography

PERIODICALS

Articles, advertisements and letters in periodicals including *Illustrated Weekly of India, Times (London), Statesman (Calcutta), Times of India, Filmindia, Sound, Indian Women's Weekly, Kaiser-I-Hind, Indian News Chronicle, The Daily Times (Pakistan), Asian Tribune, The New York Times, Dawn, Outlook, The Hindu, Hindustan Times, Village Voice, Chicago Sun Times, The Economic Times, Harvard Asia Quarterly, The TribunIndia* are cited in footnotes throughout the text.

BOOKS AND ARTICLES

Adams, Rachel, and David Savran, eds. *The Masculinity Studies Reader.* Oxford: Blackwell, 2002.

Agamben, Giorgio. *Homo Sacer: Sovereign Power and Bare Life.* Stanford: Stanford University Press, 1998.

Ageya. "No Revenge." *Writings on India's Partition.* Eds. Ramesh Mathur and Mahendra Kulasrestha. Calcutta: Simant Publications, 1976. 58–63.

Amin, Shahid. *Event, Metaphor, Memory: Chauri Chaura, 1922–1992.* Berkeley: University of California Press, 1995.

Anchal, Ishwar. "Exile." *Freedom and Fissures: An Anthology of Sindhi Partition Poetry.* Trans. Anju Makhija and Menka Shivdasani. New Delhi: Sahitya Akademi, 1998.

Anderson, Benedict R. *Imagined Communities: Reflections on the Origin and Spread of Nationalism.* London, New York: Verso, 1983.

———. "Exodus." *Critical Inquiry* 20 (Summer 1994): 738–755.

Appadurai, Arjun. *Modernity at Large: Cultural Dimensions of Globalization.* Minneapolis: University of Minnesota Press, 1996.

Appiah, Kwame Anthony. "Is the Post- in Postmodern the Post- in Postcolonial?" *Critical Inquiry* 17 (Winter 1991): 336–357.

Arendt, Hannah. *The Origins of Totalitarianism*, new edition. New York: Harcourt Brace and Company, 1979.

———. *Imperialism*. San Diego, New York, London: Harcourt Brace Jovanovich, 1968[1951].

Asad, Talal. "Religion and Politics: An Introduction." *Social Research* Spring (1992): 3–16.

Axel, Brian Keith. *The Nation's Tortured Body: Violence, Representation, and the Formation of a Sikh "Diaspora."* Durham: Duke University Press, 2001.

Balachander, Rajan. *The Dark Dancer.* New York: Simon and Schuster, 1958.

Baldwin. Shauna Singh. *What the Body Remembers.* Doubleday: New York, 1999.

Banerjee, Haimanti. *Ritwik Kumar Ghatak.* Pune, India: National Film Archive, 1985.

Banerjee, Sikata. *Make Me a Man!: Masculinity, Hinduism and Nationalism in India.* Albany: State University of New York Press, 2005.

Baral, Raj, and S. D. Muni. "Introduction: Refugees, South Asia and Security." *Refugees and Regional Security in South Asia.* Eds. S. D. Muni and Lok Raj Baral. Delhi: Konark Publishers, 1996.

Basu, Aparna. *Rebel With a Cause: Mridula Sarabhai, A Biography.* Delhi: Oxford University Press, 1995.

Bayly, Christopher Alan. *Indian society and the making of the British Empire.* Cambridge: Cambridge University Press, 1988.

Bedi, Rajinder Singh. "Lajwanti." *Stories about the Partition of India* vol I, II, III. Ed. and trans. Alok Bhalla, 22–34. New Delhi: Indus, 1994.

Benjamin, Walter. *Reflections.* Ed. Peter Demetz. Trans. Edmund Jephcott. New York: Schocken Books, 1978.

Berlant, Lauren. "Introduction." *Critical Inquiry* 24 (Winter 1998): 281–288.

———. *The Queen of America Goes to Washington City.* Durham and London: Duke University Press, 1997.

———. "'68, or Something." *Critical Inquiry* 21 (Winter 1994): 35–65.

———, and Michael Warner. "Sex in Public." *Critical Inquiry* 24.2 (Winter 1998): 547–566.

Bhabha, Homi. "Untimely ends: Homi K. Bhabha on Edward Said." *Artforum International* 42.6, 19–20. February 2004.

———. "Democracy De-realized." *Diógenes* 50.1, 27–35. 2003. .

———. "Making Difference." *Artforum International* 41.8 (Apr 2003): 73.

———. "Surviving Theory: A Conversation with Homi Bhabha." *The Pre-Occupation of Postcolonial Studies.* Eds. Kalpana Seshadri Crooks and Fawzia Afzal-Khan, 369–379. Durham and London: Duke University Press, 2000.

———. *Location of Culture.* London: Routledge, 1994.

Bhabha, Jacqueline. "Border Rights and Rites: Generalizations, Stereotypes and Gendered Migration." *Women and Immigration Law: New Variations on Classical Feminist Themes.* Eds. Sarah Van Walsum and Thomas Spijkerboer. London: Routledge-Cavendish, 2006.

———. "The Child—What Sort of Human?" *PMLA* 121.5 (2006): 1526–1535.

———. "'Not a Sack of Potatoes': Moving and Removing Children Across Borders." *Boston University Public Interest Law Journal* 15.2 (2006): 197–218.

————. "Embodied Rights: Gender Persecution, State Sovereignty and Refugees." *Public Culture* 9 (1996): 65–87.

Bhalla, Alok, ed. *Stories About the Partition of India* vol. I, II, III. New Delhi: Indus, 1994.

Bhargava, Rajeev, and Helmut Reifeld, eds. *Civil Society, Public Sphere and Citizenship: Dialogues and Perceptions.* London: Sage Publications, 2005.

Bhatia, Nandi. "Staging Resistance: The Indian People's Theatre Association." *The Politics of Culture in the Shadow of Capital.* Eds. Lisa Lowe and David Lloyd. Durham and London: Duke University Press, 1997. 432–460.

Bhattacharjea, Ajit. *Countdown to Partition: The Final Days.* New Delhi: HarperCollins Publishers India, 1997.

Bhuchar, Sudha, and Kristine Landon-Smith. *A Tainted Dawn: Images of Partition.* London: Nick Hern Books, 1999.

Bose, Brinda, and Bishnupriya Ghosh. "Introduction." *Interventions: Feminist Dialogues on Third World Literature and Film.* Eds. Bishnupriya Ghosh and Brinda Bose. New York: Garland Publishing, 1997.

Bose, Sugata, and Ayesha Jalal. *Modern South Asia; History, Culture, Political Economy.* New York: Routledge, 2004.

————. *Nationalism, Democracy & Development.* Delhi: Oxford University Press, 1997.

Brennan, Timothy. "The National Longing for Form." *Nation and Narration: Post-Structuralism and the Culture of National Identity.* Ed. Homi Bhabha. London: Routledge, 1990.

Brass, Paul R. *The Politics of India Since Independence.* Cambridge [England]; New York: Cambridge University Press, 1990.

Brown, Bill. *The Material Unconscious: American Amusement, Stephen Crane, and the Economies of Play.* Cambridge, MA: Harvard University Press, 1996.

Butalia, Urvashi. *The Other Side of Silence: Voices from the Partition of India.* New Delhi: Viking, 1998.

————. "Partition and Its Texts." *Hindu* 21 September 21, 1997.

————. "Community, State, and Gender: On Women's Agency During Partition." *Economic and Political Weekly* 28 (1995): 1125–1132.

————. "Muslims and Hindus, Men and Women." *Women and the Hindu Right.* Eds. Urvashi Butalia and Tanika Sarkar. Delhi: Kali for Women, 1995.

Butler, Judith. *Precarious Life: The Power of Mourning and Violence.* New York: Verso Books, 2004.

————. *Bodies that Matter.* New York and London: Routledge, 1993.

Campbell-Johnson, Alan. *Mission with Mountbatten.* Pennsylvania: Atheneum, 1951.

Castles, Stephen, and Mark J. Miller. *The Age of Migration: International Population Movements in the Modern World.* London: Macmillan Press, 1993.

Certeau, Michel de. *The Practice of Everyday Life.* Trans. Steven Randall. Berkeley: University of California Press, 1984.

Chakrabarty, Dipesh. *Habitations of Modernity: Essays in the Wake of Subaltern Studies.* Chicago: University of Chicago Press, 2002.

————. *Provincializing Europe: Postcolonial Thought and Historical Difference.* Princeton: Princeton University Press, 2000.

————. "Modernity and Ethnicity in India." *Politics of Violence*. Eds. John McGuire, Peter Reeves and Howard Brasted. London: Sage Publications, 1996.

————. "Remembered Villages: Representations of Hindu-Bengali Memories in the Aftermath of the Partition." *Economic and Political Weekly* 31 (1996): 1221–1125.

————. "Radical Histories and Question of Enlightenment Rationalism." *Economic and Political Weekly* 30 (1995): 1125–1130.

————. *Rethinking Working-Class History: Bengal, 1890–1940*. Princeton: Princeton University Press, 1989.

Chakravarty, Sumita. *National Identity in Indian Popular Cinema*. New Delhi, Oxford: Oxford University Press, 1996.

Chandar, Krishan. *Flame and the Flower*. Bombay: Current Book House, 1951.

————. "The Peshawar Express." *Writings on India's Partition*. Eds. Ramesh Mathur and Mahendra Kulasrestha. Delhi: Simant Publications, 1976.

Chandra, Bipin. *Selected Writings on Communalism*. Delhi: People's Publishing House, 1994.

Chatterjee, Partha. *The Nation and Its Fragments: Colonial and Postcolonial Histories*. Delhi; New York: Oxford University Press, 1994

————. "The Nationalist Resolution of the Women's Question." *Recasting Women: Essays in Colonial History*. Eds. Kumkum Sangari and Sudesh Vaid. New Delhi: Kali for Women, 1989.

Chatterji, Joya. "Right or Charity: The Debate Over Relief and Rehabilitation West Bengal, 1947–1950." *The Partitions of Memory: The Afterlife of the Division of India*. Ed. Suvir Kaul. Bloomington: Indiana University Press, 2002.

————. *Bengal Divided: Hindu Communalism and Partition, 1932–47*. Cambridge: Cambridge University Press, 1994.

Chuh, Kandice. *Imagine Otherwise: On Asian Americanist Critique*. Durham: Duke University Press, 2003.

————. "Imaginary Borders." *Orientations: Mapping Studies in the Asian Diaspora*. Eds. Kandice Chuh and Karen Shimakawa. Durham: Duke University Press, 2001.

Cohn, Bernard. *An Anthropologist Among the Historians and Other Essays*. Delhi: Oxford University Press, 1987.

Constituent Assembly of India (Legislative) Debates, 1947–50.

Daniel, Valentine E. *Charred Lullabies: Chapters in an Anthropology of Violence*. Princeton: Princeton University Press, 1996.

Das, Veena. *Life and Words: Violence and the Descent into the Ordinary*. Berkeley: University of California Press, 2007.

————. *Critical Events*. Delhi, New York: Oxford University Press, 1995.

————, ed. *Mirrors of Violence: Communities, Riots and Survivors in South Asia*. Delhi, New York: Oxford University Press, 1990.

Datta, V. N. "Punjabi Refugees and the Urban Development of Greater Delhi." *Delhi Through the Ages: Selected Essays in Urban History, Culture and Society*. Ed. R. E. Frykenberg, 251–275. Delhi: Oxford University Press, 1993.

De, Soumitra. *Nationalism and Separatism in Bengal: A Study of India's Partition*. Delhi: Vikas and Har Anand Publications, 1992.

Deleuze, Gilles and Felix Guattari. *Kafka: Toward a Minor Literature*. Trans. Dana Polan. Minneapolis: University of Minnesota Press, 1986.

Desai, Anita. *Clear Light of Day*. Middlesex, England: Penguin, with William Heinmann Ltd., 1980.

Desai, Jigna. *Beyond Bollywood: The Cultural Politics of South Asian American Film*. New York: Routledge, 2004.

Didur, Jill. *Unsettling Partition: Literature, Gender and Memory*. Toronto: University of Toronto Press, 2006.

Dumont, Louis. "Nationalism and Communalism." *Contributions to Indian Sociology* 7 (March 1964): 35–51.

Dwyer, Rachel. *Filming the Gods: Religion and Indian Cinema*. New Delhi: Routledge, 2007.

Eagleton, Terry. *Rape of Clarissa: Writing, Sexuality and Class Struggle in Samuel Richardson*. Oxford: Blackwell, 1982.

Ebright, Donald F. *Free India: The First Five Years, An Account of the 1947 Riots, Refugees, Relief and Rehabilitation*. Nashville, TN: Parthenon Press, 1954.

Eng, David. *Racial Castration: Managing Masculinity in Asian America*. Durham: Duke University Press, 2001.

Engineer, Asghar Ali, ed. *Communal Riots in Post-Independence India*. Hyderabad: Sangam Books, 1984.

———. *Communalism in India: A Historical and Empirical Study*. New Delhi: Vikas Publishing House, 1995.

Fanon, Frantz. *Black Skin, White Masks*. London: Paladin, 1970.

Feldman, Allen. *Formations of Violence*. Chicago: University of Chicago Press, 1991.

Felski, Rita. *Beyond Feminist Aesthetics: Feminist Literature and Social Change*. Cambridge: Harvard University Press, 1989.

Flemming, L. *The Life and Works of Saadat Hasan Manto*. Lahore: Vanguard, 1985.

Foucault, Michel. *Ethics: Essential Works of Foucault, 1954–1984, Volume 1*. New York: The New Press, 2006.

———. *Language, Counter-Memory, Practice: Selected Essays and Interviews*. 1977. Ithaca, NY: Cornell University Press, 1996.

———. *The Foucault* Reader. Ed. Paul Rabinow. New York: Random House, 1984.

———. "The Subject and Power." *Michel Foucault: Beyond Structuralism and Hermeneutics*. Eds. Hubert Dreyfus and Paul Rabinow. Chicago: University of Chicago Press, 1982.

———. *Power/Knowledge: Selected Interviews & Other Writings 1972–1977*. New York: Pantheon Books, 1980.

French, Patrick. *Liberty or Death: India's Journey to Independence and Division*. London: Harper Collins, 1997.

Freud, Sigmund. "The Uncanny." *Standard Edition*, XVII. Ed. J. Strachey. London: The Hogarth Press, 1974.

Gandhi, Mahatma. *The Collected Works of Mahatma Gandhi* XC. New Delhi: Publications Division, Ministry of Information and Broadcasting, Government of India, 1984.

———.*The Collected Works of Mahatma Gandhi* LXXXIX. New Delhi: Ministry of Information and Broadcasting, Government of India, 1983.

————. "Speech at a Prayer Meeting—September, 18, 1947." *Gandhi on Women.* Ed. Pushpa Joshi. Ahmedabad: Centre for Women's Development Studies and Navajivan Trust, 1988.

Gandhi, Mohandas K. *Hind Swaraj and Other Writings.* 1926. Cambridge: Cambridge University Press, 1997.

Ganti Tejaswini. *Bollywood: A Guide to Popular Hindi Cinema.* New York, London: Routledge, 2004.

Garga, B. D. *So Many Cinemas: The Motion Picture in India.* Mumbai: Eminence Designs, 1996.

Ghatak, Ritwik. *Marxist Cultural Movement in India.* Ed. Sudhi Pradhan. Calcutta: National Book Agency, 1979.

Ghosh, Amitav. *The Shadow Lines.* New York: Viking, 1989.

Ghosh, Bishnupriya. "Feminist Critiques of Nationalism and Communalism from Bangladesh and India: A Transnational Reading." *Interventions: Feminist Dialogues on Third World Literature and Film.* Eds. Bishnupriya Ghosh and Brinda Bose. New York: Garland Publishing, 1997.

Ghosh, Pratap Kumar. *The Constitution of India: How It Has Been Framed.* Calcutta: The World Press Private Ltd, 1966.

Gopal, S., ed. *Anatomy of a Confrontation: The Babri Masjid-Ram Janmabhumi Issue.* New Delhi: Penguin India, 1991.

Gopalan, Lalitha. *Cinema of Interruptions: Action Genres in Contemporary Indian Cinema.* London: BFI, 2002.

Gopinath, Gayatri. *Impossible Desires: Queer Diasporas and South Asian Public Cultures.* Durham: Duke University Press, 2005.

Gorra, Michael. *After Empire: Scott, Naipaul, Rushdie.* Chicago: University of Chicago Press, 1997.

Government of India. Annual *Report of the Ministry of Rehabilitation 1952–53.*

————. *Annual Report of the Ministry for Rehabilitation 1953–54.*

————. *Annual Report of the Ministry for Rehabilitation 1954–55.*

————. *Parliamentary Debates: House of the People, 1950–55.*

Government of Pakistan. *The Journey to Pakistan: A Documentation on refugees of 1947.* National Document Centre, 1993.

Green, Peter. "Eye-Witness to the End of an Empire." *The Canberra Times* August 15, 1987. MSS Eur C 416, OIOC Collection, British Library.

Grewal, Inderpal. *Transnational America: Feminisms, Diasporas, Neoliberalisms.* Durham: Duke University Press, 2005.

Guha, Ranajit, and Gayatri Chakravorty Spivak, eds. *Selected Subaltern Studies.* New York: Oxford University Press, 1988.

Gupta, Amar Devi. *A 1947 Tragedy of Jammu and Kashmir State: The Cleansing of Mirpur,* unpublished memoirs manuscript. OIOC Collection, British Library, London.

Gupta, Dipankar. "Communalism and Fundamentalism: Some Notes on the Nature of Ethnic Politics in India." *Economic and Political Weekly,* Annual Number (March 1991): 1155–1175.

Gupta, Raj Narain. *Indian Constitution and Civic Life.* Bombay: Kitab Mahal, Allahabad 1963.

Habermas, Jurgen. *The Structural Transformation of the Public Sphere.* Cambridge: MIT Press, 1989.

Hamid, Shahid. *Disastrous Twilight: A Personal Record of the Partition of India.* London: Leo Cooper in association with Secker & Warburg, 1986.

Hansen, Miriam. *Babel and Babylon: Spectatorship in American Silent Film.* Cambridge: Harvard University Press, 1991.

———. "Benjamin, Cinema and Experience: 'The Blue Flower in the Land of Technology.'" *New German Critique* 40 (Winter 1987): 23–50.

Hasan, Khalid, ed. "Introduction." *Mottled Dawn: Fifty Sketches and Stories of Partition* by S. H. Manto. Trans. Khalid Hasan, 1–6. Delhi: Penguin India, 1997.

Hasan, Mushirul. *India Partitioned: The Other Face of Freedom* (Volumes I & II). New Delhi: Roli Books, 1995.

———, ed. *India's Partition: Process, Strategy and Mobilization.* Delhi; Oxford: Oxford University Press, 1994 [1993].

Heard, S. H. *A Doctor Remembers: IMS Days.* OIOC Collection, British Library, London, 1947.

Heller, Agnes. *Everyday Life.* London: Routledge and Kegan Paul, 1984.

Herzfeld, Michael. *Cultural Intimacy: Social Poetics in the Nation-State.* New York: Routledge, 1997.

Hodson, H. V. *The Great Divide.* London: Hutchinson, 1969.

Holt, Thomas C. *The Problem of Race in the 21st Century.* Cambridge, MA: Harvard University Press, 2002.

Hussain, Akmal. "The Karachi Riots of December 1986: Crisis of State and Civil Society in Pakistan." *Mirrors of Violence: Communities, Riots and Survivors in South Asia.* Ed. Veena Das. Delhi: Oxford University Press, 1990.

Jalal, Ayesha. "Exploding Communalism." *Nationalism, Democracy and Development.* Eds. Sugata Bose and Ayesha Jalal. Delhi: Oxford University Press, 1998.

———. "Secularists, Subalterns and the Stigma of 'Communalism': Partition Historiography Revisited." *Modern Asian Studies* 30:3 (1996): 78–95.

———. *The Sole Spokesman: Jinnah, the Muslim League and the Demand for Pakistan.* New York: Cambridge University Press, 1985.

Jayawardena, Kumari, and Malathi de Alwis, eds. *Embodied Violence: Communalising Women's Sexuality in South Asia.* Delhi: Kali for Women, 1996.

Jenkins, Evan. *Confidential Reports (April 1947).* Oriental and India Office Collection, British Library, London.

Kakar, Sudhir. *The Colours of Violence.* New Delhi: Viking, 1995.

Karnad, Girish. "Comments from the Gallery." *India International Centre Quarterly* 8, 1(1981): 104.

Kaplan Amy. "Romancing the Empire: The Embodiment of American Masculinity in the Popular Historical Novel of the 1890s." *Postcolonial Theory and the United States: Race, Ethnicity and Literature.* Eds. Amritjit Singh and Peter Schmidt. Jackson: University Press of Mississippi, 2000.

Karaka, D. F. *Freedom Must Not Stink.* Delhi: Kutub, 1948.

Karma, Sukeshi. *Bearing Witness: Partition, Independence, End of the Raj.* Calgary: University of Calgary Press, 2002.

Kaul, Suvir, ed. *The Partitions of Memory: The Afterlife of the Division of India.* Bloomington: Indiana University Press, 2002.

Kavka, Misha. "Introduction." *Feminist Consequences: Theory for a New Century.* Eds. Elisabeth Bronfen and Misha Kavka. New York: Columbia University Press, 2001.

Khilnani, Sunil. *The Idea of India.* London: Hamish Hamilton, 1997.

Kipnis, Laura. "Adultery." *Critical Inquiry* 24. 2 (Winter 1998): 289–327.

Kumar, Sukrita Paul, and Muhammad Ali Siddiqui, eds. *Mapping Memories: Urdu Stories from India and Pakistan.* Delhi: Katha, 1998.

Lahiri, Jhumpa. *The Interpreter of Maladies.* New York: Mariner, 1999.

Lefebvre, Henri. *Critique of Everyday Life* vol. I. Trans. John Moore. London: Verso [1947] 1992.

———. *Everyday Life in the Modern World.* New York: Harper & Row, 1971.

Lowe, Lisa. *Immigrant Acts: On Asian American Politics.* Durham and London: Duke University Press, 1996.

Ludden, David, ed. *Making India Hindu: Religion, Community, and the Politics of Democracy in India.* Delhi: Oxford University Press, 1996.

Makhija, Anju, and Menka Shivdasani, eds. *Freedom and Fissures: An Anthology of Sindhi Partition Poetry.* New Delhi: Sahitya Akademi, 1998.

Malkki, Liisa H. *Purity and Exile: Violence, Memory, and National Cosmology among Hutu Refugees in Tanzania.* Chicago: University of Chicago Press, 1995.

Mani, Lata. *Contentious Traditions: The Debate on Sati in Colonial India.* Berkeley and Los Angeles: University of California Press, 1998.

Mankekar, Purnima. *Screening Culture, Viewing Politics: An Ethnography of Television, Womanhood and Nation in Postcolonial India.* Durham: Duke University Press, 1999.

Manto, Saadat Hasan. *Kingdom's End and Other Stories.* Trans. Khalid Hasan. Delhi: Penguin, 1989.

———. *The Best of Manto: A Collection of His Short Stories.* Trans. Jai Ratan and Romen Basu. New Delhi: Sterling Publishers, 1989.

———. *Mottled Dawn: Fifty Sketches and Stories of Partition.* Trans. Khalid Hasan. 1975. New Delhi: Penguin Books, 1997.

———. *Black Milk: A Collection of Short Stories.* Lahore: Pakistan Alkitab, 1956.

Mayaram, Shail. "Speech, Silence, and the Making of Partition Violence in Mewat." *Subaltern Studies IX.* Eds. Shahid Amin and Dipesh Chakrabarty. Delhi: Oxford University Press, 1996.

Mazumdar, Sucheta. "The Politics of Religion and National Origin: Rediscovering Hindu Indian Identity in the United States." *Antinomies of Modernity: Essays on Race, Orient, Nation.* Eds. Vasant Kaiwar and Sucheta Mazumdar. Durham: Duke University Press, 2003.

McClintock, Anne. "'No Longer in a Future Heaven': Gender, Race and Nationalism." *Dangerous Liaisons: Gender, Nation and Postcolonial Perspectives.* Eds. Anne McClintock, Aamir Mufti, and Ella Shohat. Minneapolis, London: University of Minnesota Press, 1997.

———. *Imperial Leather: Race, Gender, and Sexuality in the Colonial Conquest.* New York: Routledge, 1995.

McLane, J. R. *Indian Nationalism and the Early Congress.* Princeton: Princeton University Press, 1977.

Menon, Ritu, and Kamla Bhasin. *Borders & Boundaries: Women in India's Partition.* New Delhi: Kali for Women, 1998.

————. "Abducted Women, the State and Questions of Honour: Three perspectives on the Recovery of Operation in Post-Partition India." *Embodied Violence: Communalising Women's Sexuality in South Asia*. Eds. Kumari Jayawardena and Malathi de Alwis. Delhi: Kali for Women, 1996.

Mishra, Vijay. *Bollywood Cinema: Temples of Desire*. London and New York: Routledge, 2002.

Monteiro, Anjali. "Official Television and Unofficial Fabrications of the Self." *The Secret Politics of our Desires*. Ed. Ashish Nandy. London: Zed Books, 1998.

Moon, Penderel. *Divide and Quit*. London: Chatto & Windus, 1961.

Mufti, Aamir R. "Auerbach in Istanbul: Edward Said, Secular Criticism, and the Question of Minority Culture." *Edward Said and the Work of the Critic: Speaking Truth to Power*. Ed. Paul A. Bove. Durham: Duke University Press, 2000.

Naficy, Hamid. *An Accented Cinema: Exilic and Diasporic Filmmaking*. Princeton University Press, 2001.

Naim, C. M. *Ambiguities of Heritage: Fictions and Polemics*. Karachi: City Press, 1999.

Nanda, J. (Mrs.). *Punjab Uprooted: A Survey of the Punjab Riots and Rehabilitation Problems*. Bombay: Hind Kitab Publishers, April 1948.

Nandy, Ashish. "Introduction: Indian Popular Cinema as a Slum's Eye View of Politics." *The Secret Politics of our Desires: Innocence, Culpability and Indian Popular Cinema*. Ed. Ashis Nandy. London: Zed Books, 1999.

————. "Too Painful for Words." *Sunday Times of India*, July 20, 1997.

————. *The Intimate Enemy: Loss and recovery of self under colonialism*. Delhi: Oxford, 1983.

Negt, Oskar, and Alexander Kluge. *Public Sphere and Experience: Toward an Analysis of the Bourgeois and Proletarian Public Sphere*. Trans. Peter Labanyi, Jamie Owel Daniel, and Assenka Oksiloff. Foreword by Miriam Hansen. Minneapolis: University of Minnesota Press, 1993.

Nehru, Jawaharlal. *Selected Works of Jawaharlal Nehru* vol. 7. Delhi: Orient Longman, 1975.

————. *The Discovery of India*. Garden City, New York: Doubleday & Company, 1960.

————. "Speech on the Granting of Indian Independence, August 14, 1947." *Penguin Book of Twentieth Century Speeches*. Ed. Brian McArthur. London: Penguin Viking, 1992.

Nijhawan, Dina Nath, and R. D. Chopra. *Exhaustive Commentary on The Displaced Persons (Compensation and Rehabilitation) Act 1954 and The Displaced Persons (Compensation and Rehabilitation) Rules 1955*. Delhi: Federal Law Depot, Law Publishers, 1955.

O'Donnell, Erin. "'Woman' and 'homeland' in Ritwik Ghatak's films: Constructing post-Independence Bengali cultural identity." *Jump Cut: A Review of Contemporary Media*. No. 47 (2004). http://www.ejumpcut.org (accessed May 14, 2005).

O'Hanlon, Rosalind. "Issues of Masculinity in North Indian History: The Bangash Nawabs of Farrukhabad." *Indian Journal of Gender Studies*. 4(1997): 1–19.

Ojha, Rajendra. *80 Glorious Years of Indian Cinema: Complete Filmography of All Silent & Hindi Films Released Between 1913–1993 Along With Cast, Credits, Year of Release and Category with Alphabetical Index*. Bombay: Screen World Publication, 1993.

Ondaatje, Michael. *Anil's Ghost*. New York: Vintage Books, 2000.

Orsini, Francesca. *The Hindi Public Sphere 1920–1940: Language and Literature in the Age of Nationalism*. New York: Oxford University Press, 2002.

Pandey, Gyan. *Remembering Partition: Violence, Nationalism and History in India*. Cambridge: Cambridge University Press, 2001.

———. "Memory, History and Political Violence: Recollections of India's Partition." Unpublished paper, 1999.

———. "The Prose of Otherness." *Subaltern Studies* VIII. Eds. David Arnold and David Hardiman. Delhi: Oxford University Press, 1994.

———. "In Defence of the Fragment: Writing About Hindu-Muslim Riots in India Today." *Economic and Political Weekly* Annual Number (March 1991): 559–572.

Patel, Vallabhbhai. *Speeches of Patel: For a United India*. Delhi: Publications Division, Old Secretariat, 1950.

Prasad, Madhava M. *Ideology of the Hindi Film: A Historical Construction*. Delhi: Oxford University Press, 1998.

Prashad, Vijay. *The Karma of Brown Folk*. Minneapolis: University of Minnesota Press, 2000.

———. "Crafting Solidarities." *Apart, Yet Apart: South Asians in Asian America*. Eds. Lavina Dhingra Shankar and Rajini Srikanth. Philadelphia: Temple University Press, 1998.

Pritam, Amrita. *A Slice of Life—Selected Works*. New Delhi: UBS Publishers, 1996.

Rajadhyaksha, Ashish. "Strange Attractions." *Sight and Sound* 6 (1996): 36–57.

———, and Paul Willemen, eds. *Encyclopaedia of Indian Cinema*. New Delhi; New York: Oxford University Press, 1995.

———. *A Return to the Epic*. Screen Unit, 1982.

Rajagopal, Arvind. *Politics After Television: Hindu Nationalism and the Reshaping of the Indian Public*. New York: Cambridge University Press, 2001.

Ramaswamy, Sumathi. "Catastrophic Cartographies: Mapping the Lost Continent of Lemuria." *Representations* 67(Summer 1999): 115–142.

Rao, V. K. R. V., and P. B. Desai. *Greater Delhi: A Study in Urbanization 1940–1957*. Bombay: New York: Asia Publication House, 1965.

Ravikant. "Partition: Strategies of Oblivion, Ways of Remembering." *Translating Partition*. Eds. Ravikant and Tarun K. Saint. Delhi: Katha, 2001.

Ravikant and Tarun K. Saint, eds. *Translating Partition*. Delhi: Katha, 2001.

Ray, Sangeeta. *En-Gendering India: Woman and Nation in Colonial and Postcolonial Narratives*. Durham: Duke University Press, 2000.

Rees, T. W. Papers of Evan Jenkins. "Report on the Punjab Boundary Force 1 August–1 September 1947 prepared in New Delhi on 15 November 1947." OIOC Collection, British Library, London.

Reetz, Dietrich. *Islam in the Public Sphere: Religious Groups in India, 1900–1947*. New York: Oxford University Press, 2006.

Robbins, Bruce, and Pheng Cheah, eds. *Cosmopolitics: Thinking and Feeling Beyond the Nation*. Minneapolis: University of Minnesota Press, 1998.

Rudolph, Lloyd, and Susanne Rudolph. *In Pursuit of Lakshmi: The Political Economy of the Indian State*. Chicago: University of Chicago Press, 1987.

———. *The Modernity of Tradition: Political Development in India*. Chicago: University of Chicago Press, 1967.

Rushdie, Salman. *Shalimar, the Clown*. New York, Random House, 2005.

———. "Damme, This Is the Oriental Scene For You!" *The New Yorker*, 23–30 June 1997.

———. *Imaginary Homelands*. London; New York: Granta in association with Penguin, 1991.

———. *Shame: A Novel*. New York: Knopf, 1983.

———. *Midnight's Children*. New York: Avon Books, 1981.

Rushdie, Salman, and Elizabeth West, eds. *Mirrorwork: 50 Years of Indian writing, 1947–1997*. New York: H. Holt & Co., 1997.

Sahni, Bhisham. *We Have Arrived in Amritsar and Other Stories*. Trans. Jai Ratan. Hyderabad: Disha Books, 1990.

———. *Tamas (Darkness)*. New Delhi; New York: Penguin, 1988.

Sangari, Kumkum, and Sudesh Vaid, eds. *Recasting Women: Essays in Colonial History*. New Delhi: Kali for Women, 1993.

Sarang, Vilas. *Indian English Poetry Since 1950: An Anthology*. London: Sangam, 1990.

Sarkar, Sumit. *Modern India 1885–1947*. New Delhi: Macmillan India, 1983.

Sassen, Saskia. *Guests and Aliens*. New York: The New Press, 1999.

———. *Globalization and Its Discontents: Selected Essays 1984–1998*. New York: The New Press, 1998.

Scarry, Elaine. *The Body in Pain: The Making and Unmaking of the World*. New York: Oxford University Press, 1985.

Schwartz, Henry. "Mission Impossible: Introducing Postcolonial Studies in the US Academy." *A Companion to Postcolonial Studies*. Eds. Henry Schwarz and Sangeeta Ray. Oxford, U.K.: Blackwell Publishers, 2000.

———. "Sexing the Pundits: Gender, Romance and Realism in the Cultural Politics of Colonial Bengal." *Reading the Shape of the World*. Eds. Henry Schwarz and Richard Dienst. Boulder, CO: Westview Press, 1996.

Seshadri, H. V. *Tragic Story of Partition*. Bangalore, 1982.

Shaheed, Farida. "The Pathan-Muhajir Conflicts, 1985–6: A National Perspective." *Mirrors of Violence: Communities, Riots and Survivors in South Asia*. Ed. Veena Das. Delhi: Oxford University Press, 1990.

Shankar, S. "Passage to North America." *Contours of the Heart: South Asians Map North America*. Eds. Sunaina Maira and Rajini Srikanth. New York: The Asian American Writers' Workshop, 1996.

Sidhwa, Bapsi. *Cracking India*. Minneapolis: Milkweed Editions, 1991.

Sikand, Yoginder. *Muslims in India Since 1947: Islamic Perspectives on Inter-Faith Relations*. London: Routledge, 2004.

Singh, Amritjit, and Peter Schmidt, eds. *Postcolonial Theory and the United States: Race, Ethnicity and Literature*. Jackson: University Press of Mississippi, 2000.

Singh, Ghanda. *India Partitioned: The Other Face of Freedom*, vol. 2. Ed. Mushirul Hasan. Delhi: Roli International, 1997.

Singh, Khushdeva. *Love Is Stronger than Hate (A Remembrance of 1947)*. Patiala, India: Guru Nanak Mission, 1973.

Singh, Khushwant. *Train to Pakistan*. 1956. New Delhi: Ravi Dayal and Orient Longman, 1997.

———. *The Unending Trail*. Delhi: Rajkamal Publications, 1957.

Sinha, Mrinalini. *Colonial Masculinity: The "Manly Englishman" and the "Effeminate Bengali" in the Late 19th Century*. Manchester: Manchester University Press, 1995.

Spillers, Hortense J. "Mama's Baby, Papa's Maybe: An American Grammar Book." *Diacritics* 17 (Summer 1987): 32–61.

Spivak, Gayatri Chakravarty. *A Critique of Postcolonial Reason: Toward a History of the Vanishing Present*. Cambridge: Harvard University Press, 1999.

———. *Outside in the Teaching Machine*. New York: Routledge, 1993.

———. "Subaltern Studies: Deconstructing Historiography." *Selected Subaltern Studies*. Eds. Ranajit Guha and Gayatri Chakravarty Spivak. New York, Oxford: Oxford University Press, 1988.

———. "Introduction." *Selected Subaltern Studies*. Eds. Ranajit Guha and Gayatri Chakravarty Spivak. New York, Oxford: Oxford University Press, 1988.

———. *In Other Worlds: Essays in Cultural Politics*. New York: Methuen, 1987.

Srikanth, Rajini. *The World Next Door: South Asian American Literature and the Idea of America*. Philadelphia: Temple, 2004.

Srivastava, Sanjay, ed. *Sexual Sites, Seminal Attitudes Sexualities, Masculinities and Culture*. New Delhi: Sage Publications, 2004.

Stam, Robert, and Ella Shohat. *Flagging Patriotism: Crises of Narcissism and Anti Americanism*. New York: Routledge, 2007.

Sunder Rajan, Rajeswari. *The Scandal of the State: Women, Law and Citizenship in India*. Durham and London: Duke University Press, 2003.

———. *Real and Imagined Women*. London: Routledge, 1993.

Talbot, Ian. "Literature and the Human Drama of the 1947 Partition." *South Asia*, Special Issue, xviii (1995): 15–25.

Tambiah, Stanley. J. *Leveling Crowds: Ethnonationalist Conflicts and Collective Violence in South Asia*. Berkeley: University of California Press, 1996.

Tandon, Prakash. *Punjabi Century: 1857–1947*. London: Chatto and Windus, 1961.

Tharu, Susie. "Rendering Account of the Nation: Partition Narratives and Other Genres of the Passive Revolution." *Oxford Literature Review* 16 (1994): 23–45.

Thoraval, Yves. *The Cinemas of India (1896–2000)*. Delhi: Macmillan India, 2000.

Turner, Victor. *The Ritual Process: Structure and Anti-Structure*. Chicago: Aldine, 1969.

———. *The Forest of Symbols: Aspects of Ndembu Ritual*. Ithaca, NY: Cornell University Press, 1967.

Vanaik, Achin. *The Painful Transition: Bourgeois Democracy in India*. London: Verso, 1990.

Vasudevan, Ravi. "Addressing the Spectator of a 'Third World' National Cinema: The Bombay 'Social' Film of the 1940s and 1950s." *Screen* 36.4 (Fall 2004): 305–324.

———. "Dislocations: The Cinematic Imagining of a New Society in 1950s in India." *Oxford Literary Review* 16 (1994): 93–124.

Wallbank, Walter T., ed. *The Partition of India: Causes and Responsibilities*. Boston: D. C. Heath & Company, 1966.

Whitehead, Stephen M., and Frank J. Barrett, eds. *The Masculinities Reader*. New York: Polity Press, 2001.

Zakaria, Rafiq. *Price of Partition: Recollections and Reflections*. Mumbai: Bharatiya Vidya Bhavan, 1998.

Index

Veer Zaara (Chopra), 43, 53, 151, 161–167, 182
Vishwa Hindu Parishad, 151
Violence
    against women, 85, 97, 99, 142,
      see abduction, rape, intra-ethnic
      violence
    against men, *see* castration, circumci-
      sion, masculinity
    of the idea of nation, 185, 187, 191, 198
    of the modern state, 144–148, 200,
      202,
    and terror, 1–3, 201, 204–206,
      207–209

Waqt (Chopra), 154
war films, 167–174
Water (Mehta), 57
What the Body Remembers (Baldwin), 85–86
women, *see also* gender, body
    as nationalist, 189
    as symbols, 40–41, 43, 75, 96
    as minor agents, 79, 196–198

Yahaan (Sircar), 181
Yun Hota To Kya Hota (Shah), 201

Zils, Paul, 88

Kavita Daiya is Associate Professor of English at the George Washington University in Washington, D.C.